BLUE PERIOD 9

TSUBASA YAMAGUCHI

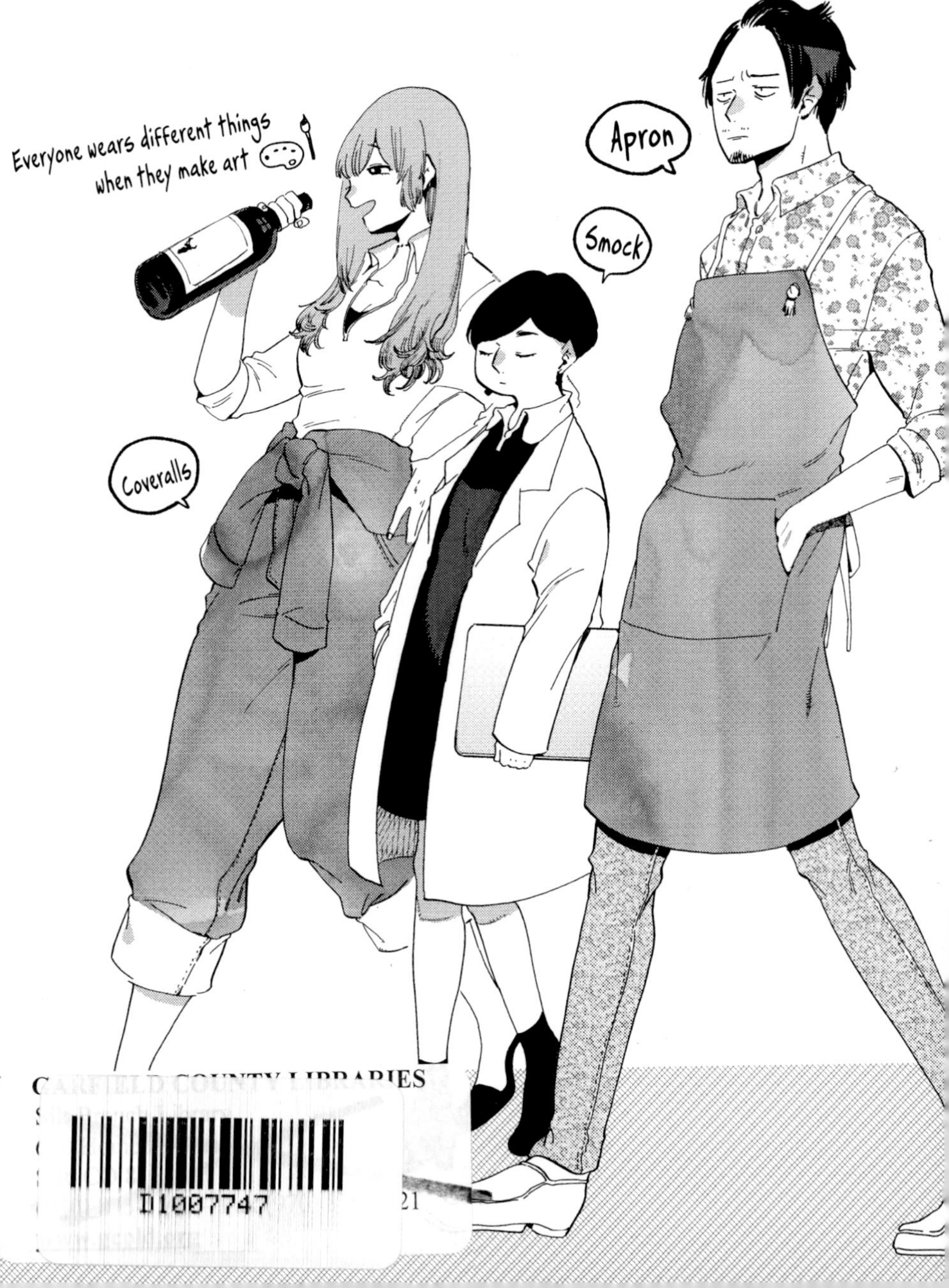

Everyone wears different things when they make art
Apron
Smock
Coveralls

CHARACTERS

Kinemi Miki
The one who broke Yatora's mirror during TUA's first exam. She's serving as a mikoshi-team captain at this year's Geisai.

Yotasuke Takahashi
After quitting the prep school that he and Yatora had been attending, he studied on his own and passed TUA's exams on his first attempt. His talent, skills, and unsociable character inspire Yatora to be a better artist.

Yatora Yaguchi
After getting hooked on the joy of making art, he studied to get into Tokyo University of the Arts, the most competitive of all Japanese art colleges, and passed on his first attempt. He's a hardworking normie.

Kenji Hachiro
Also goes by the name Hacchan. He often hangs out with Murai.

Yakumo Murai
An all-around knowledgeable guy who is constantly redefining what it means to be "the strongest." He's taken a liking to Yatora.

Ayano Aizawa
She attended the same prep school as Kinemi, and is good friends with her. She's a mikoshi-team vice-captain.

TABLE OF CONTENTS

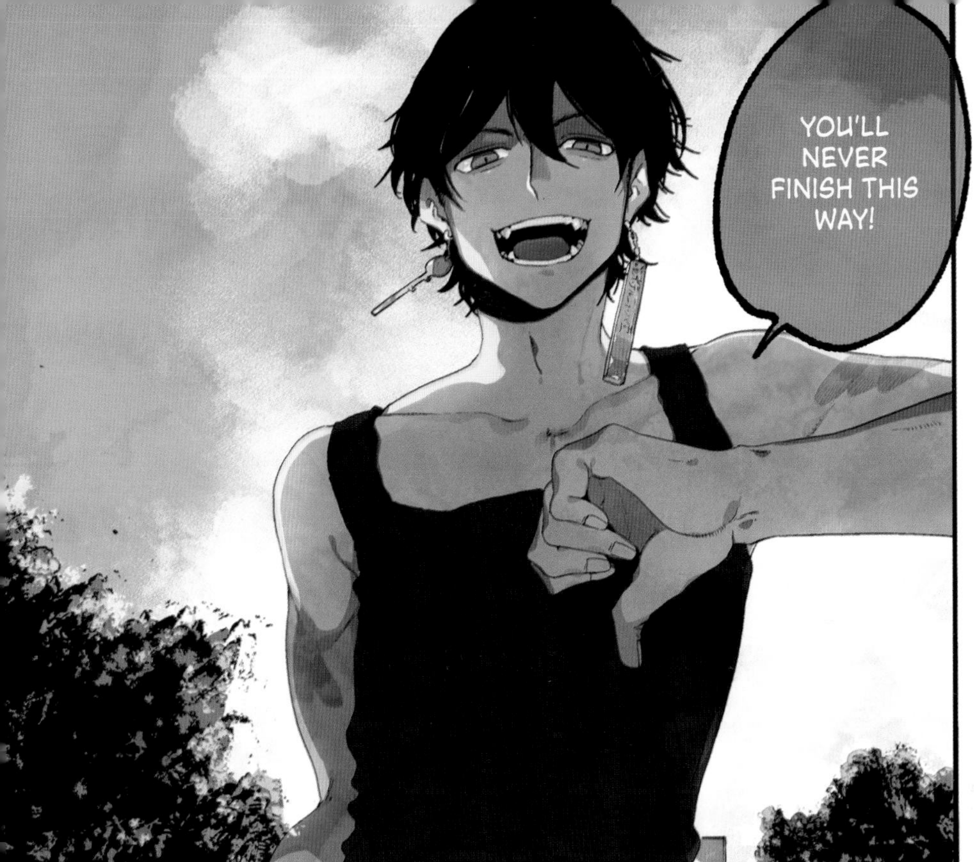
YOU'LL NEVER FINISH THIS WAY!
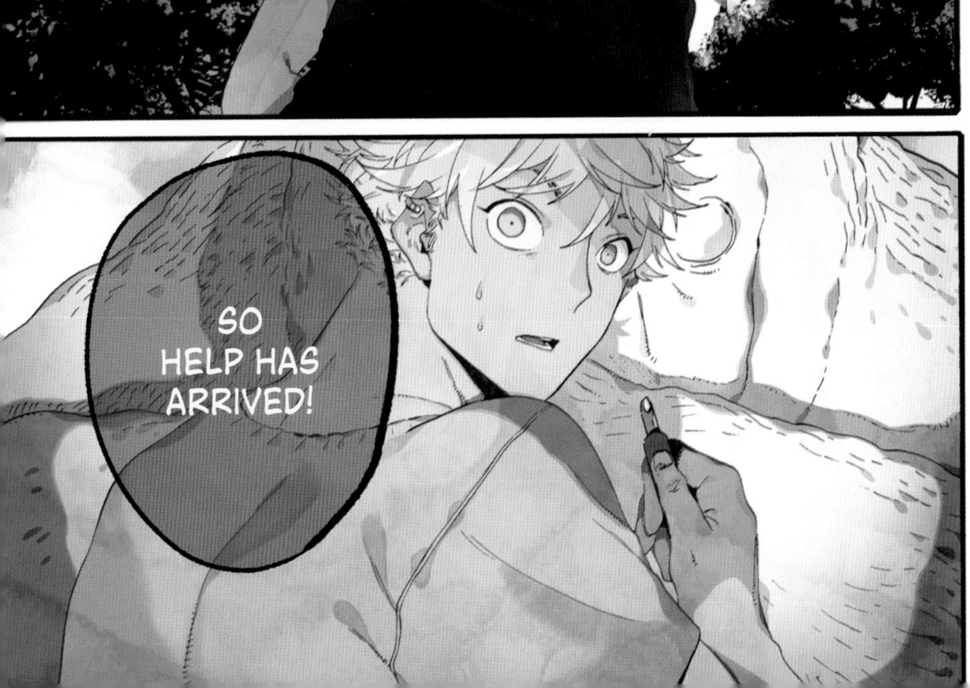
SO HELP HAS ARRIVED!

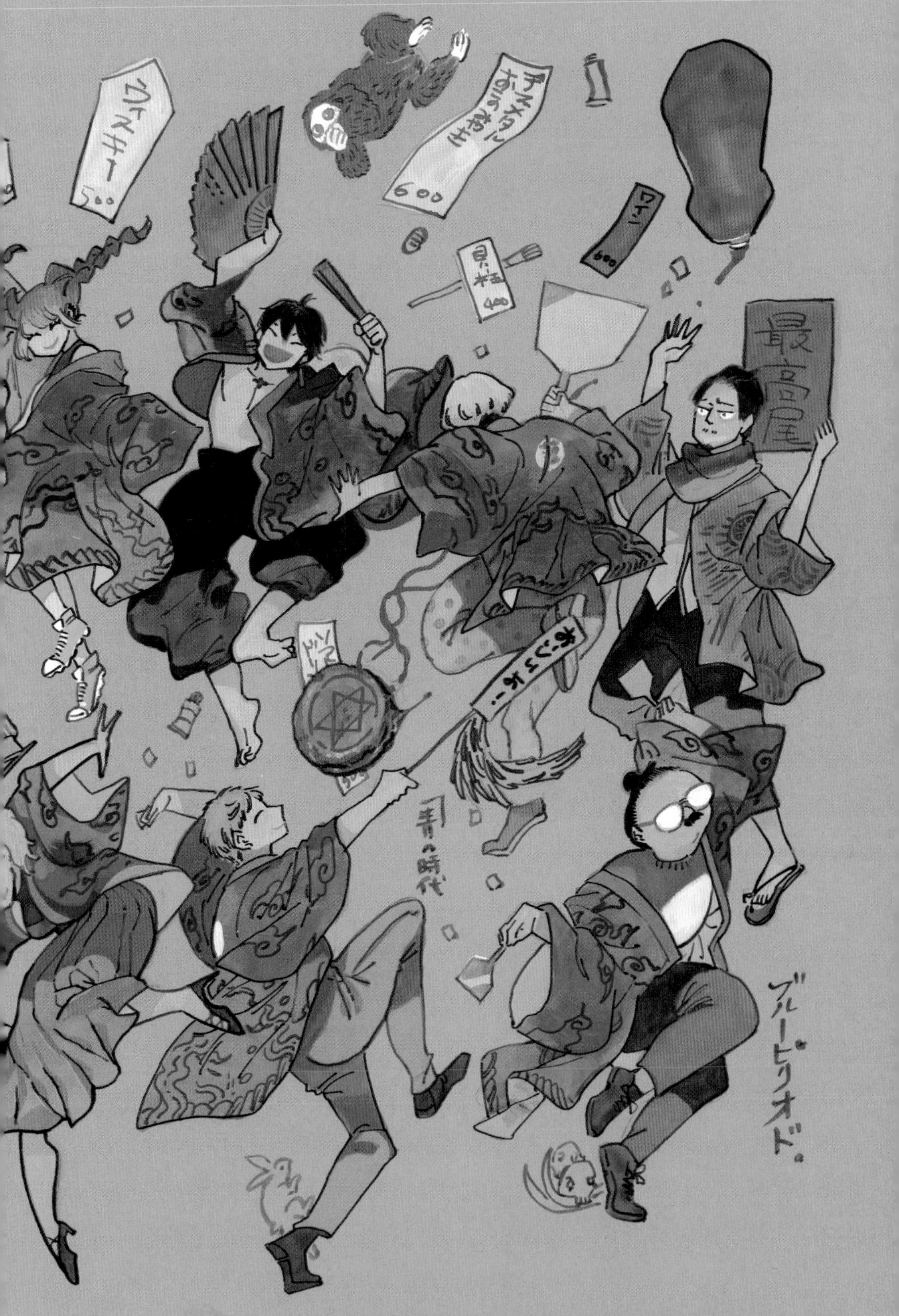
ウィスキー
500
600
ワイン
600
最高屋
青の時代
ブルーピリオド。

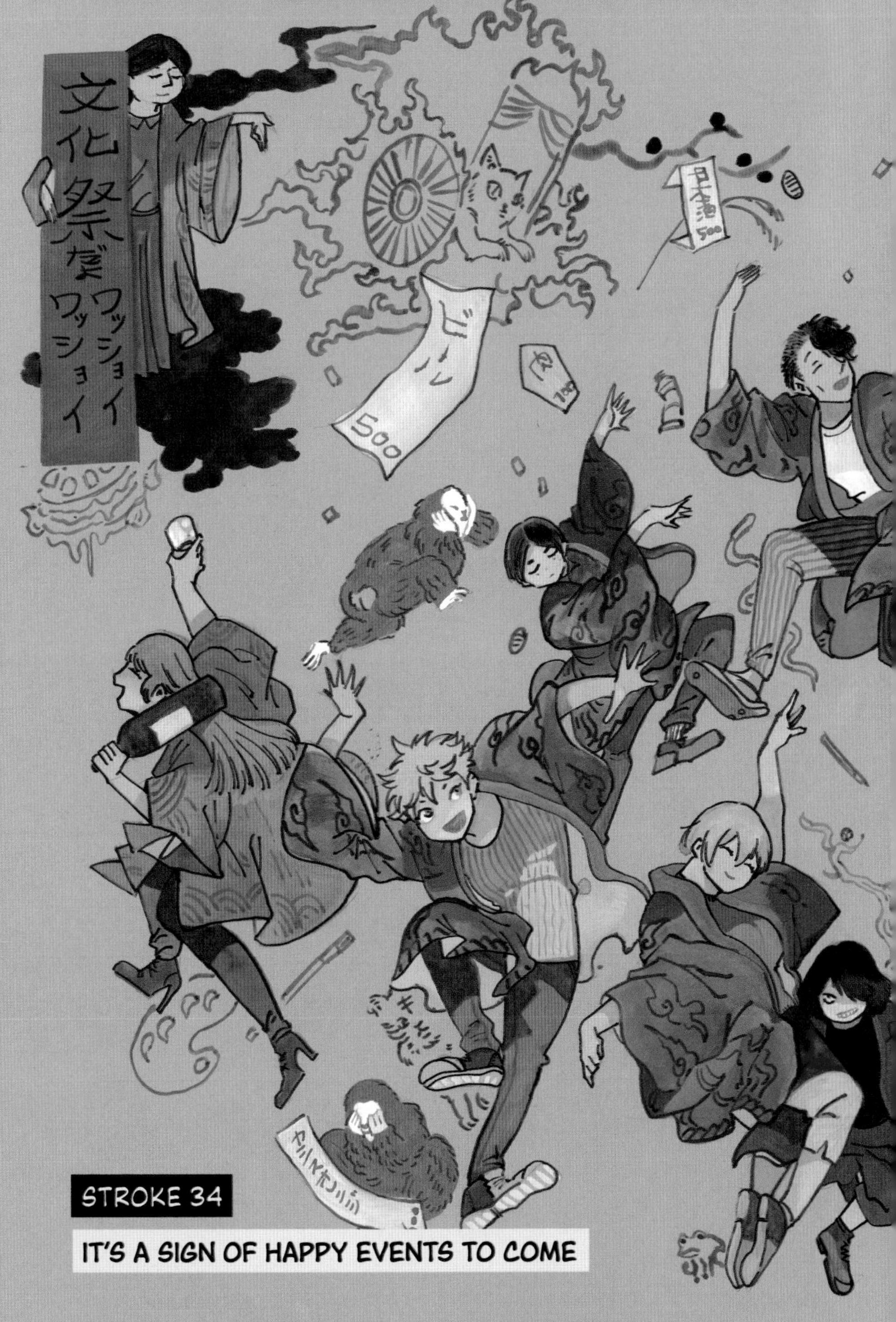
文化祭だワッショイワッショイ
500

STROKE 34

IT'S A SIGN OF HAPPY EVENTS TO COME

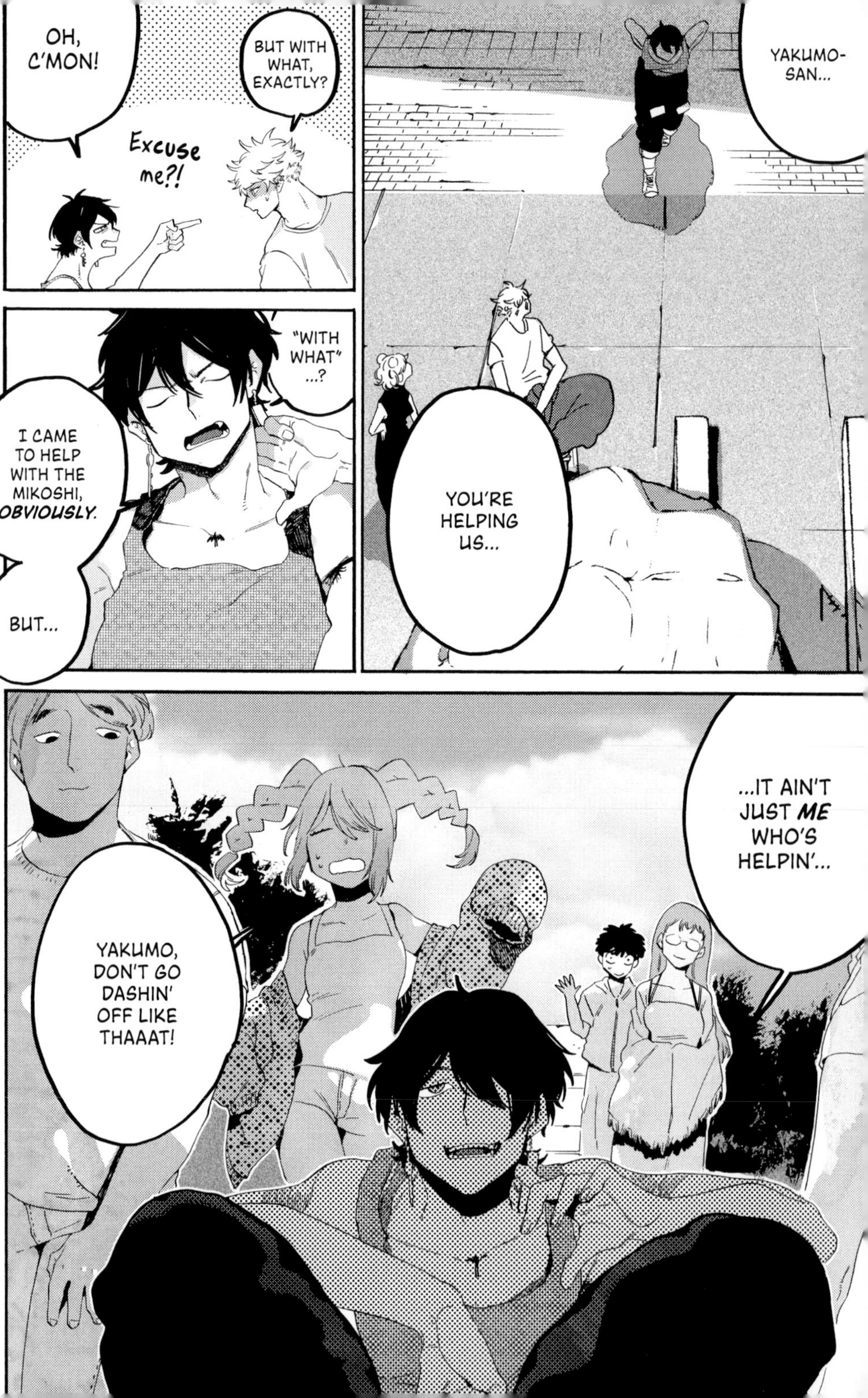
YAKUMO-SAN...
YOU'RE HELPING US...
BUT WITH WHAT, EXACTLY?
OH, C'MON!
Excuse me?!
"WITH WHAT" ...?
I CAME TO HELP WITH THE MIKOSHI, *OBVIOUSLY*.
BUT...
...IT AIN'T JUST *ME* WHO'S HELPIN'...
YAKUMO, DON'T GO DASHIN' OFF LIKE THAAAT!

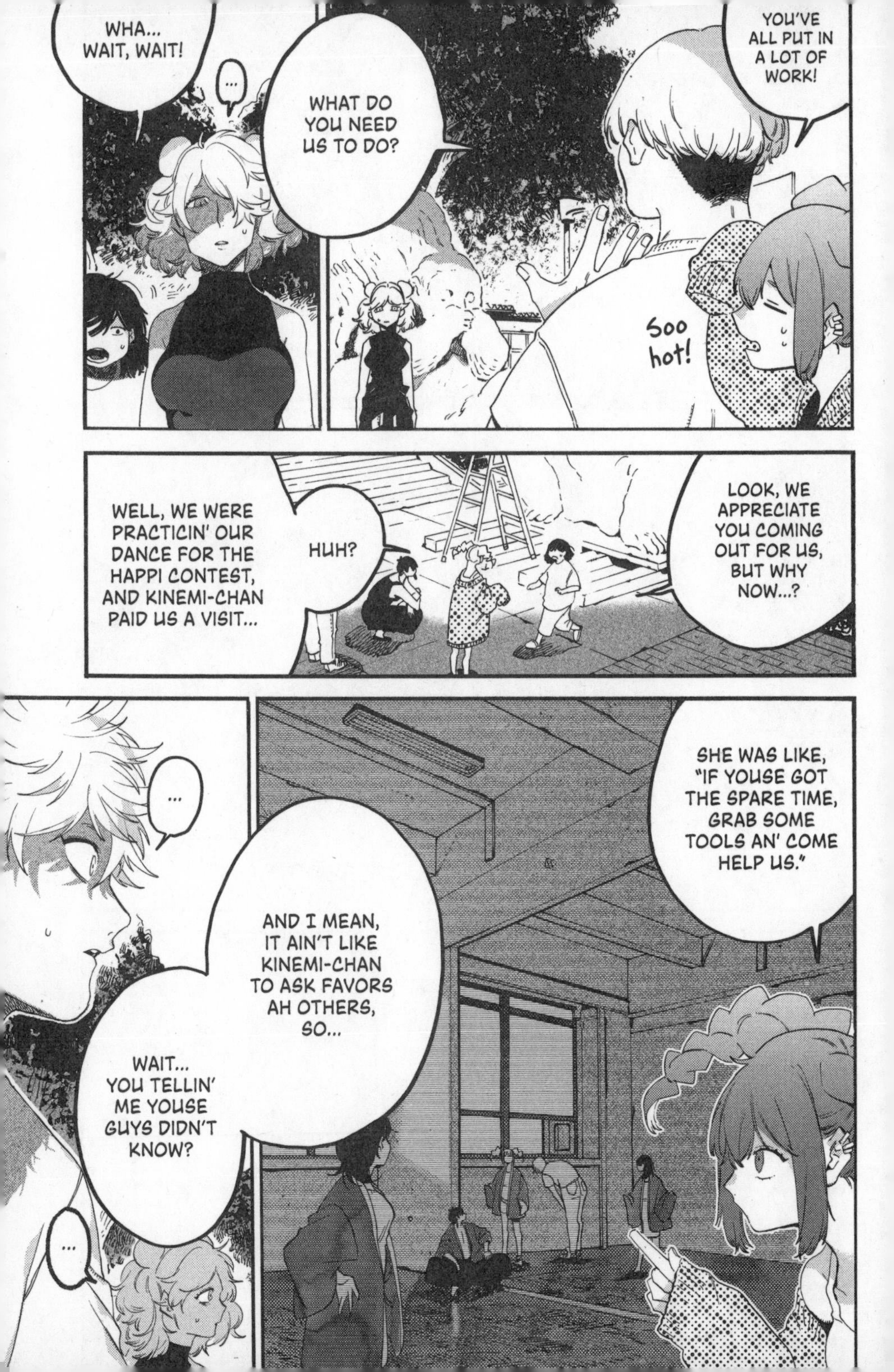
YOU'VE ALL PUT IN A LOT OF WORK!
WHAT DO YOU NEED US TO DO?
Soo hot!
WHA... WAIT, WAIT!
...
LOOK, WE APPRECIATE YOU COMING OUT FOR US, BUT WHY NOW...?
HUH?
WELL, WE WERE PRACTICIN' OUR DANCE FOR THE HAPPI CONTEST, AND KINEMI-CHAN PAID US A VISIT...
SHE WAS LIKE, "IF YOUSE GOT THE SPARE TIME, GRAB SOME TOOLS AN' COME HELP US."
AND I MEAN, IT AIN'T LIKE KINEMI-CHAN TO ASK FAVORS AH OTHERS, SO...
...
WAIT... YOU TELLIN' ME YOUSE GUYS DIDN'T KNOW?
...

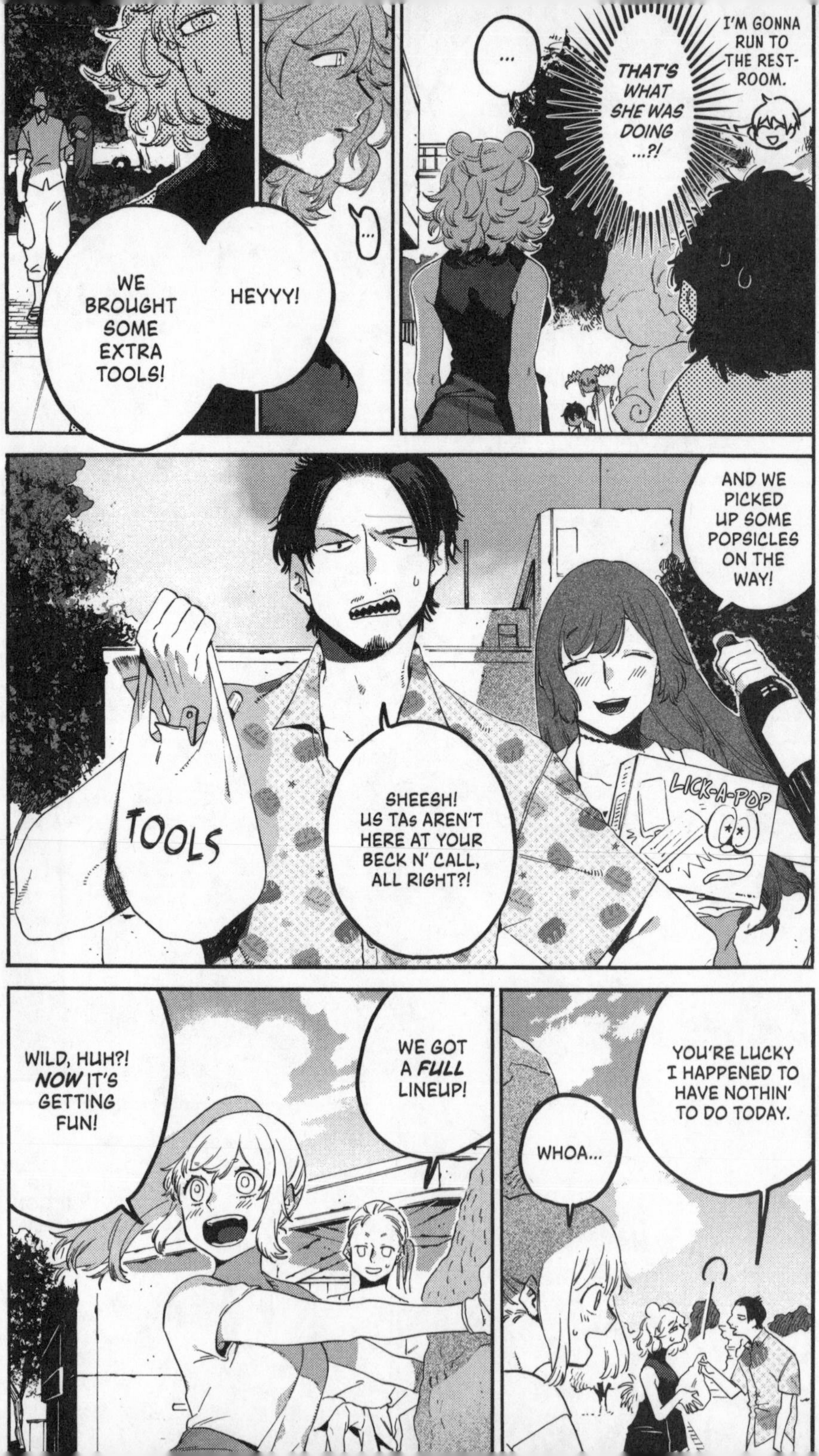
I'M GONNA RUN TO THE REST-ROOM.
THAT'S WHAT SHE WAS DOING ...?!
...
...
HEYYY!
WE BROUGHT SOME EXTRA TOOLS!
AND WE PICKED UP SOME POPSICLES ON THE WAY!
LICK-A-POP
SHEESH! US TAs AREN'T HERE AT YOUR BECK N' CALL, ALL RIGHT?!
TOOLS
YOU'RE LUCKY I HAPPENED TO HAVE NOTHIN' TO DO TODAY.
WHOA...
WE GOT A *FULL* LINEUP!
WILD, HUH?! *NOW* IT'S GETTING FUN!

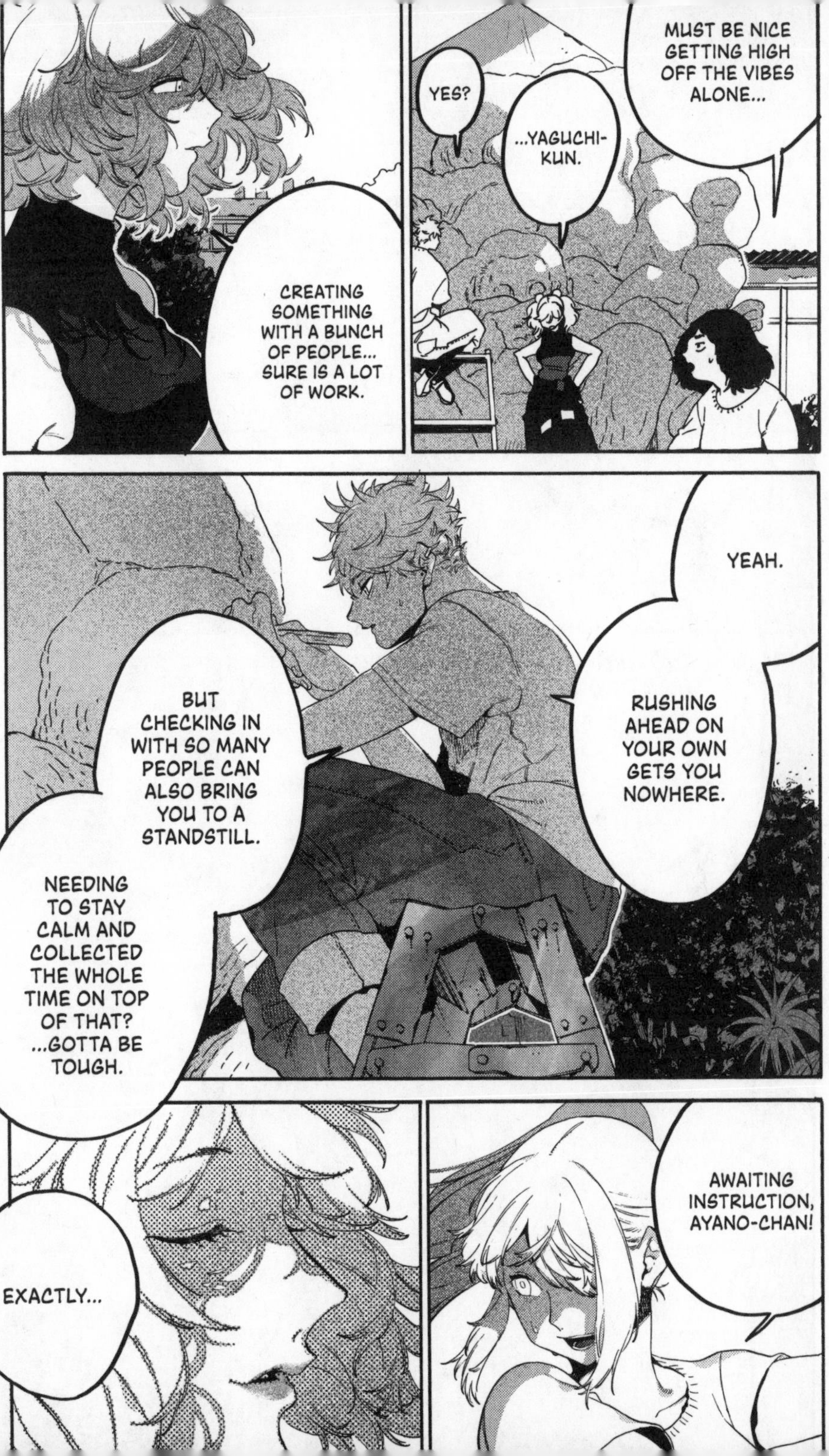
MUST BE NICE GETTING HIGH OFF THE VIBES ALONE...
...YAGUCHI-KUN.
YES?
CREATING SOMETHING WITH A BUNCH OF PEOPLE... SURE IS A LOT OF WORK.
YEAH.
RUSHING AHEAD ON YOUR OWN GETS YOU NOWHERE.
BUT CHECKING IN WITH SO MANY PEOPLE CAN ALSO BRING YOU TO A STANDSTILL.
NEEDING TO STAY CALM AND COLLECTED THE WHOLE TIME ON TOP OF THAT? ...GOTTA BE TOUGH.
AWAITING INSTRUCTION, AYANO-CHAN!
EXACTLY...

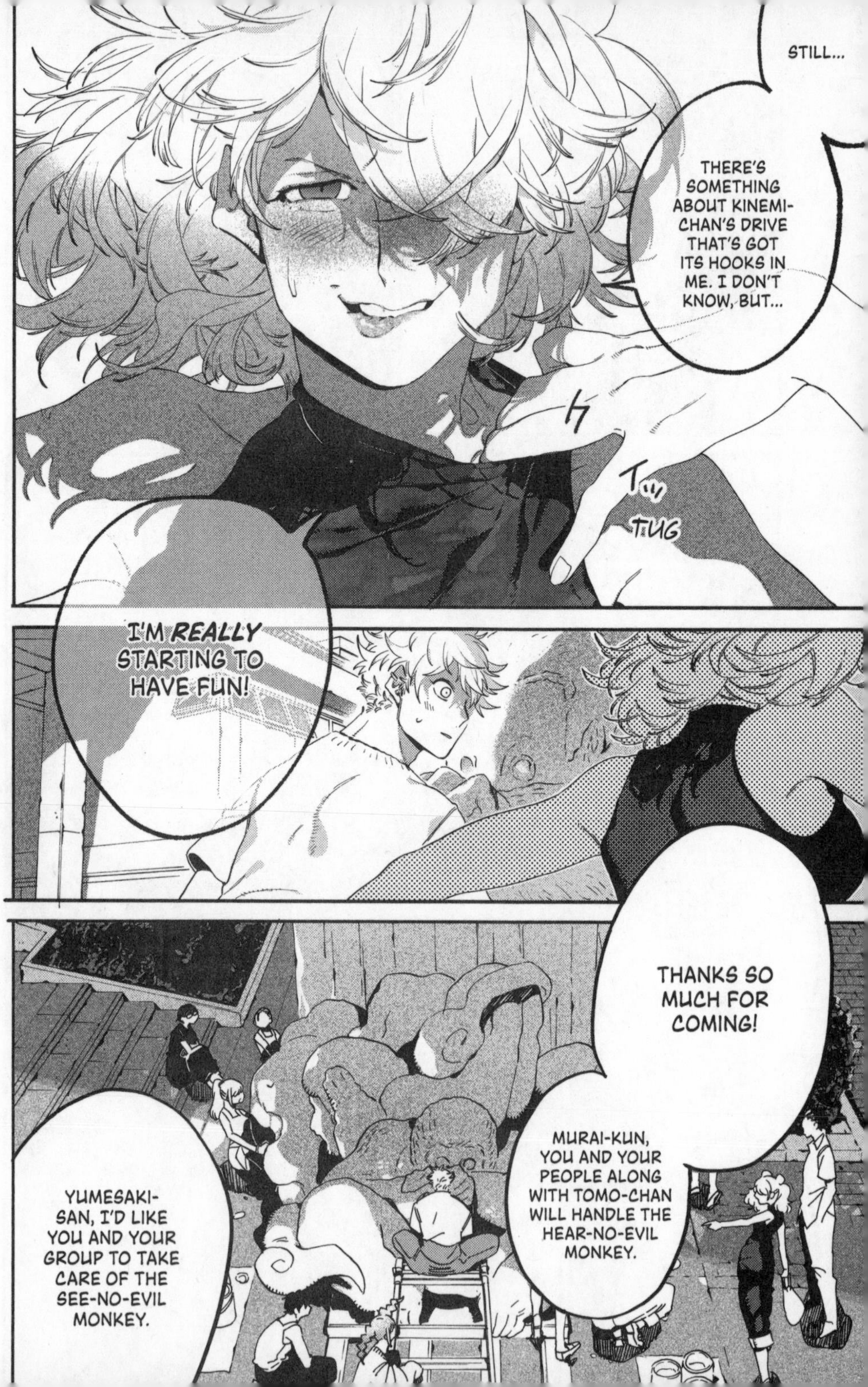
STILL...
THERE'S SOMETHING ABOUT KINEMI-CHAN'S DRIVE THAT'S GOT ITS HOOKS IN ME. I DON'T KNOW, BUT...
TUG
I'M *REALLY* STARTING TO HAVE FUN!
THANKS SO MUCH FOR COMING!
MURAI-KUN, YOU AND YOUR PEOPLE ALONG WITH TOMO-CHAN WILL HANDLE THE HEAR-NO-EVIL MONKEY.
YUMESAKI-SAN, I'D LIKE YOU AND YOUR GROUP TO TAKE CARE OF THE SEE-NO-EVIL MONKEY.

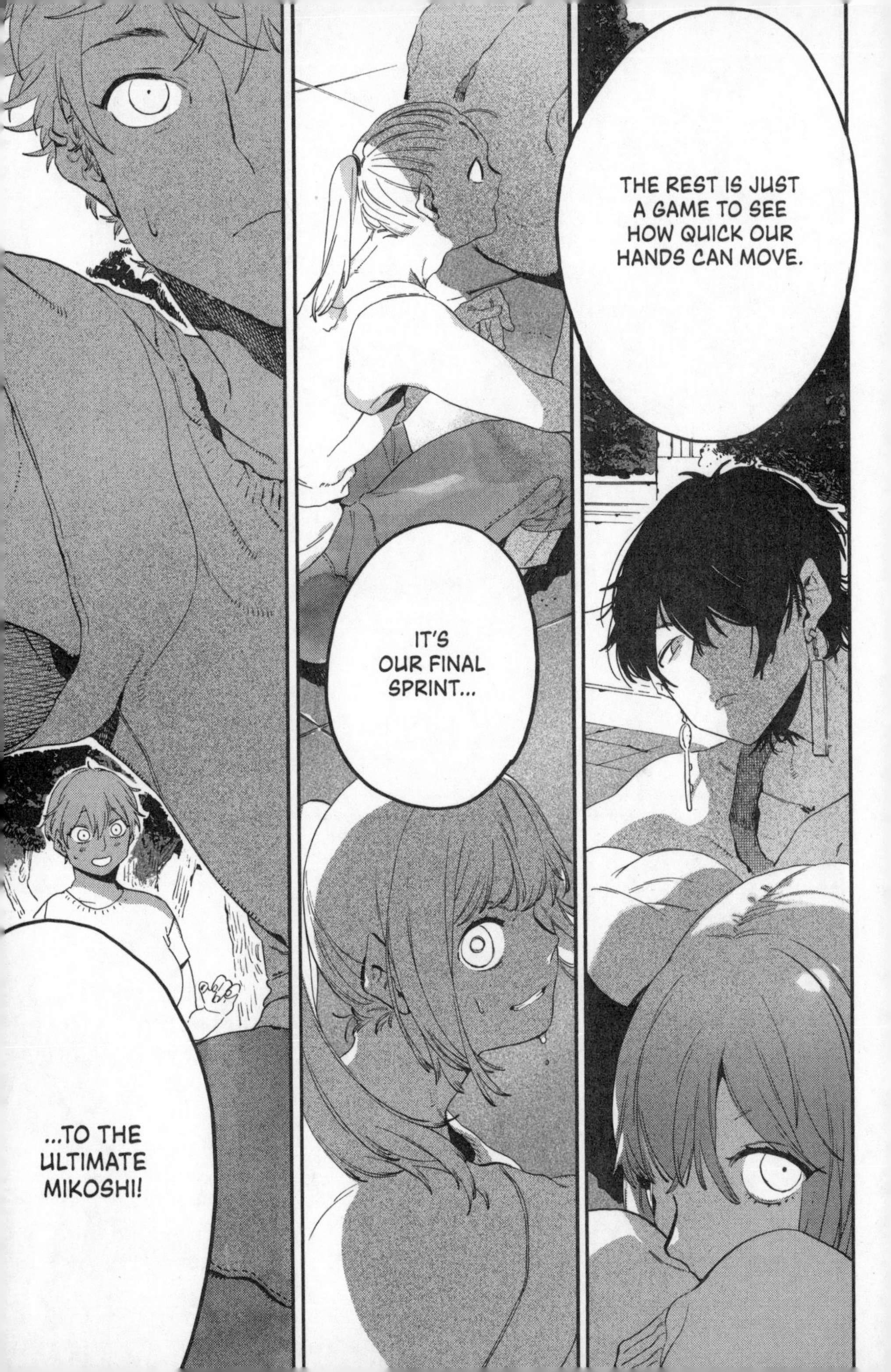
THE REST IS JUST A GAME TO SEE HOW QUICK OUR HANDS CAN MOVE.
IT'S OUR FINAL SPRINT...
...TO THE ULTIMATE MIKOSHI!

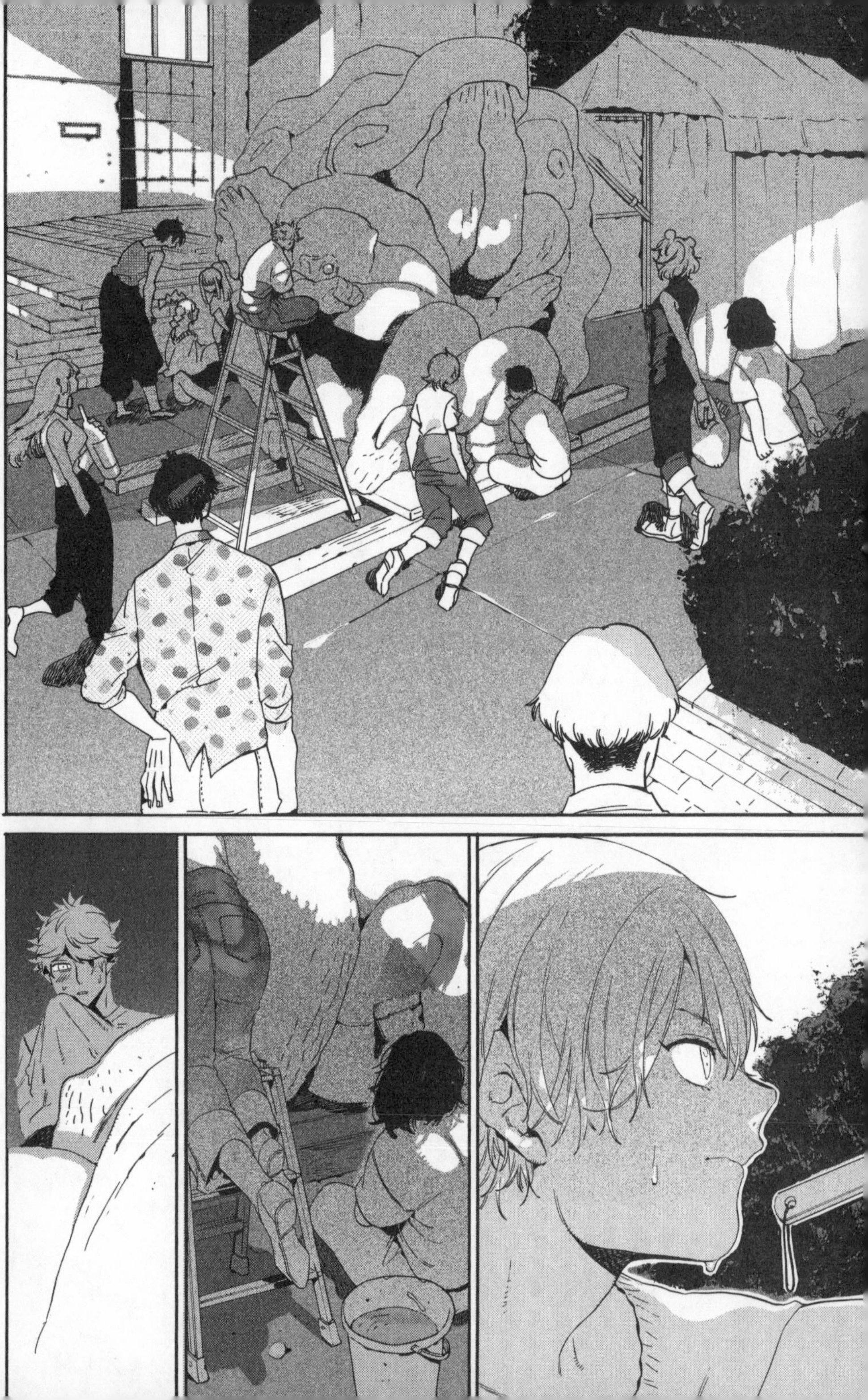

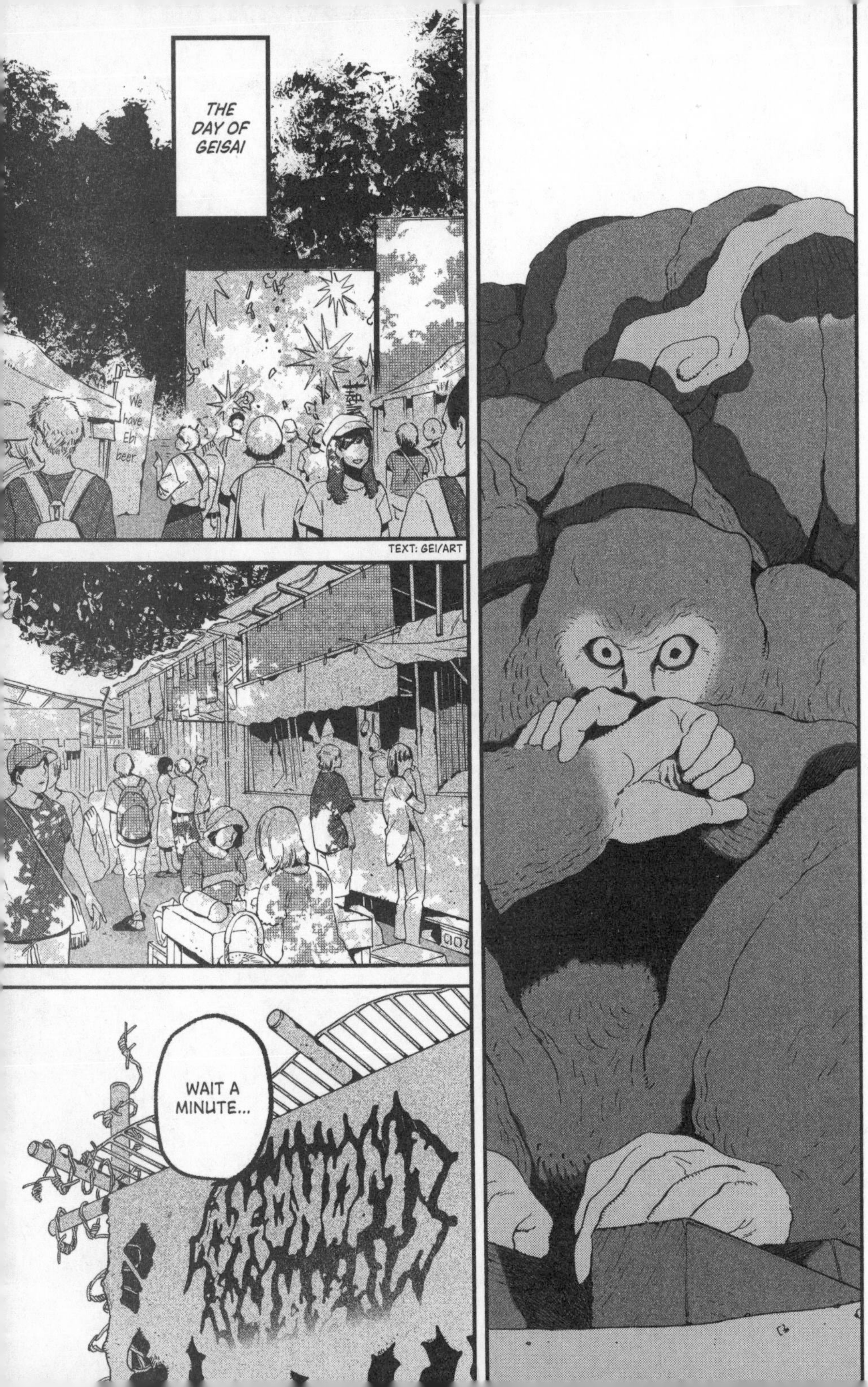
THE DAY OF GEISAI
We have Ebi beer.
藝
TEXT: GEI/ART
WAIT A MINUTE...

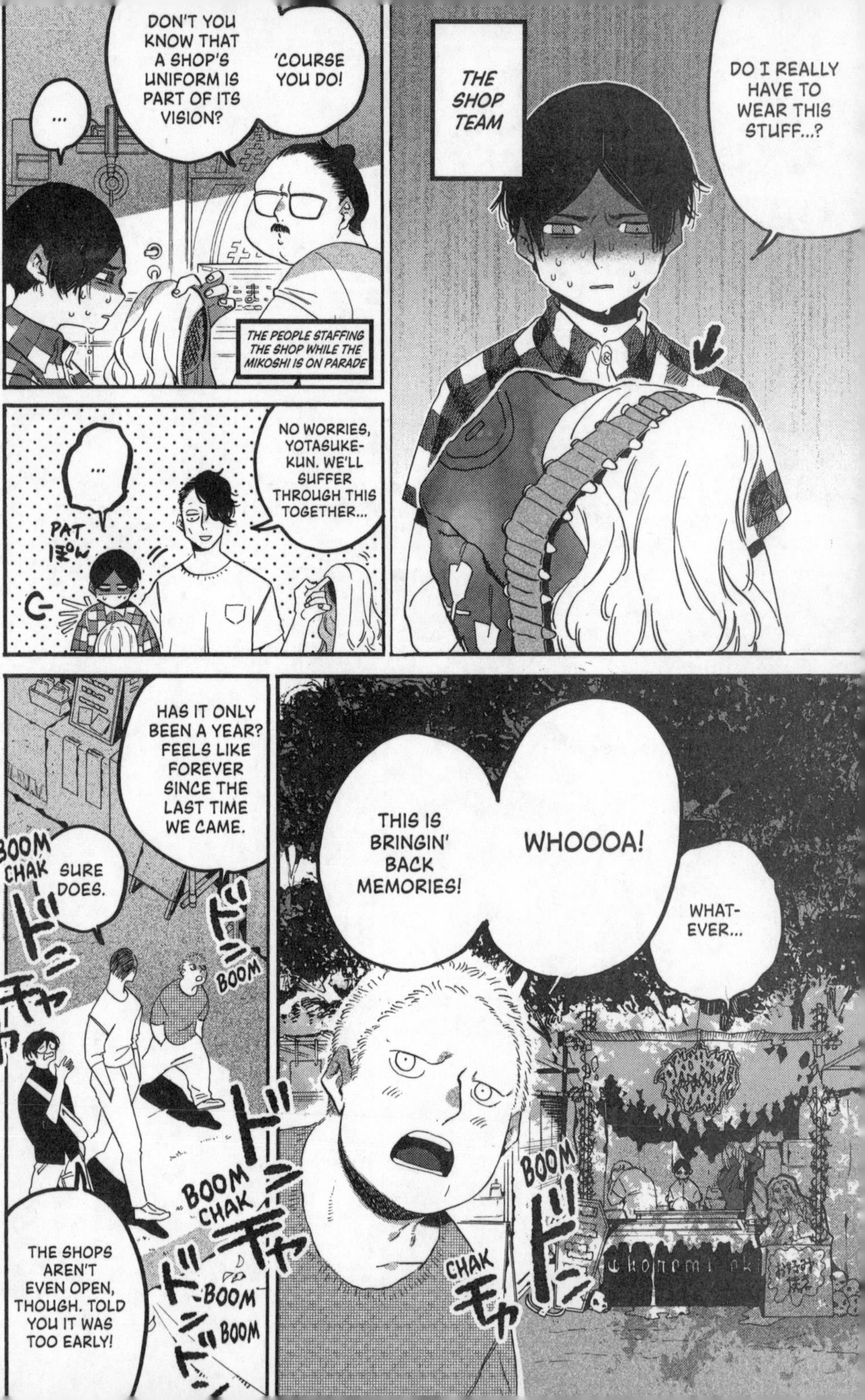
THE SHOP TEAM
DO I REALLY HAVE TO WEAR THIS STUFF...?
'COURSE YOU DO!
DON'T YOU KNOW THAT A SHOP'S UNIFORM IS PART OF ITS VISION?
...
THE PEOPLE STAFFING THE SHOP WHILE THE MIKOSHI IS ON PARADE
NO WORRIES, YOTASUKE-KUN. WE'LL SUFFER THROUGH THIS TOGETHER...
...
PAT
WHOOOA!
THIS IS BRINGIN' BACK MEMORIES!
WHAT-EVER...
BOOM
CHAK
HAS IT ONLY BEEN A YEAR? FEELS LIKE FOREVER SINCE THE LAST TIME WE CAME.
SURE DOES.
BOOM CHAK
BOOM
BOOM CHAK
BOOM
BOOM
THE SHOPS AREN'T EVEN OPEN, THOUGH. TOLD YOU IT WAS TOO EARLY!

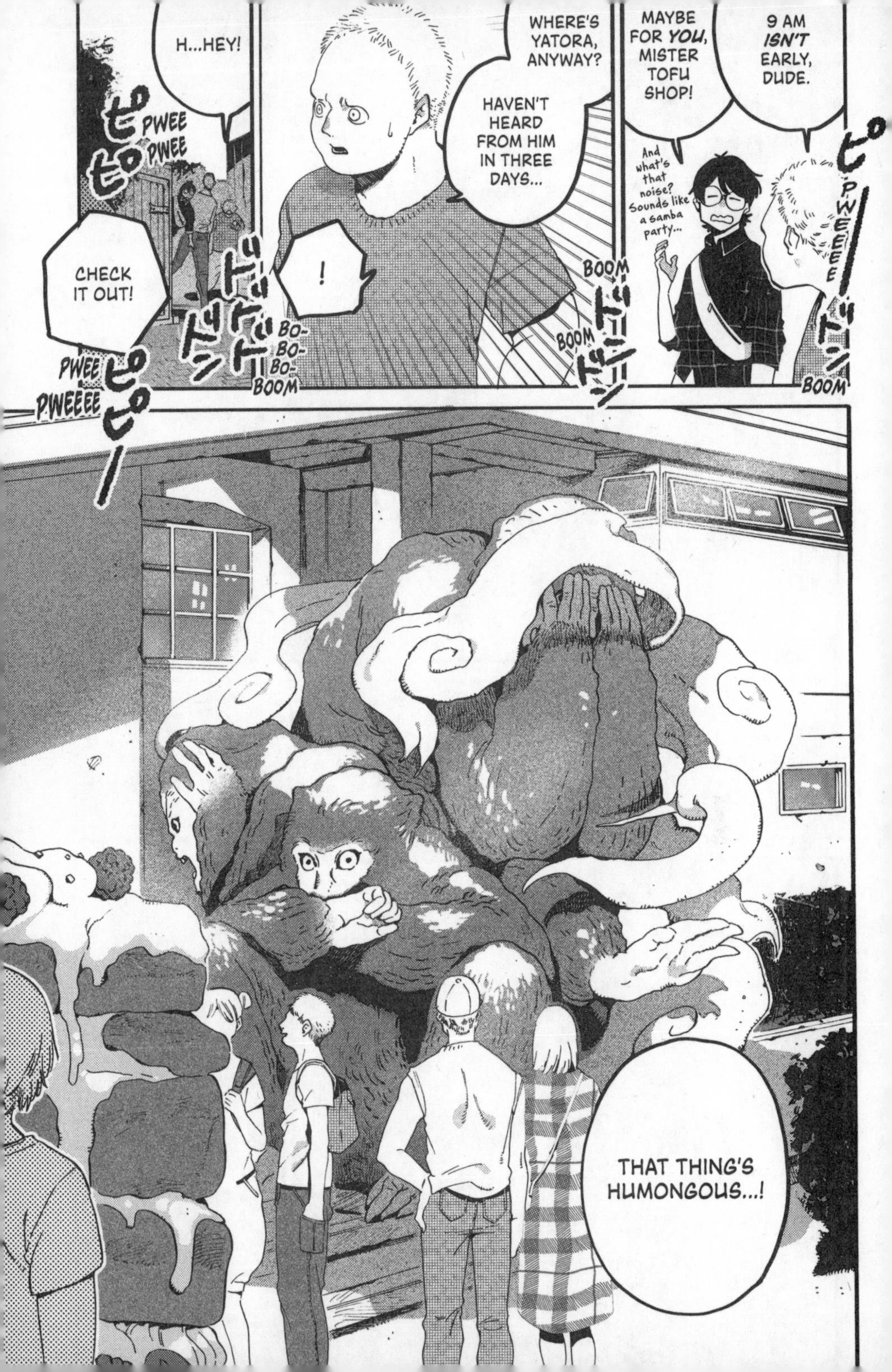
9 AM ISN'T EARLY, DUDE.
MAYBE FOR YOU, MISTER TOFU SHOP!
And what's that noise? Sounds like a samba party...
PWEEEEE
BOOM
BOOM
BOOM
WHERE'S YATORA, ANYWAY?
HAVEN'T HEARD FROM HIM IN THREE DAYS...
!
BO-BO-BO-BOOM
H...HEY!
PWEE PWEE
CHECK IT OUT!
PWEE PWEEEEE
THAT THING'S HUMONGOUS...!

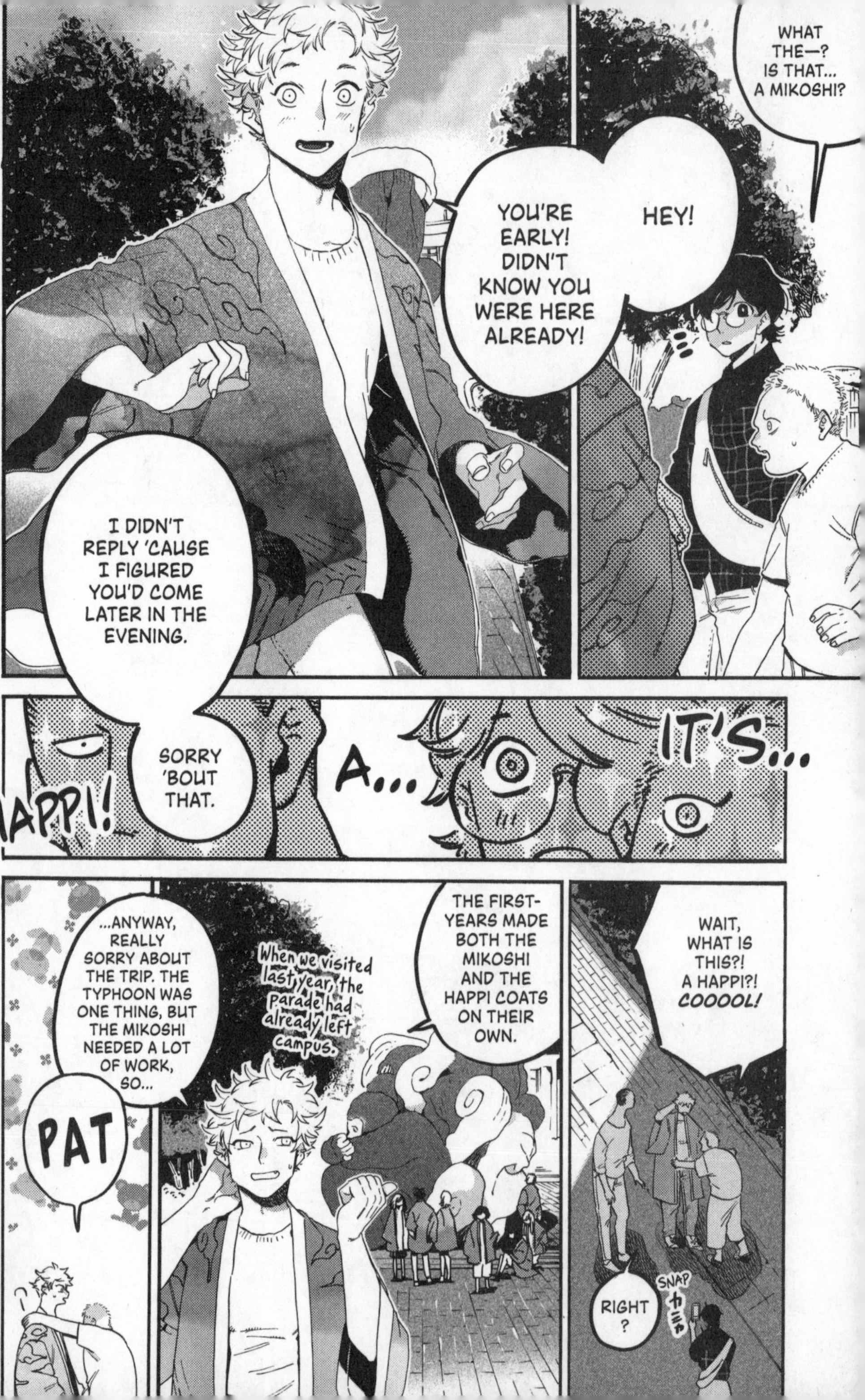
WHAT THE—? IS THAT... A MIKOSHI?
HEY!
YOU'RE EARLY! DIDN'T KNOW YOU WERE HERE ALREADY!
I DIDN'T REPLY 'CAUSE I FIGURED YOU'D COME LATER IN THE EVENING.
SORRY 'BOUT THAT.
IT'S...
A...
HAPPI!
WAIT, WHAT IS THIS?! A HAPPI?! *COOOOL!*
SNAP
カシャ
RIGHT?
THE FIRST-YEARS MADE BOTH THE MIKOSHI AND THE HAPPI COATS ON THEIR OWN.
When we visited last year, the parade had already left campus.
...ANYWAY, REALLY SORRY ABOUT THE TRIP. THE TYPHOON WAS ONE THING, BUT THE MIKOSHI NEEDED A LOT OF WORK, SO...
PAT

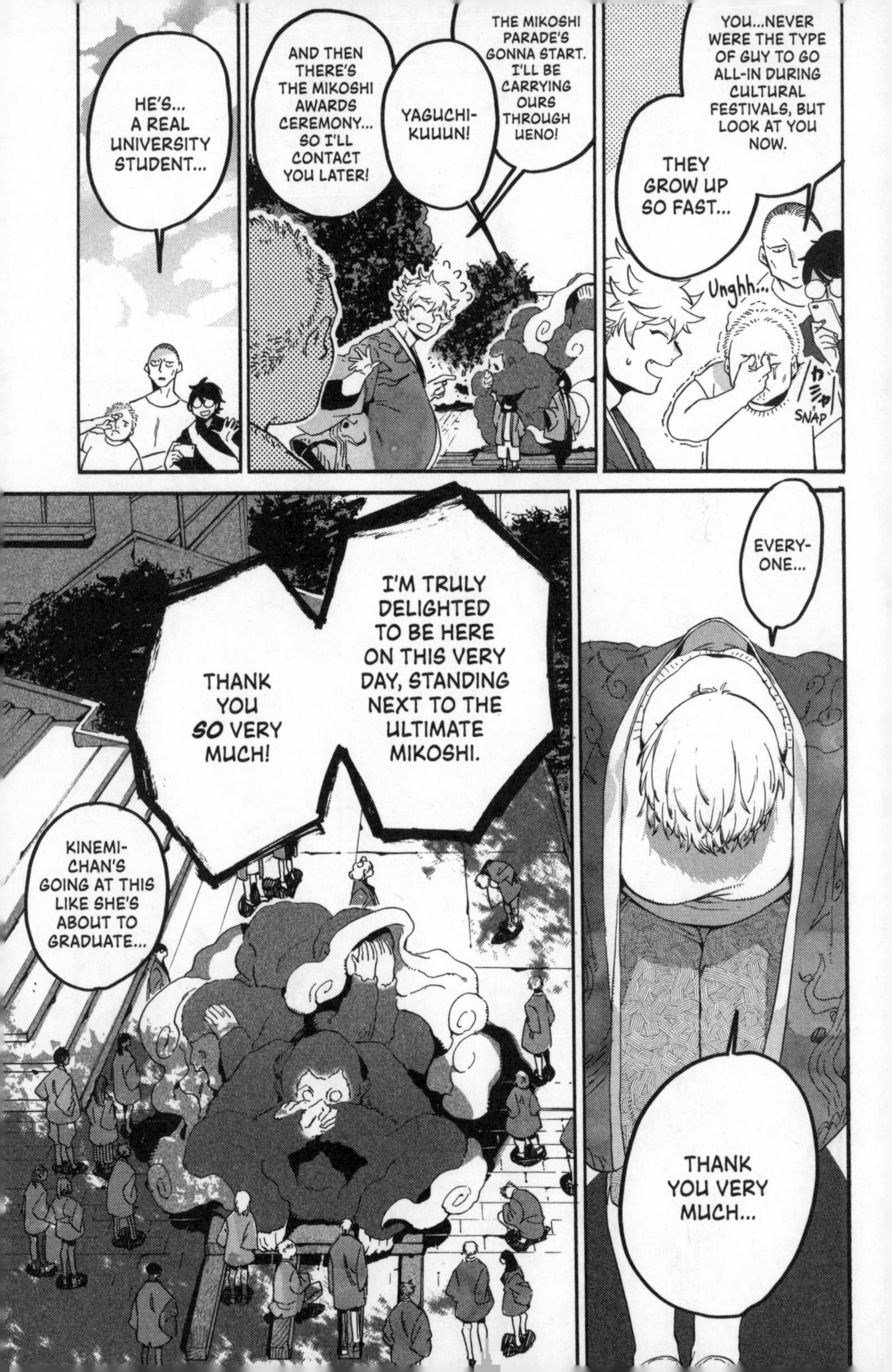
YOU...NEVER WERE THE TYPE OF GUY TO GO ALL-IN DURING CULTURAL FESTIVALS, BUT LOOK AT YOU NOW.
THEY GROW UP SO FAST...
Unghh...
SNAP
THE MIKOSHI PARADE'S GONNA START. I'LL BE CARRYING OURS THROUGH UENO!
YAGUCHI-KUUUN!
AND THEN THERE'S THE MIKOSHI AWARDS CEREMONY... SO I'LL CONTACT YOU LATER!
HE'S... A REAL UNIVERSITY STUDENT...
EVERY-ONE...
THANK YOU VERY MUCH...
I'M TRULY DELIGHTED TO BE HERE ON THIS VERY DAY, STANDING NEXT TO THE ULTIMATE MIKOSHI.
THANK YOU *SO* VERY MUCH!
KINEMI-CHAN'S GOING AT THIS LIKE SHE'S ABOUT TO GRADUATE...

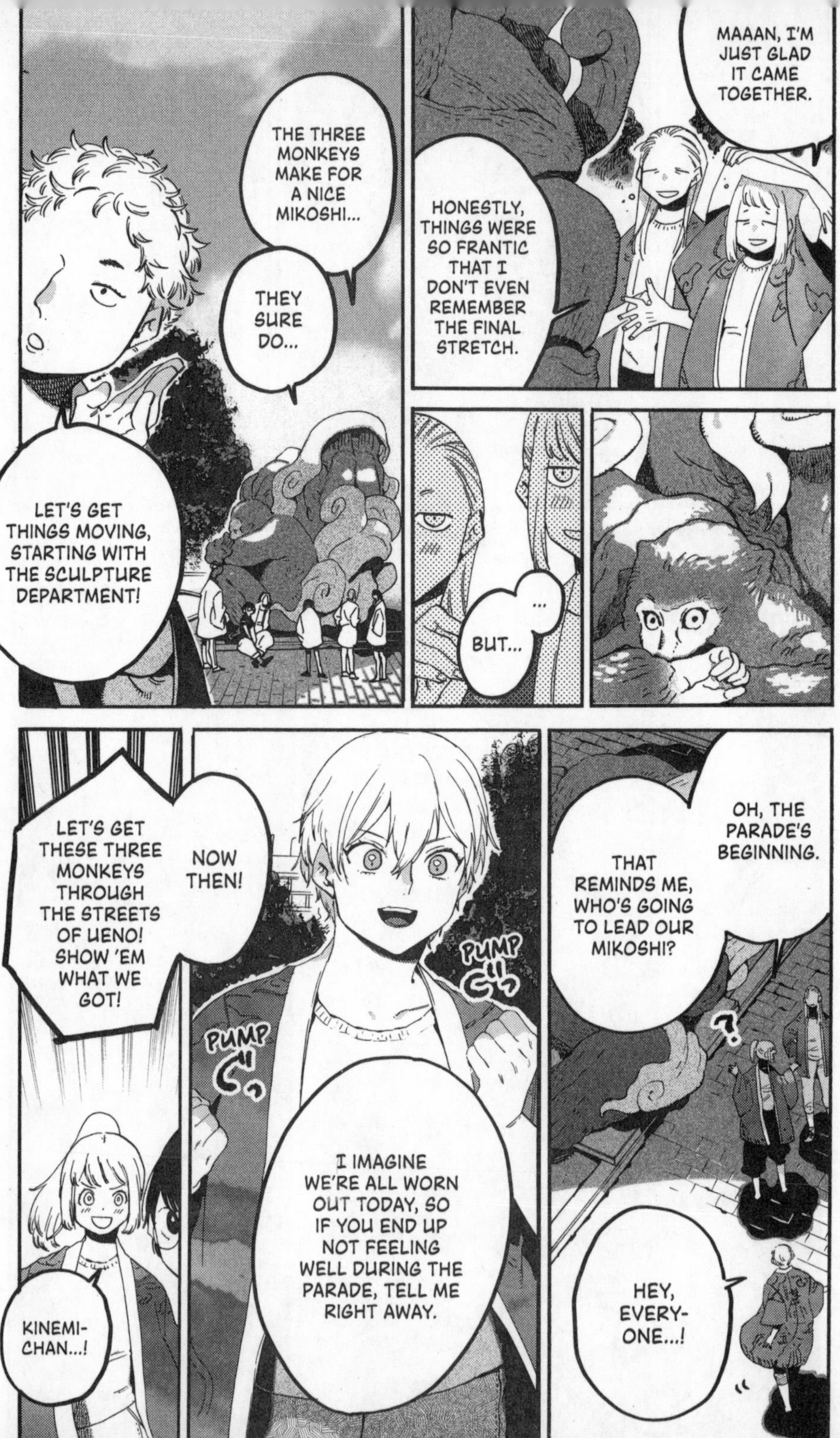
MAAAN, I'M JUST GLAD IT CAME TOGETHER.
HONESTLY, THINGS WERE SO FRANTIC THAT I DON'T EVEN REMEMBER THE FINAL STRETCH.
...
BUT...
THE THREE MONKEYS MAKE FOR A NICE MIKOSHI...
THEY SURE DO...
LET'S GET THINGS MOVING, STARTING WITH THE SCULPTURE DEPARTMENT!
OH, THE PARADE'S BEGINNING.
THAT REMINDS ME, WHO'S GOING TO LEAD OUR MIKOSHI?
?
HEY, EVERY-ONE...!
PUMP
PUMP
I IMAGINE WE'RE ALL WORN OUT TODAY, SO IF YOU END UP NOT FEELING WELL DURING THE PARADE, TELL ME RIGHT AWAY.
NOW THEN!
LET'S GET THESE THREE MONKEYS THROUGH THE STREETS OF UENO! SHOW 'EM WHAT WE GOT!
KINEMI-CHAN...!

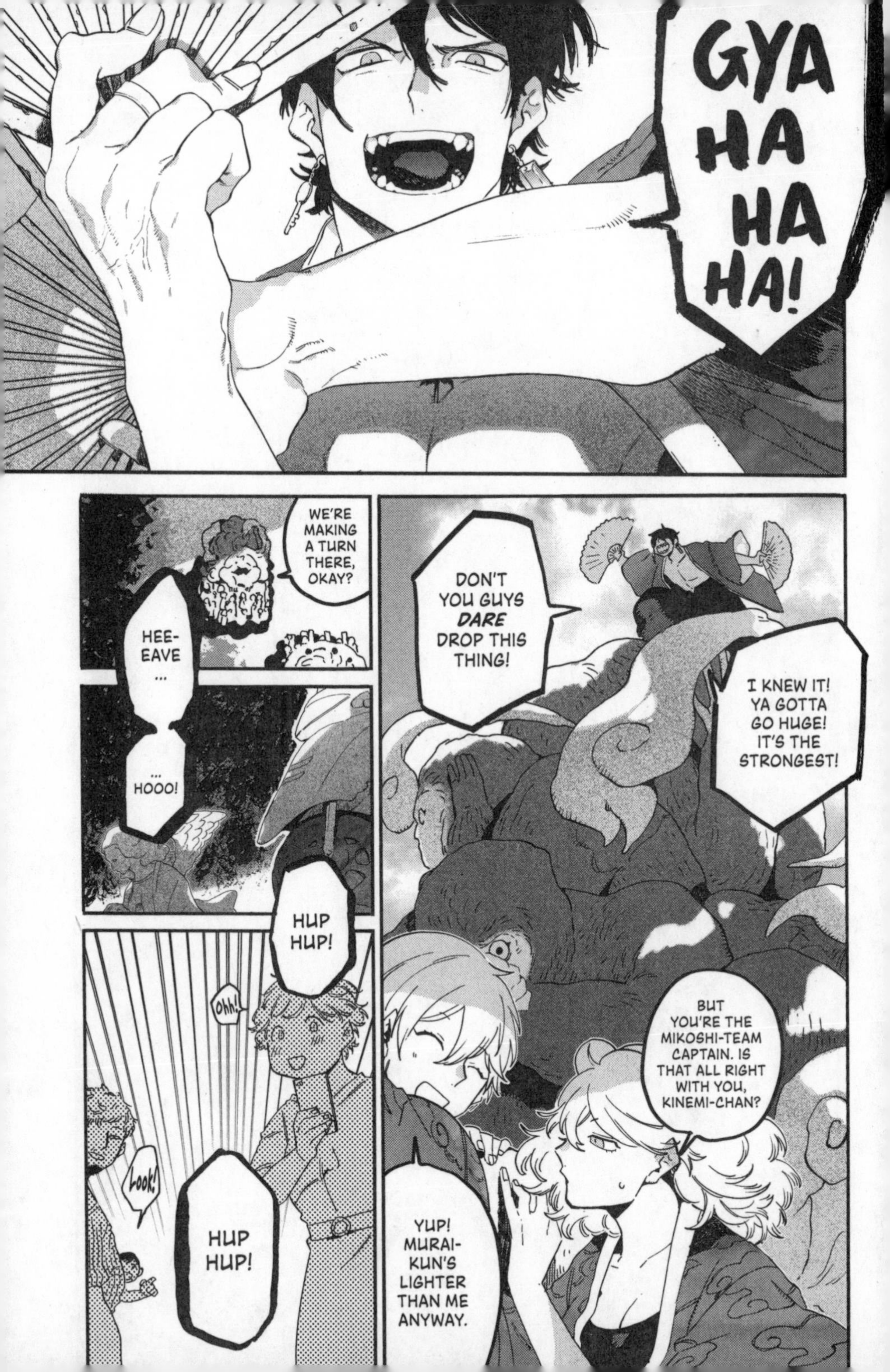
GYA HA HA HA HA!
DON'T YOU GUYS DARE DROP THIS THING!
I KNEW IT! YA GOTTA GO HUGE! IT'S THE STRONGEST!
BUT YOU'RE THE MIKOSHI-TEAM CAPTAIN. IS THAT ALL RIGHT WITH YOU, KINEMI-CHAN?
YUP! MURAI-KUN'S LIGHTER THAN ME ANYWAY.
WE'RE MAKING A TURN THERE, OKAY?
HEE-EAVE...
...HOOO!
HUP HUP!
Ohh!
HUP HUP!
Look!

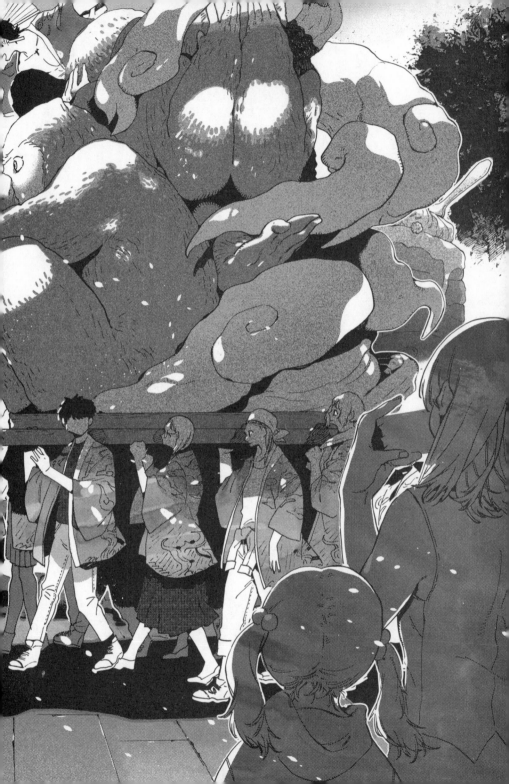

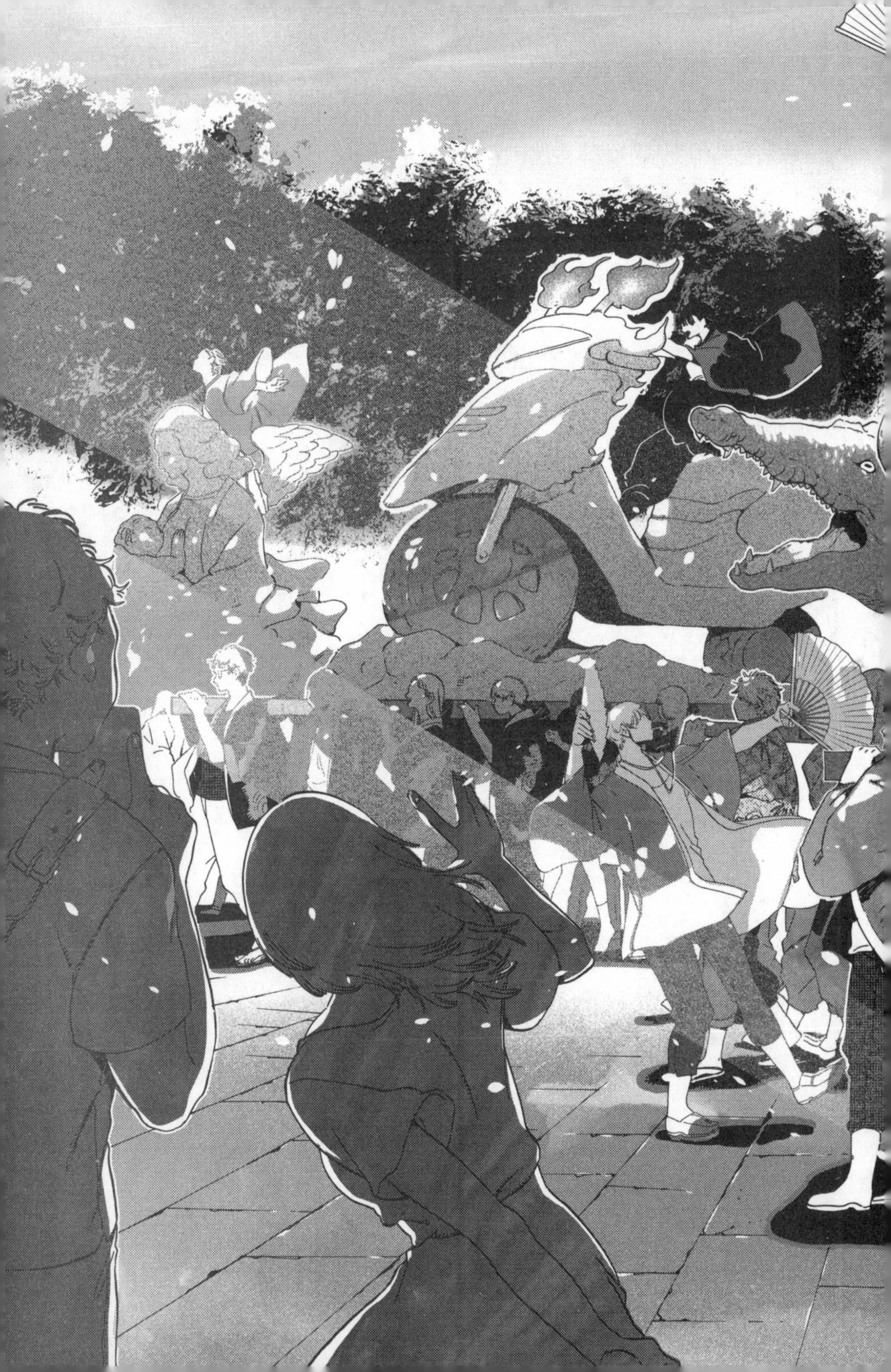

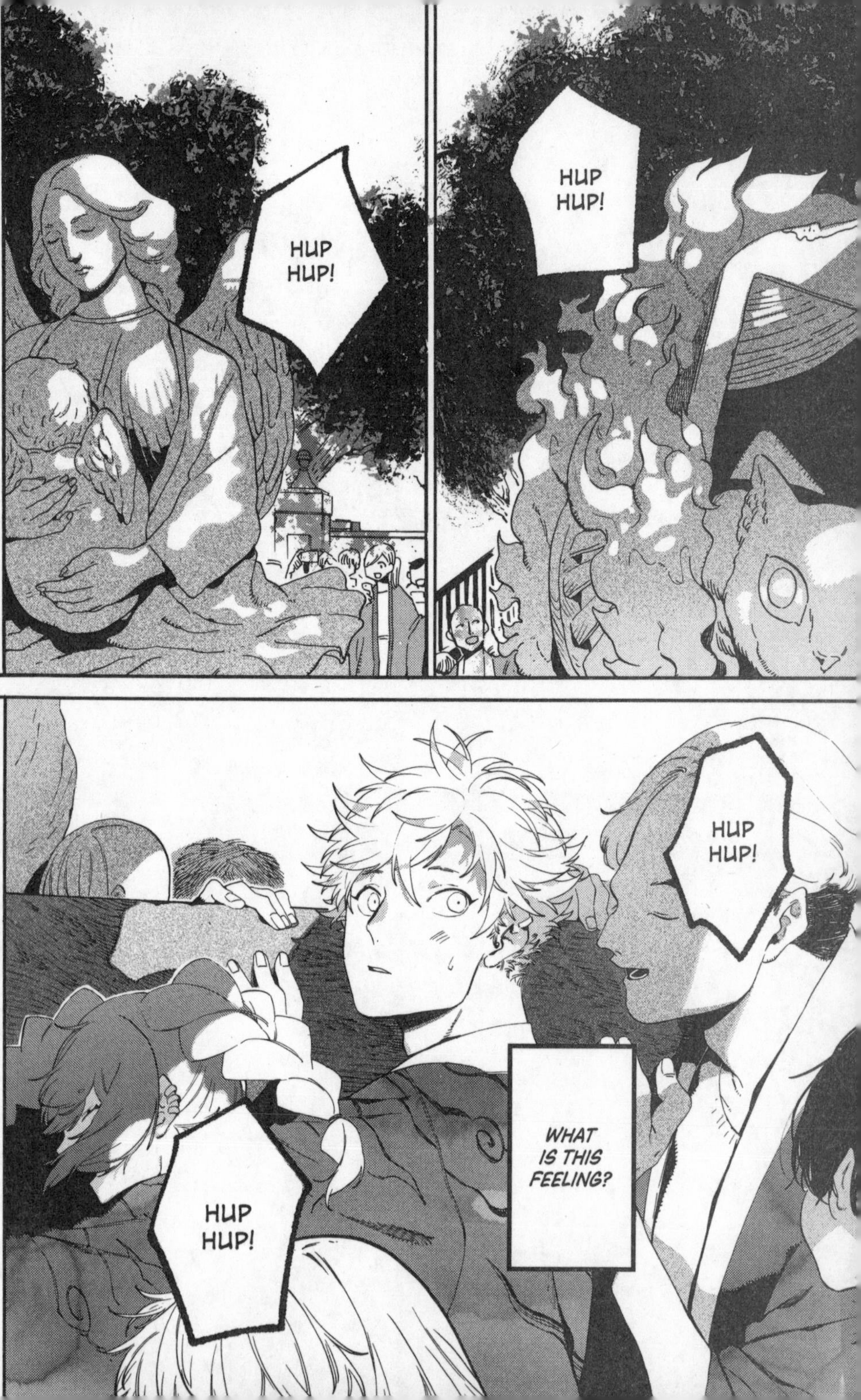
HUP HUP!
HUP HUP!
HUP HUP!
WHAT IS THIS FEELING?
HUP HUP!

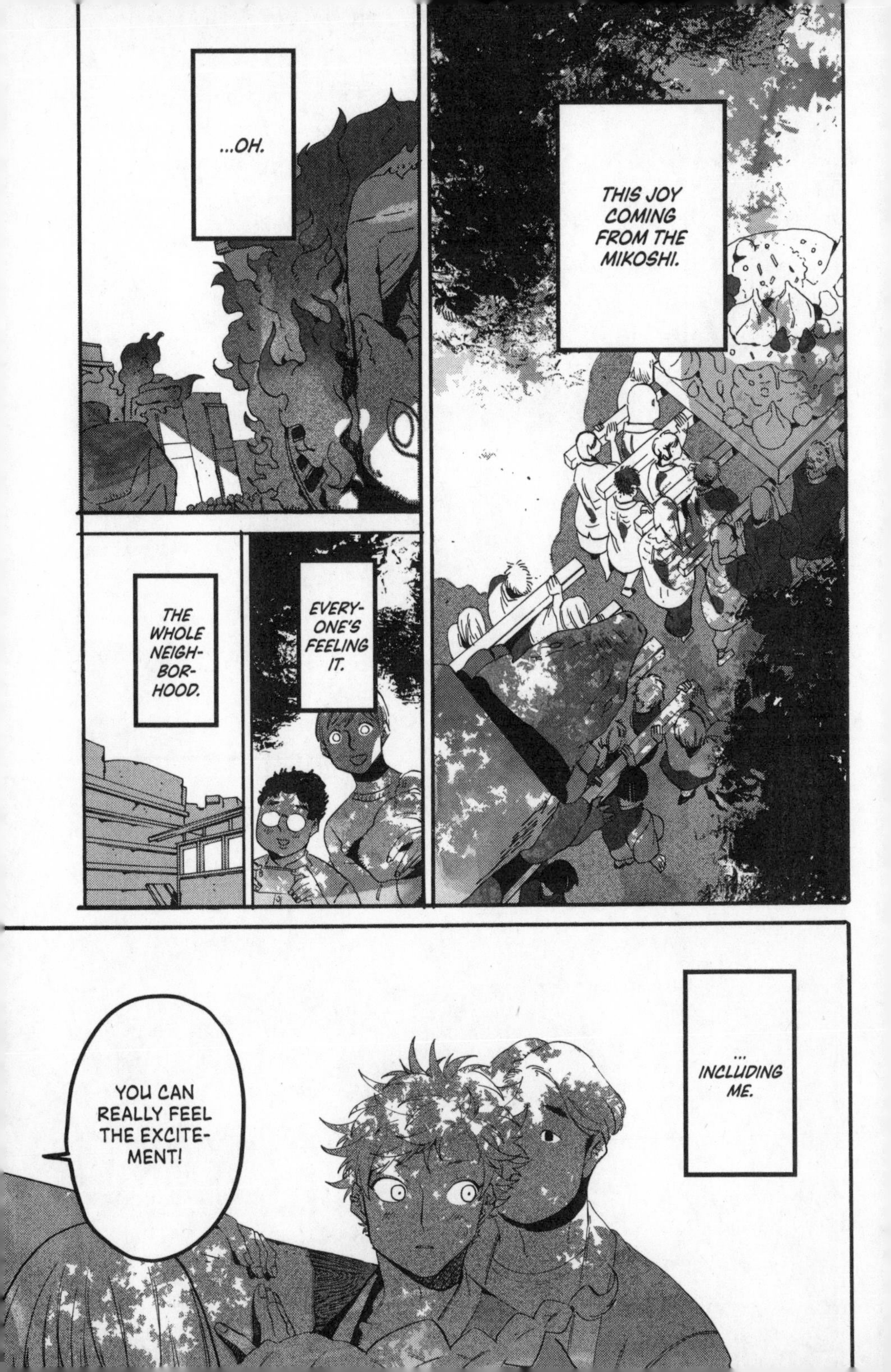
THIS JOY COMING FROM THE MIKOSHI.
...OH.
EVERY-ONE'S FEELING IT.
THE WHOLE NEIGH-BOR-HOOD.
...INCLUDING ME.
YOU CAN REALLY FEEL THE EXCITE-MENT!

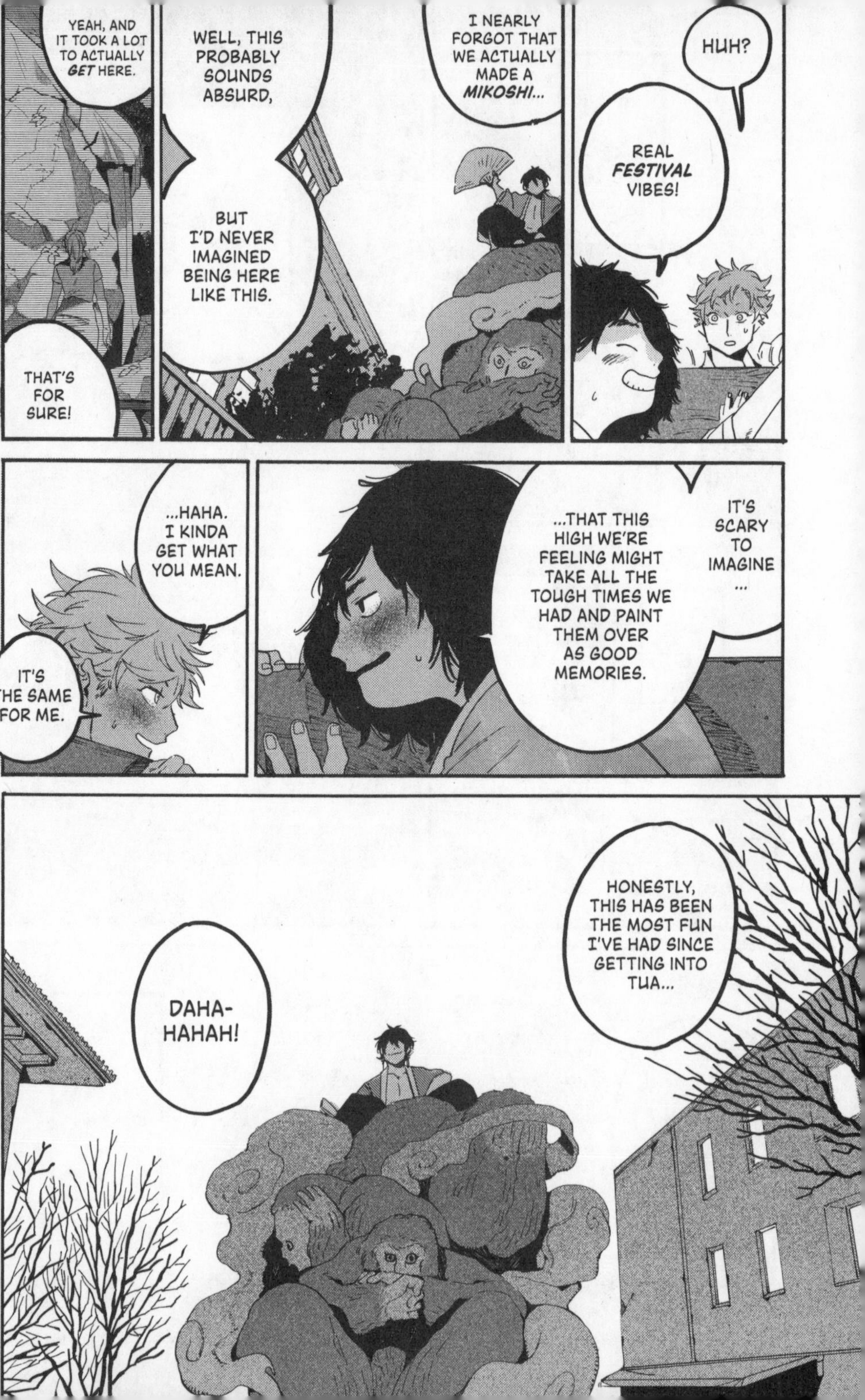
HUH?
REAL *FESTIVAL* VIBES!
I NEARLY FORGOT THAT WE ACTUALLY MADE A *MIKOSHI*...
WELL, THIS PROBABLY SOUNDS ABSURD,
BUT I'D NEVER IMAGINED BEING HERE LIKE THIS.
YEAH, AND IT TOOK A LOT TO ACTUALLY *GET* HERE.
THAT'S FOR SURE!
IT'S SCARY TO IMAGINE ...
...THAT THIS HIGH WE'RE FEELING MIGHT TAKE ALL THE TOUGH TIMES WE HAD AND PAINT THEM OVER AS GOOD MEMORIES.
...HAHA. I KINDA GET WHAT YOU MEAN.
IT'S THE SAME FOR ME.
HONESTLY, THIS HAS BEEN THE MOST FUN I'VE HAD SINCE GETTING INTO TUA...
DAHA-HAHAH!

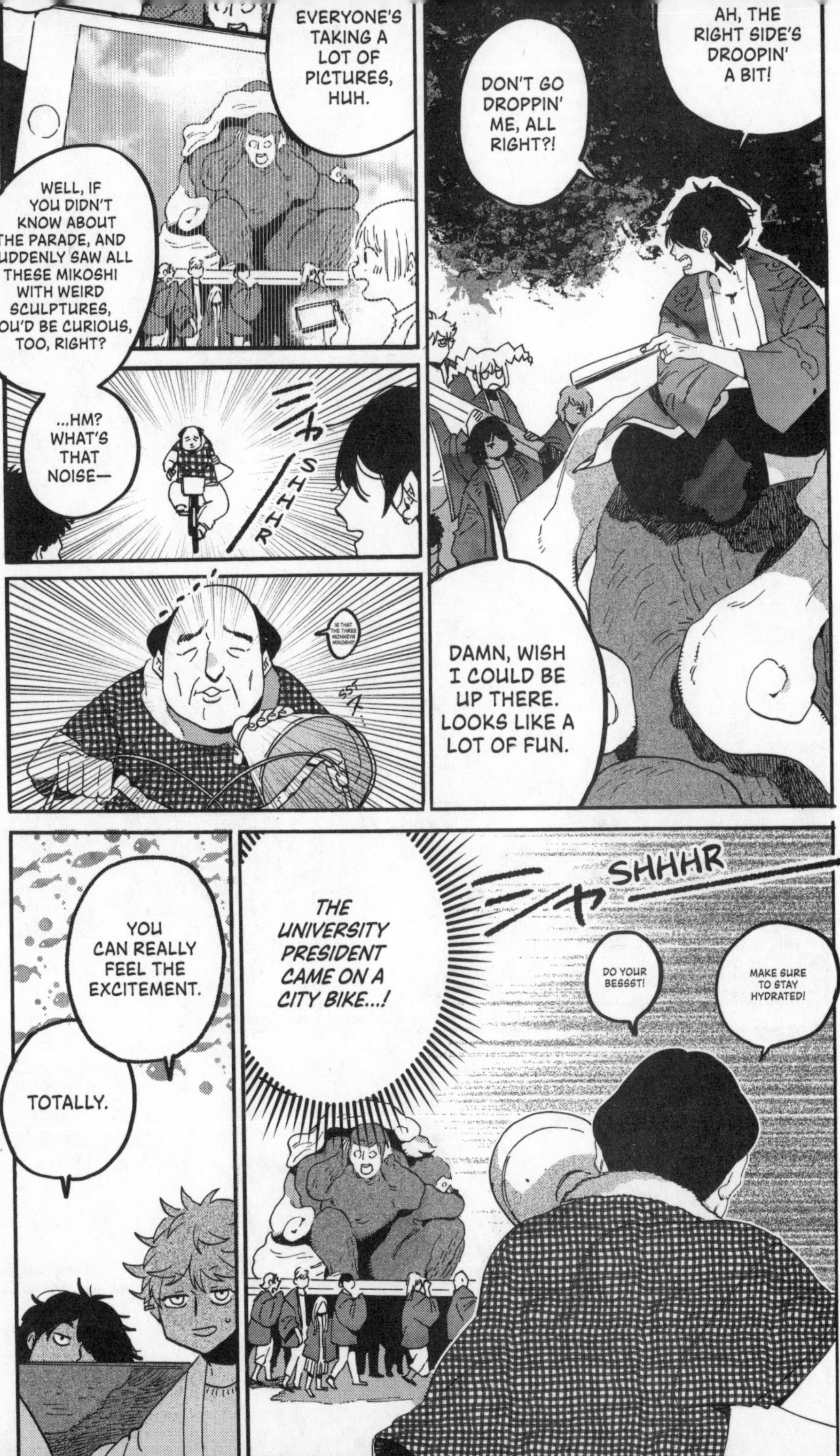
AH, THE RIGHT SIDE'S DROOPIN' A BIT!
DON'T GO DROPPIN' ME, ALL RIGHT?!
DAMN, WISH I COULD BE UP THERE. LOOKS LIKE A LOT OF FUN.
EVERYONE'S TAKING A LOT OF PICTURES, HUH.
WELL, IF YOU DIDN'T KNOW ABOUT THE PARADE, AND SUDDENLY SAW ALL THESE MIKOSHI WITH WEIRD SCULPTURES, YOU'D BE CURIOUS, TOO, RIGHT?
SHHHR
...HM? WHAT'S THAT NOISE—
IS THAT THE THREE MONKEYS MIKOSHI?
SST
SHHHR
MAKE SURE TO STAY HYDRATED!
DO YOUR BESSST!
THE UNIVERSITY PRESIDENT CAME ON A CITY BIKE...!
YOU CAN REALLY FEEL THE EXCITEMENT.
TOTALLY.

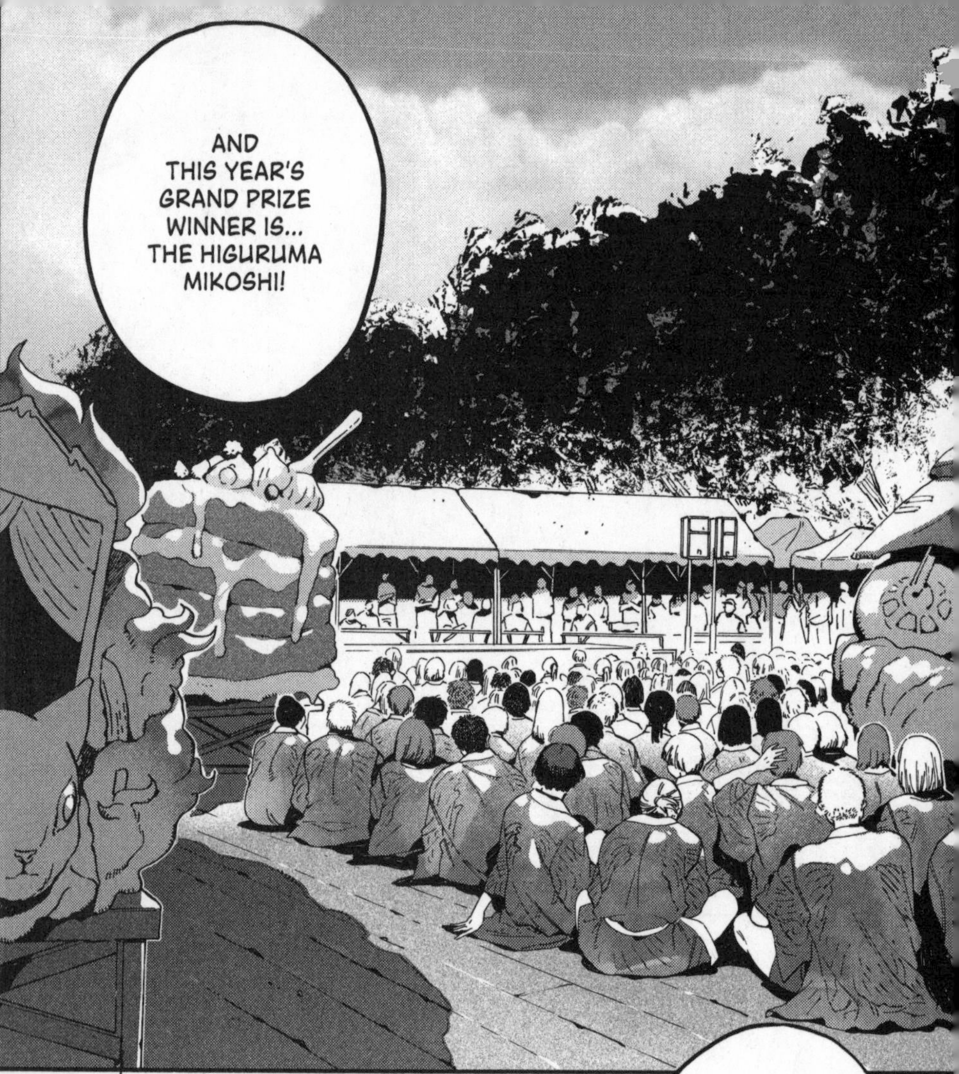
AND THIS YEAR'S GRAND PRIZE WINNER IS... THE HIGURUMA MIKOSHI!

*GAGAKU = JAPANESE ANCIENT COURT MUSIC.

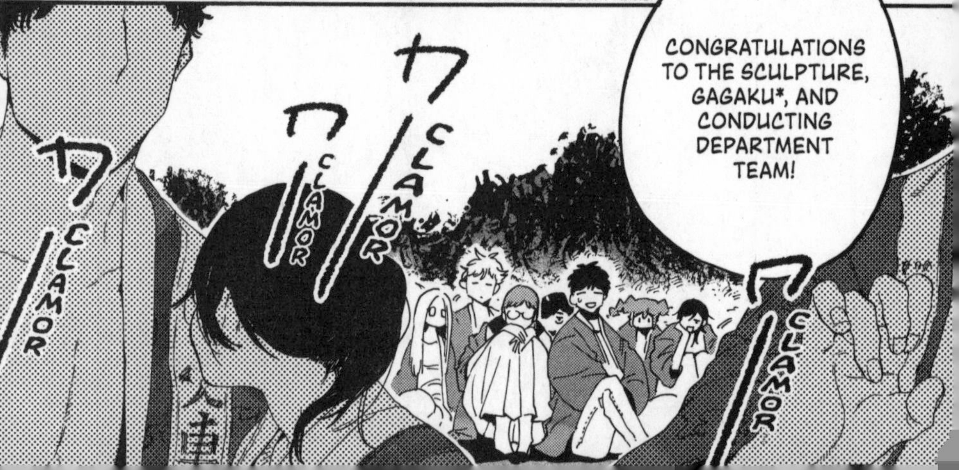
CONGRATULATIONS TO THE SCULPTURE, GAGAKU*, AND CONDUCTING DEPARTMENT TEAM!
CLAMOR
CLAMOR
CLAMOR
CLAMOR
CLAMOR

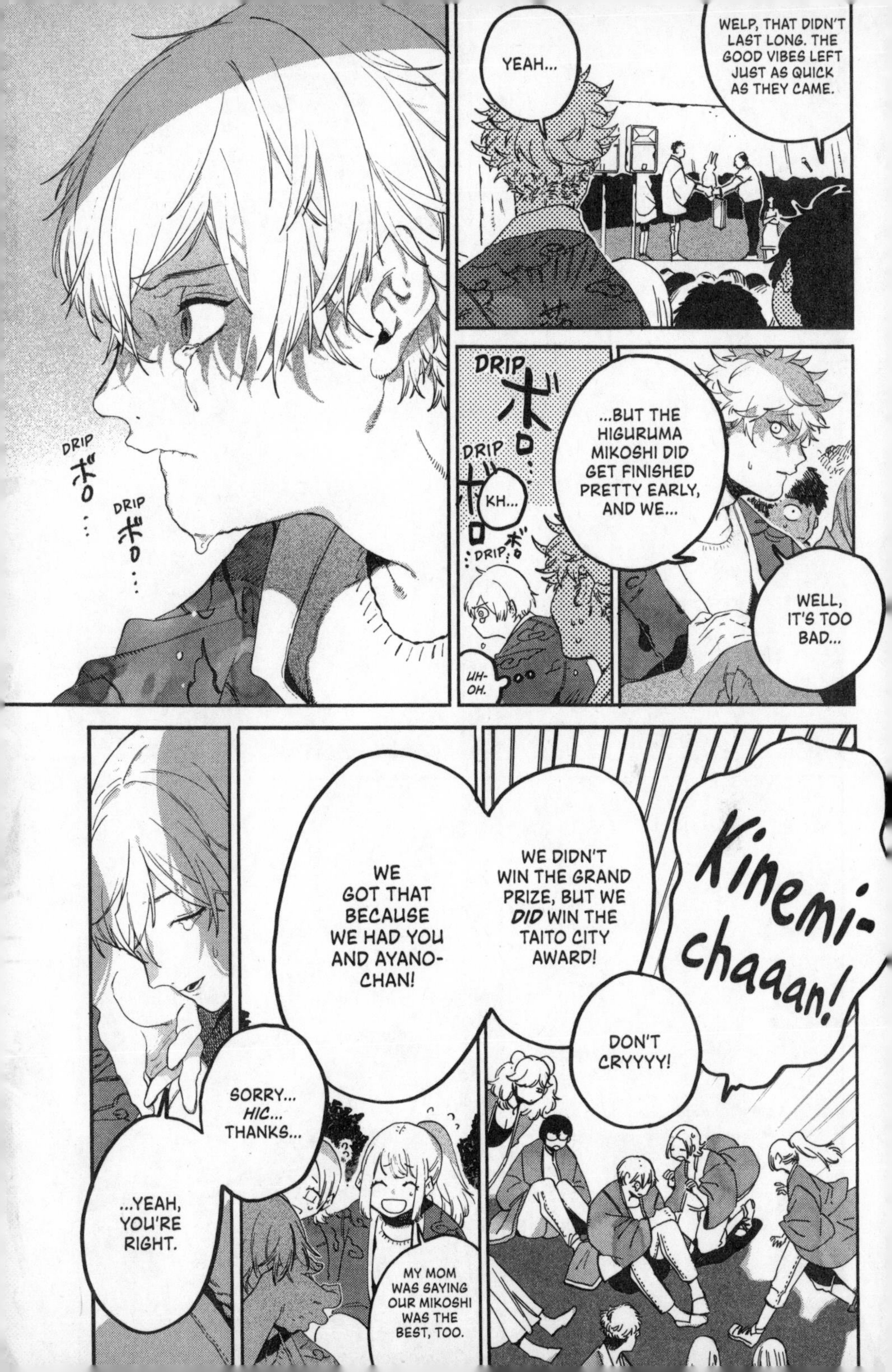
WELP, THAT DIDN'T LAST LONG. THE GOOD VIBES LEFT JUST AS QUICK AS THEY CAME.
YEAH...
...BUT THE HIGURUMA MIKOSHI DID GET FINISHED PRETTY EARLY, AND WE...
WELL, IT'S TOO BAD...
DRIP
DRIP
KH...
DRIP
UH-OH.
DRIP
DRIP
Kinemi-chaaaan!
WE DIDN'T WIN THE GRAND PRIZE, BUT WE *DID* WIN THE TAITO CITY AWARD!
WE GOT THAT BECAUSE WE HAD YOU AND AYANO-CHAN!
DON'T CRYYYY!
MY MOM WAS SAYING OUR MIKOSHI WAS THE BEST, TOO.
SORRY... *HIC*... THANKS...
...YEAH, YOU'RE RIGHT.

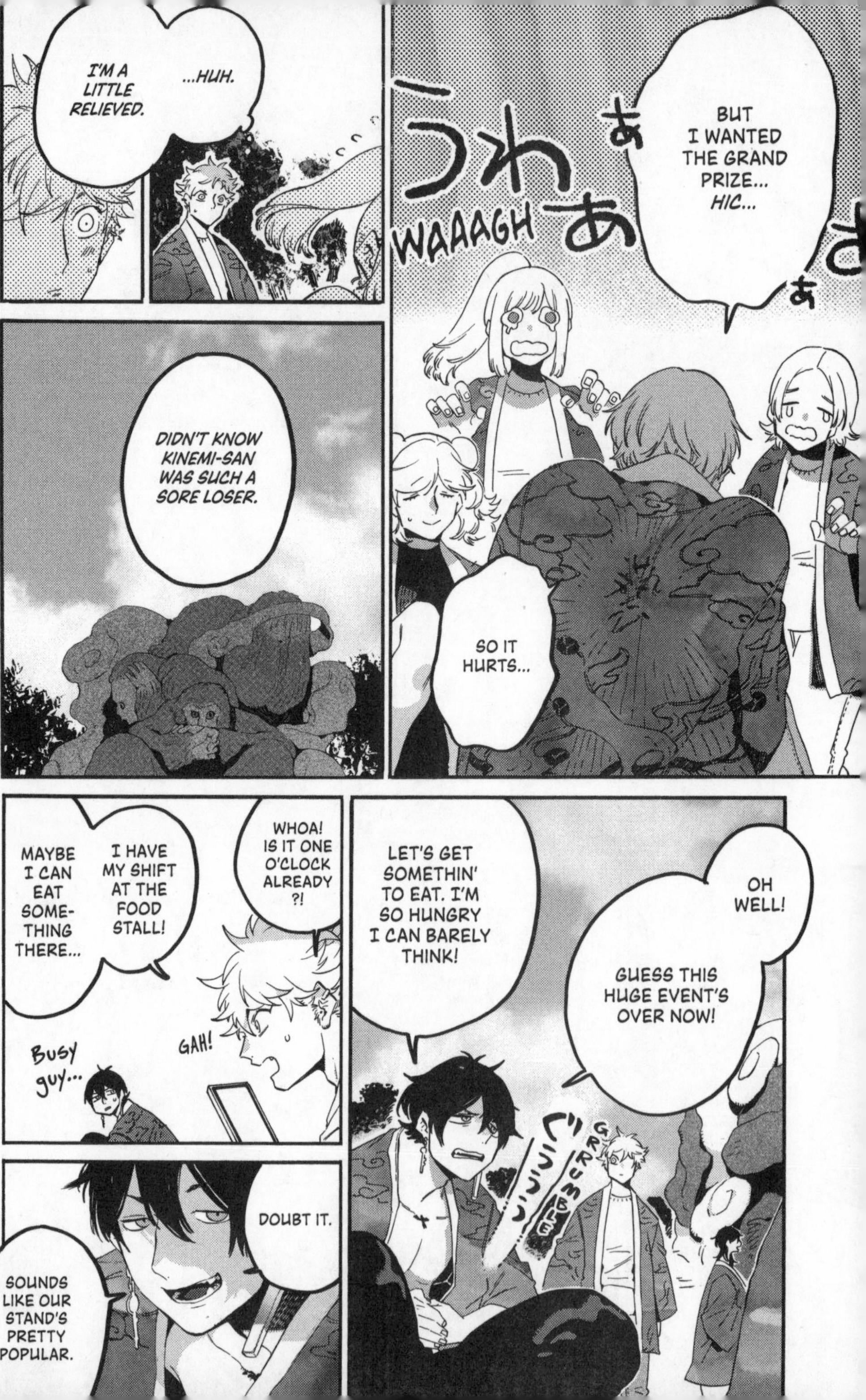
うわあああ
WAAAGH
BUT I WANTED THE GRAND PRIZE... HIC...
SO IT HURTS...
...HUH.
I'M A LITTLE RELIEVED.
DIDN'T KNOW KINEMI-SAN WAS SUCH A SORE LOSER.
OH WELL!
GUESS THIS HUGE EVENT'S OVER NOW!
LET'S GET SOMETHIN' TO EAT. I'M SO HUNGRY I CAN BARELY THINK!
GRRUMBLE
WHOA! IS IT ONE O'CLOCK ALREADY?!
GAH!
I HAVE MY SHIFT AT THE FOOD STALL!
MAYBE I CAN EAT SOMETHING THERE...
Busy guy...
DOUBT IT.
SOUNDS LIKE OUR STAND'S PRETTY POPULAR.

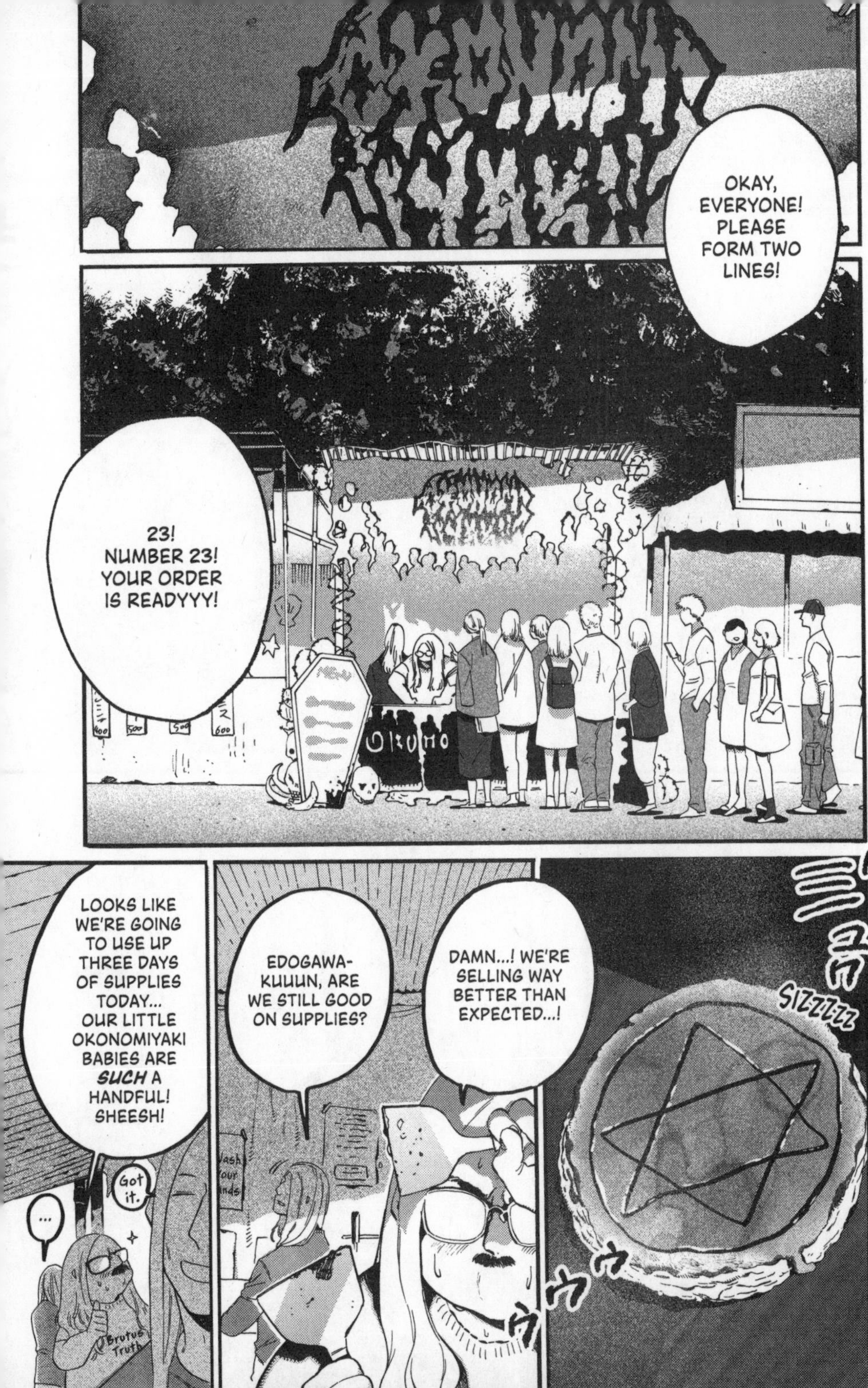
OKAY, EVERYONE! PLEASE FORM TWO LINES!
23! NUMBER 23! YOUR ORDER IS READYYY!
SIZZZZZ
DAMN...! WE'RE SELLING WAY BETTER THAN EXPECTED...!
EDOGAWA-KUUUN, ARE WE STILL GOOD ON SUPPLIES?
Got it.
LOOKS LIKE WE'RE GOING TO USE UP THREE DAYS OF SUPPLIES TODAY... OUR LITTLE OKONOMIYAKI BABIES ARE *SUCH* A HANDFUL! SHEESH!
...
Brutus Truth

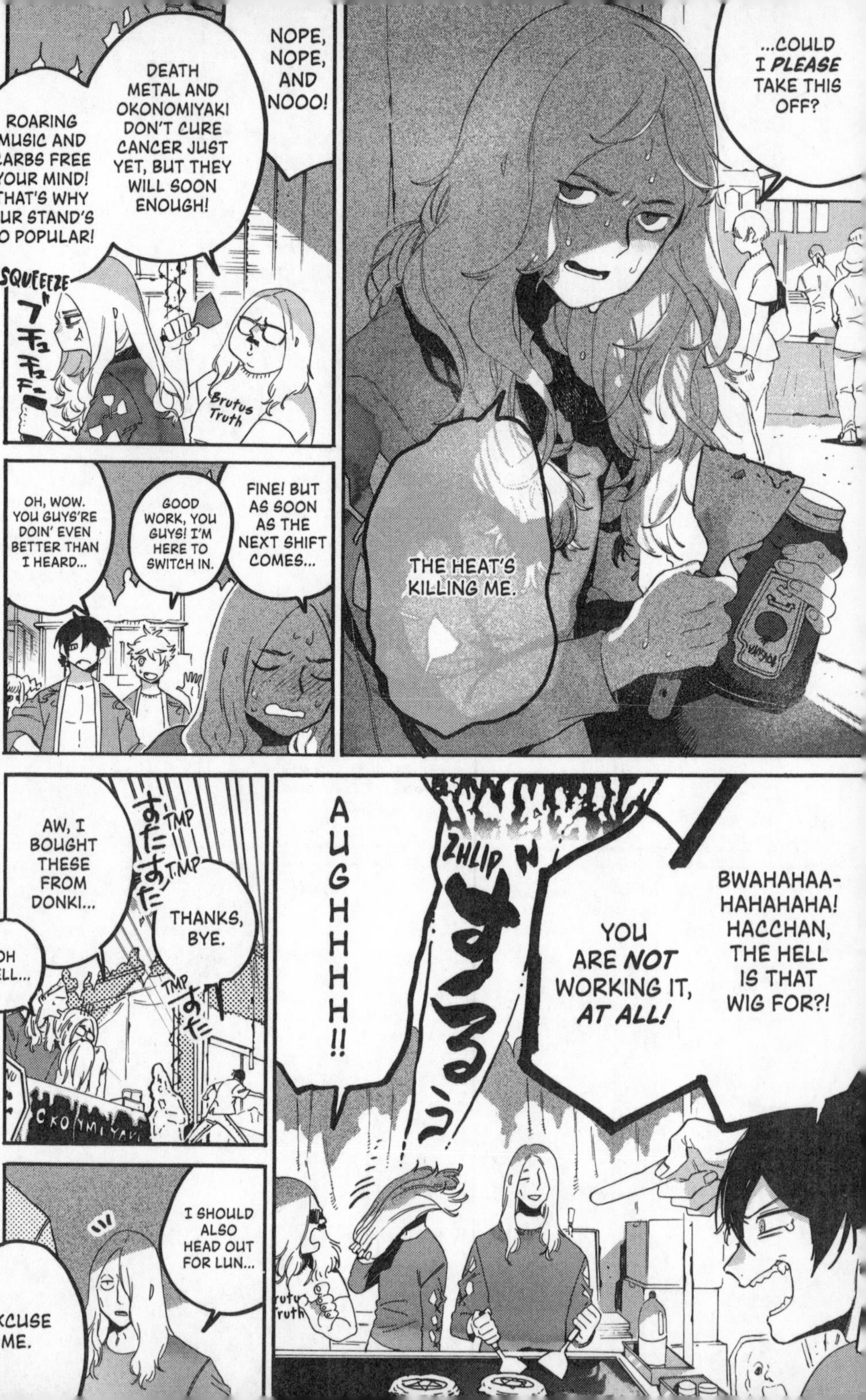
...COULD I *PLEASE* TAKE THIS OFF?
THE HEAT'S KILLING ME.
NOPE, NOPE, AND NOOO!
DEATH METAL AND OKONOMIYAKI DON'T CURE CANCER JUST YET, BUT THEY WILL SOON ENOUGH!
ROARING MUSIC AND CARBS FREE YOUR MIND! THAT'S WHY OUR STAND'S SO POPULAR!
SQUEEEZE
Brutus Truth
FINE! BUT AS SOON AS THE NEXT SHIFT COMES...
GOOD WORK, YOU GUYS! I'M HERE TO SWITCH IN.
OH, WOW. YOU GUYS'RE DOIN' EVEN BETTER THAN I HEARD...
BWAHAHAA-HAHAHAHA! HACCHAN, THE HELL IS THAT WIG FOR?!
YOU ARE *NOT* WORKING IT, *AT ALL!*
AUGHHHH!!
ZHLIP
Brutus Truth
TMP
TMP
THANKS, BYE.
TMP
AW, I BOUGHT THESE FROM DONKI...
OH WELL...
I SHOULD ALSO HEAD OUT FOR LUN...
EXCUSE ME.

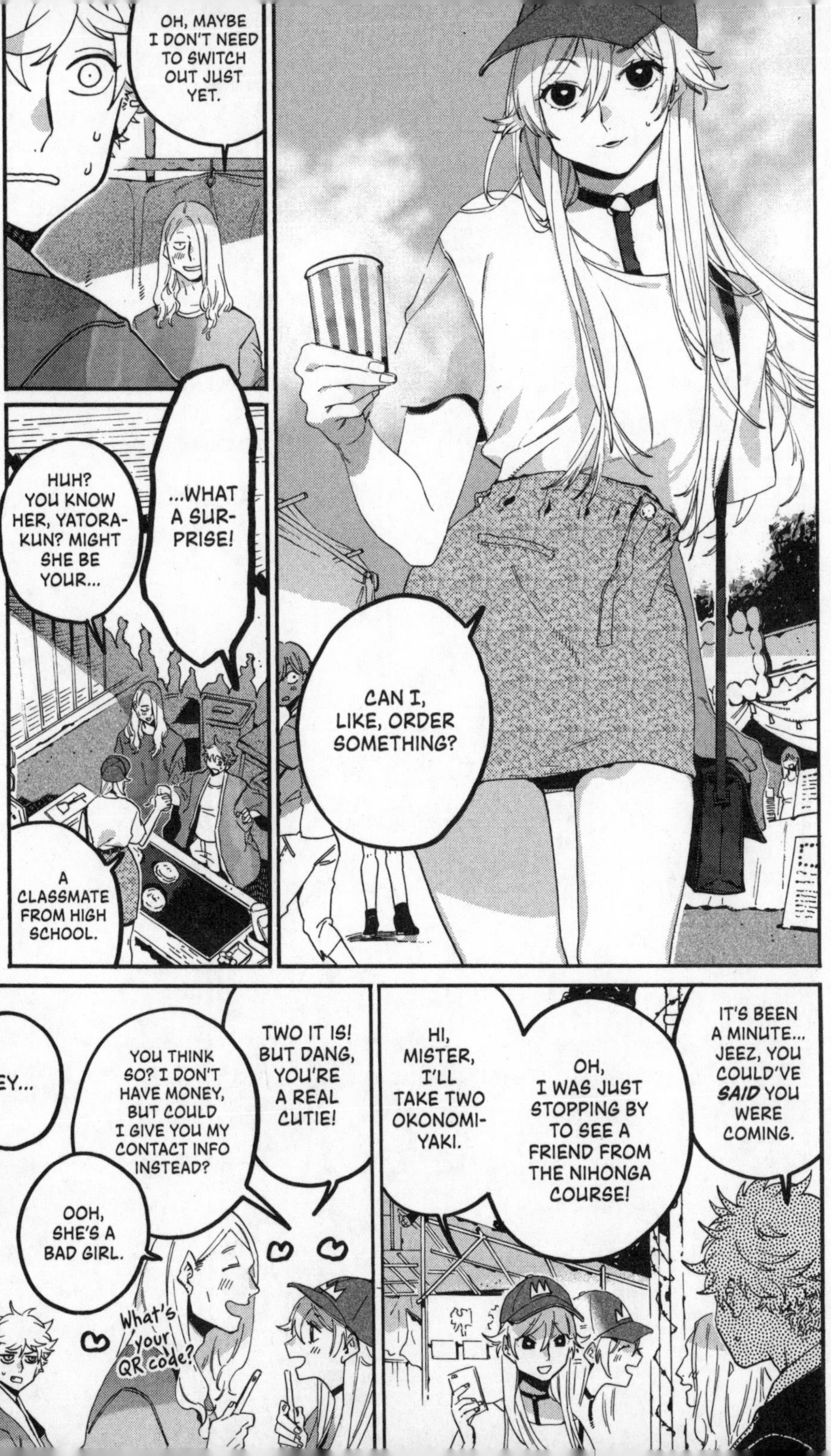
CAN I, LIKE, ORDER SOMETHING?
OH, MAYBE I DON'T NEED TO SWITCH OUT JUST YET.
...WHAT A SUR-PRISE!
HUH? YOU KNOW HER, YATORA-KUN? MIGHT SHE BE YOUR...
A CLASSMATE FROM HIGH SCHOOL.
IT'S BEEN A MINUTE... JEEZ, YOU COULD'VE *SAID* YOU WERE COMING.
OH, I WAS JUST STOPPING BY TO SEE A FRIEND FROM THE NIHONGA COURSE!
HI, MISTER, I'LL TAKE TWO OKONOMI-YAKI.
TWO IT IS! BUT DANG, YOU'RE A REAL CUTIE!
YOU THINK SO? I DON'T HAVE MONEY, BUT COULD I GIVE YOU MY CONTACT INFO INSTEAD?
HEY...
OOH, SHE'S A BAD GIRL.
What's your QR code?

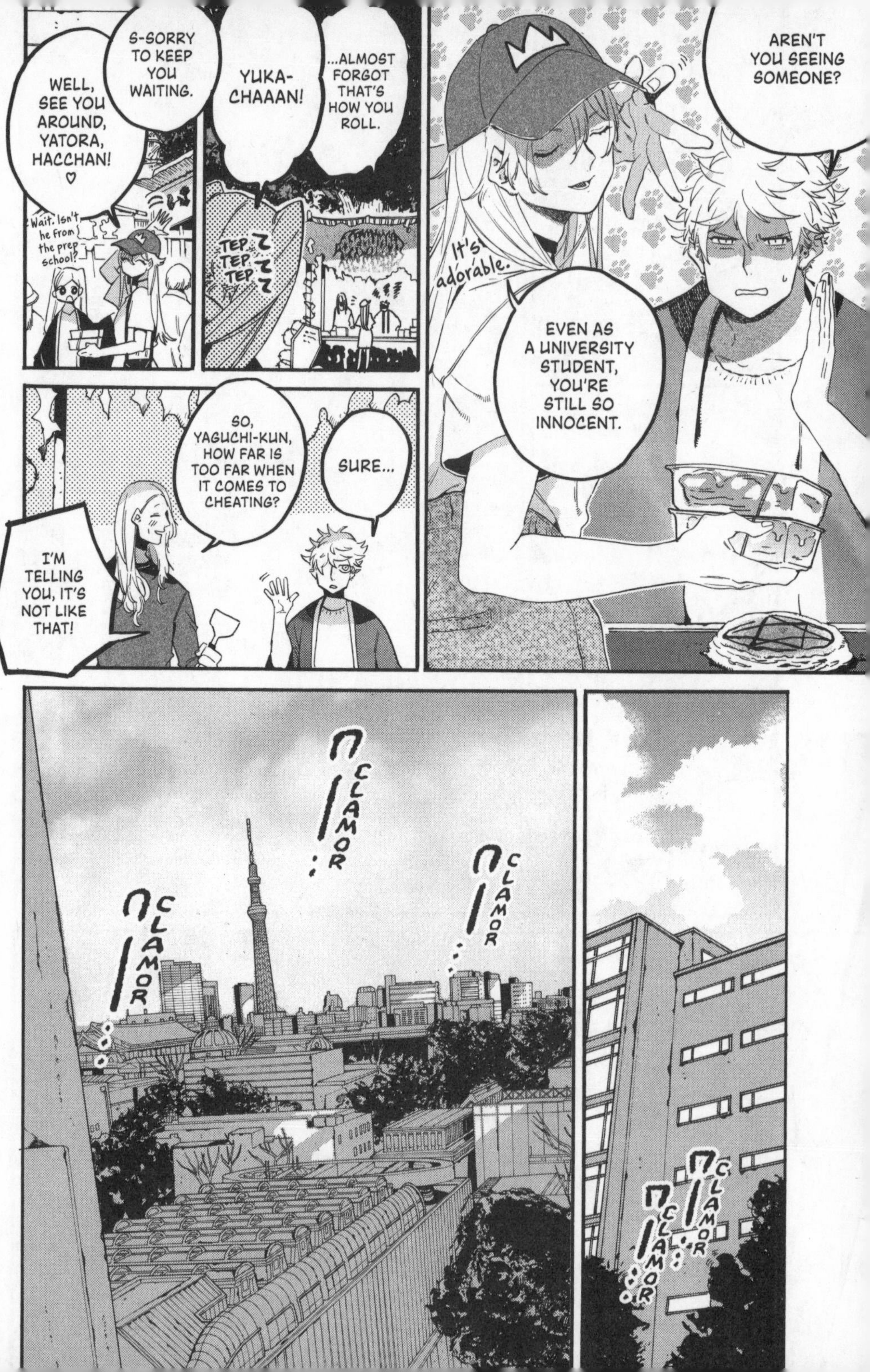
AREN'T YOU SEEING SOMEONE?
It's adorable.
EVEN AS A UNIVERSITY STUDENT, YOU'RE STILL SO INNOCENT.
...ALMOST FORGOT THAT'S HOW YOU ROLL.
YUKA-CHAAAN!
TEP TEP TEP
S-SORRY TO KEEP YOU WAITING.
WELL, SEE YOU AROUND, YATORA, HACCHAN! ♡
Wait. Isn't he from the prep school?
SURE...
SO, YAGUCHI-KUN, HOW FAR IS TOO FAR WHEN IT COMES TO CHEATING?
I'M TELLING YOU, IT'S NOT LIKE THAT!
CLAMOR
CLAMOR
CLAMOR
CLAMOR
CLAMOR

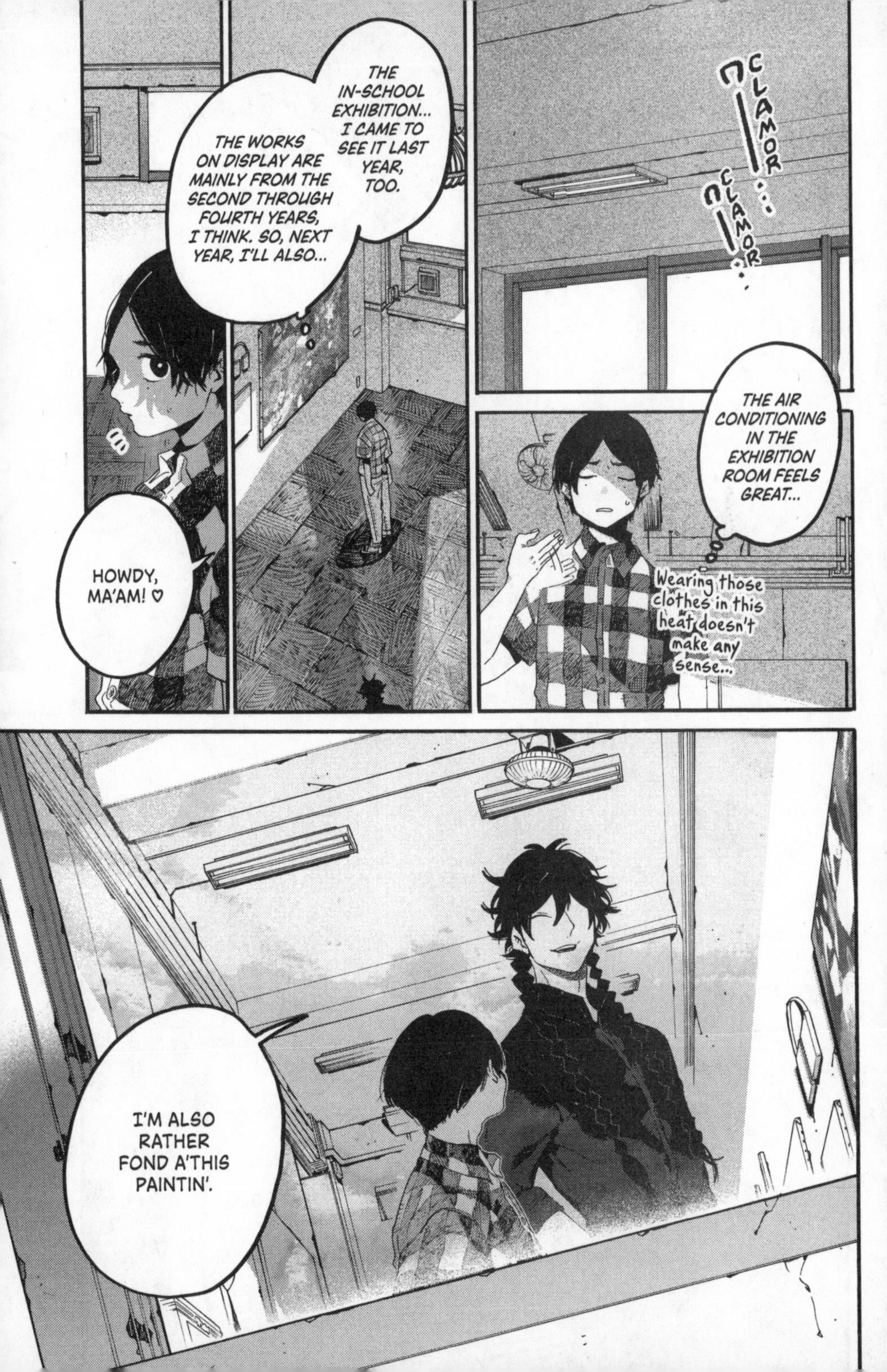
CLAMOR...
CLAMOR...
THE AIR CONDITIONING IN THE EXHIBITION ROOM FEELS GREAT...
Wearing those clothes in this heat doesn't make any sense...
THE IN-SCHOOL EXHIBITION... I CAME TO SEE IT LAST YEAR, TOO.
THE WORKS ON DISPLAY ARE MAINLY FROM THE SECOND THROUGH FOURTH YEARS, I THINK. SO, NEXT YEAR, I'LL ALSO...
HOWDY, MA'AM! ♡
I'M ALSO RATHER FOND A'THIS PAINTIN'.

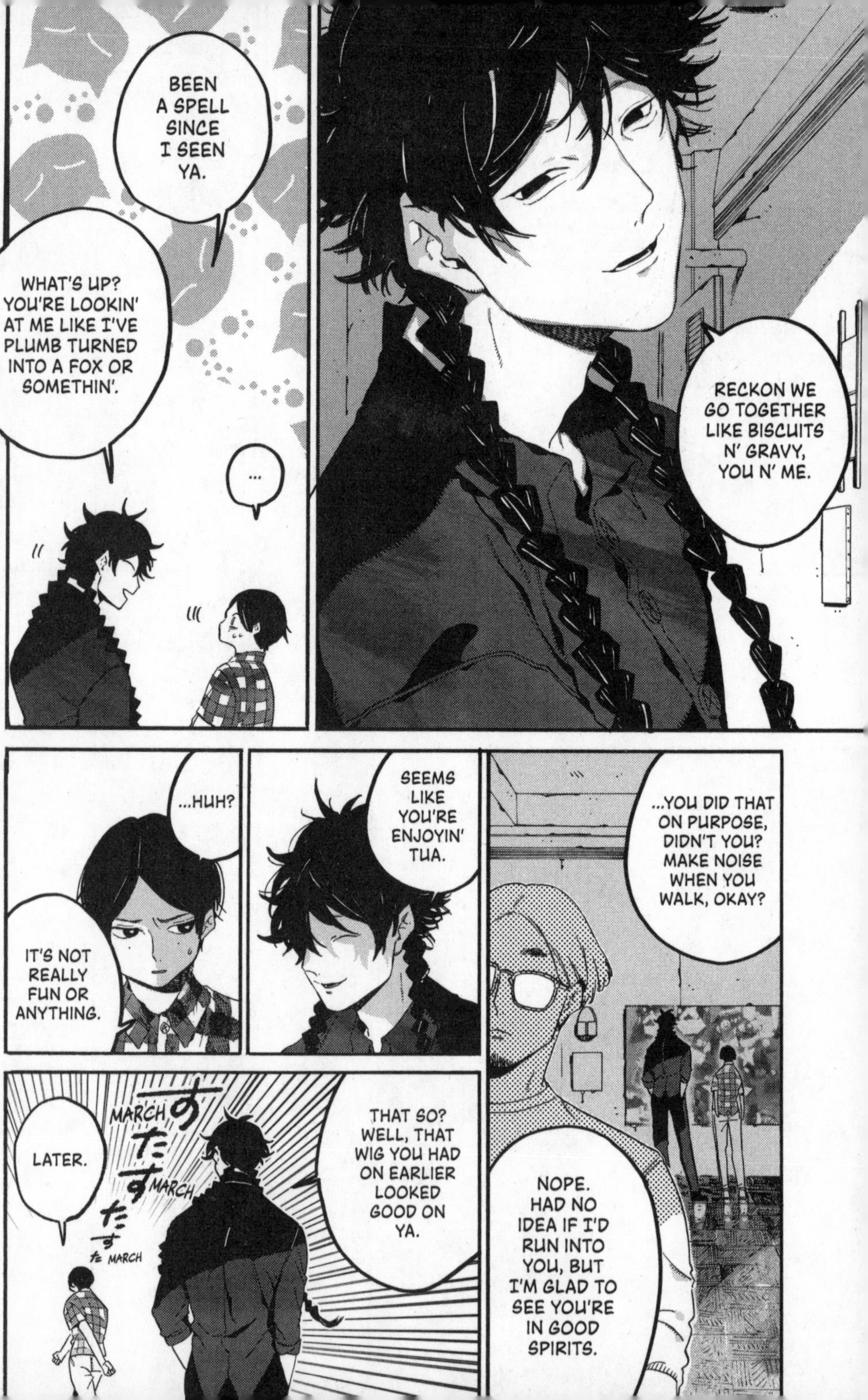
RECKON WE GO TOGETHER LIKE BISCUITS N' GRAVY, YOU N' ME.
BEEN A SPELL SINCE I SEEN YA.
WHAT'S UP? YOU'RE LOOKIN' AT ME LIKE I'VE PLUMB TURNED INTO A FOX OR SOMETHIN'.
...
...YOU DID THAT ON PURPOSE, DIDN'T YOU? MAKE NOISE WHEN YOU WALK, OKAY?
NOPE. HAD NO IDEA IF I'D RUN INTO YOU, BUT I'M GLAD TO SEE YOU'RE IN GOOD SPIRITS.
SEEMS LIKE YOU'RE ENJOYIN' TUA.
...HUH?
IT'S NOT REALLY FUN OR ANYTHING.
THAT SO? WELL, THAT WIG YOU HAD ON EARLIER LOOKED GOOD ON YA.
MARCH
MARCH
MARCH
LATER.

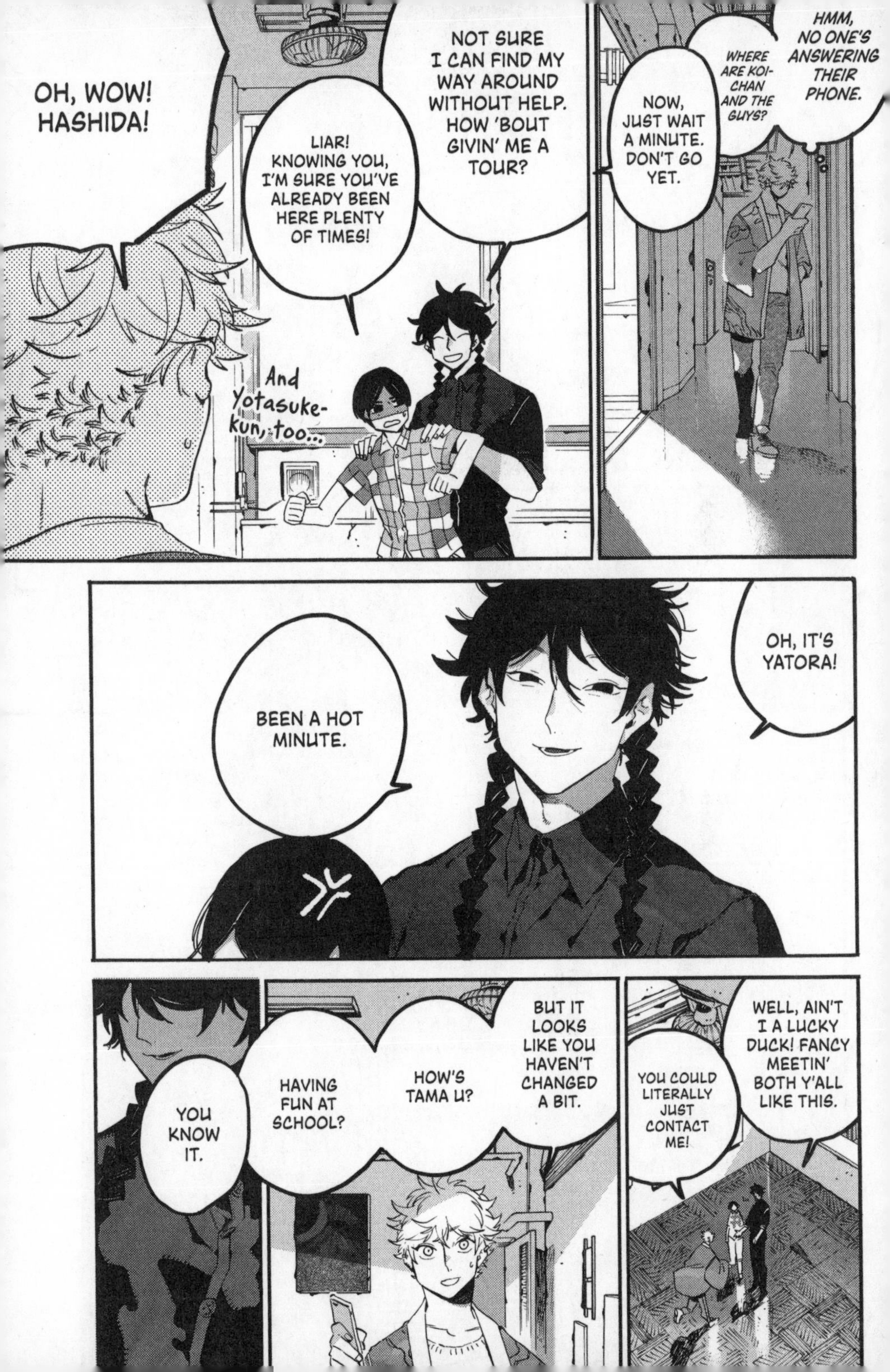
HMM, NO ONE'S ANSWERING THEIR PHONE.
WHERE ARE KOI-CHAN AND THE GUYS?
NOW, JUST WAIT A MINUTE. DON'T GO YET.
NOT SURE I CAN FIND MY WAY AROUND WITHOUT HELP. HOW 'BOUT GIVIN' ME A TOUR?
LIAR! KNOWING YOU, I'M SURE YOU'VE ALREADY BEEN HERE PLENTY OF TIMES!
OH, WOW! HASHIDA!
And Yotasuke-kun, too...
OH, IT'S YATORA!
BEEN A HOT MINUTE.
WELL, AIN'T I A LUCKY DUCK! FANCY MEETIN' BOTH Y'ALL LIKE THIS.
YOU COULD LITERALLY JUST CONTACT ME!
BUT IT LOOKS LIKE YOU HAVEN'T CHANGED A BIT.
HOW'S TAMA U?
HAVING FUN AT SCHOOL?
YOU KNOW IT.

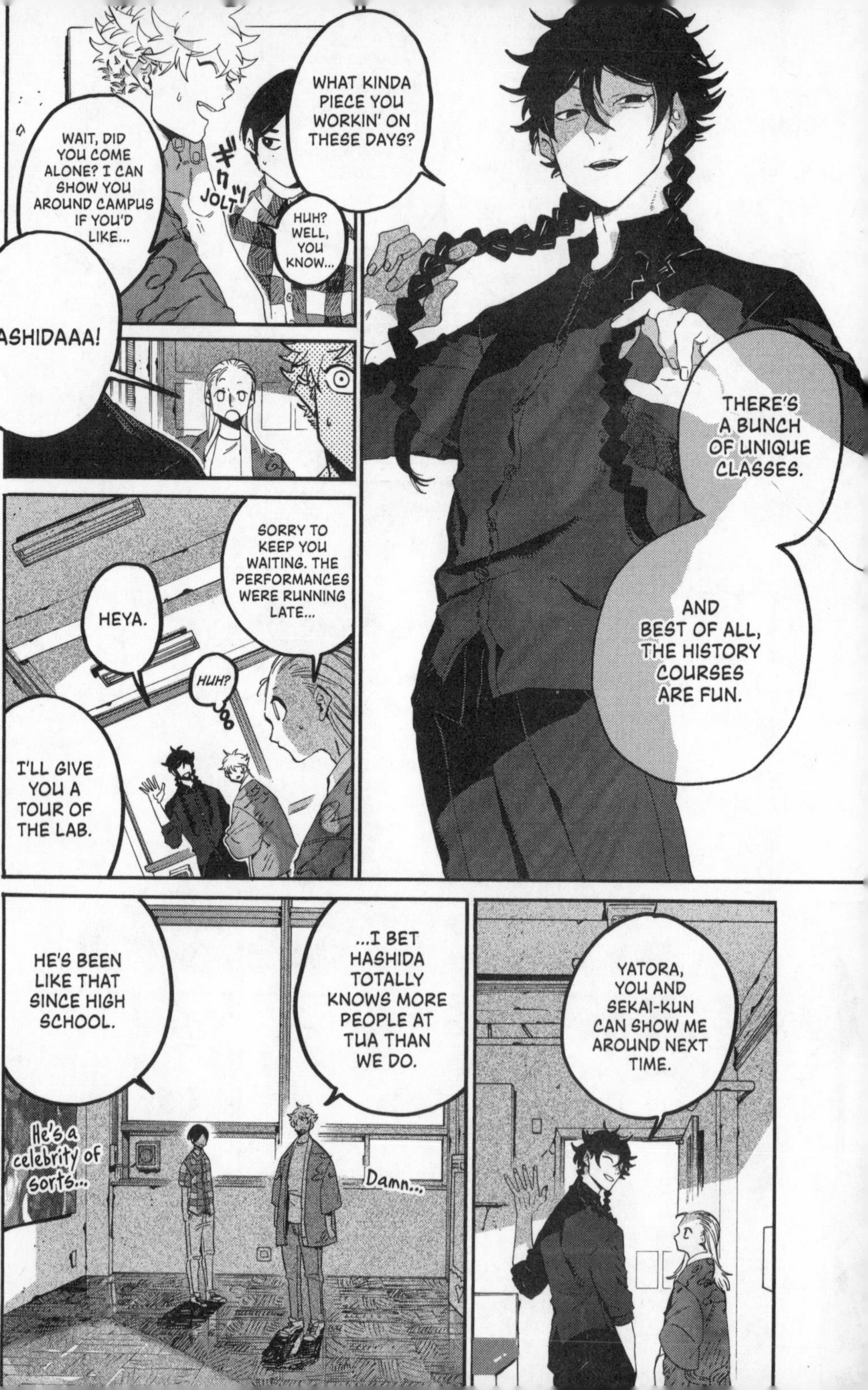
THERE'S A BUNCH OF UNIQUE CLASSES.
AND BEST OF ALL, THE HISTORY COURSES ARE FUN.
WHAT KINDA PIECE YOU WORKIN' ON THESE DAYS?
WAIT, DID YOU COME ALONE? I CAN SHOW YOU AROUND CAMPUS IF YOU'D LIKE...
JOLT
HUH? WELL, YOU KNOW...
HASHIDAAA!
SORRY TO KEEP YOU WAITING. THE PERFORMANCES WERE RUNNING LATE...
HEYA.
HUH?
I'LL GIVE YOU A TOUR OF THE LAB.
YATORA, YOU AND SEKAI-KUN CAN SHOW ME AROUND NEXT TIME.
...I BET HASHIDA TOTALLY KNOWS MORE PEOPLE AT TUA THAN WE DO.
HE'S BEEN LIKE THAT SINCE HIGH SCHOOL.
Damn...
He's a celebrity of sorts...

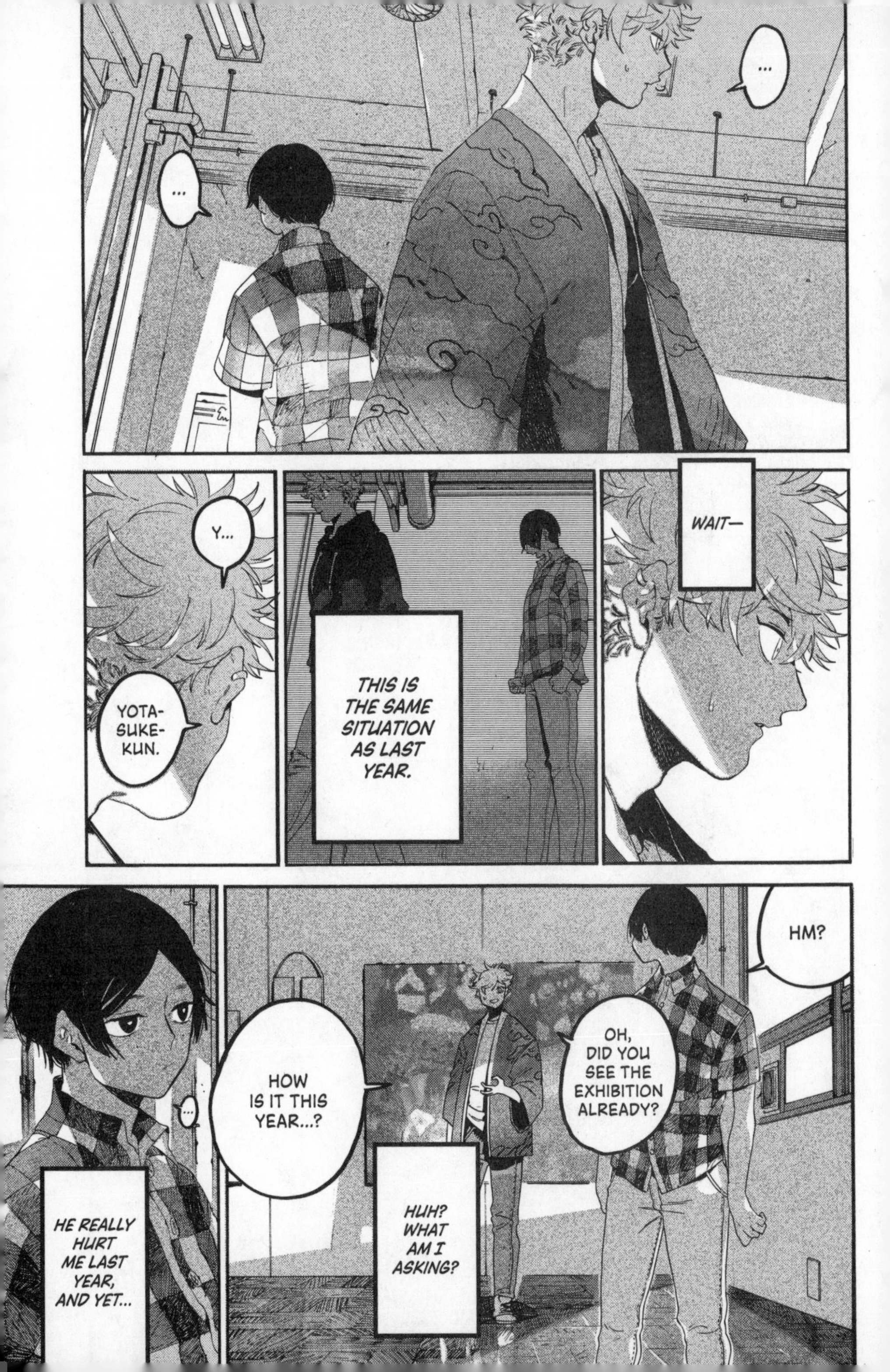
...
...
WAIT—
THIS IS THE SAME SITUATION AS LAST YEAR.
Y...
YOTA-SUKE-KUN.
HM?
OH, DID YOU SEE THE EXHIBITION ALREADY?
HOW IS IT THIS YEAR...?
HUH? WHAT AM I ASKING?
...
HE REALLY HURT ME LAST YEAR, AND YET...

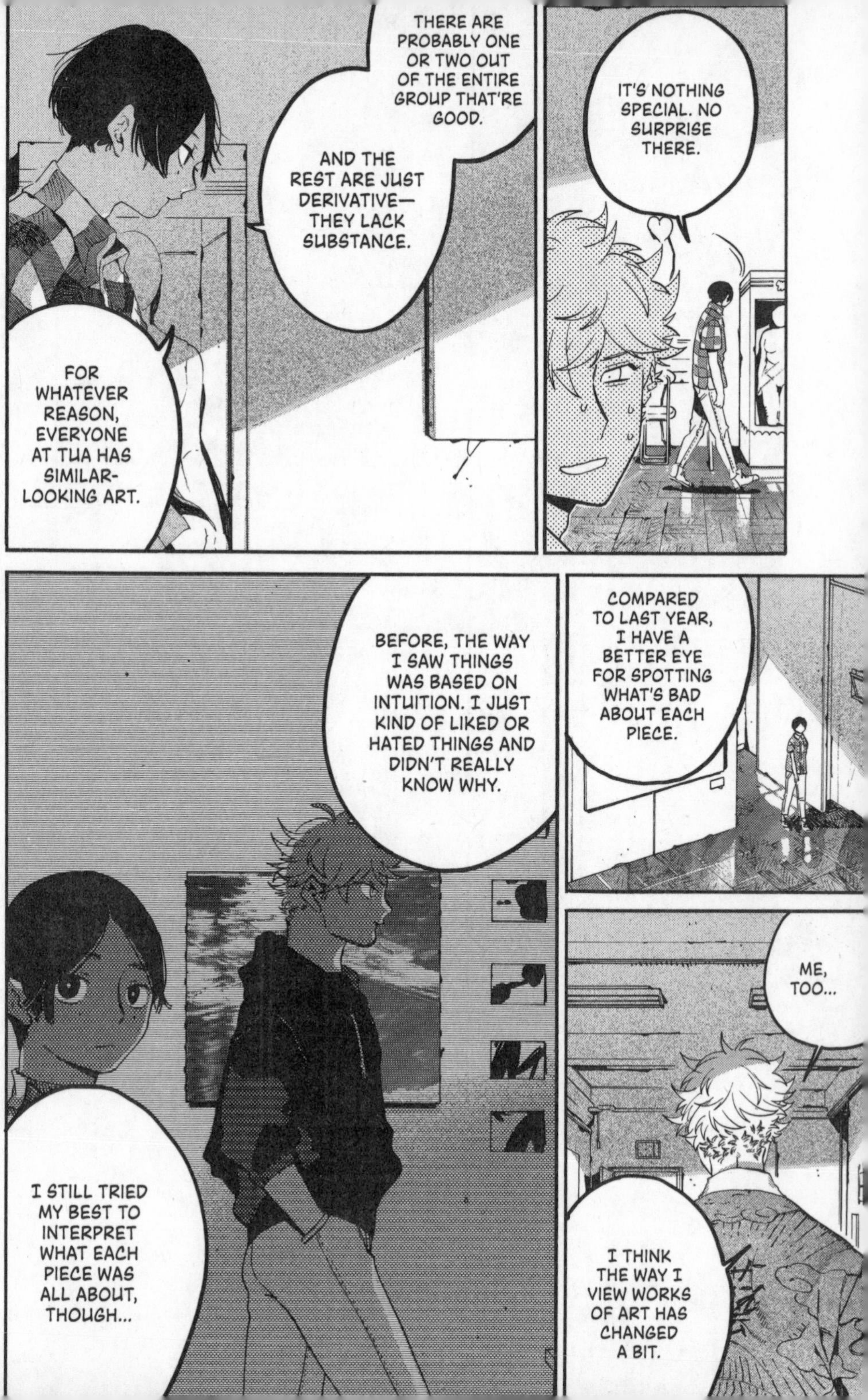
IT'S NOTHING SPECIAL. NO SURPRISE THERE.
THERE ARE PROBABLY ONE OR TWO OUT OF THE ENTIRE GROUP THAT'RE GOOD.
AND THE REST ARE JUST DERIVATIVE— THEY LACK SUBSTANCE.
FOR WHATEVER REASON, EVERYONE AT TUA HAS SIMILAR-LOOKING ART.
COMPARED TO LAST YEAR, I HAVE A BETTER EYE FOR SPOTTING WHAT'S BAD ABOUT EACH PIECE.
ME, TOO...
I THINK THE WAY I VIEW WORKS OF ART HAS CHANGED A BIT.
BEFORE, THE WAY I SAW THINGS WAS BASED ON INTUITION. I JUST KIND OF LIKED OR HATED THINGS AND DIDN'T REALLY KNOW WHY.
I STILL TRIED MY BEST TO INTERPRET WHAT EACH PIECE WAS ALL ABOUT, THOUGH...

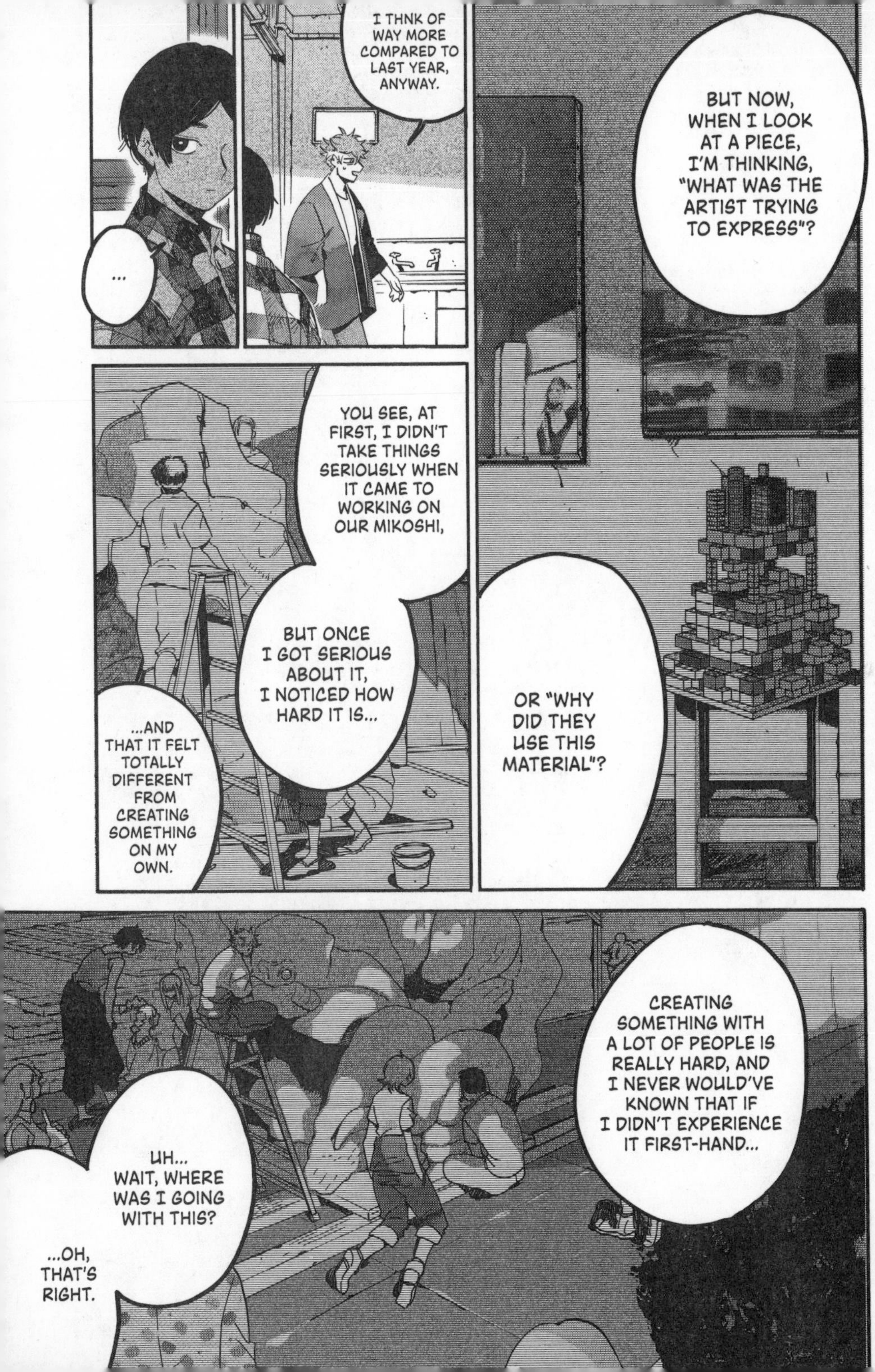
BUT NOW, WHEN I LOOK AT A PIECE, I'M THINKING, "WHAT WAS THE ARTIST TRYING TO EXPRESS"?
OR "WHY DID THEY USE THIS MATERIAL"?
I THNK OF WAY MORE COMPARED TO LAST YEAR, ANYWAY.
...
YOU SEE, AT FIRST, I DIDN'T TAKE THINGS SERIOUSLY WHEN IT CAME TO WORKING ON OUR MIKOSHI,
BUT ONCE I GOT SERIOUS ABOUT IT, I NOTICED HOW HARD IT IS...
...AND THAT IT FELT TOTALLY DIFFERENT FROM CREATING SOMETHING ON MY OWN.
CREATING SOMETHING WITH A LOT OF PEOPLE IS REALLY HARD, AND I NEVER WOULD'VE KNOWN THAT IF I DIDN'T EXPERIENCE IT FIRST-HAND...
UH... WAIT, WHERE WAS I GOING WITH THIS?
...OH, THAT'S RIGHT.

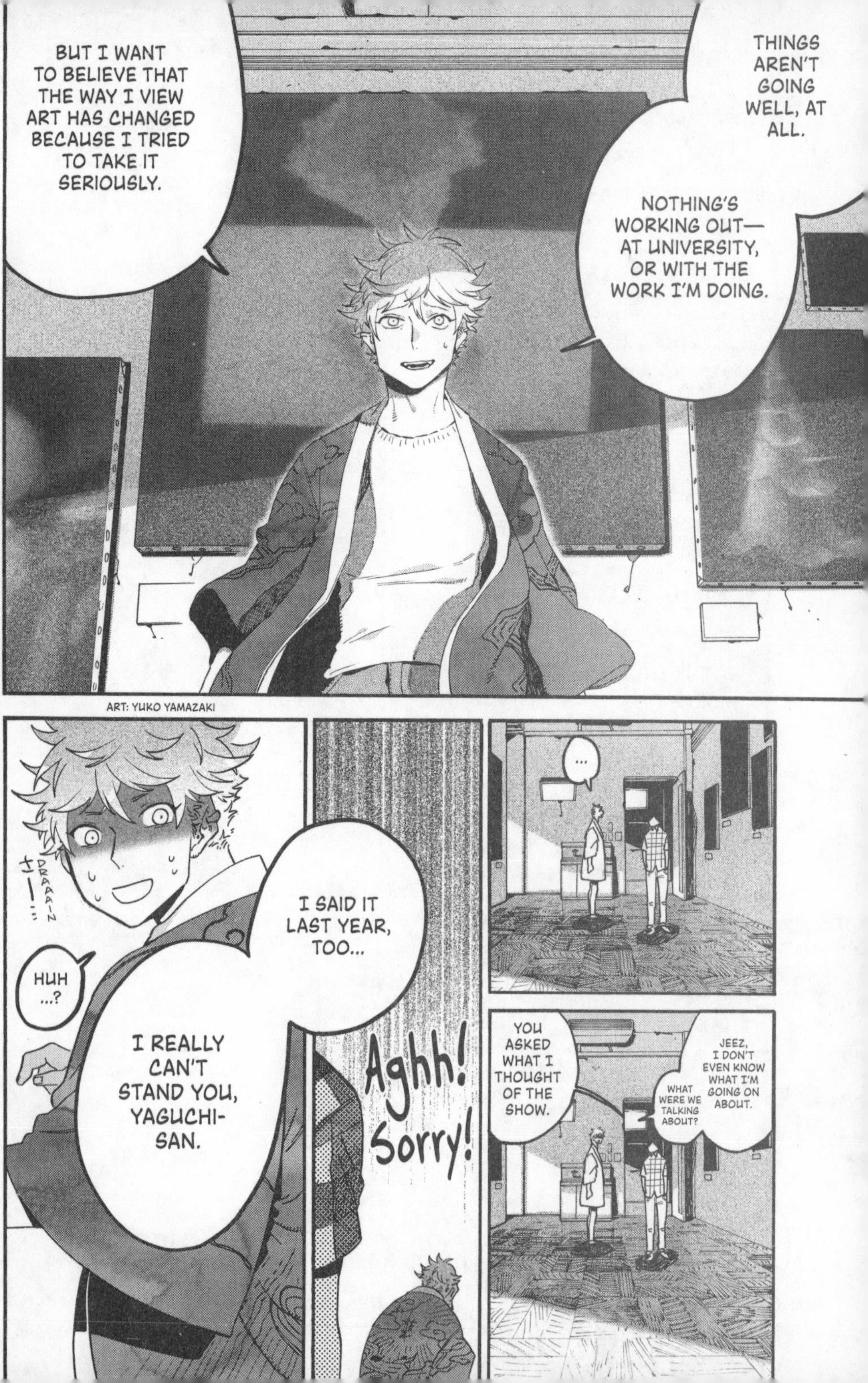
THINGS AREN'T GOING WELL, AT ALL.
NOTHING'S WORKING OUT—AT UNIVERSITY, OR WITH THE WORK I'M DOING.
BUT I WANT TO BELIEVE THAT THE WAY I VIEW ART HAS CHANGED BECAUSE I TRIED TO TAKE IT SERIOUSLY.
ART: YUKO YAMAZAKI
...
JEEZ, I DON'T EVEN KNOW WHAT I'M GOING ON ABOUT.
WHAT WERE WE TALKING ABOUT?
YOU ASKED WHAT I THOUGHT OF THE SHOW.
Aghh! Sorry!
I SAID IT LAST YEAR, TOO...
DRAAAIN
HUH ...?
I REALLY CAN'T STAND YOU, YAGUCHI-SAN.

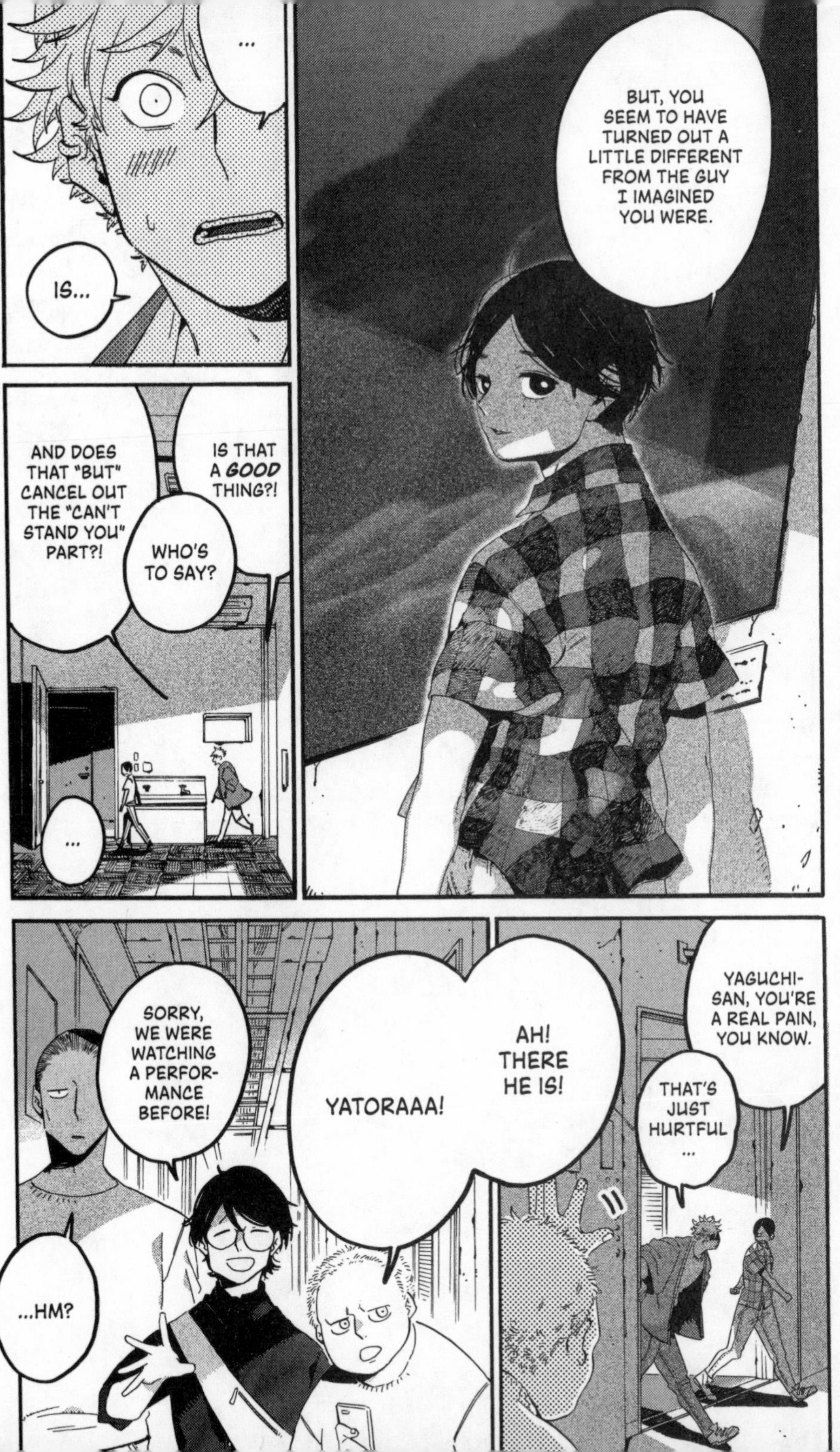

BUT, YOU SEEM TO HAVE TURNED OUT A LITTLE DIFFERENT FROM THE GUY I IMAGINED YOU WERE.
...
IS...
IS THAT A **GOOD** THING?!
AND DOES THAT "BUT" CANCEL OUT THE "CAN'T STAND YOU" PART?!
WHO'S TO SAY?
...
YAGUCHI-SAN, YOU'RE A REAL PAIN, YOU KNOW.
THAT'S JUST HURTFUL...
AH! THERE HE IS!
YATORAAA!
SORRY, WE WERE WATCHING A PERFORMANCE BEFORE!
...HM?

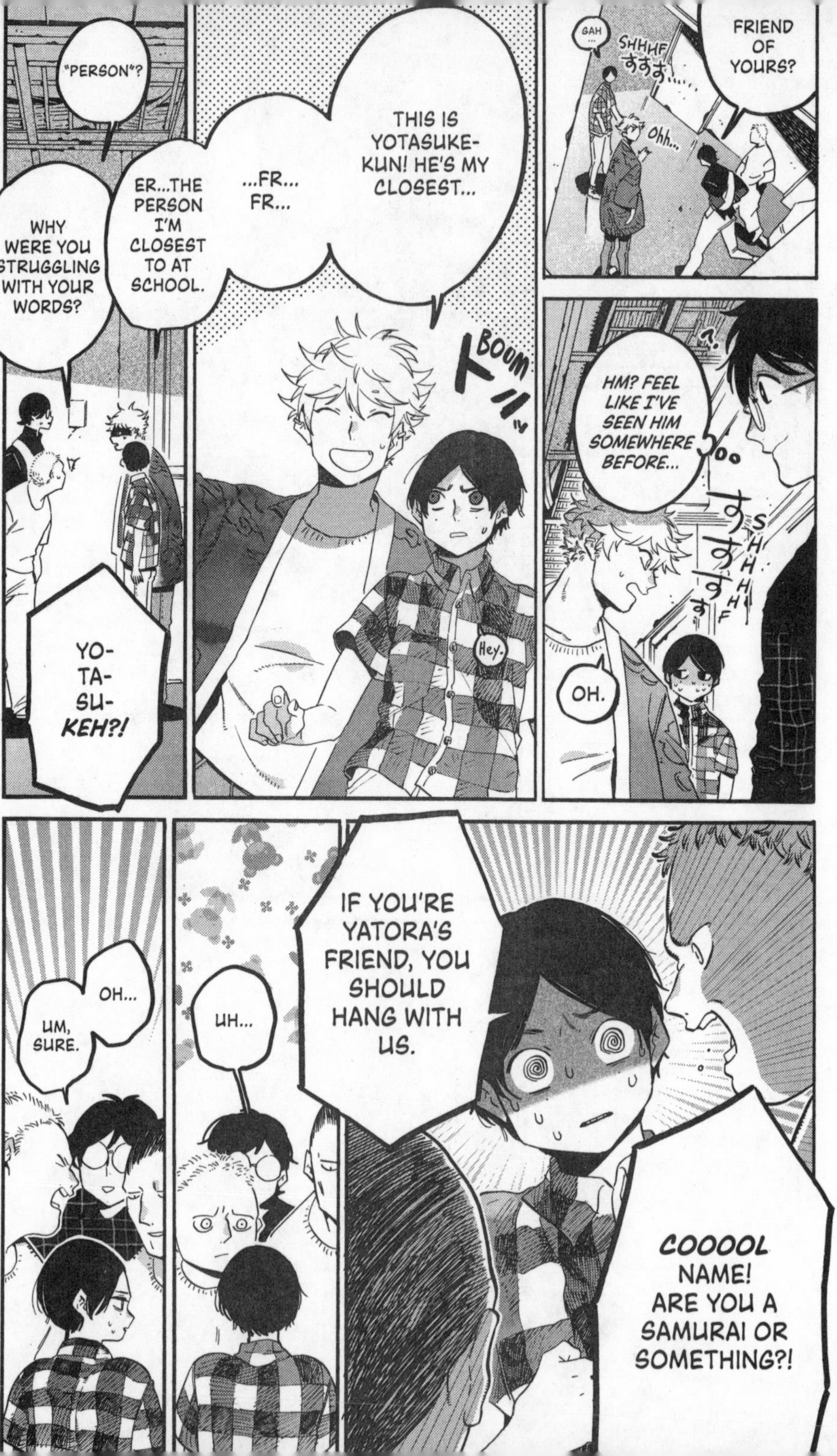
FRIEND OF YOURS?
GAH...
SHHHF すすす...
Ohh...
HM? FEEL LIKE I'VE SEEN HIM SOMEWHERE BEFORE...
すすすす SHHHHHF
OH.
THIS IS YOTASUKE-KUN! HE'S MY CLOSEST...
...FR... FR...
BOOM
Hey.
ER...THE PERSON I'M CLOSEST TO AT SCHOOL.
"PERSON"?
WHY WERE YOU STRUGGLING WITH YOUR WORDS?
YO-TA-SU-KEH?!
IF YOU'RE YATORA'S FRIEND, YOU SHOULD HANG WITH US.
COOOOL NAME! ARE YOU A SAMURAI OR SOMETHING?!
UH...
OH...
UM, SURE.

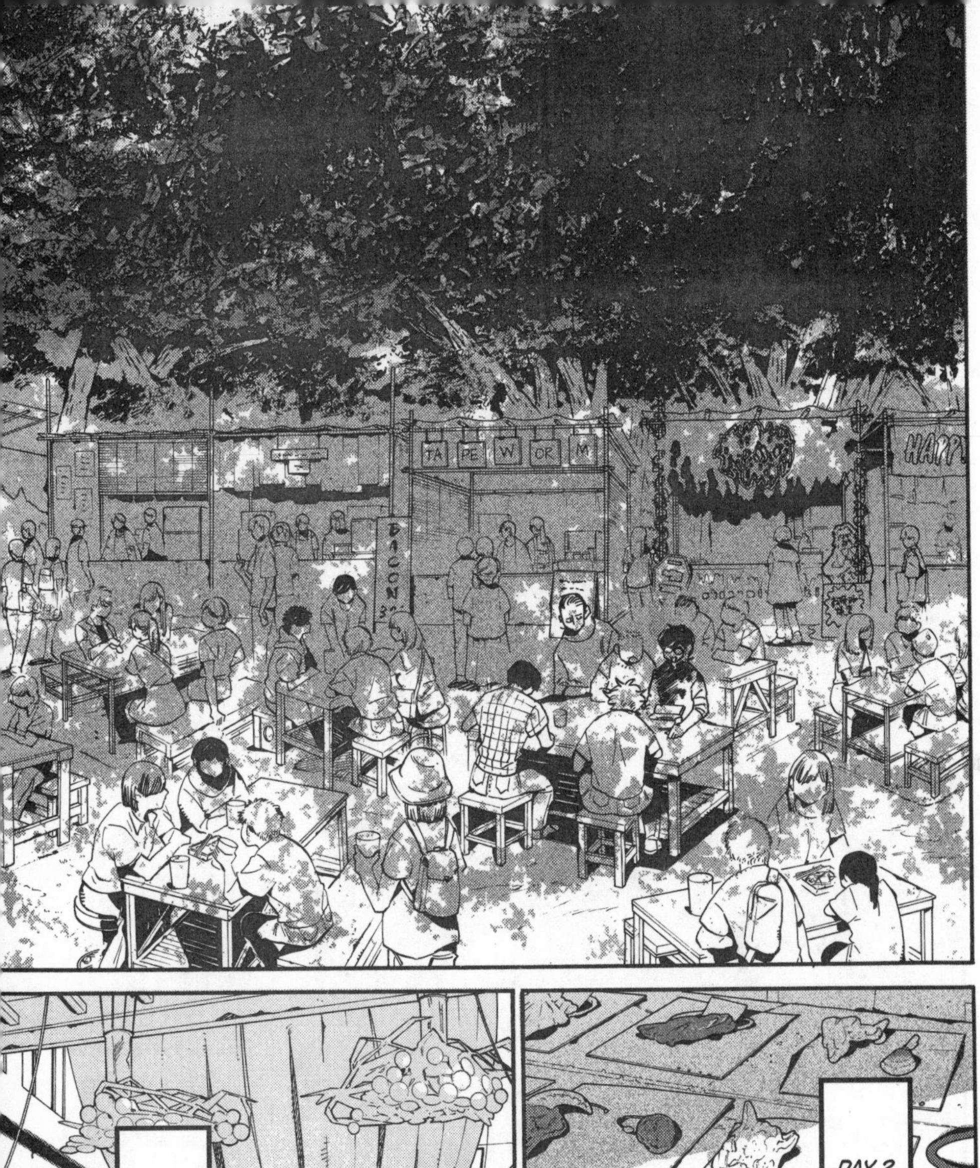
TA PE W OR M

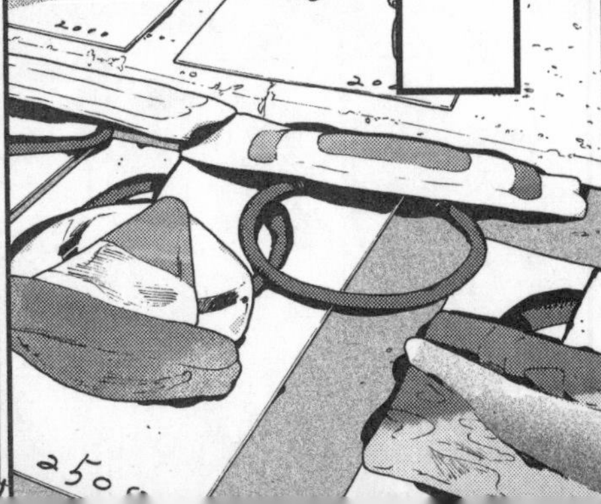
DAY 2

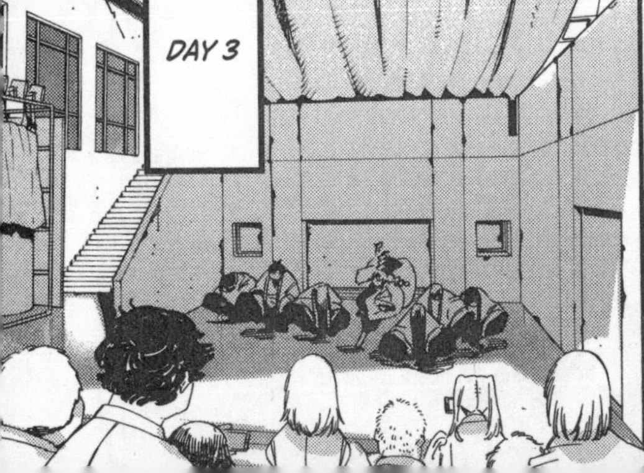
DAY 3

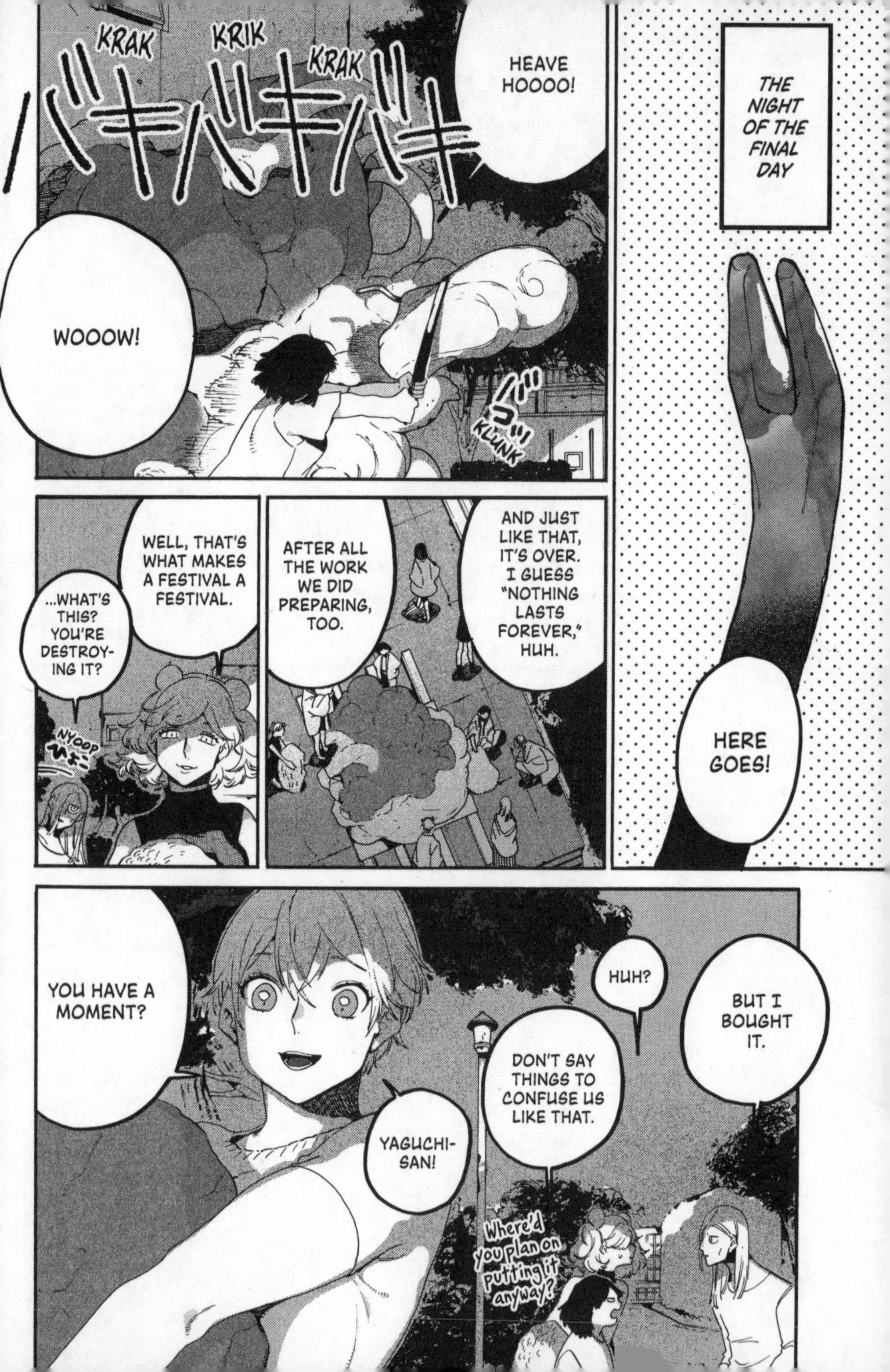
THE NIGHT OF THE FINAL DAY
HERE GOES!
HEAVE HOOOO!
バキバキバキ
KRAK
KRIK
KRAK
ゴッ
KLUNK
WOOOW!
AND JUST LIKE THAT, IT'S OVER. I GUESS "NOTHING LASTS FOREVER," HUH.
AFTER ALL THE WORK WE DID PREPARING, TOO.
WELL, THAT'S WHAT MAKES A FESTIVAL A FESTIVAL.
...WHAT'S THIS? YOU'RE DESTROYING IT?
ひょこ
NYOOP
BUT I BOUGHT IT.
HUH?
DON'T SAY THINGS TO CONFUSE US LIKE THAT.
Where'd you plan on putting it anyway?
YAGUCHI-SAN!
YOU HAVE A MOMENT?

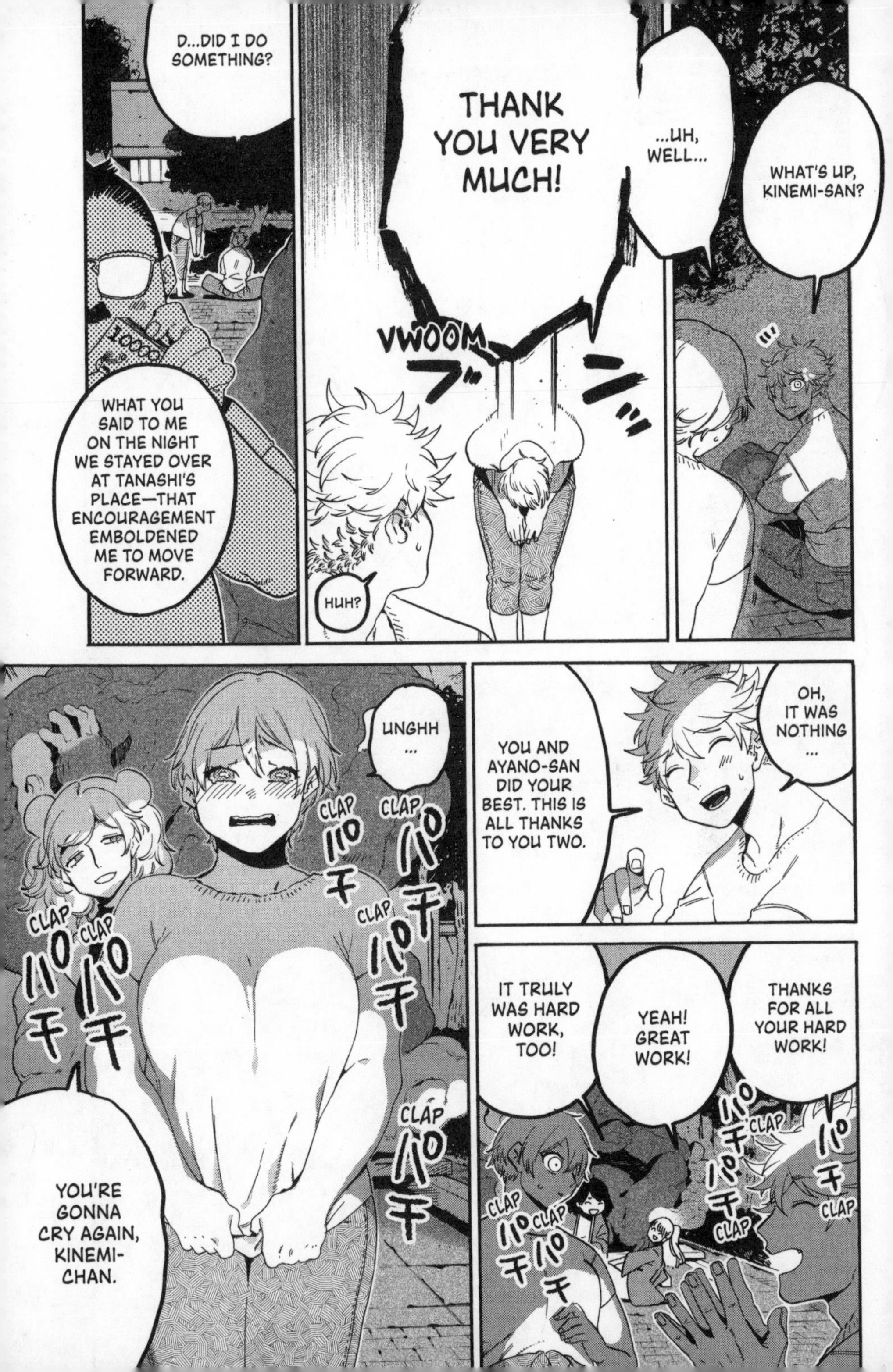
WHAT'S UP, KINEMI-SAN?
...UH, WELL...
THANK YOU VERY MUCH!
VWOOM
HUH?
D...DID I DO SOMETHING?
WHAT YOU SAID TO ME ON THE NIGHT WE STAYED OVER AT TANASHI'S PLACE—THAT ENCOURAGEMENT EMBOLDENED ME TO MOVE FORWARD.
OH, IT WAS NOTHING ...
YOU AND AYANO-SAN DID YOUR BEST. THIS IS ALL THANKS TO YOU TWO.
THANKS FOR ALL YOUR HARD WORK!
YEAH! GREAT WORK!
IT TRULY WAS HARD WORK, TOO!
CLAP CLAP CLAP CLAP CLAP
UNGHH ...
CLAP CLAP CLAP CLAP CLAP
YOU'RE GONNA CRY AGAIN, KINEMI-CHAN.

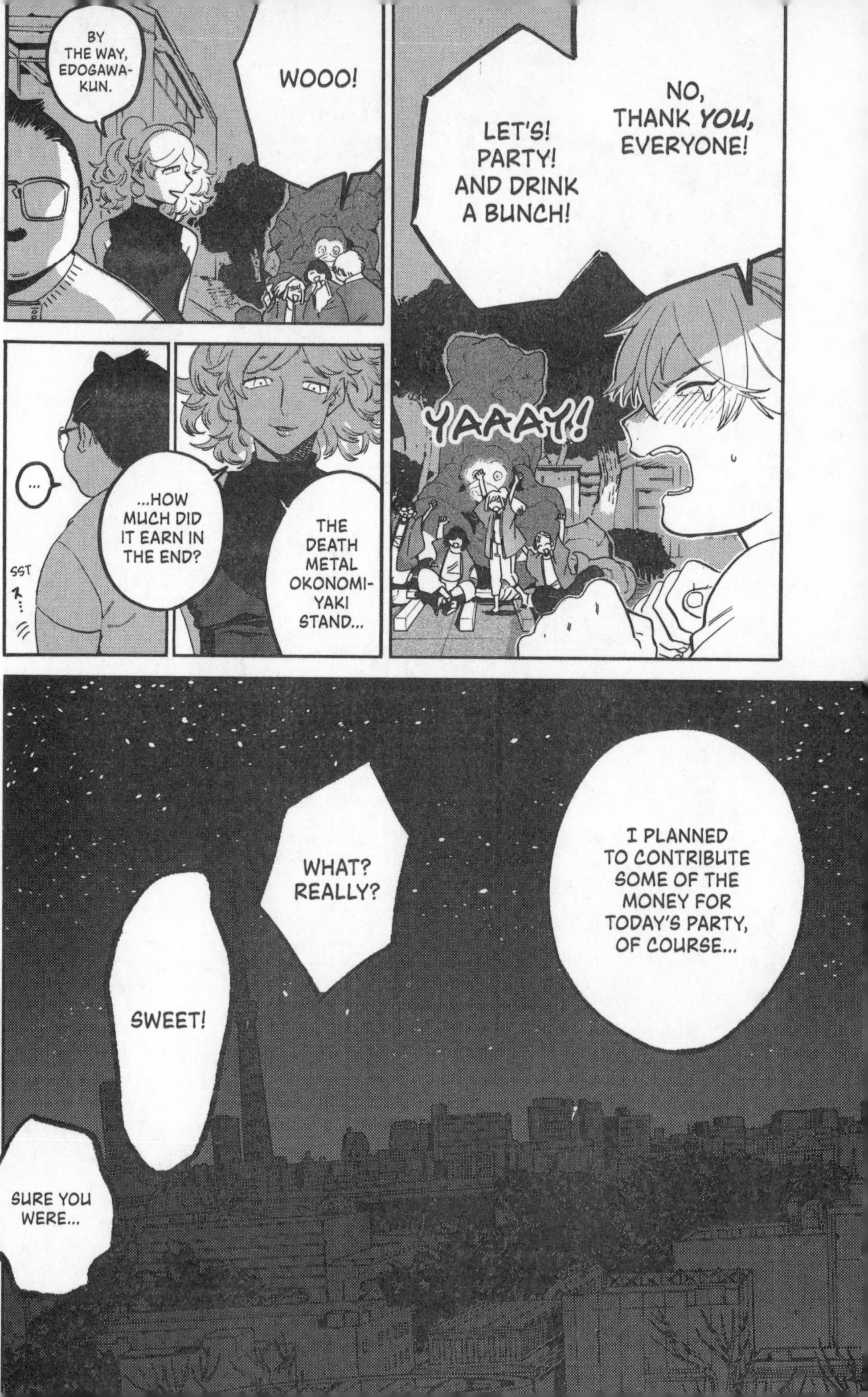
NO, THANK YOU, EVERYONE!
LET'S! PARTY! AND DRINK A BUNCH!
YAAAY!
WOOO!
BY THE WAY, EDOGAWA-KUN.
THE DEATH METAL OKONOMIYAKI STAND...
...HOW MUCH DID IT EARN IN THE END?
...
SST
I PLANNED TO CONTRIBUTE SOME OF THE MONEY FOR TODAY'S PARTY, OF COURSE...
WHAT? REALLY?
SWEET!
SURE YOU WERE...

STROKE 34 END

I made it.

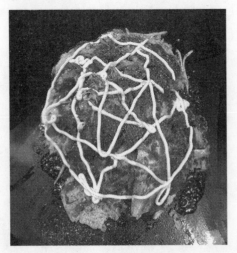

BLUE PERIOD

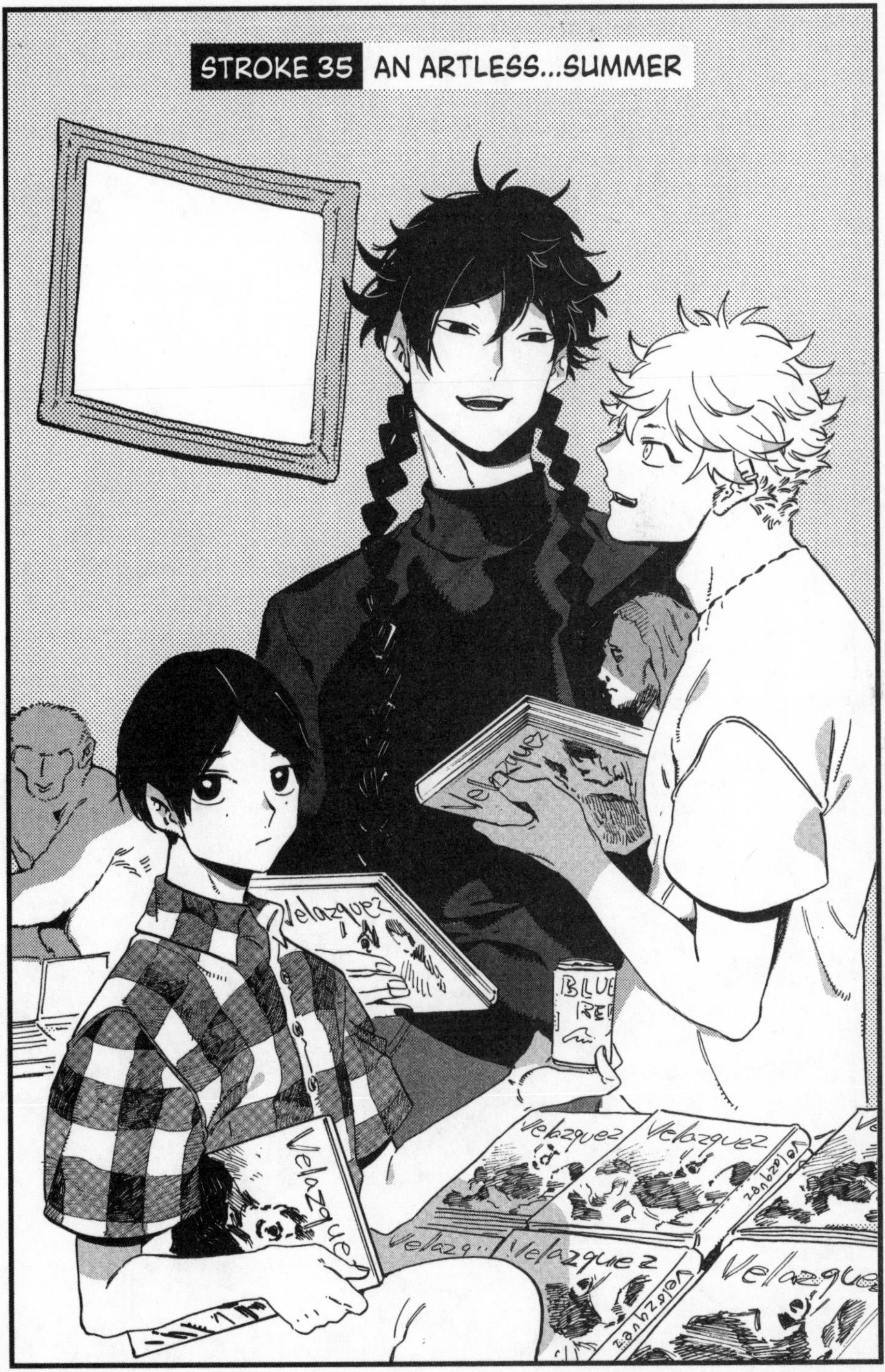
STROKE 35 AN ARTLESS...SUMMER
Velazquez
Velazquez
BLUE RE
Velazquez
Velazquez
Velazquez
Velazquez
Velazg...
Velazquez
Velazquez
Velazque

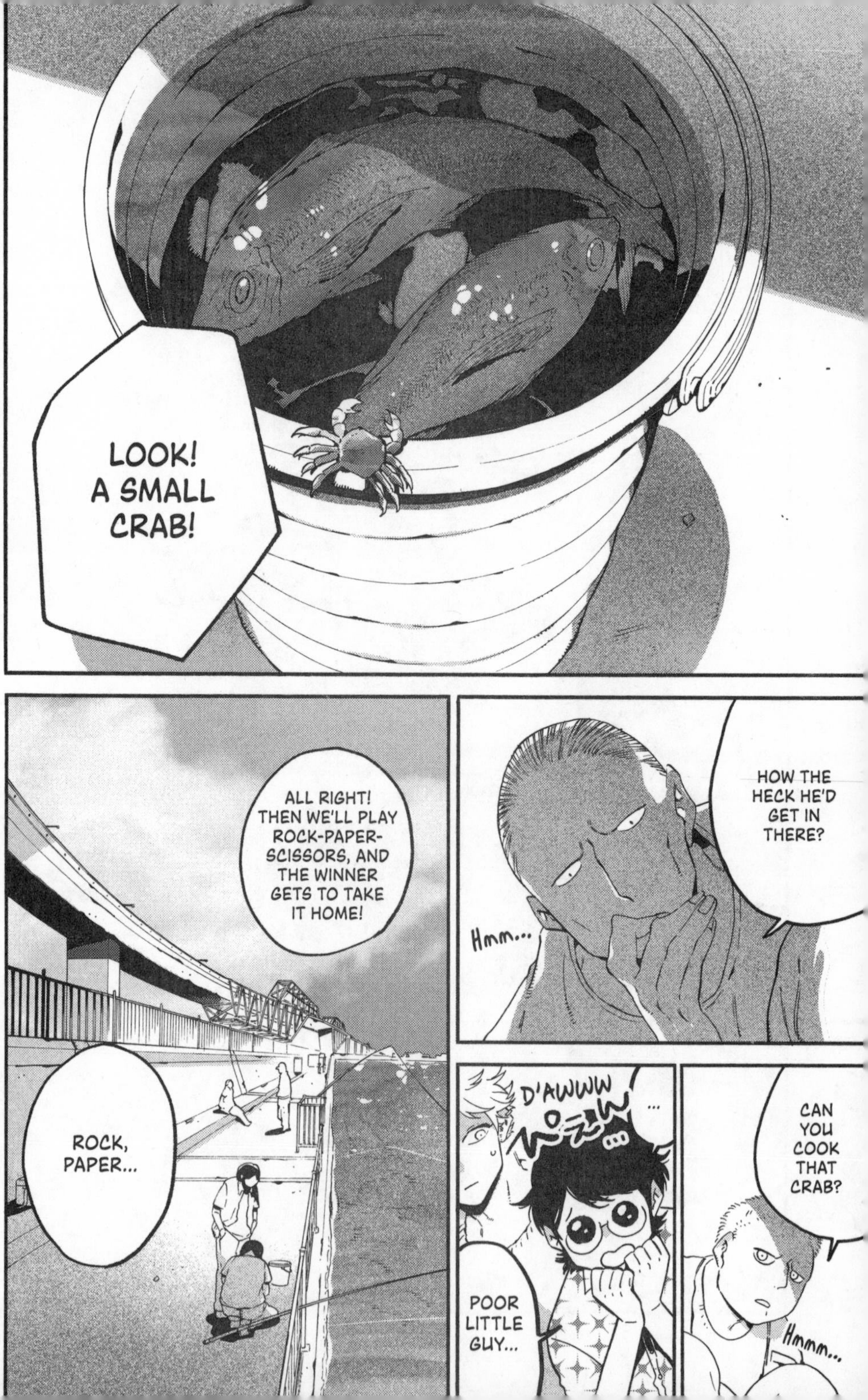
LOOK! A SMALL CRAB!
HOW THE HECK HE'D GET IN THERE?
Hmm...
CAN YOU COOK THAT CRAB?
Hmmm...
D'AWWW
...
POOR LITTLE GUY...
ALL RIGHT! THEN WE'LL PLAY ROCK-PAPER-SCISSORS, AND THE WINNER GETS TO TAKE IT HOME!
ROCK, PAPER...

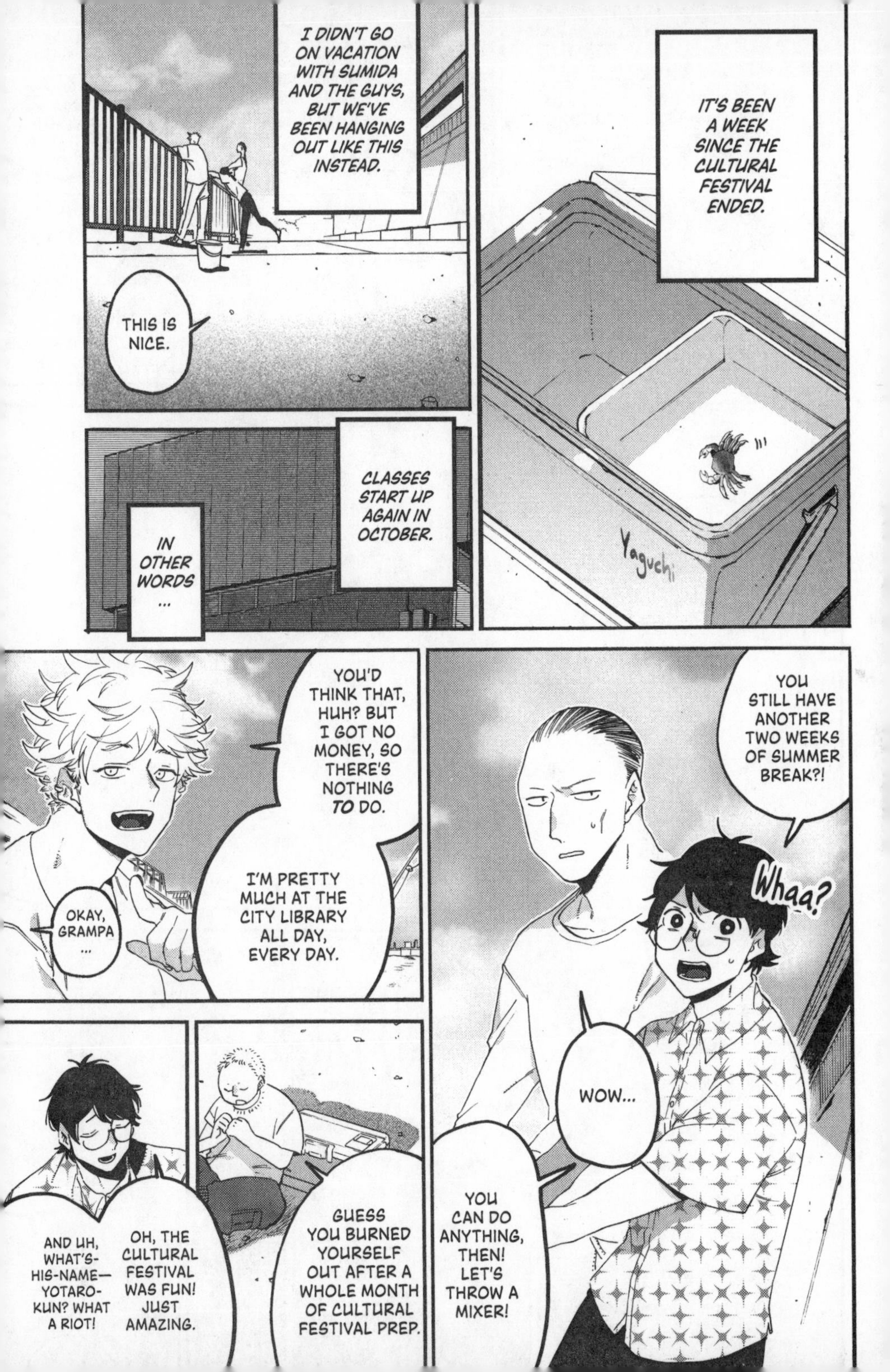
IT'S BEEN A WEEK SINCE THE CULTURAL FESTIVAL ENDED.
Yaguchi
I DIDN'T GO ON VACATION WITH SUMIDA AND THE GUYS, BUT WE'VE BEEN HANGING OUT LIKE THIS INSTEAD.
THIS IS NICE.
CLASSES START UP AGAIN IN OCTOBER.
IN OTHER WORDS...
YOU STILL HAVE ANOTHER TWO WEEKS OF SUMMER BREAK?!
Whaa?
WOW...
YOU CAN DO ANYTHING, THEN! LET'S THROW A MIXER!
YOU'D THINK THAT, HUH? BUT I GOT NO MONEY, SO THERE'S NOTHING TO DO.
I'M PRETTY MUCH AT THE CITY LIBRARY ALL DAY, EVERY DAY.
OKAY, GRAMPA...
GUESS YOU BURNED YOURSELF OUT AFTER A WHOLE MONTH OF CULTURAL FESTIVAL PREP.
OH, THE CULTURAL FESTIVAL WAS FUN! JUST AMAZING.
AND UH, WHAT'S-HIS-NAME—YOTARO-KUN? WHAT A RIOT!

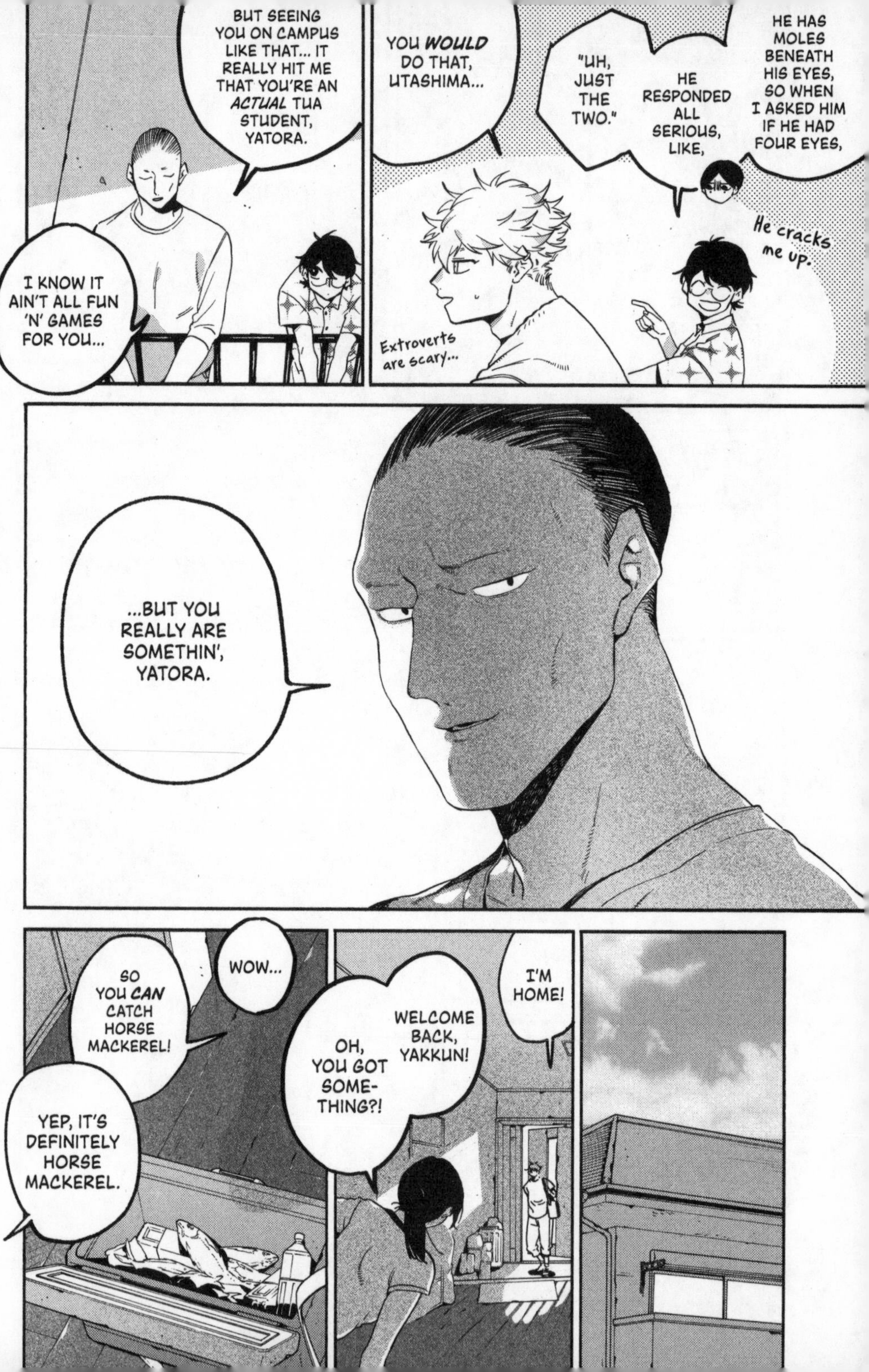
HE HAS MOLES BENEATH HIS EYES, SO WHEN I ASKED HIM IF HE HAD FOUR EYES,
HE RESPONDED ALL SERIOUS, LIKE,
"UH, JUST THE TWO."
He cracks me up.
YOU *WOULD* DO THAT, UTASHIMA...
Extroverts are scary...
BUT SEEING YOU ON CAMPUS LIKE THAT... IT REALLY HIT ME THAT YOU'RE AN *ACTUAL* TUA STUDENT, YATORA.
I KNOW IT AIN'T ALL FUN 'N' GAMES FOR YOU...
...BUT YOU REALLY ARE SOMETHIN', YATORA.
I'M HOME!
WELCOME BACK, YAKKUN!
OH, YOU GOT SOME-THING?!
WOW...
SO YOU *CAN* CATCH HORSE MACKEREL!
YEP, IT'S DEFINITELY HORSE MACKEREL.

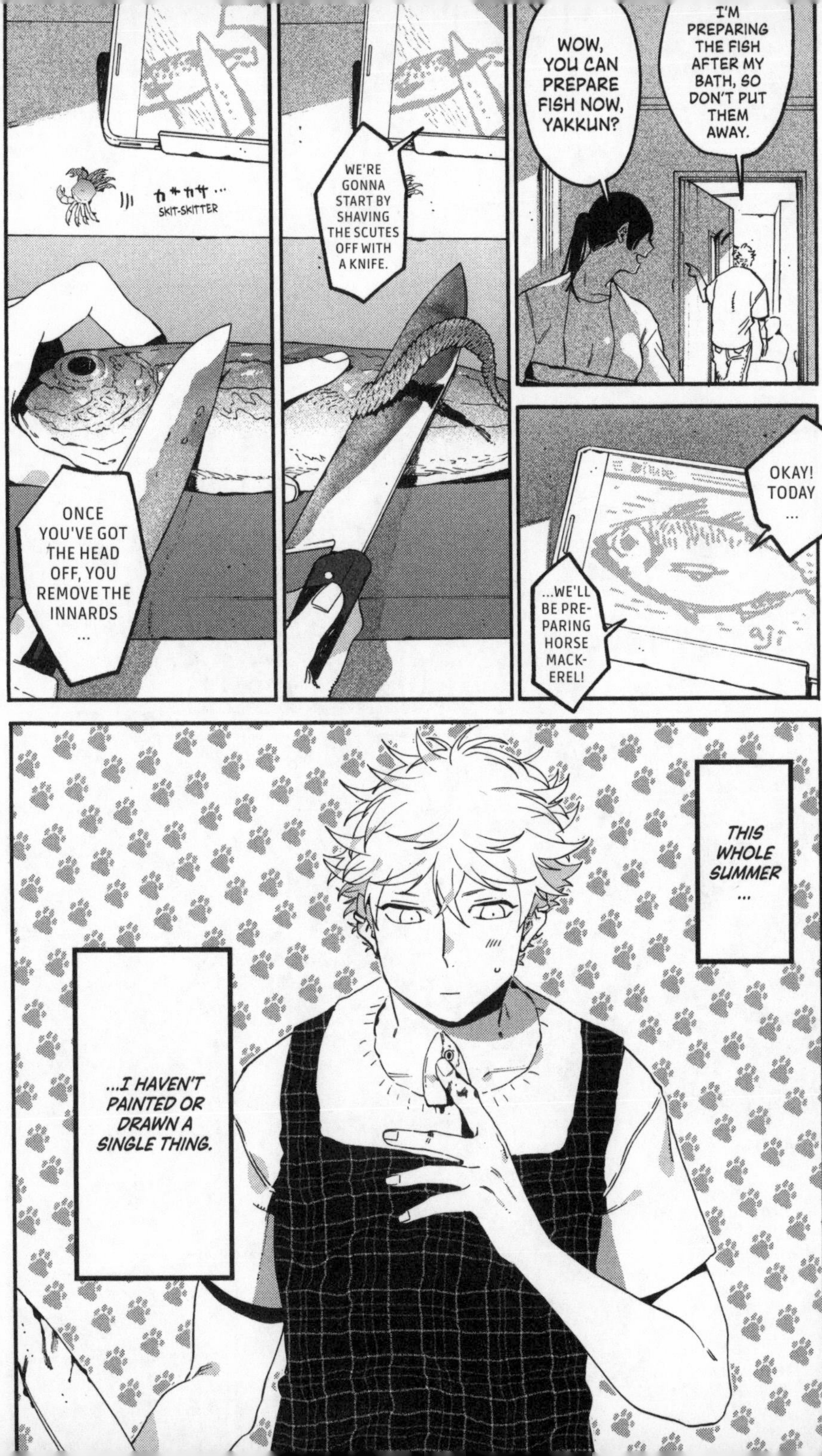
I'M PREPARING THE FISH AFTER MY BATH, SO DON'T PUT THEM AWAY.
WOW, YOU CAN PREPARE FISH NOW, YAKKUN?
OKAY! TODAY ...
...WE'LL BE PRE-PARING HORSE MACK-EREL!
WE'RE GONNA START BY SHAVING THE SCUTES OFF WITH A KNIFE.
カサカサ…
SKIT-SKITTER
ONCE YOU'VE GOT THE HEAD OFF, YOU REMOVE THE INNARDS ...
THIS WHOLE SUMMER ...
...I HAVEN'T PAINTED OR DRAWN A SINGLE THING.

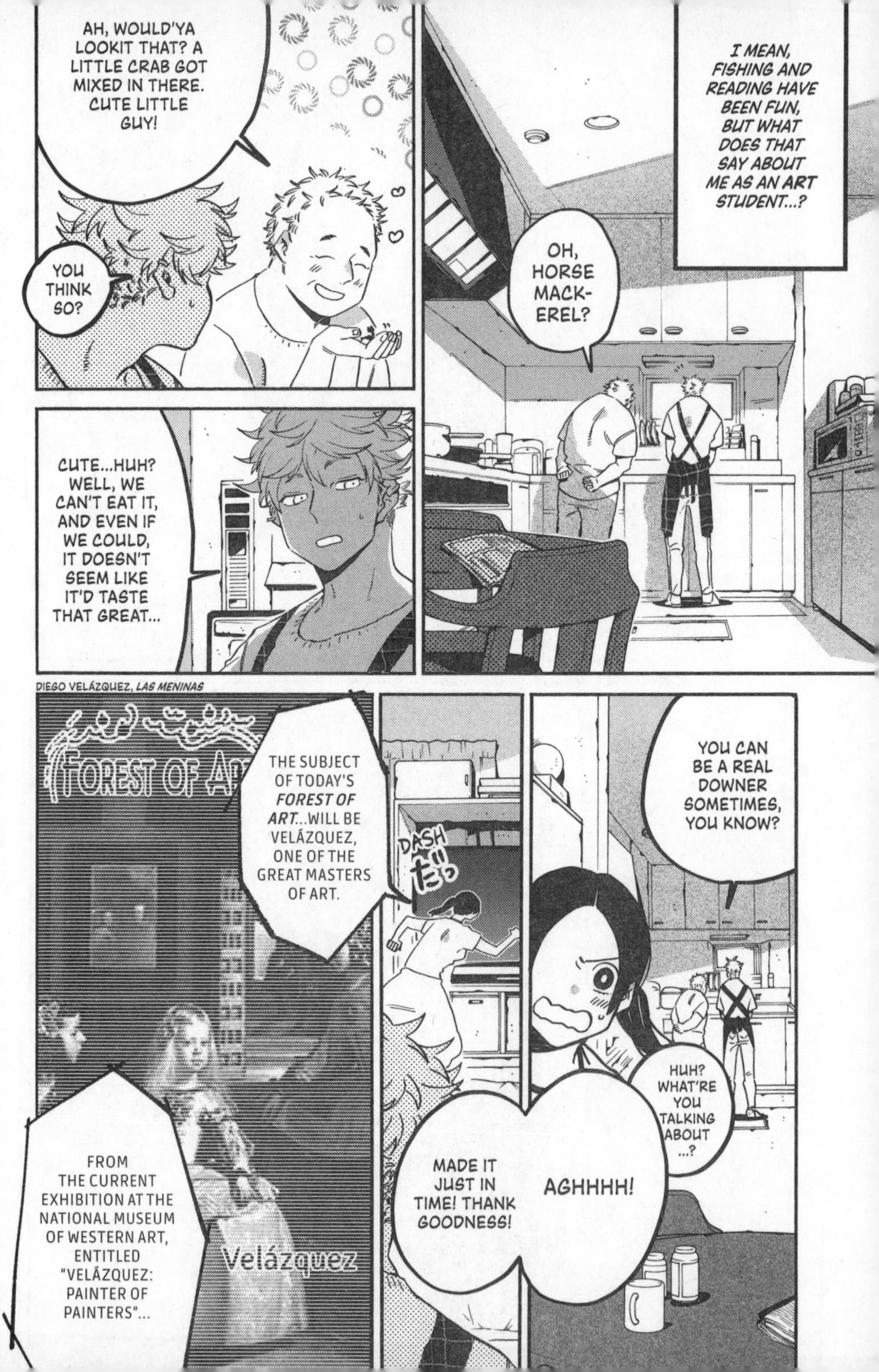
I MEAN, FISHING AND READING HAVE BEEN FUN, BUT WHAT DOES THAT SAY ABOUT ME AS AN ART STUDENT...?
OH, HORSE MACK-EREL?
AH, WOULD'YA LOOKIT THAT? A LITTLE CRAB GOT MIXED IN THERE. CUTE LITTLE GUY!
YOU THINK SO?
CUTE...HUH? WELL, WE CAN'T EAT IT, AND EVEN IF WE COULD, IT DOESN'T SEEM LIKE IT'D TASTE THAT GREAT...
DIEGO VELÁZQUEZ, *LAS MENINAS*
YOU CAN BE A REAL DOWNER SOMETIMES, YOU KNOW?
HUH? WHAT'RE YOU TALKING ABOUT ...?
AGHHHH!
DASH
だっ
MADE IT JUST IN TIME! THANK GOODNESS!
FOREST OF AR
THE SUBJECT OF TODAY'S *FOREST OF ART*...WILL BE VELÁZQUEZ, ONE OF THE GREAT MASTERS OF ART.
FROM THE CURRENT EXHIBITION AT THE NATIONAL MUSEUM OF WESTERN ART, ENTITLED "VELÁZQUEZ: PAINTER OF PAINTERS"...
Velázquez

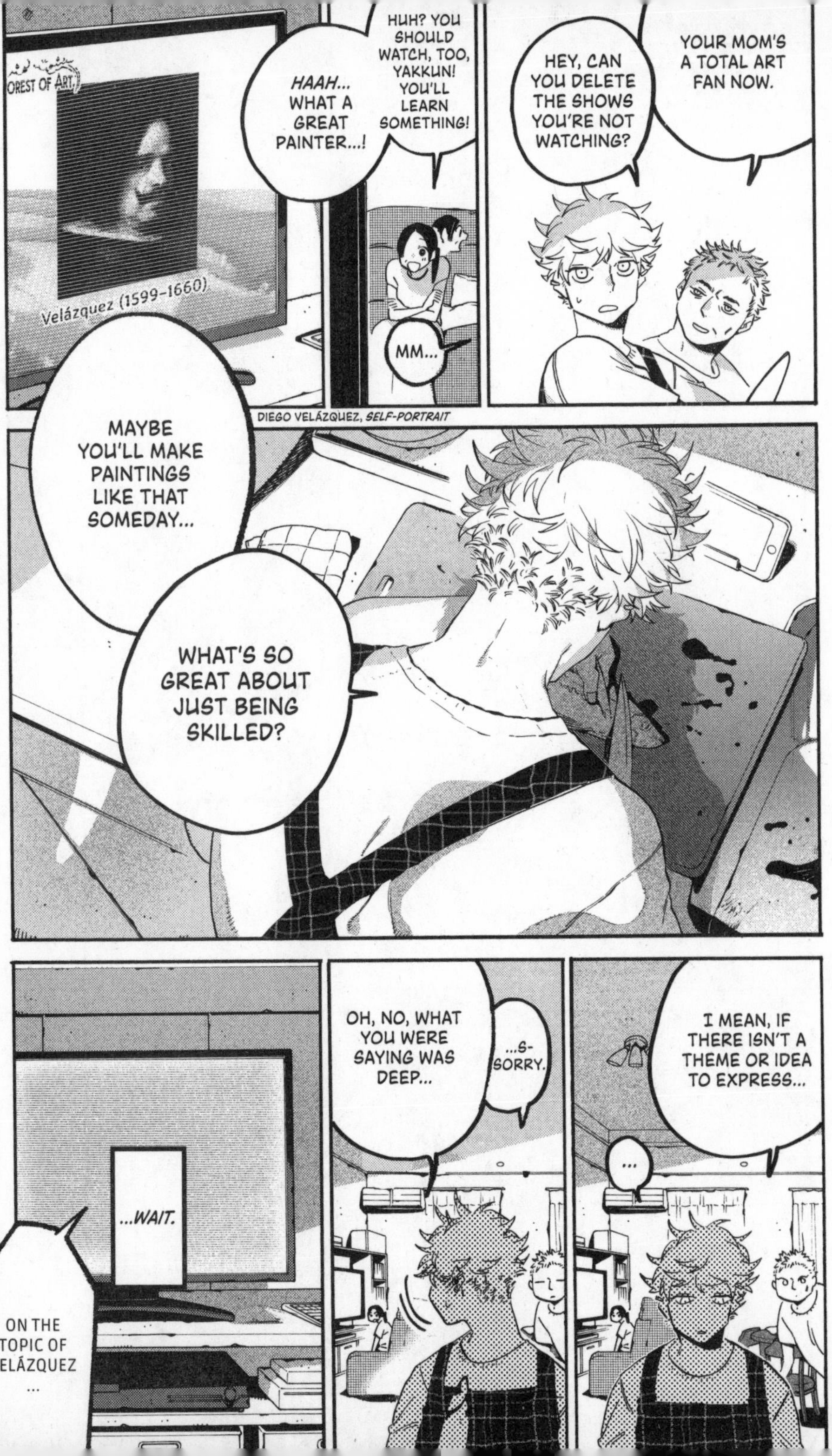
YOUR MOM'S A TOTAL ART FAN NOW.
HEY, CAN YOU DELETE THE SHOWS YOU'RE NOT WATCHING?
HUH? YOU SHOULD WATCH, TOO, YAKKUN! YOU'LL LEARN SOMETHING!
HAAH... WHAT A GREAT PAINTER...!
MM...
OREST OF ART
Velázquez (1599-1660)
DIEGO VELÁZQUEZ, SELF-PORTRAIT
MAYBE YOU'LL MAKE PAINTINGS LIKE THAT SOMEDAY...
WHAT'S SO GREAT ABOUT JUST BEING SKILLED?
I MEAN, IF THERE ISN'T A THEME OR IDEA TO EXPRESS...
...
...S-SORRY.
OH, NO, WHAT YOU WERE SAYING WAS DEEP...
...WAIT.
ON THE TOPIC OF VELÁZQUEZ ...

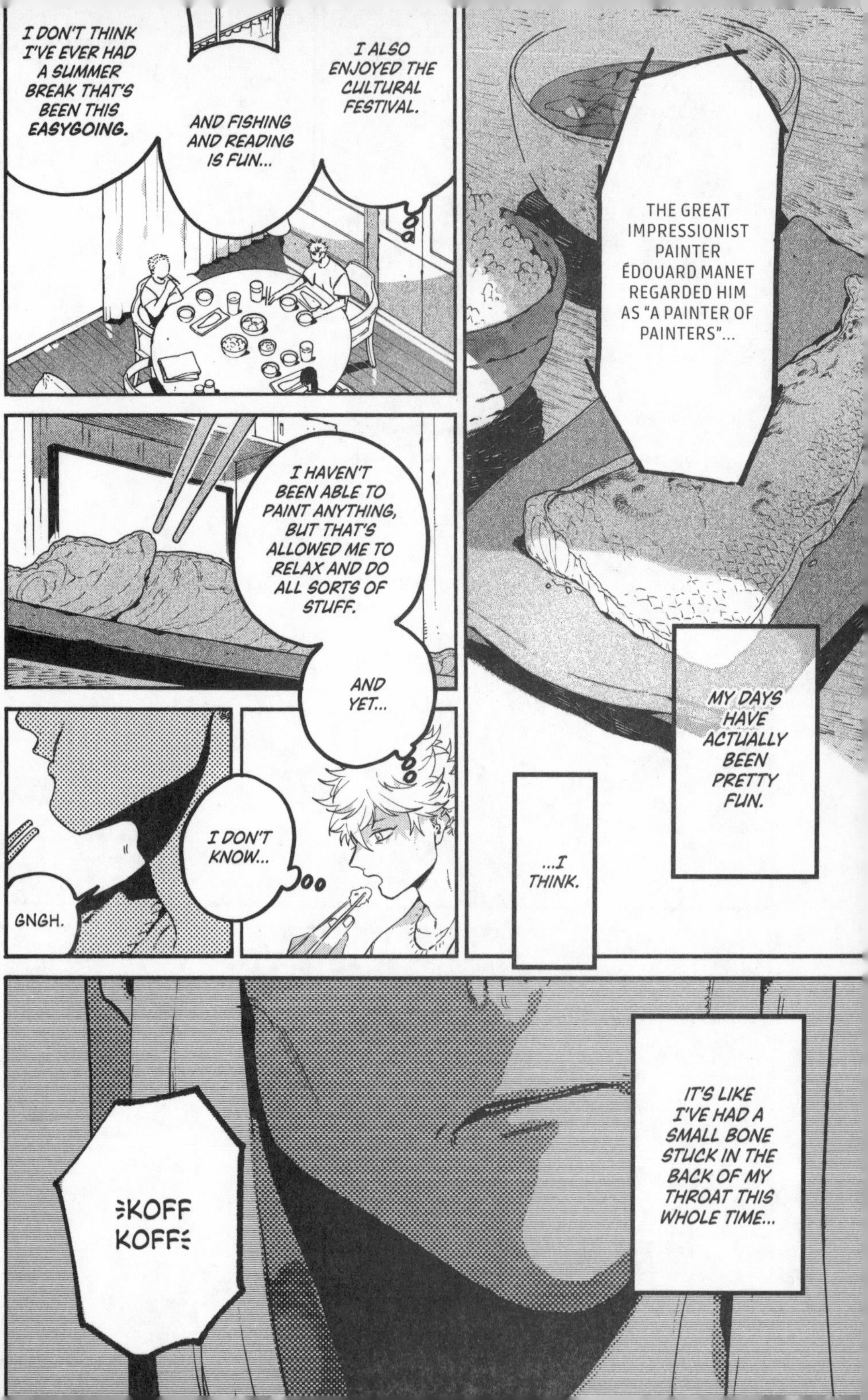

THE GREAT IMPRESSIONIST PAINTER ÉDOUARD MANET REGARDED HIM AS "A PAINTER OF PAINTERS"...
MY DAYS HAVE ACTUALLY BEEN PRETTY FUN.
...I THINK.
I ALSO ENJOYED THE CULTURAL FESTIVAL.
AND FISHING AND READING IS FUN...
I DON'T THINK I'VE EVER HAD A SUMMER BREAK THAT'S BEEN THIS EASYGOING.
I HAVEN'T BEEN ABLE TO PAINT ANYTHING, BUT THAT'S ALLOWED ME TO RELAX AND DO ALL SORTS OF STUFF.
AND YET...
I DON'T KNOW...
GNGH.
IT'S LIKE I'VE HAD A SMALL BONE STUCK IN THE BACK OF MY THROAT THIS WHOLE TIME...
KOFF KOFF

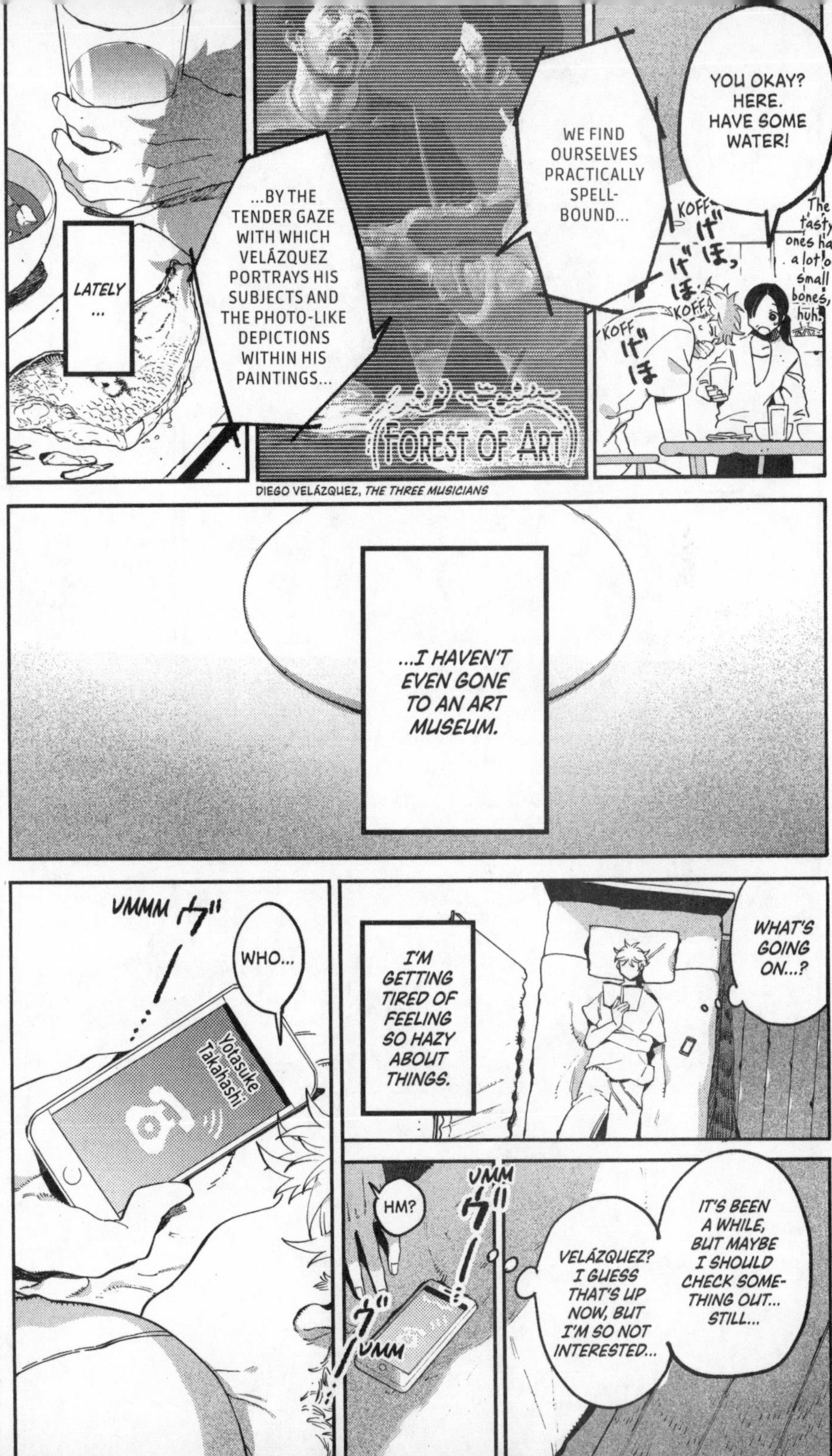
YOU OKAY? HERE. HAVE SOME WATER!
KOFF げほっ
げほ KOFF
KOFF げほ
The tasty ones have a lot of small bones, huh.
WE FIND OURSELVES PRACTICALLY SPELL-BOUND...
...BY THE TENDER GAZE WITH WHICH VELÁZQUEZ PORTRAYS HIS SUBJECTS AND THE PHOTO-LIKE DEPICTIONS WITHIN HIS PAINTINGS...
Forest of Art
LATELY ...
...I HAVEN'T EVEN GONE TO AN ART MUSEUM.
WHAT'S GOING ON...?
I'M GETTING TIRED OF FEELING SO HAZY ABOUT THINGS.
UMMM ヴ"
WHO...
Yotasuke Takahashi
IT'S BEEN A WHILE, BUT MAYBE I SHOULD CHECK SOME-THING OUT... STILL...
VELÁZQUEZ? I GUESS THAT'S UP NOW, BUT I'M SO NOT INTERESTED...
UMM ヴ
HM?
ヴ UMM

DIEGO VELÁZQUEZ, *THE THREE MUSICIANS*

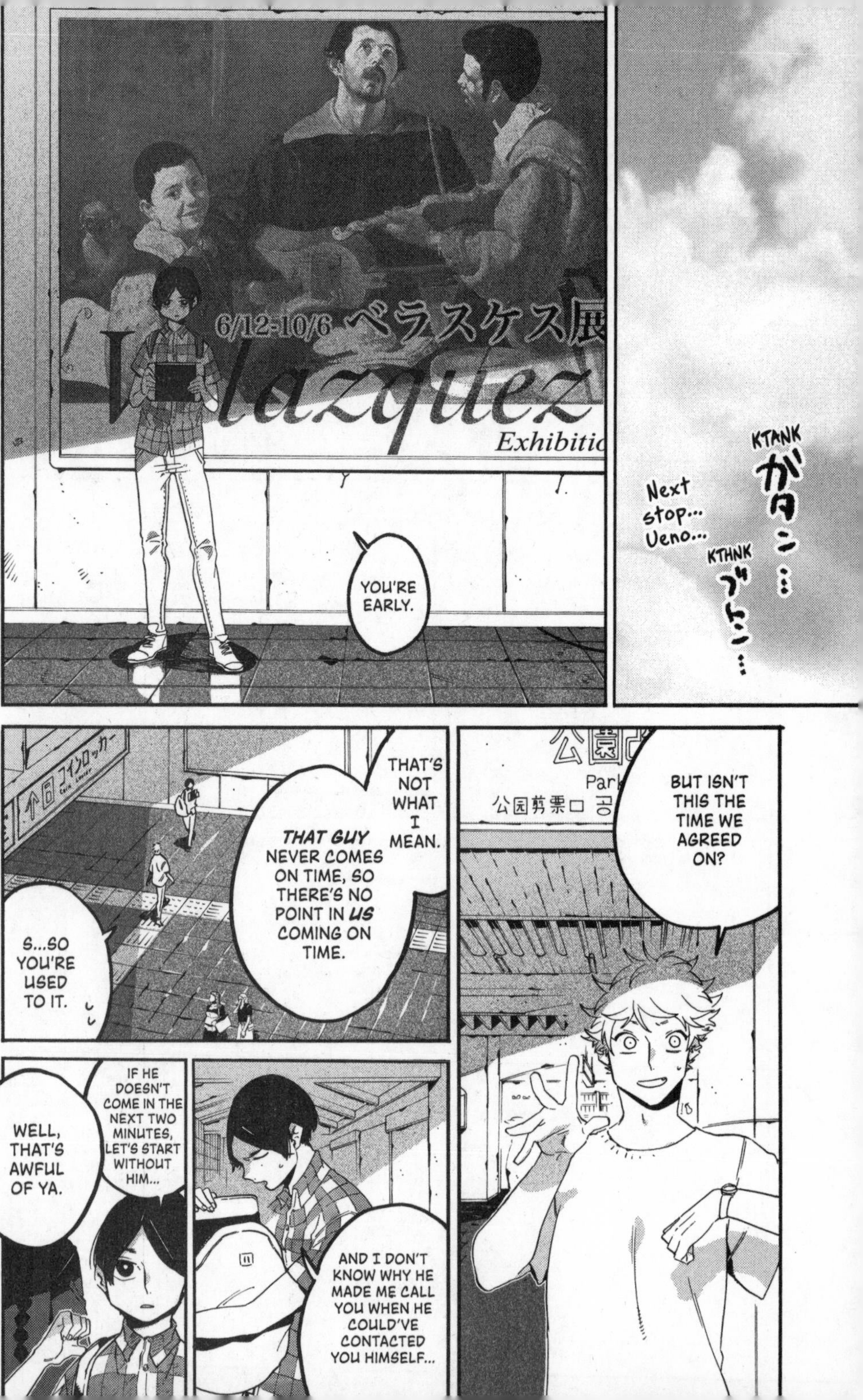
KTANK
ガタン…
Next stop... Ueno...
KTHNK
ゴトン…
6/12-10/6 ベラスケス展
lazquez
Exhibitio
YOU'RE EARLY.
公園口
Park
公园剪票口 공
BUT ISN'T THIS THE TIME WE AGREED ON?
コインロッカー
THAT'S NOT WHAT I MEAN.
THAT GUY NEVER COMES ON TIME, SO THERE'S NO POINT IN *US* COMING ON TIME.
S...SO YOU'RE USED TO IT.
IF HE DOESN'T COME IN THE NEXT TWO MINUTES, LET'S START WITHOUT HIM...
AND I DON'T KNOW WHY HE MADE ME CALL YOU WHEN HE COULD'VE CONTACTED YOU HIMSELF...
WELL, THAT'S AWFUL OF YA.

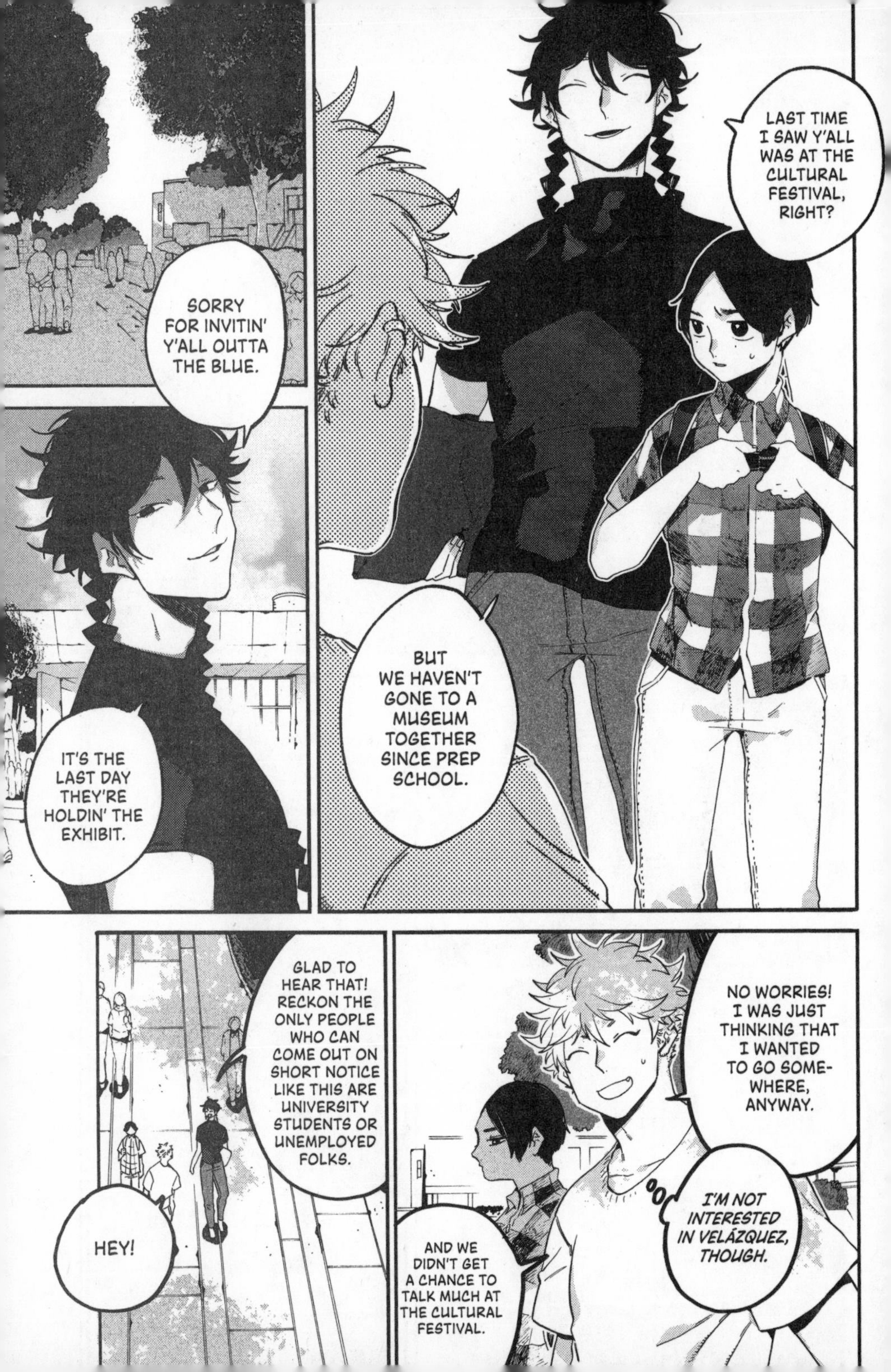
LAST TIME I SAW Y'ALL WAS AT THE CULTURAL FESTIVAL, RIGHT?
BUT WE HAVEN'T GONE TO A MUSEUM TOGETHER SINCE PREP SCHOOL.
SORRY FOR INVITIN' Y'ALL OUTTA THE BLUE.
IT'S THE LAST DAY THEY'RE HOLDIN' THE EXHIBIT.
NO WORRIES! I WAS JUST THINKING THAT I WANTED TO GO SOME-WHERE, ANYWAY.
I'M NOT INTERESTED IN VELÁZQUEZ, THOUGH.
AND WE DIDN'T GET A CHANCE TO TALK MUCH AT THE CULTURAL FESTIVAL.
GLAD TO HEAR THAT! RECKON THE ONLY PEOPLE WHO CAN COME OUT ON SHORT NOTICE LIKE THIS ARE UNIVERSITY STUDENTS OR UNEMPLOYED FOLKS.
HEY!

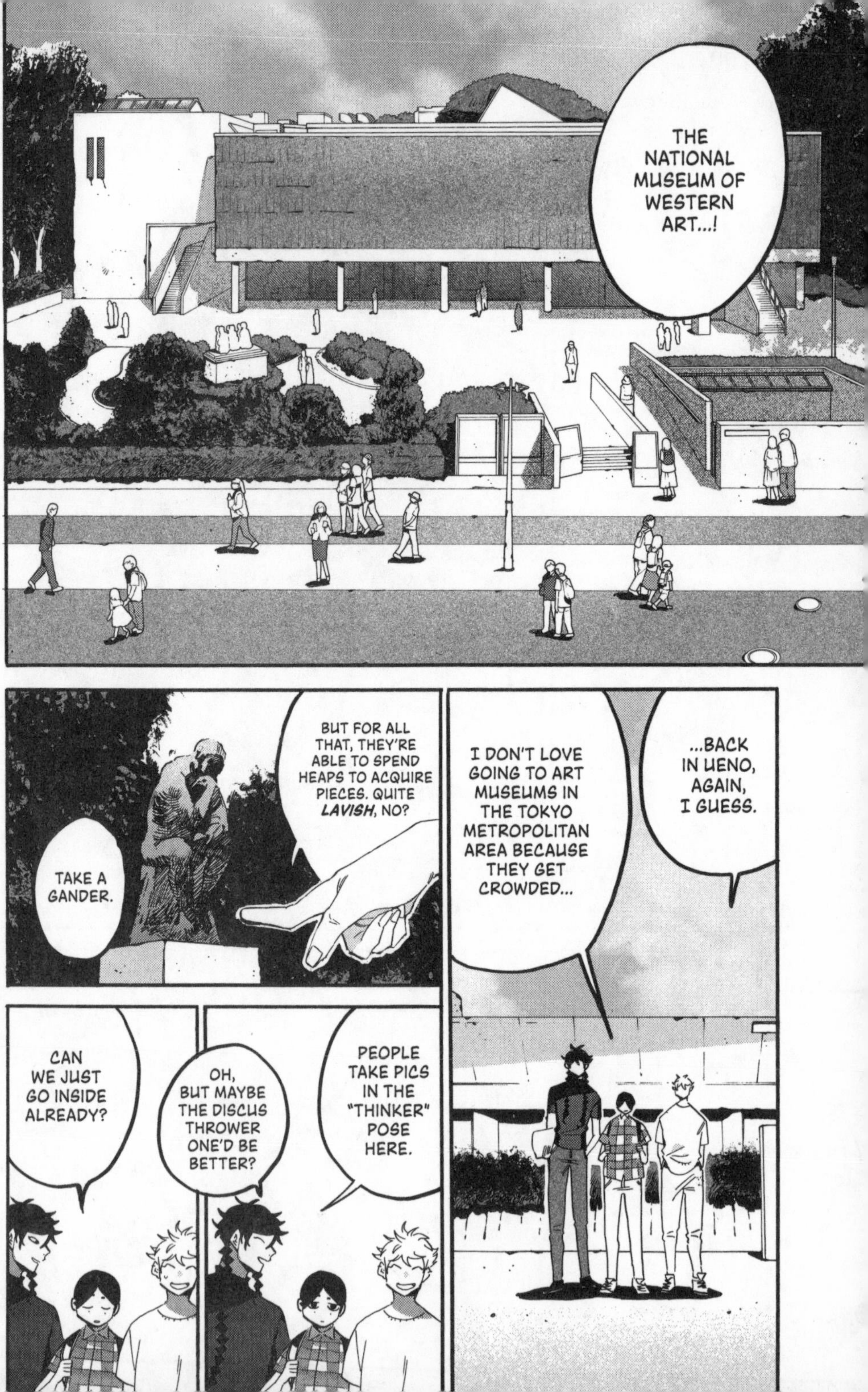
THE NATIONAL MUSEUM OF WESTERN ART...!
...BACK IN UENO, AGAIN, I GUESS.
I DON'T LOVE GOING TO ART MUSEUMS IN THE TOKYO METROPOLITAN AREA BECAUSE THEY GET CROWDED...
BUT FOR ALL THAT, THEY'RE ABLE TO SPEND HEAPS TO ACQUIRE PIECES. QUITE *LAVISH*, NO?
TAKE A GANDER.
PEOPLE TAKE PICS IN THE "THINKER" POSE HERE.
OH, BUT MAYBE THE DISCUS THROWER ONE'D BE BETTER?
CAN WE JUST GO INSIDE ALREADY?

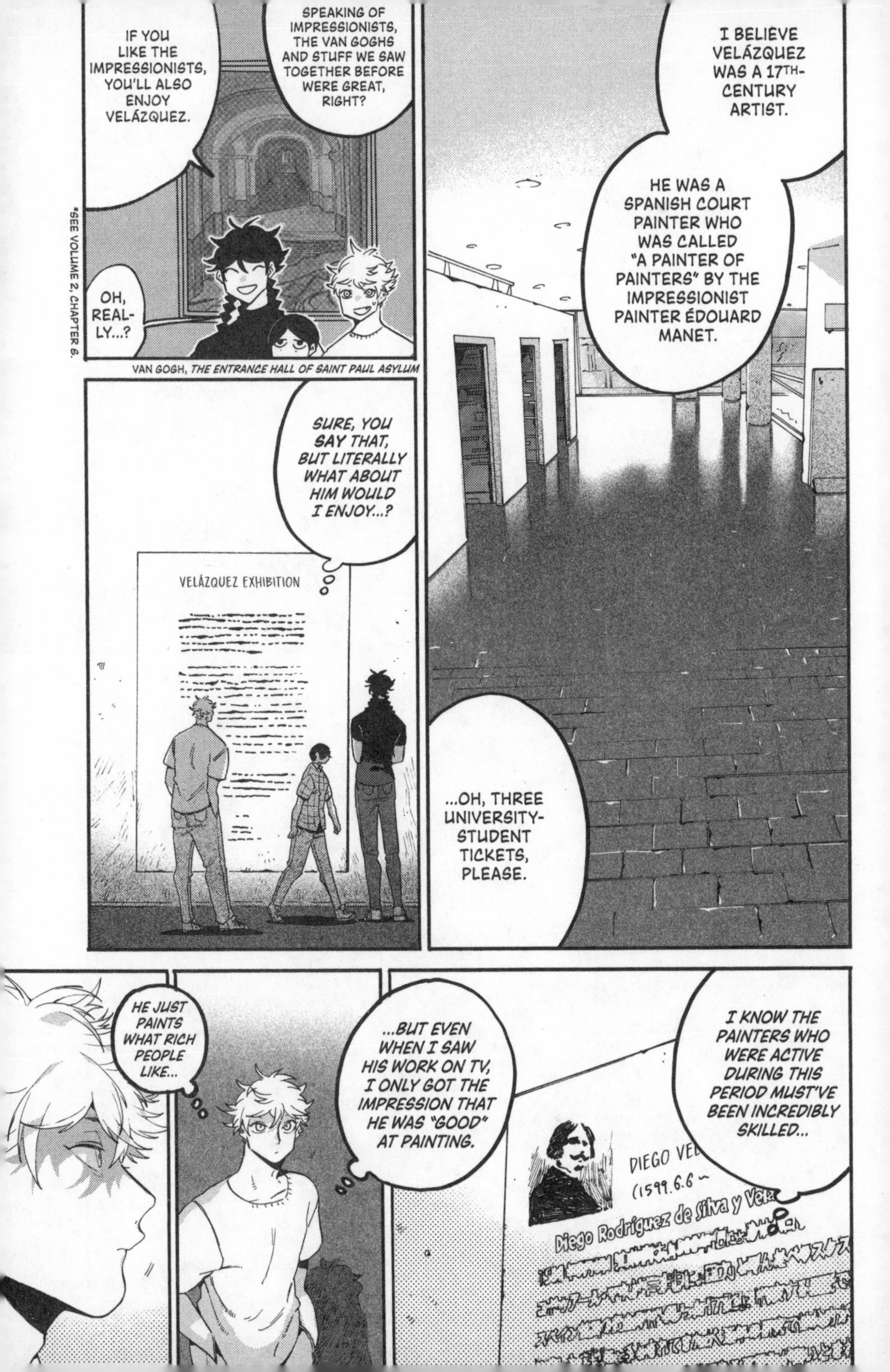
I BELIEVE VELÁZQUEZ WAS A 17TH-CENTURY ARTIST.
HE WAS A SPANISH COURT PAINTER WHO WAS CALLED "A PAINTER OF PAINTERS" BY THE IMPRESSIONIST PAINTER ÉDOUARD MANET.
...OH, THREE UNIVERSITY-STUDENT TICKETS, PLEASE.
SPEAKING OF IMPRESSIONISTS, THE VAN GOGHS AND STUFF WE SAW TOGETHER BEFORE WERE GREAT, RIGHT?
IF YOU LIKE THE IMPRESSIONISTS, YOU'LL ALSO ENJOY VELÁZQUEZ.
OH, REAL-LY...?
*SEE VOLUME 2, CHAPTER 6.
VAN GOGH, THE ENTRANCE HALL OF SAINT PAUL ASYLUM
SURE, YOU SAY THAT, BUT LITERALLY WHAT ABOUT HIM WOULD I ENJOY...?
VELÁZQUEZ EXHIBITION
I KNOW THE PAINTERS WHO WERE ACTIVE DURING THIS PERIOD MUST'VE BEEN INCREDIBLY SKILLED...
...BUT EVEN WHEN I SAW HIS WORK ON TV, I ONLY GOT THE IMPRESSION THAT HE WAS "GOOD" AT PAINTING.
HE JUST PAINTS WHAT RICH PEOPLE LIKE...
(1599.6.6 ~

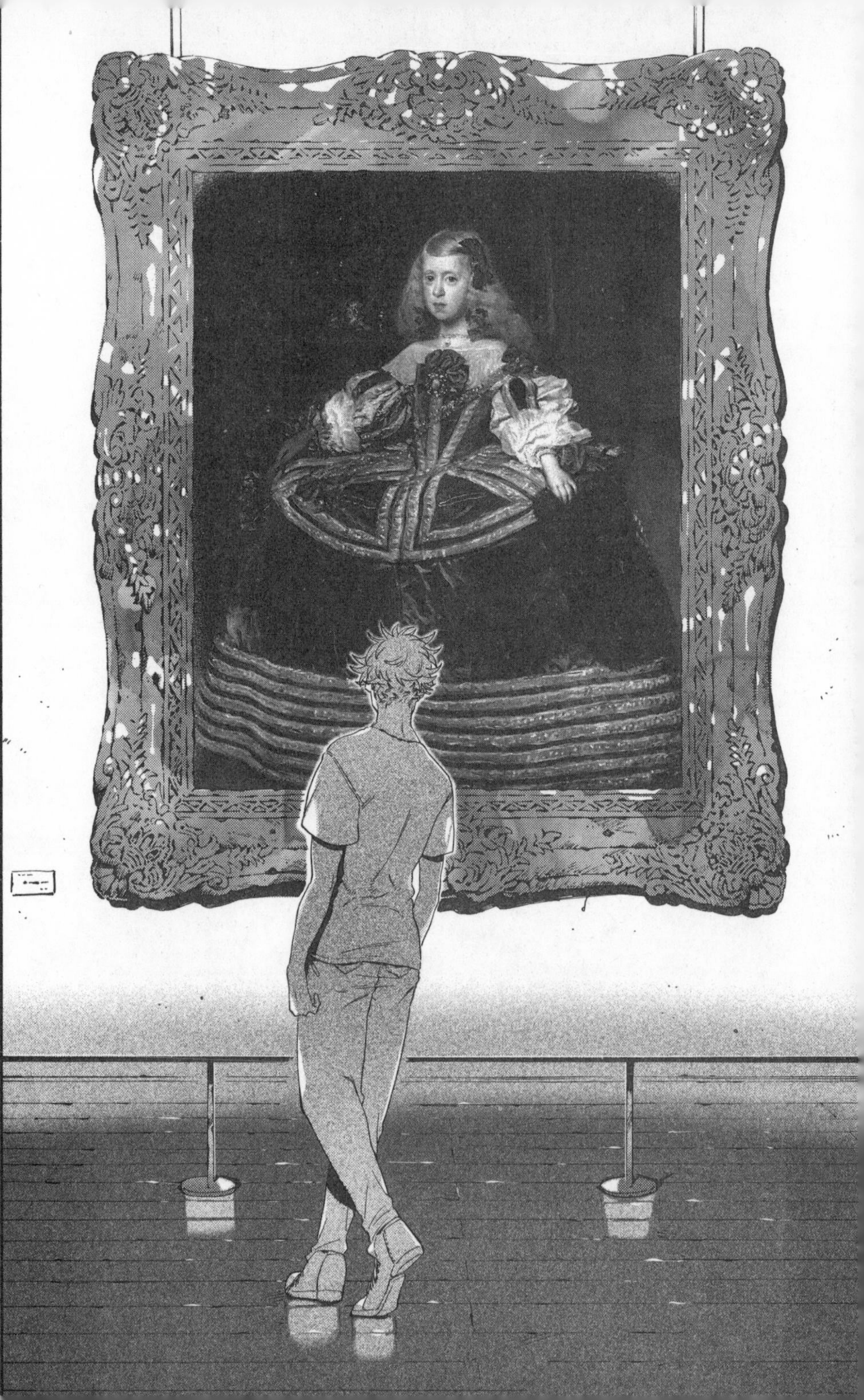

DIEGO VELÁZQUEZ, *INFANTA MARGARITA TERESA IN A BLUE DRESS*

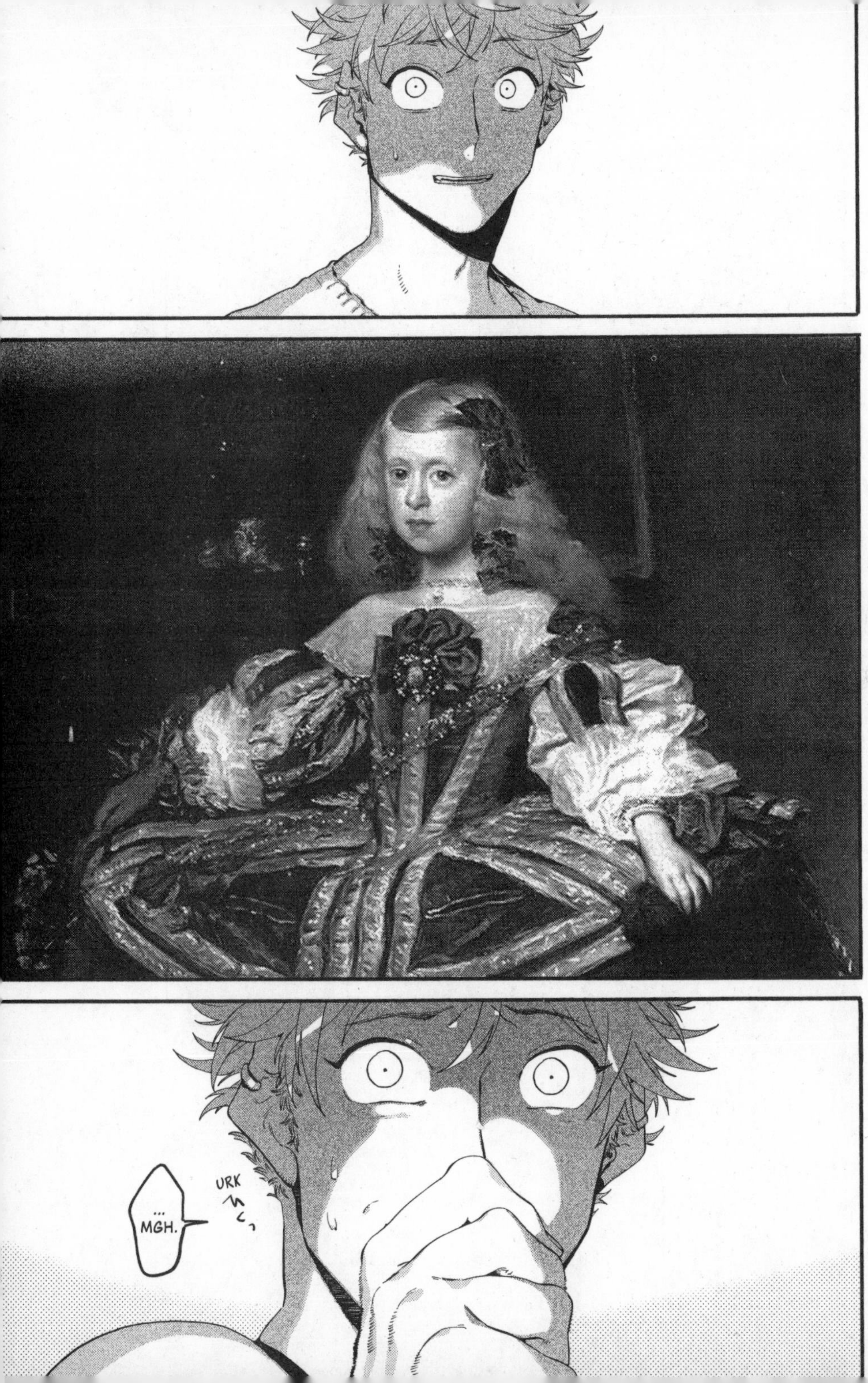
URK
...MGH.

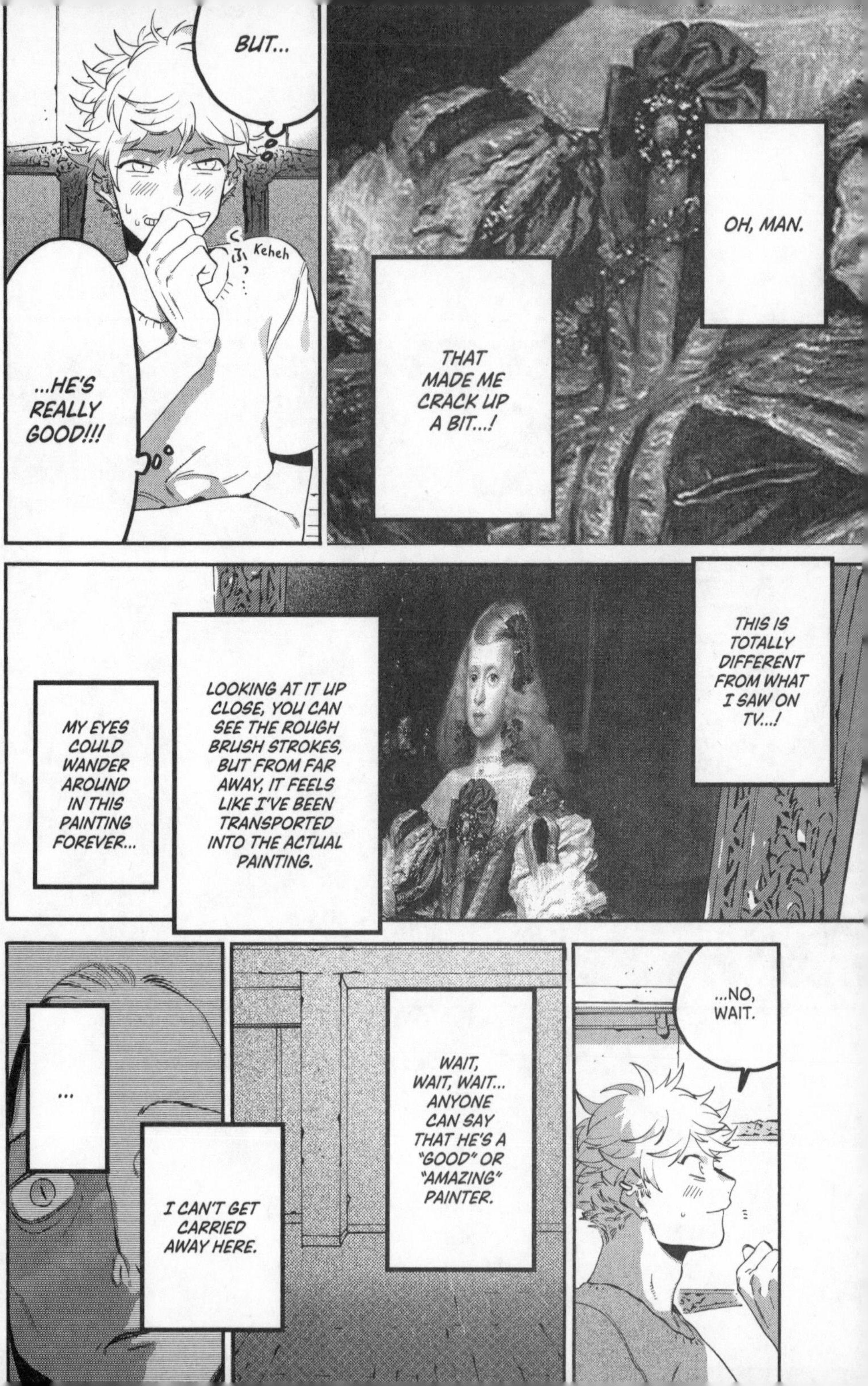
OH, MAN.
THAT MADE ME CRACK UP A BIT...!
BUT...
Keheh
...HE'S REALLY GOOD!!!
THIS IS TOTALLY DIFFERENT FROM WHAT I SAW ON TV...!
LOOKING AT IT UP CLOSE, YOU CAN SEE THE ROUGH BRUSH STROKES, BUT FROM FAR AWAY, IT FEELS LIKE I'VE BEEN TRANSPORTED INTO THE ACTUAL PAINTING.
MY EYES COULD WANDER AROUND IN THIS PAINTING FOREVER...
...NO, WAIT.
WAIT, WAIT, WAIT... ANYONE CAN SAY THAT HE'S A "GOOD" OR "AMAZING" PAINTER.
...
I CAN'T GET CARRIED AWAY HERE.

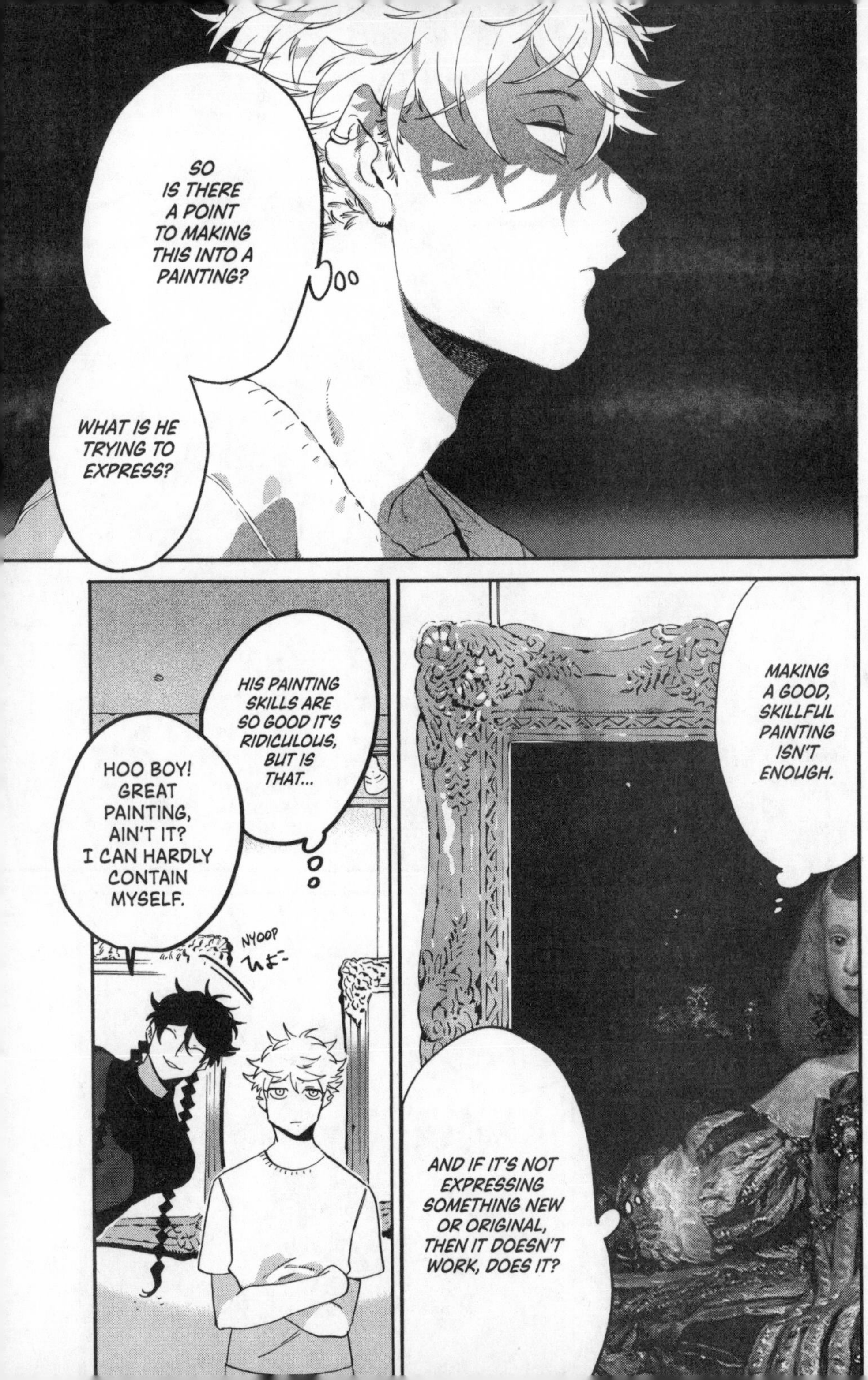
SO IS THERE A POINT TO MAKING THIS INTO A PAINTING?
WHAT IS HE TRYING TO EXPRESS?
MAKING A GOOD, SKILLFUL PAINTING ISN'T ENOUGH.
AND IF IT'S NOT EXPRESSING SOMETHING NEW OR ORIGINAL, THEN IT DOESN'T WORK, DOES IT?
HIS PAINTING SKILLS ARE SO GOOD IT'S RIDICULOUS, BUT IS THAT...
HOO BOY! GREAT PAINTING, AIN'T IT? I CAN HARDLY CONTAIN MYSELF.
NYOOP
ひょー

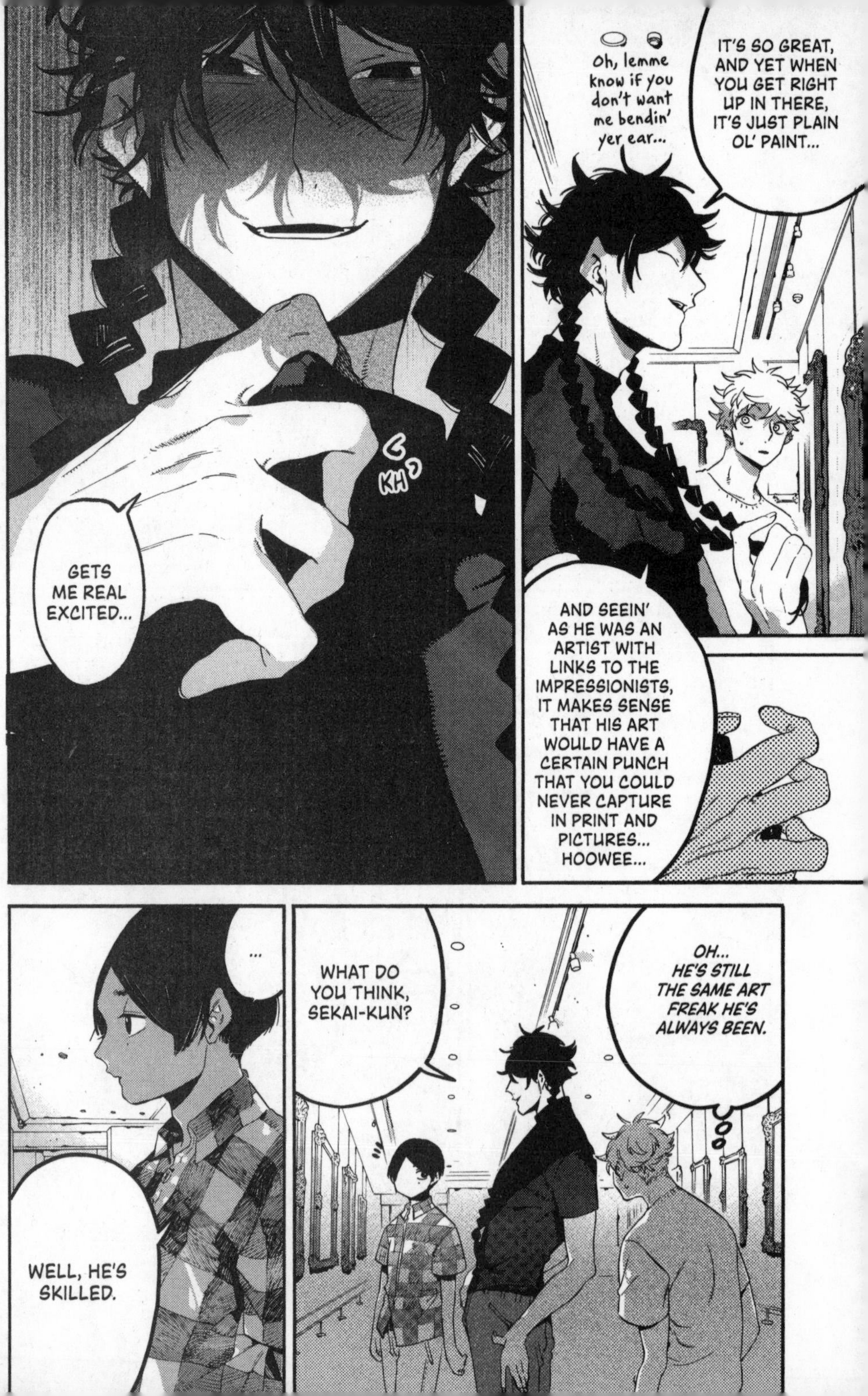

IT'S SO GREAT, AND YET WHEN YOU GET RIGHT UP IN THERE, IT'S JUST PLAIN OL' PAINT...
Oh, lemme know if you don't want me bendin' yer ear...
AND SEEIN' AS HE WAS AN ARTIST WITH LINKS TO THE IMPRESSIONISTS, IT MAKES SENSE THAT HIS ART WOULD HAVE A CERTAIN PUNCH THAT YOU COULD NEVER CAPTURE IN PRINT AND PICTURES... HOOWEE...
KH
GETS ME REAL EXCITED...
OH... HE'S STILL THE SAME ART FREAK HE'S ALWAYS BEEN.
WHAT DO YOU THINK, SEKAI-KUN?
...
WELL, HE'S SKILLED.

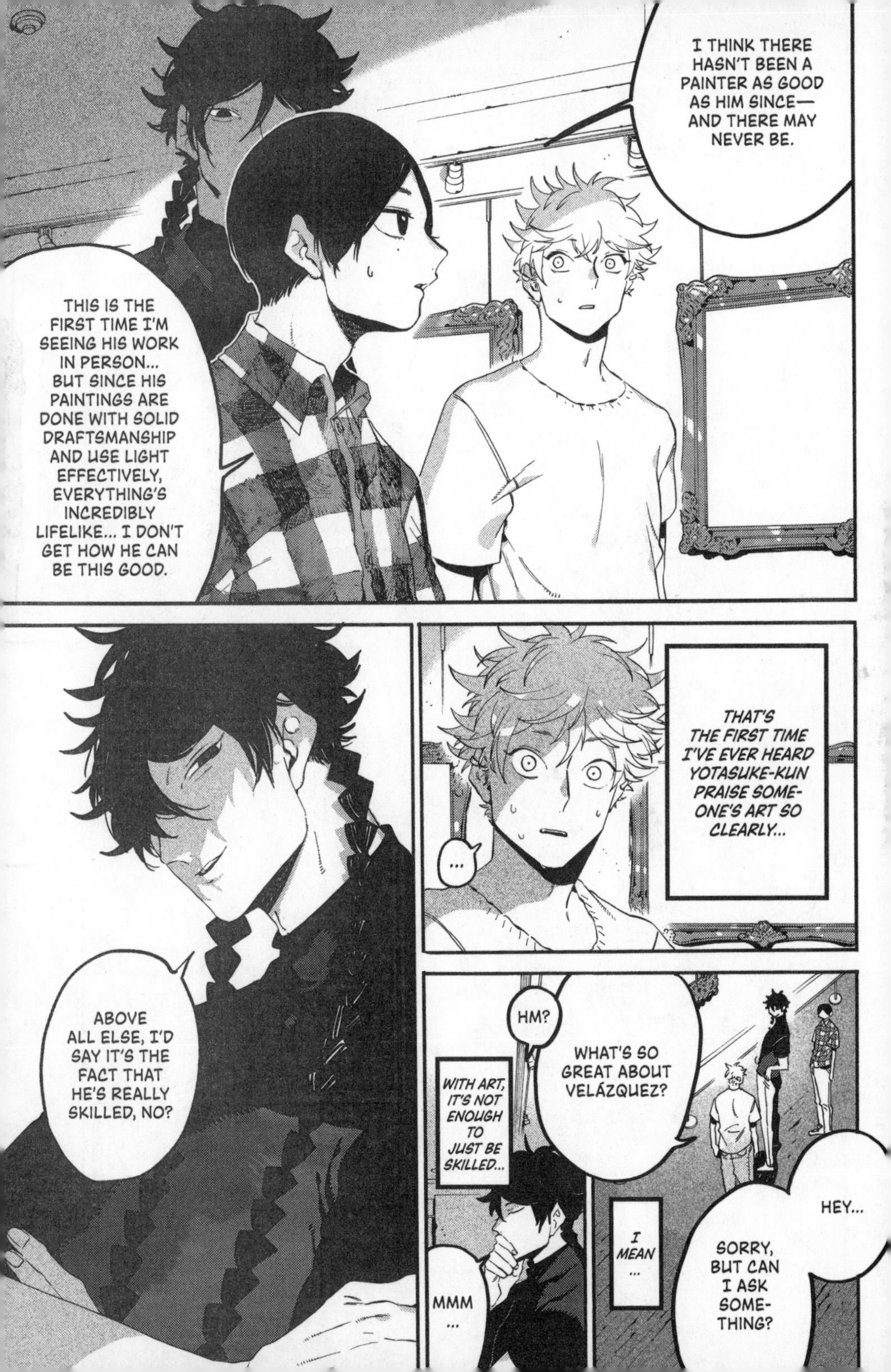
I THINK THERE HASN'T BEEN A PAINTER AS GOOD AS HIM SINCE—AND THERE MAY NEVER BE.
THIS IS THE FIRST TIME I'M SEEING HIS WORK IN PERSON... BUT SINCE HIS PAINTINGS ARE DONE WITH SOLID DRAFTSMANSHIP AND USE LIGHT EFFECTIVELY, EVERYTHING'S INCREDIBLY LIFELIKE... I DON'T GET HOW HE CAN BE THIS GOOD.
THAT'S THE FIRST TIME I'VE EVER HEARD YOTASUKE-KUN PRAISE SOME-ONE'S ART SO CLEARLY...
...
HEY...
SORRY, BUT CAN I ASK SOME-THING?
HM?
WHAT'S SO GREAT ABOUT VELÁZQUEZ?
I MEAN ...
WITH ART, IT'S NOT ENOUGH TO JUST BE SKILLED...
MMM ...
ABOVE ALL ELSE, I'D SAY IT'S THE FACT THAT HE'S REALLY SKILLED, NO?

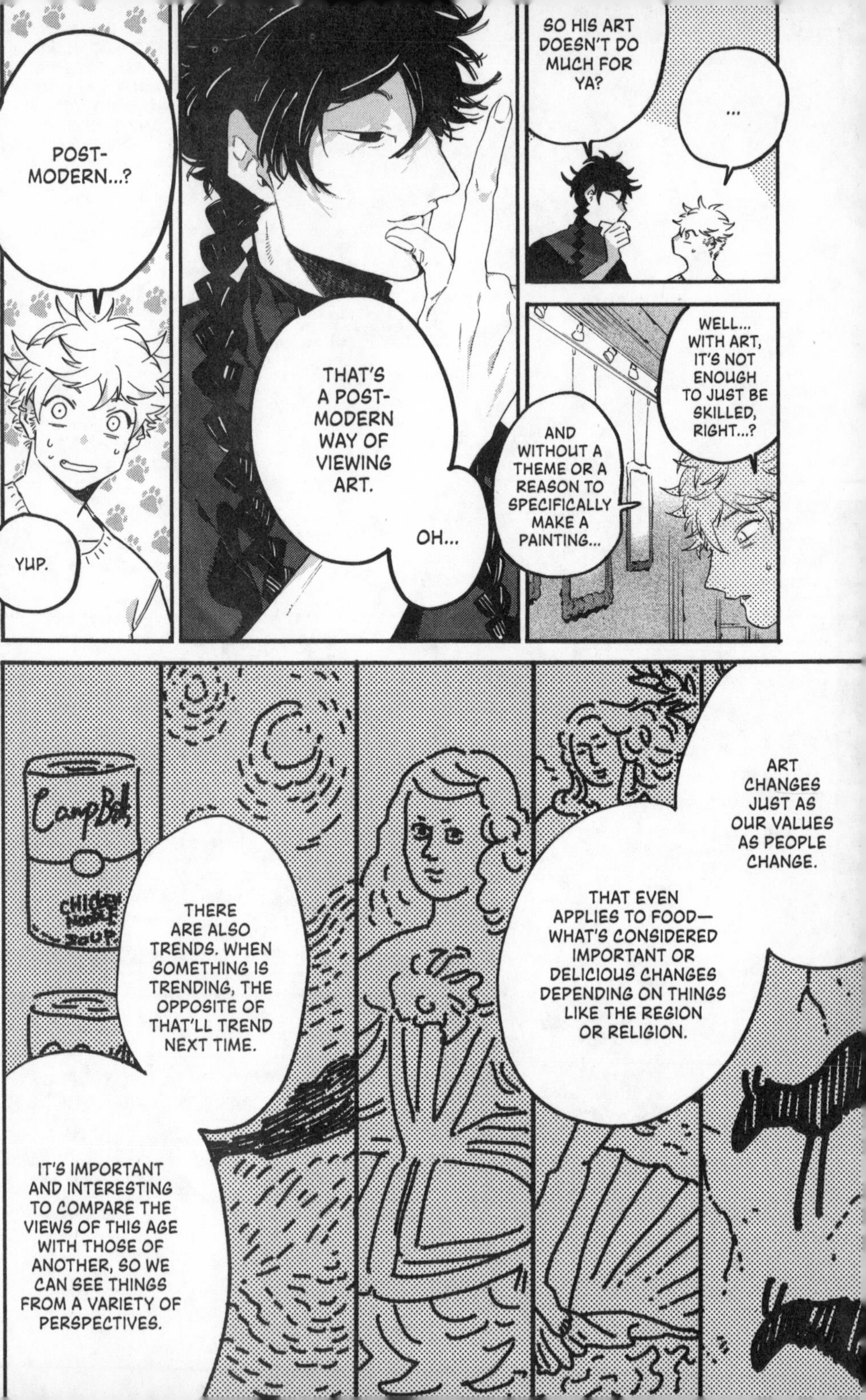
SO HIS ART DOESN'T DO MUCH FOR YA?
...
WELL... WITH ART, IT'S NOT ENOUGH TO JUST BE SKILLED, RIGHT...?
AND WITHOUT A THEME OR A REASON TO SPECIFICALLY MAKE A PAINTING...
THAT'S A POST-MODERN WAY OF VIEWING ART.
OH...
POST-MODERN...?
YUP.
ART CHANGES JUST AS OUR VALUES AS PEOPLE CHANGE.
THAT EVEN APPLIES TO FOOD—WHAT'S CONSIDERED IMPORTANT OR DELICIOUS CHANGES DEPENDING ON THINGS LIKE THE REGION OR RELIGION.
THERE ARE ALSO TRENDS. WHEN SOMETHING IS TRENDING, THE OPPOSITE OF THAT'LL TREND NEXT TIME.
IT'S IMPORTANT AND INTERESTING TO COMPARE THE VIEWS OF THIS AGE WITH THOSE OF ANOTHER, SO WE CAN SEE THINGS FROM A VARIETY OF PERSPECTIVES.

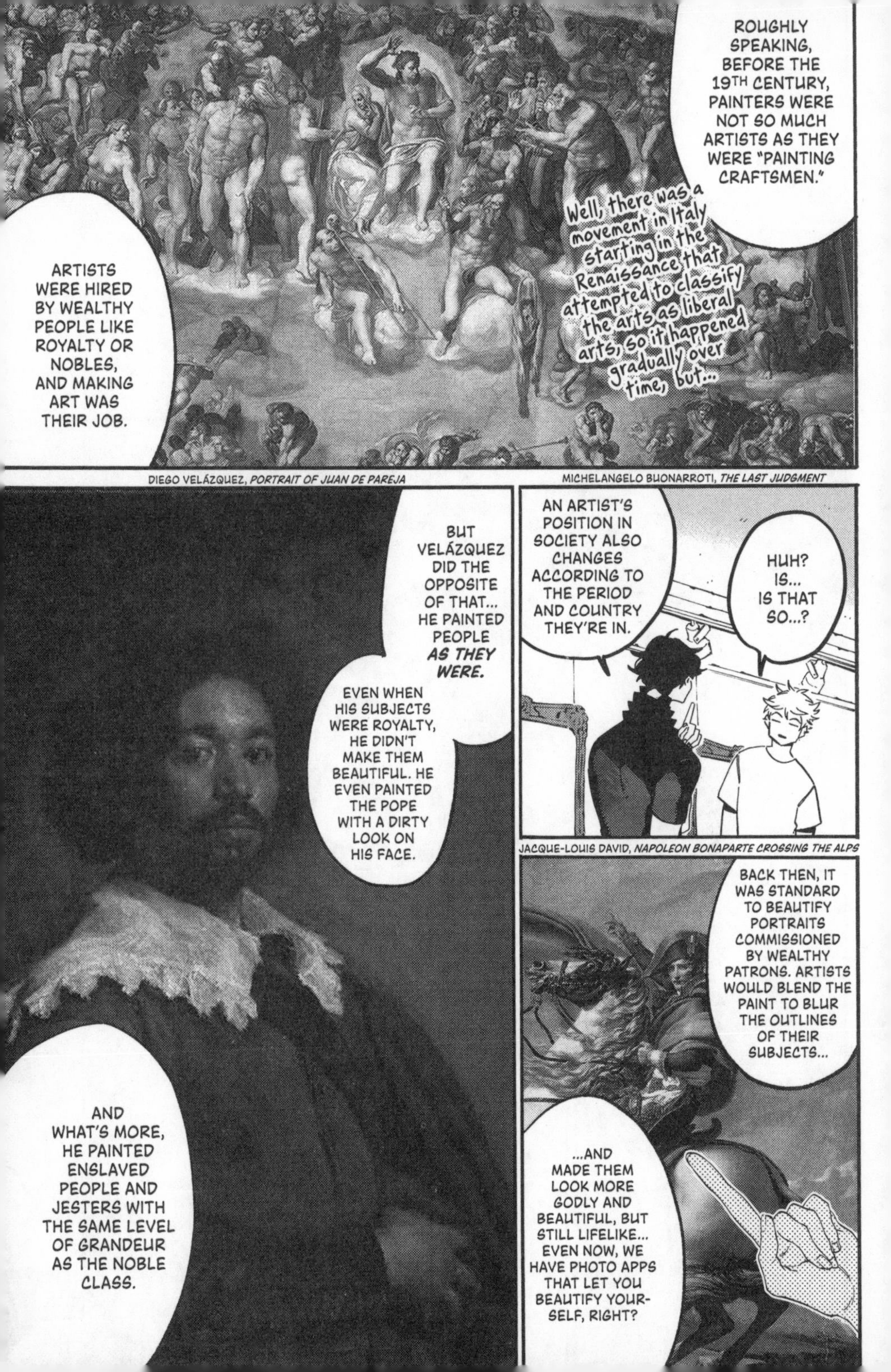

ROUGHLY SPEAKING, BEFORE THE 19TH CENTURY, PAINTERS WERE NOT SO MUCH ARTISTS AS THEY WERE "PAINTING CRAFTSMEN."
Well, there was a movement in Italy starting in the Renaissance that attempted to classify the arts as liberal arts, so it happened gradually over time, but...
ARTISTS WERE HIRED BY WEALTHY PEOPLE LIKE ROYALTY OR NOBLES, AND MAKING ART WAS THEIR JOB.
MICHELANGELO BUONARROTI, *THE LAST JUDGMENT*
AN ARTIST'S POSITION IN SOCIETY ALSO CHANGES ACCORDING TO THE PERIOD AND COUNTRY THEY'RE IN.
HUH? IS... IS THAT SO...?
JACQUE-LOUIS DAVID, *NAPOLEON BONAPARTE CROSSING THE ALPS*
BACK THEN, IT WAS STANDARD TO BEAUTIFY PORTRAITS COMMISSIONED BY WEALTHY PATRONS. ARTISTS WOULD BLEND THE PAINT TO BLUR THE OUTLINES OF THEIR SUBJECTS...
...AND MADE THEM LOOK MORE GODLY AND BEAUTIFUL, BUT STILL LIFELIKE... EVEN NOW, WE HAVE PHOTO APPS THAT LET YOU BEAUTIFY YOUR-SELF, RIGHT?
DIEGO VELÁZQUEZ, *PORTRAIT OF JUAN DE PAREJA*
BUT VELÁZQUEZ DID THE OPPOSITE OF THAT... HE PAINTED PEOPLE ***AS THEY WERE.***
EVEN WHEN HIS SUBJECTS WERE ROYALTY, HE DIDN'T MAKE THEM BEAUTIFUL. HE EVEN PAINTED THE POPE WITH A DIRTY LOOK ON HIS FACE.
AND WHAT'S MORE, HE PAINTED ENSLAVED PEOPLE AND JESTERS WITH THE SAME LEVEL OF GRANDEUR AS THE NOBLE CLASS.

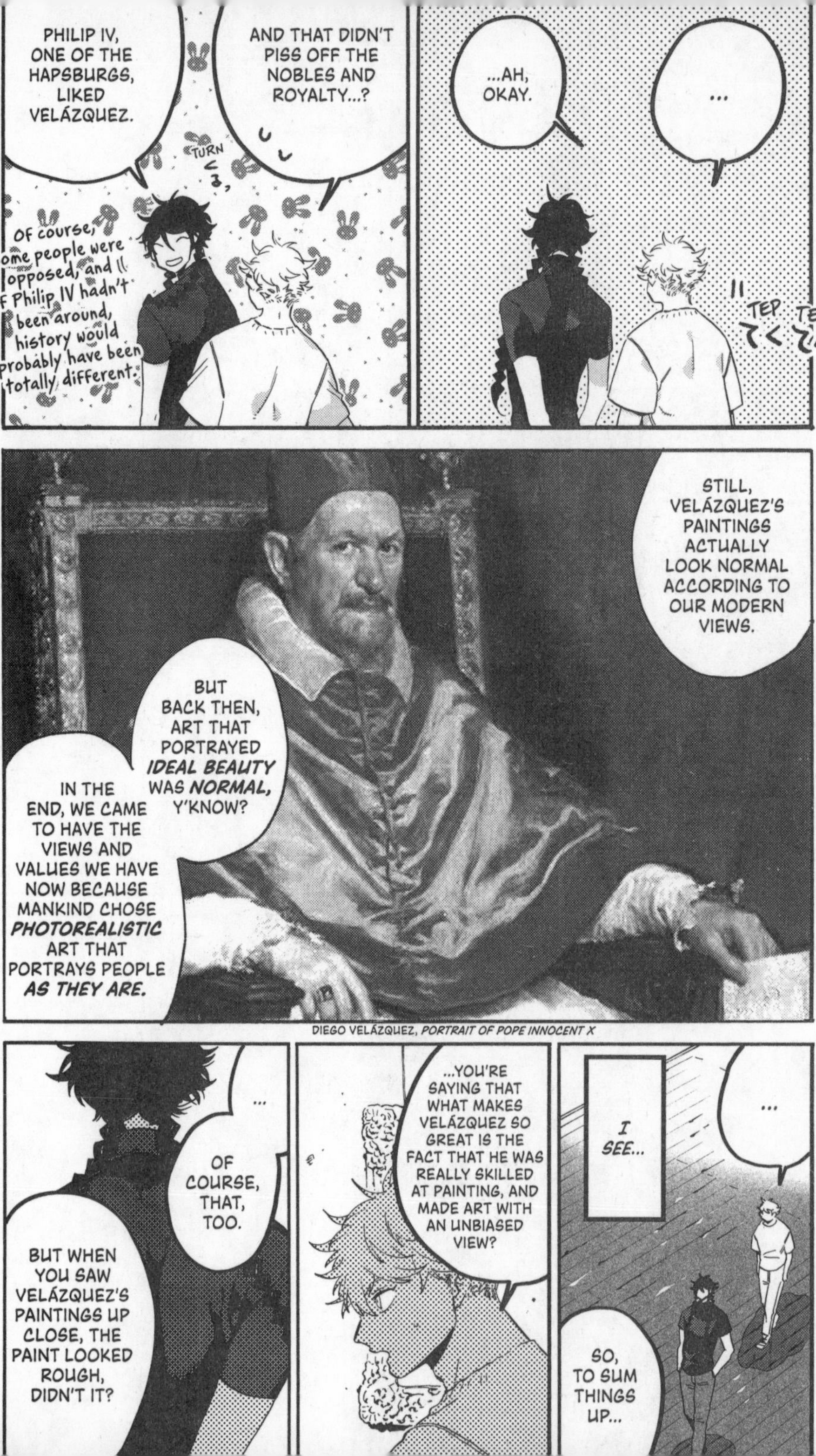
...
...AH, OKAY.
TEP TEP
AND THAT DIDN'T PISS OFF THE NOBLES AND ROYALTY...?
PHILIP IV, ONE OF THE HAPSBURGS, LIKED VELÁZQUEZ.
TURN
Of course, some people were opposed, and if Philip IV hadn't been around, history would probably have been totally different.
STILL, VELÁZQUEZ'S PAINTINGS ACTUALLY LOOK NORMAL ACCORDING TO OUR MODERN VIEWS.
BUT BACK THEN, ART THAT PORTRAYED IDEAL BEAUTY WAS NORMAL, Y'KNOW?
IN THE END, WE CAME TO HAVE THE VIEWS AND VALUES WE HAVE NOW BECAUSE MANKIND CHOSE PHOTOREALISTIC ART THAT PORTRAYS PEOPLE AS THEY ARE.
DIEGO VELÁZQUEZ, PORTRAIT OF POPE INNOCENT X
...
I SEE...
SO, TO SUM THINGS UP...
...YOU'RE SAYING THAT WHAT MAKES VELÁZQUEZ SO GREAT IS THE FACT THAT HE WAS REALLY SKILLED AT PAINTING, AND MADE ART WITH AN UNBIASED VIEW?
...
OF COURSE, THAT, TOO.
BUT WHEN YOU SAW VELÁZQUEZ'S PAINTINGS UP CLOSE, THE PAINT LOOKED ROUGH, DIDN'T IT?

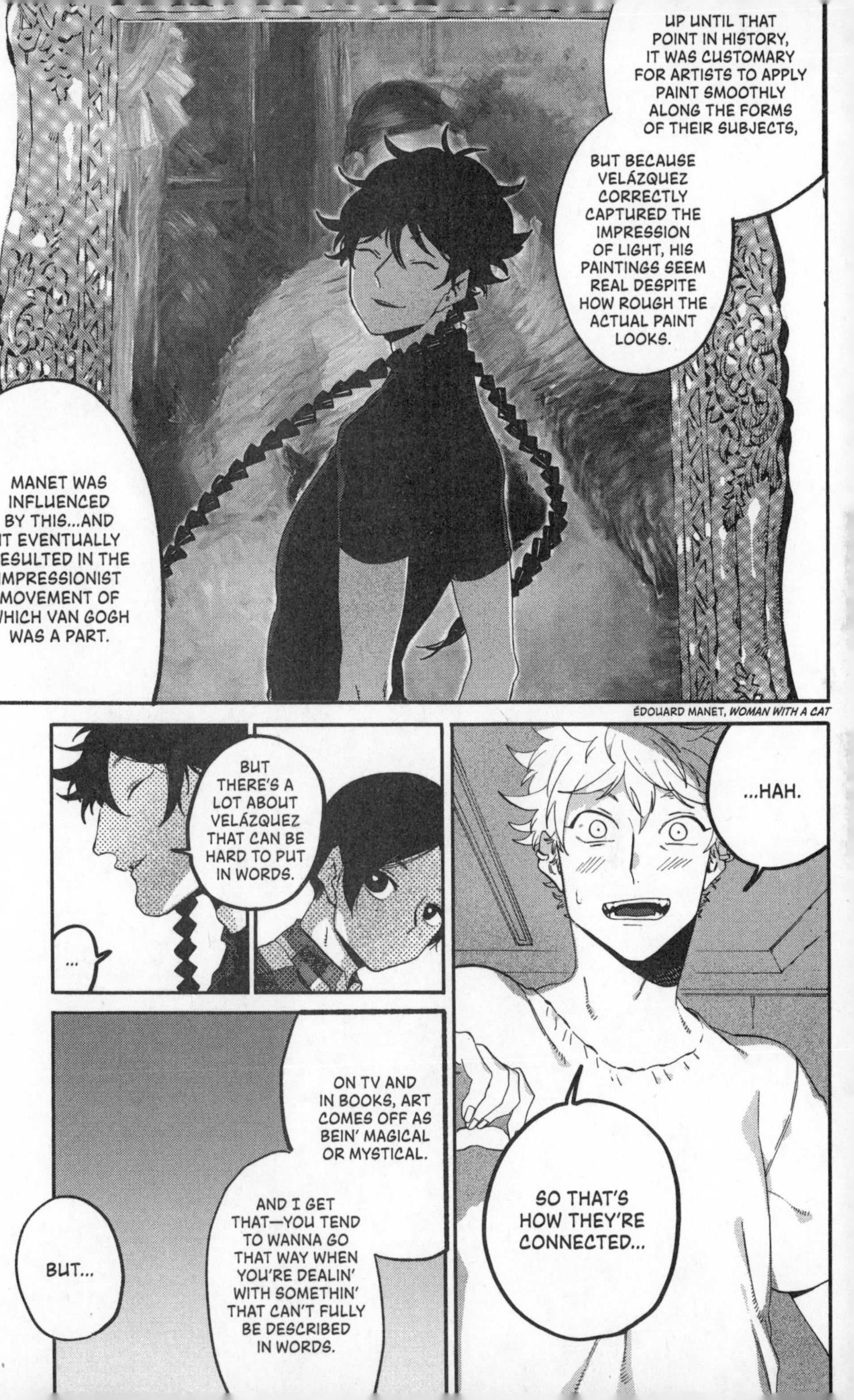
UP UNTIL THAT POINT IN HISTORY, IT WAS CUSTOMARY FOR ARTISTS TO APPLY PAINT SMOOTHLY ALONG THE FORMS OF THEIR SUBJECTS,
BUT BECAUSE VELÁZQUEZ CORRECTLY CAPTURED THE IMPRESSION OF LIGHT, HIS PAINTINGS SEEM REAL DESPITE HOW ROUGH THE ACTUAL PAINT LOOKS.
MANET WAS INFLUENCED BY THIS...AND IT EVENTUALLY RESULTED IN THE IMPRESSIONIST MOVEMENT OF WHICH VAN GOGH WAS A PART.
...HAH.
BUT THERE'S A LOT ABOUT VELÁZQUEZ THAT CAN BE HARD TO PUT IN WORDS.
...
SO THAT'S HOW THEY'RE CONNECTED...
ON TV AND IN BOOKS, ART COMES OFF AS BEIN' MAGICAL OR MYSTICAL.
AND I GET THAT—YOU TEND TO WANNA GO THAT WAY WHEN YOU'RE DEALIN' WITH SOMETHIN' THAT CAN'T FULLY BE DESCRIBED IN WORDS.
BUT...
ÉDOUARD MANET, *WOMAN WITH A CAT*

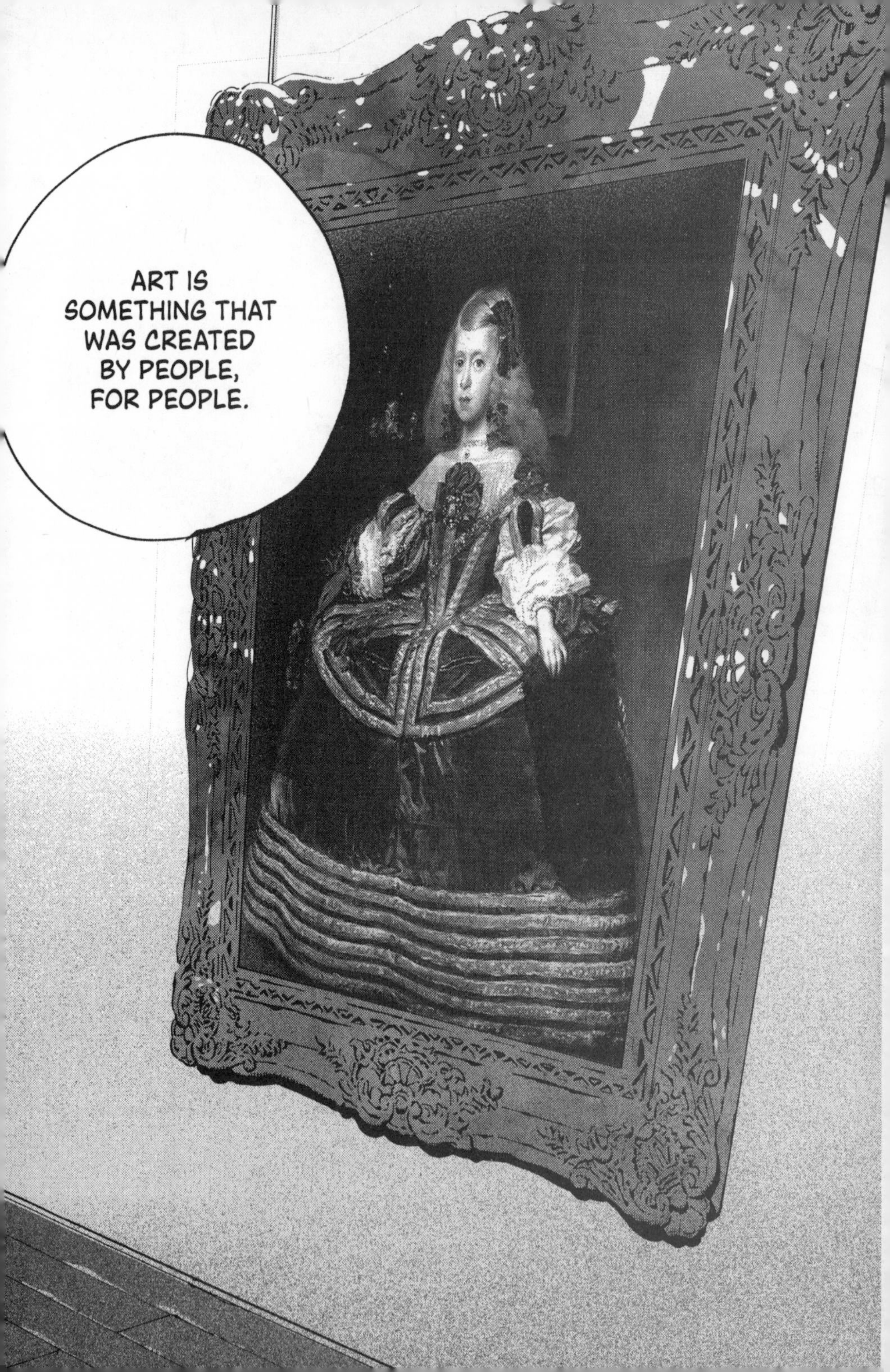
ART IS SOMETHING THAT WAS CREATED BY PEOPLE, FOR PEOPLE.

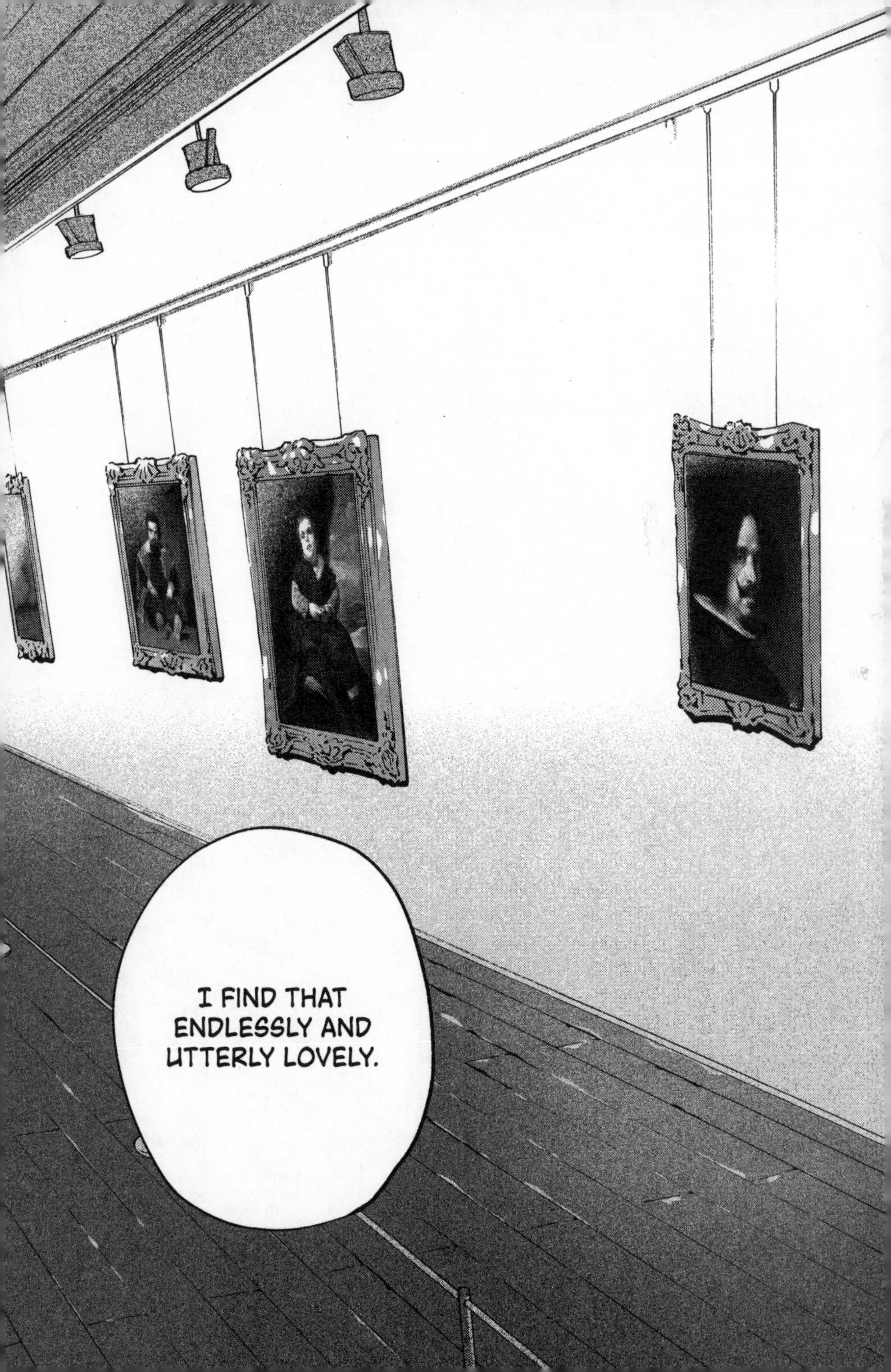
I FIND THAT ENDLESSLY AND UTTERLY LOVELY.

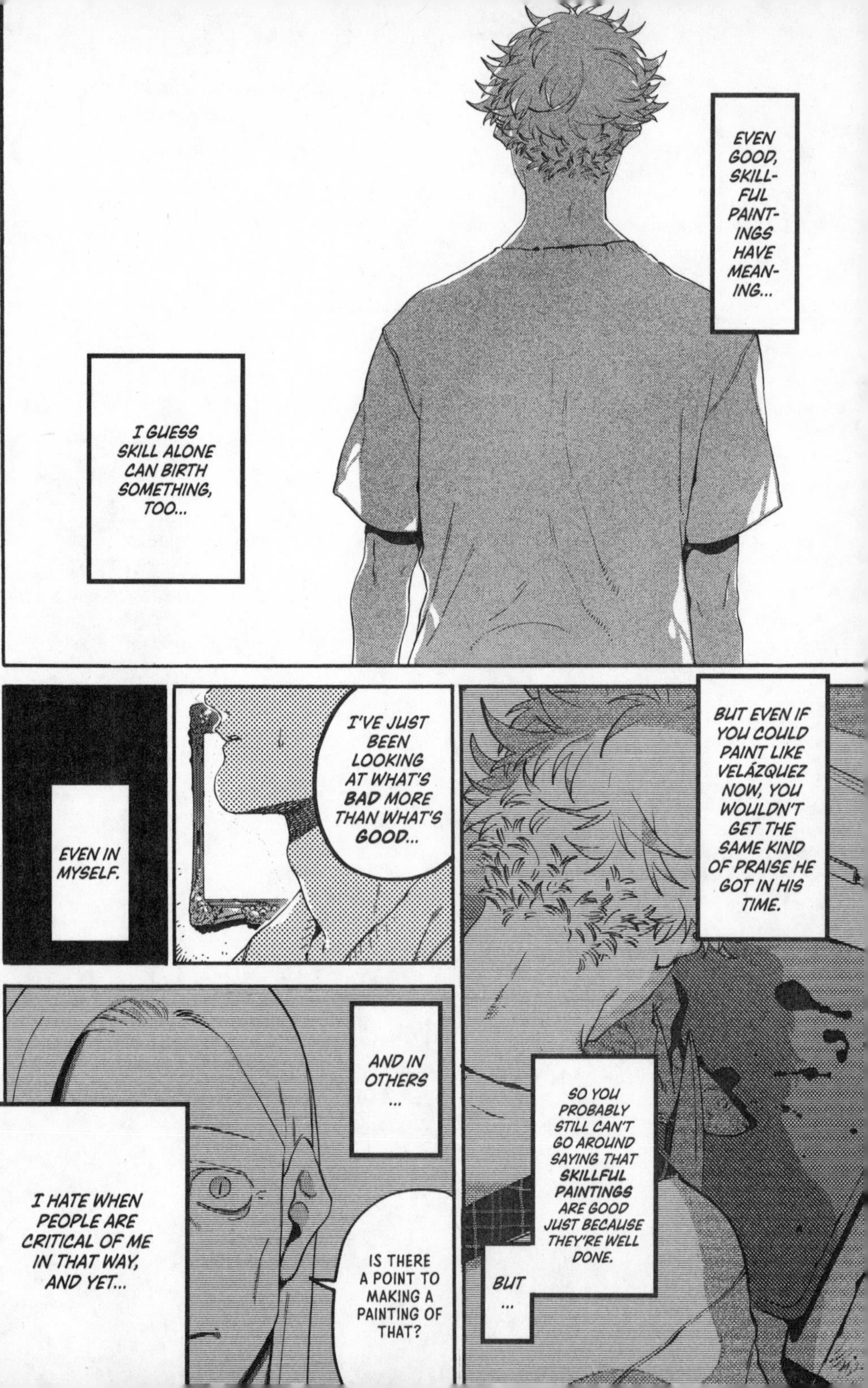
EVEN GOOD, SKILL-FUL PAINT-INGS HAVE MEAN-ING...
I GUESS SKILL ALONE CAN BIRTH SOMETHING, TOO...
BUT EVEN IF YOU COULD PAINT LIKE VELÁZQUEZ NOW, YOU WOULDN'T GET THE SAME KIND OF PRAISE HE GOT IN HIS TIME.
SO YOU PROBABLY STILL CAN'T GO AROUND SAYING THAT **SKILLFUL PAINTINGS** ARE GOOD JUST BECAUSE THEY'RE WELL DONE.
BUT ...
I'VE JUST BEEN LOOKING AT WHAT'S **BAD** MORE THAN WHAT'S **GOOD**...
EVEN IN MYSELF.
AND IN OTHERS ...
I HATE WHEN PEOPLE ARE CRITICAL OF ME IN THAT WAY, AND YET...
IS THERE A POINT TO MAKING A PAINTING OF THAT?

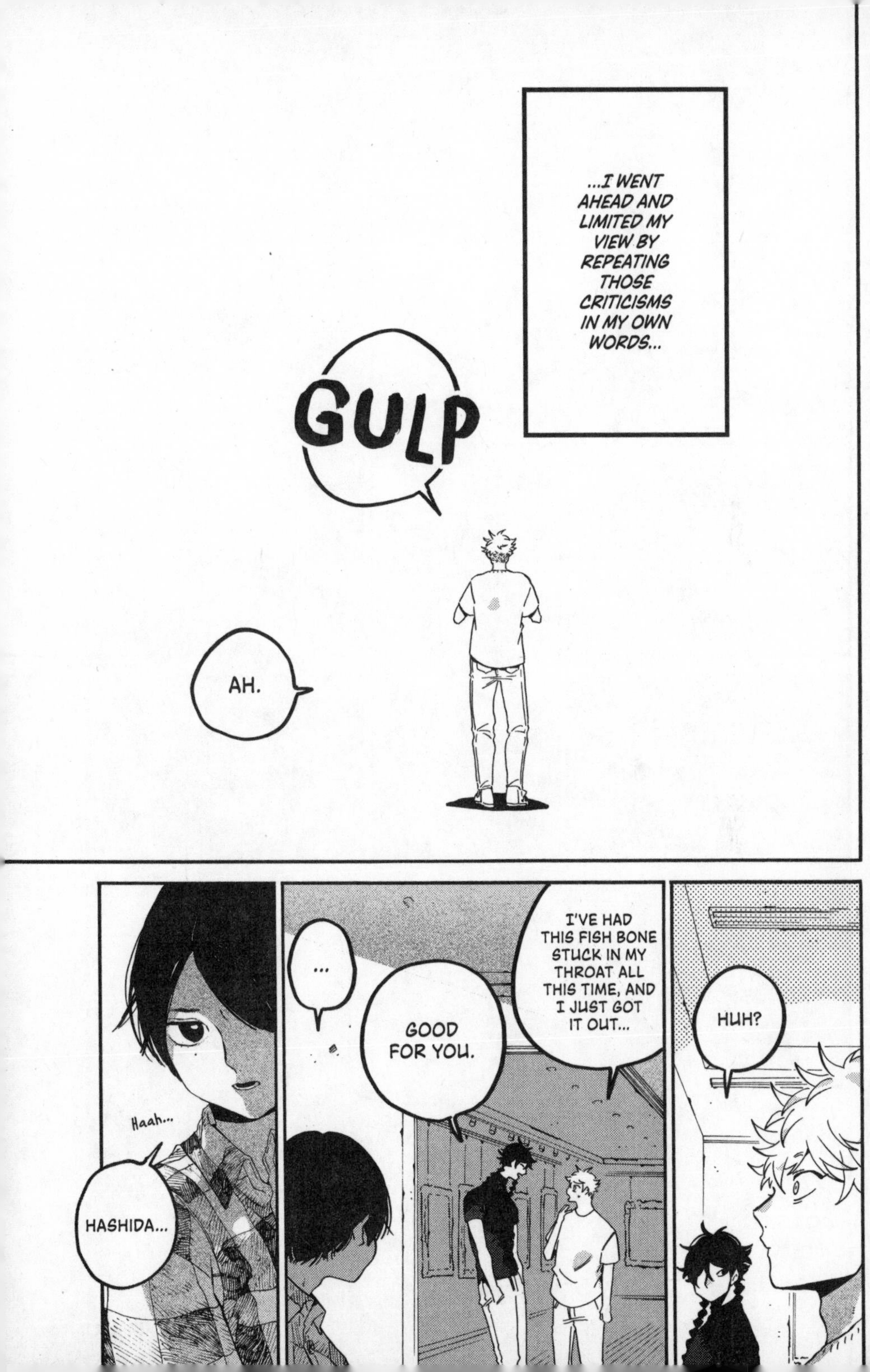
...I WENT AHEAD AND LIMITED MY VIEW BY REPEATING THOSE CRITICISMS IN MY OWN WORDS...
GULP
AH.
HUH?
I'VE HAD THIS FISH BONE STUCK IN MY THROAT ALL THIS TIME, AND I JUST GOT IT OUT...
GOOD FOR YOU.
...
Haah...
HASHIDA...

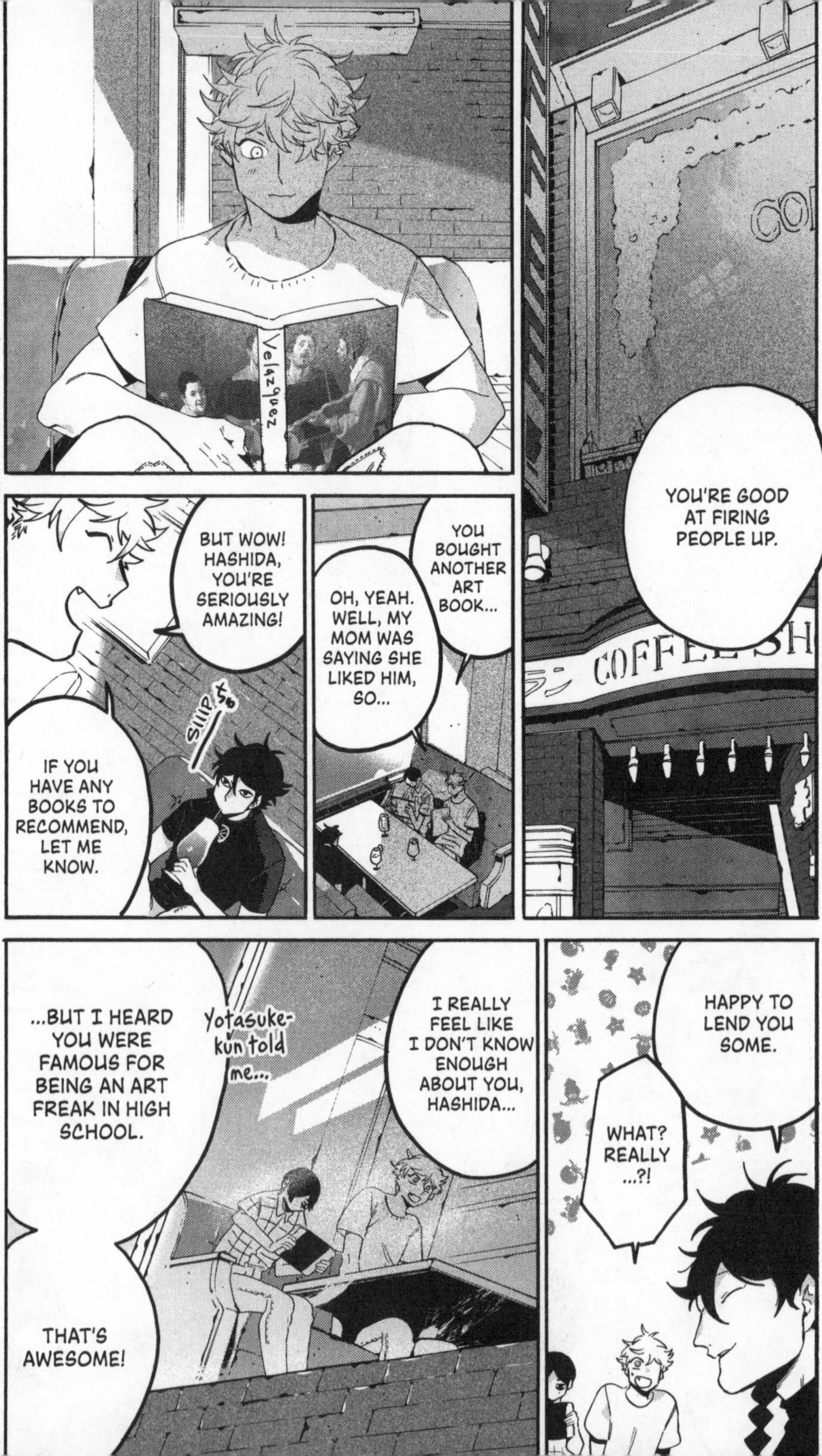
YOU'RE GOOD AT FIRING PEOPLE UP.
Velazquez
YOU BOUGHT ANOTHER ART BOOK...
OH, YEAH. WELL, MY MOM WAS SAYING SHE LIKED HIM, SO...
BUT WOW! HASHIDA, YOU'RE SERIOUSLY AMAZING!
SHIP
IF YOU HAVE ANY BOOKS TO RECOMMEND, LET ME KNOW.
HAPPY TO LEND YOU SOME.
WHAT? REALLY ...?!
I REALLY FEEL LIKE I DON'T KNOW ENOUGH ABOUT YOU, HASHIDA...
Yotasuke-kun told me...
...BUT I HEARD YOU WERE FAMOUS FOR BEING AN ART FREAK IN HIGH SCHOOL.
THAT'S AWESOME!

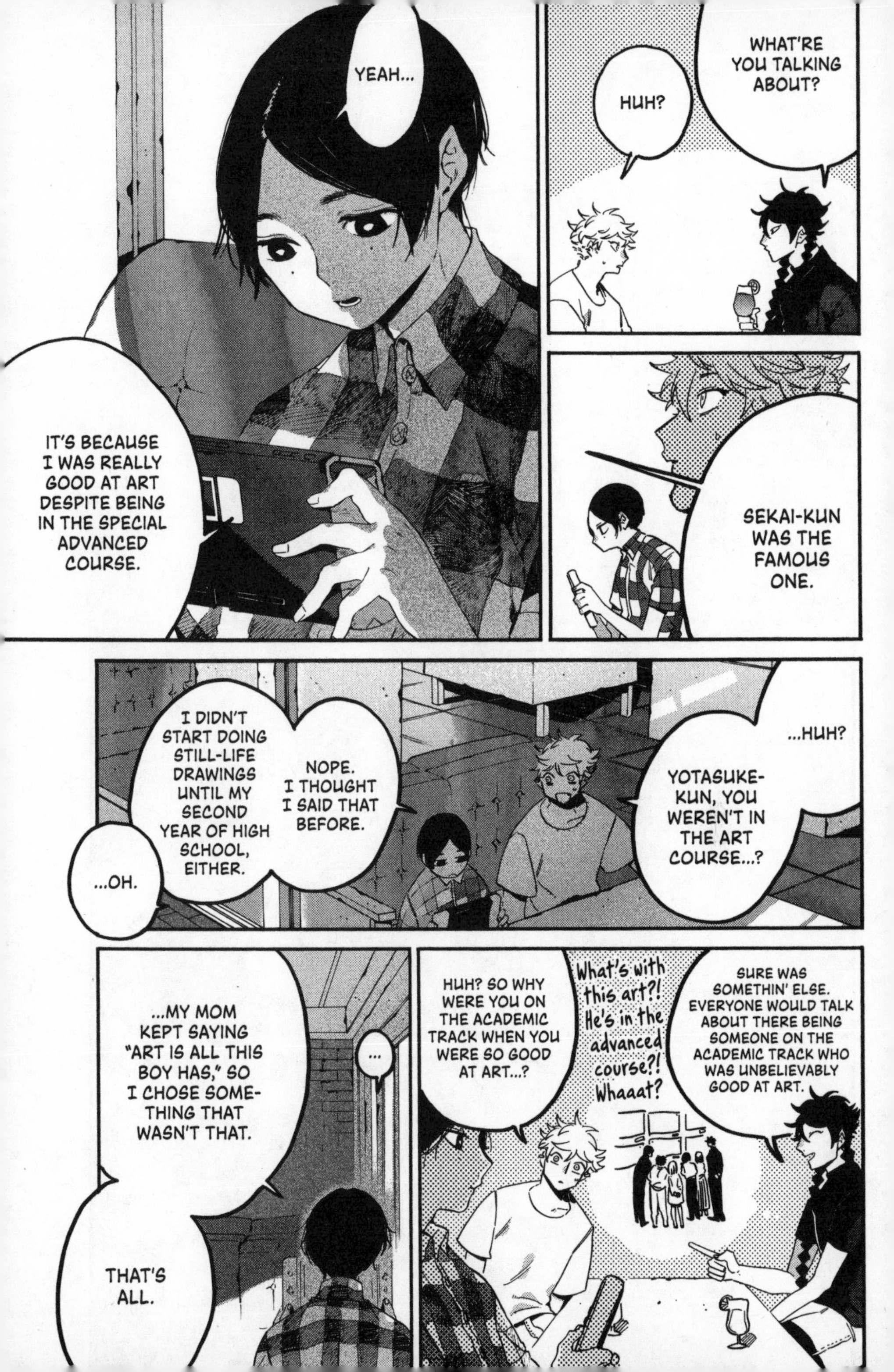

WHAT'RE YOU TALKING ABOUT?
HUH?
SEKAI-KUN WAS THE FAMOUS ONE.
YEAH...
IT'S BECAUSE I WAS REALLY GOOD AT ART DESPITE BEING IN THE SPECIAL ADVANCED COURSE.
...HUH?
YOTASUKE-KUN, YOU WEREN'T IN THE ART COURSE...?
NOPE. I THOUGHT I SAID THAT BEFORE.
I DIDN'T START DOING STILL-LIFE DRAWINGS UNTIL MY SECOND YEAR OF HIGH SCHOOL, EITHER.
...OH.
SURE WAS SOMETHIN' ELSE. EVERYONE WOULD TALK ABOUT THERE BEING SOMEONE ON THE ACADEMIC TRACK WHO WAS UNBELIEVABLY GOOD AT ART.
What's with this art?! He's in the advanced course?! Whaaat?
HUH? SO WHY WERE YOU ON THE ACADEMIC TRACK WHEN YOU WERE SO GOOD AT ART...?
...
...MY MOM KEPT SAYING "ART IS ALL THIS BOY HAS," SO I CHOSE SOME-THING THAT WASN'T THAT.
THAT'S ALL.

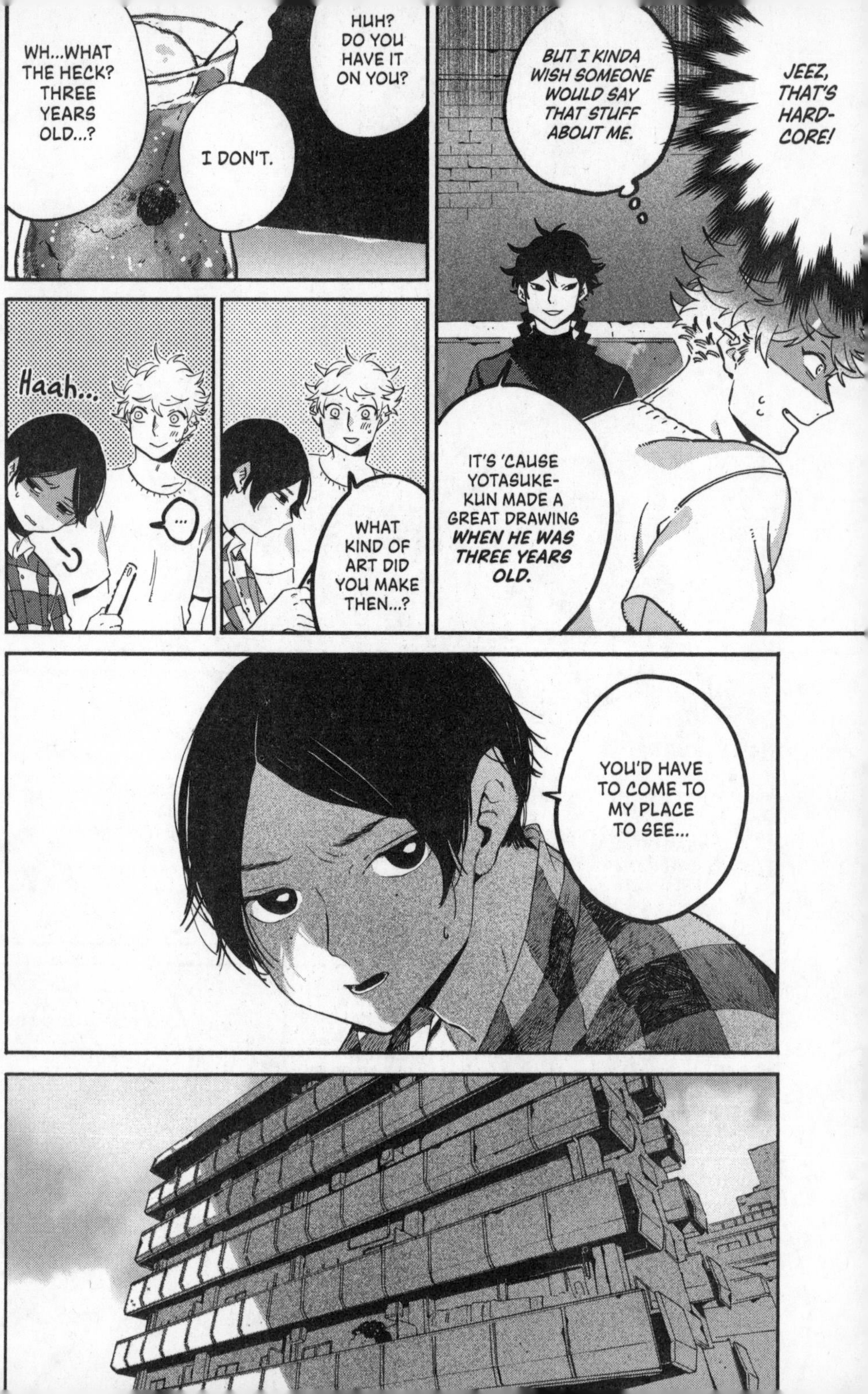
JEEZ, THAT'S HARDCORE!
BUT I KINDA WISH SOMEONE WOULD SAY THAT STUFF ABOUT ME.
IT'S 'CAUSE YOTASUKE-KUN MADE A GREAT DRAWING *WHEN HE WAS THREE YEARS OLD.*
HUH? DO YOU HAVE IT ON YOU?
WH...WHAT THE HECK? THREE YEARS OLD...?
I DON'T.
WHAT KIND OF ART DID YOU MAKE THEN...?
Haah...
...
YOU'D HAVE TO COME TO MY PLACE TO SEE...

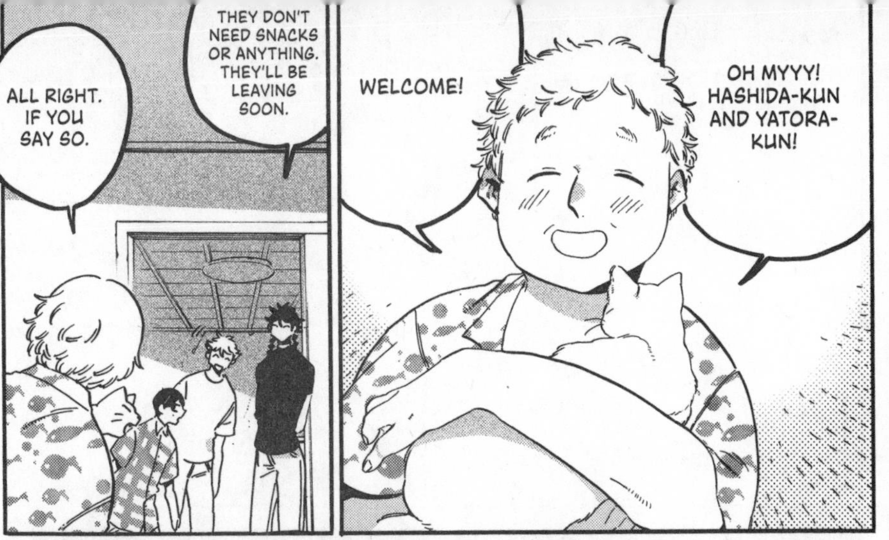
OH MYYY! HASHIDA-KUN AND YATORA-KUN!
WELCOME!
THEY DON'T NEED SNACKS OR ANYTHING. THEY'LL BE LEAVING SOON.
ALL RIGHT. IF YOU SAY SO.

ART: CHIHARU OTSUKA

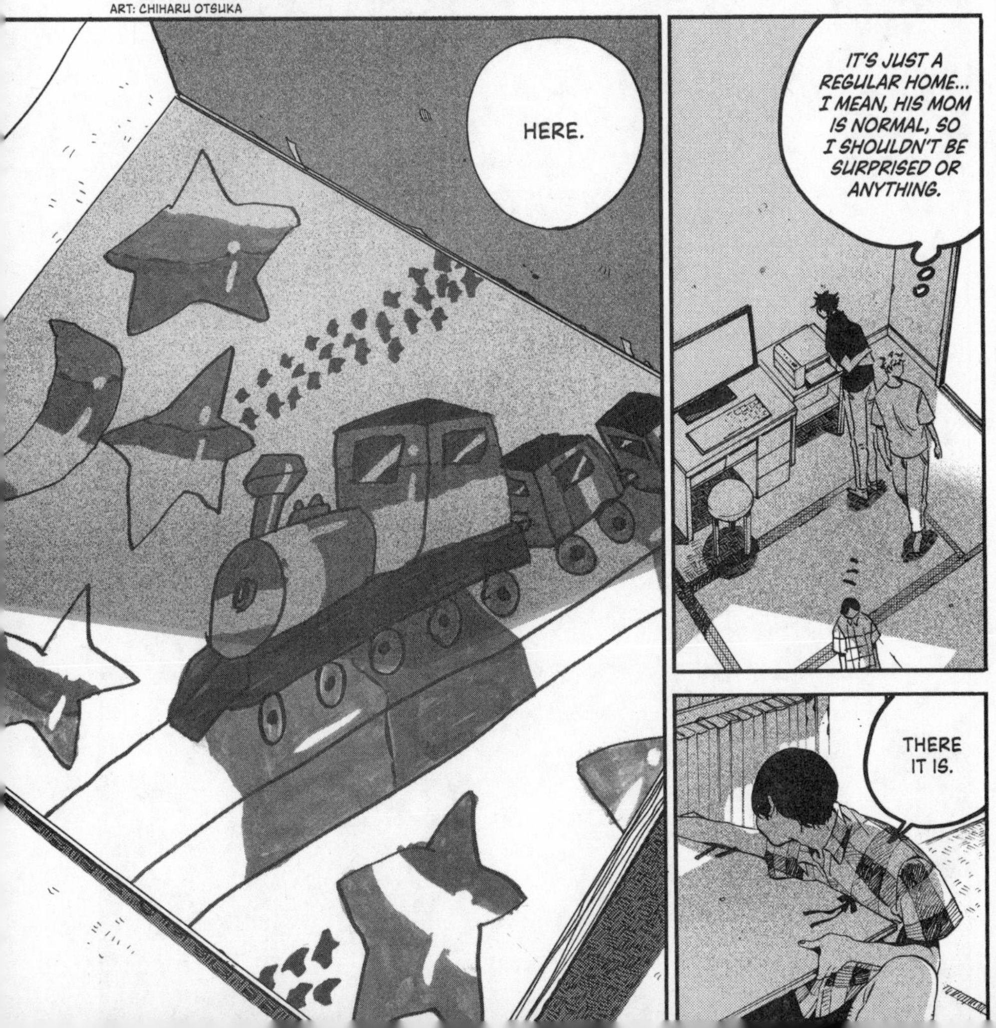
IT'S JUST A REGULAR HOME... I MEAN, HIS MOM IS NORMAL, SO I SHOULDN'T BE SURPRISED OR ANYTHING.
THERE IT IS.
HERE.

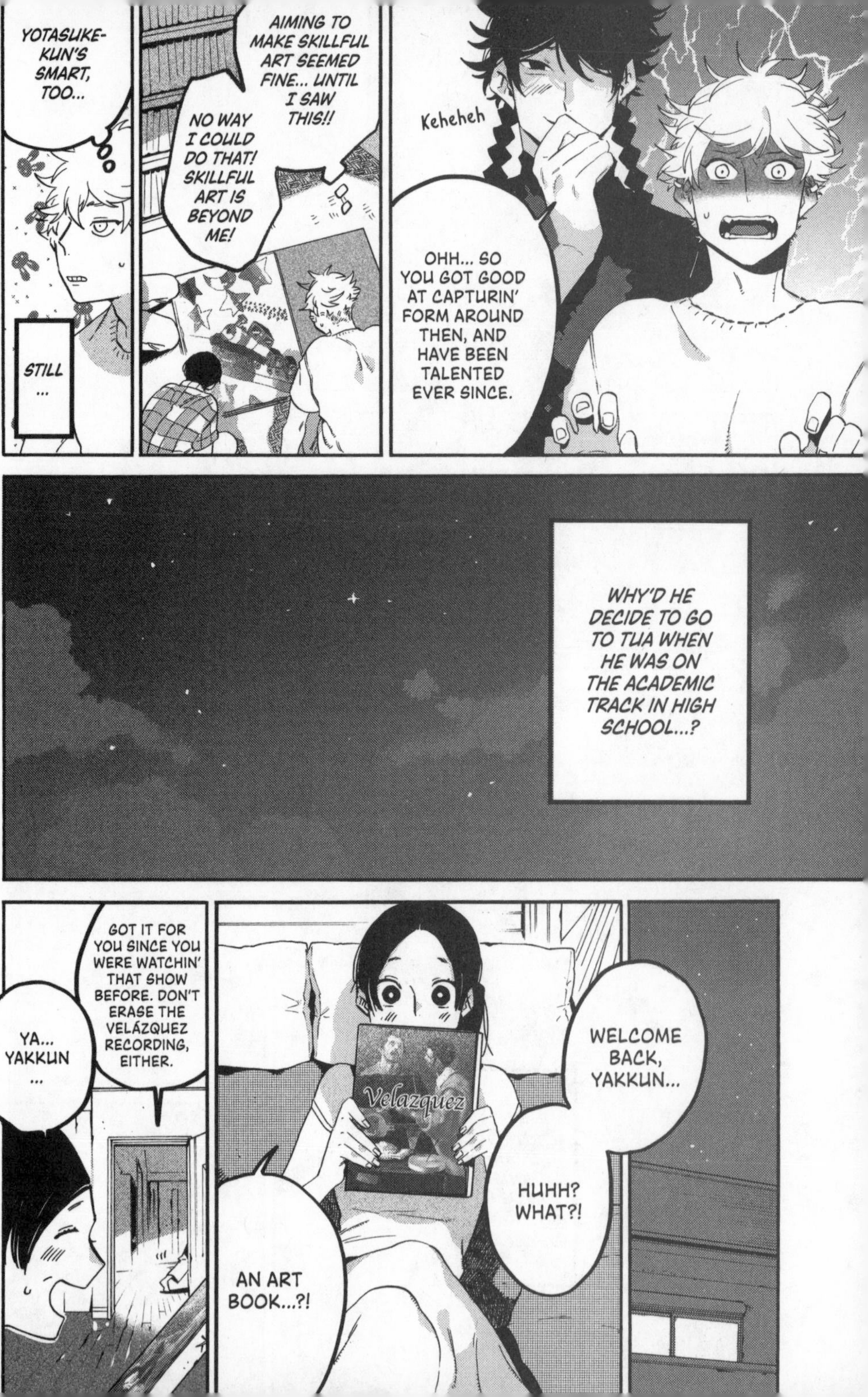
Keheheh
OHH... SO YOU GOT GOOD AT CAPTURIN' FORM AROUND THEN, AND HAVE BEEN TALENTED EVER SINCE.
AIMING TO MAKE SKILLFUL ART SEEMED FINE... UNTIL I SAW THIS!!
NO WAY I COULD DO THAT! SKILLFUL ART IS BEYOND ME!
YOTASUKE-KUN'S SMART, TOO...
STILL ...
WHY'D HE DECIDE TO GO TO TUA WHEN HE WAS ON THE ACADEMIC TRACK IN HIGH SCHOOL...?
WELCOME BACK, YAKKUN...
HUHH? WHAT?!
Velazquez
AN ART BOOK...?!
GOT IT FOR YOU SINCE YOU WERE WATCHIN' THAT SHOW BEFORE. DON'T ERASE THE VELÁZQUEZ RECORDING, EITHER.
YA... YAKKUN ...

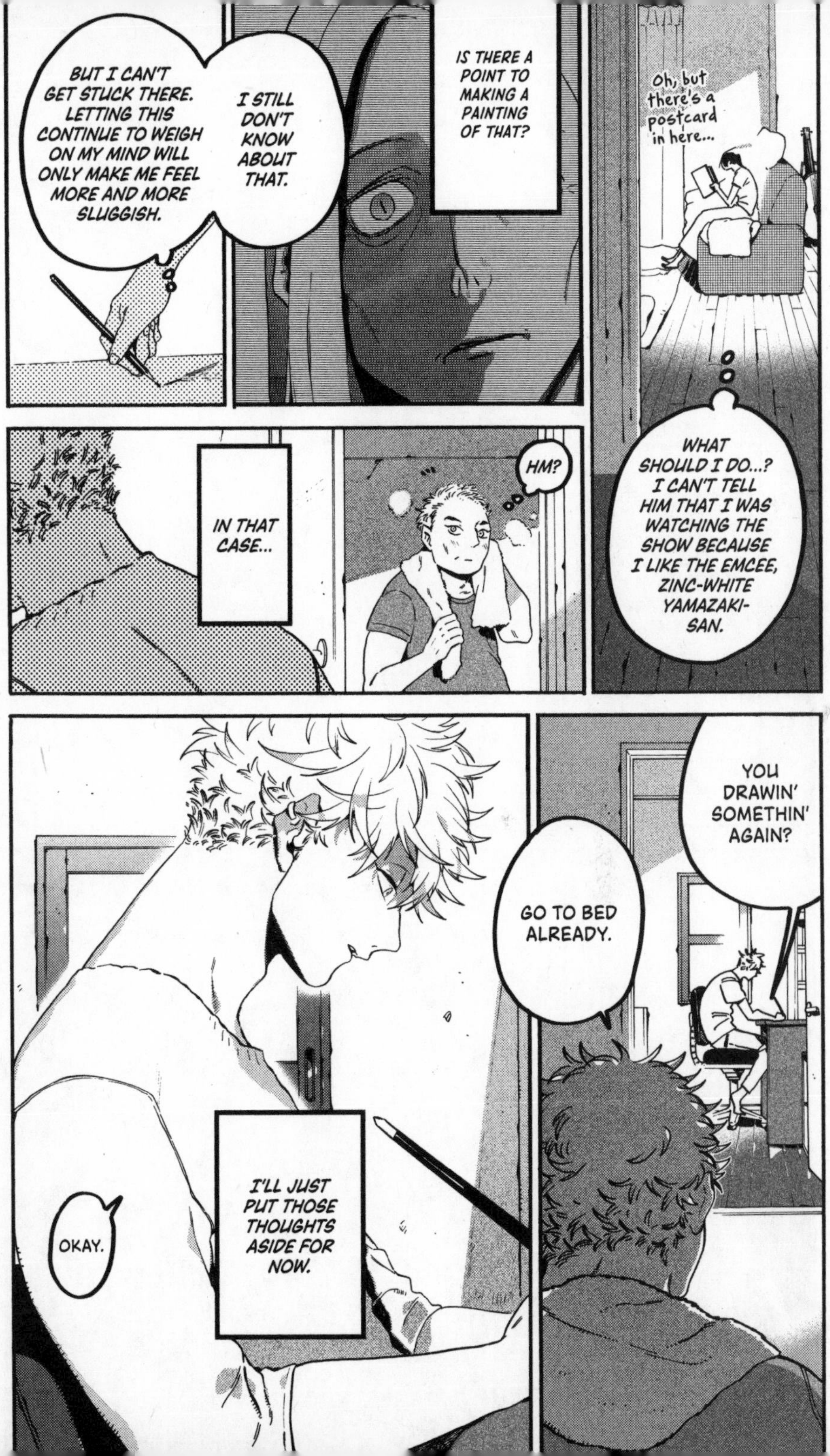
Oh, but there's a postcard in here...
WHAT SHOULD I DO...? I CAN'T TELL HIM THAT I WAS WATCHING THE SHOW BECAUSE I LIKE THE EMCEE, ZINC-WHITE YAMAZAKI-SAN.
IS THERE A POINT TO MAKING A PAINTING OF THAT?
I STILL DON'T KNOW ABOUT THAT.
BUT I CAN'T GET STUCK THERE. LETTING THIS CONTINUE TO WEIGH ON MY MIND WILL ONLY MAKE ME FEEL MORE AND MORE SLUGGISH.
HM?
IN THAT CASE...
YOU DRAWIN' SOMETHIN' AGAIN?
GO TO BED ALREADY.
I'LL JUST PUT THOSE THOUGHTS ASIDE FOR NOW.
OKAY.

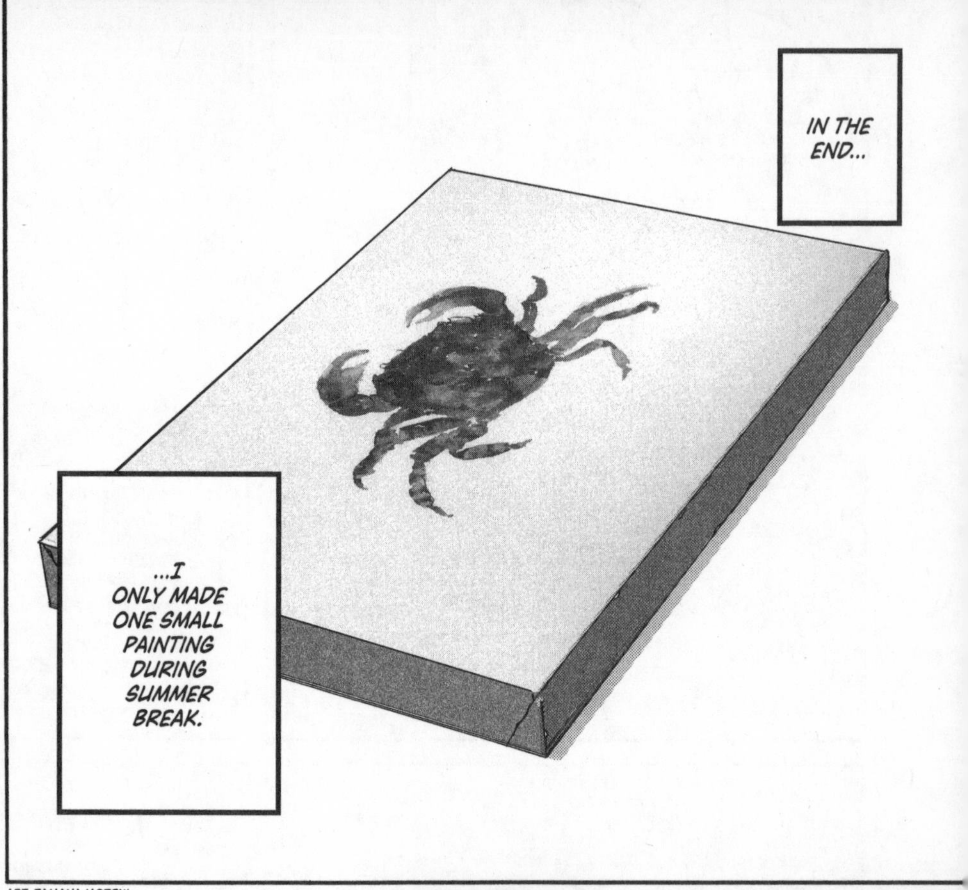
IN THE END...
...I ONLY MADE ONE SMALL PAINTING DURING SUMMER BREAK.

ART: TAMANA MOTEKI

SIGN: UENO STATION

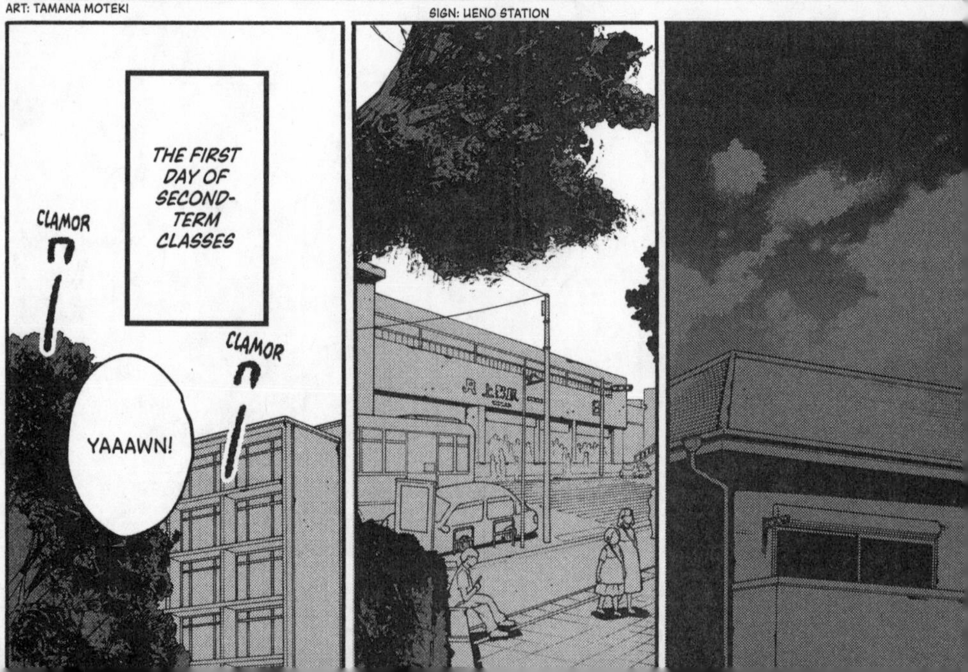
THE FIRST DAY OF SECOND-TERM CLASSES
CLAMOR
CLAMOR
YAAAWN!

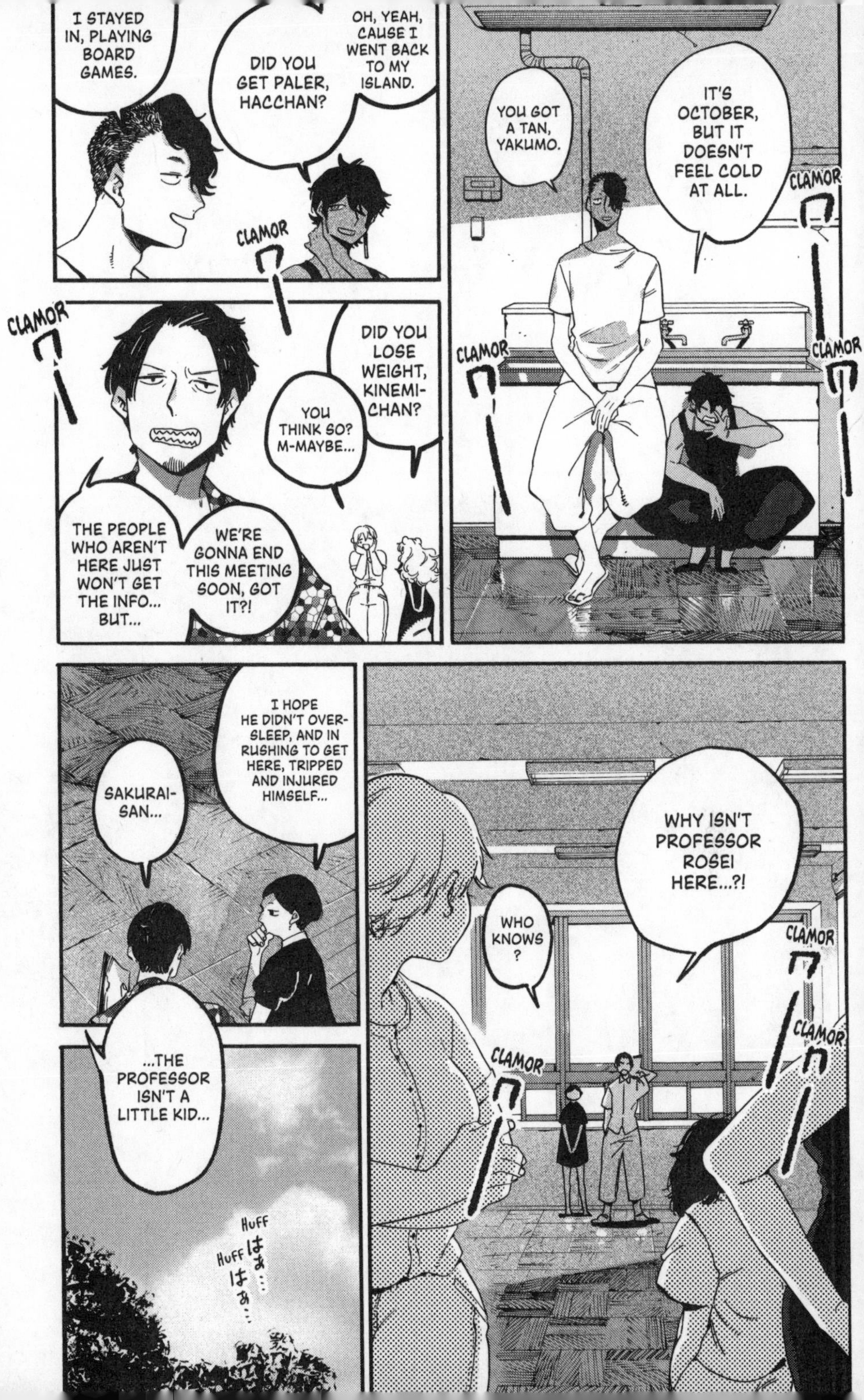
IT'S OCTOBER, BUT IT DOESN'T FEEL COLD AT ALL.
CLAMOR
YOU GOT A TAN, YAKUMO.
CLAMOR
CLAMOR
OH, YEAH, CAUSE I WENT BACK TO MY ISLAND.
DID YOU GET PALER, HACCHAN?
I STAYED IN, PLAYING BOARD GAMES.
CLAMOR
DID YOU LOSE WEIGHT, KINEMI-CHAN?
YOU THINK SO? M-MAYBE...
CLAMOR
WE'RE GONNA END THIS MEETING SOON, GOT IT?!
THE PEOPLE WHO AREN'T HERE JUST WON'T GET THE INFO... BUT...
WHY ISN'T PROFESSOR ROSEI HERE...?!
CLAMOR
WHO KNOWS?
CLAMOR
CLAMOR
I HOPE HE DIDN'T OVER-SLEEP, AND IN RUSHING TO GET HERE, TRIPPED AND INJURED HIMSELF...
SAKURAI-SAN...
...THE PROFESSOR ISN'T A LITTLE KID...
HUFF はぁ…
HUFF はぁ…

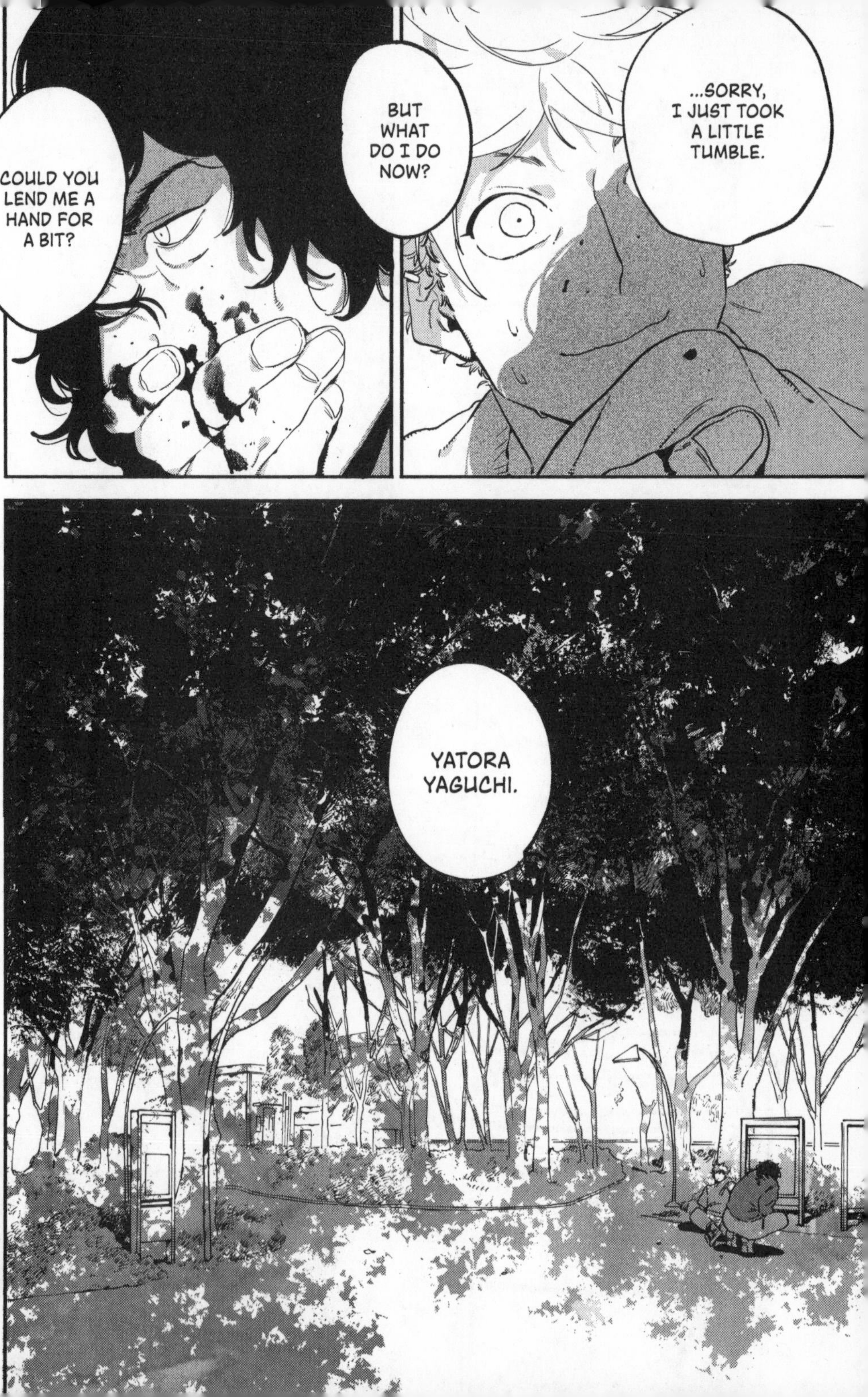
...SORRY, I JUST TOOK A LITTLE TUMBLE.
BUT WHAT DO I DO NOW?
COULD YOU LEND ME A HAND FOR A BIT?
YATORA YAGUCHI.

STROKE 35 END

He kept it as a pet for a little while.

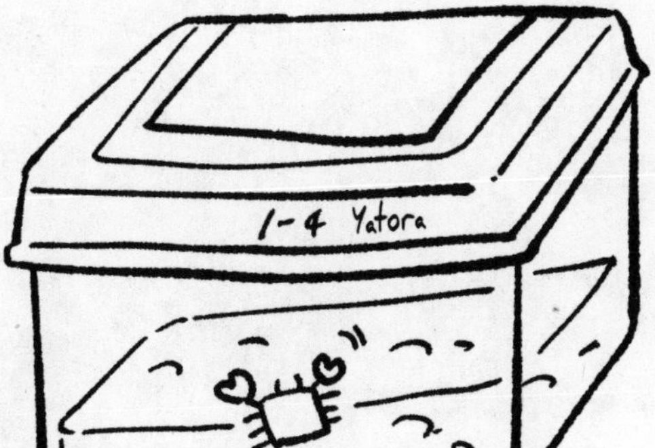
1-4 Yatora

BLUE PERIOD

STROKE 36 HELLO, WORLD!

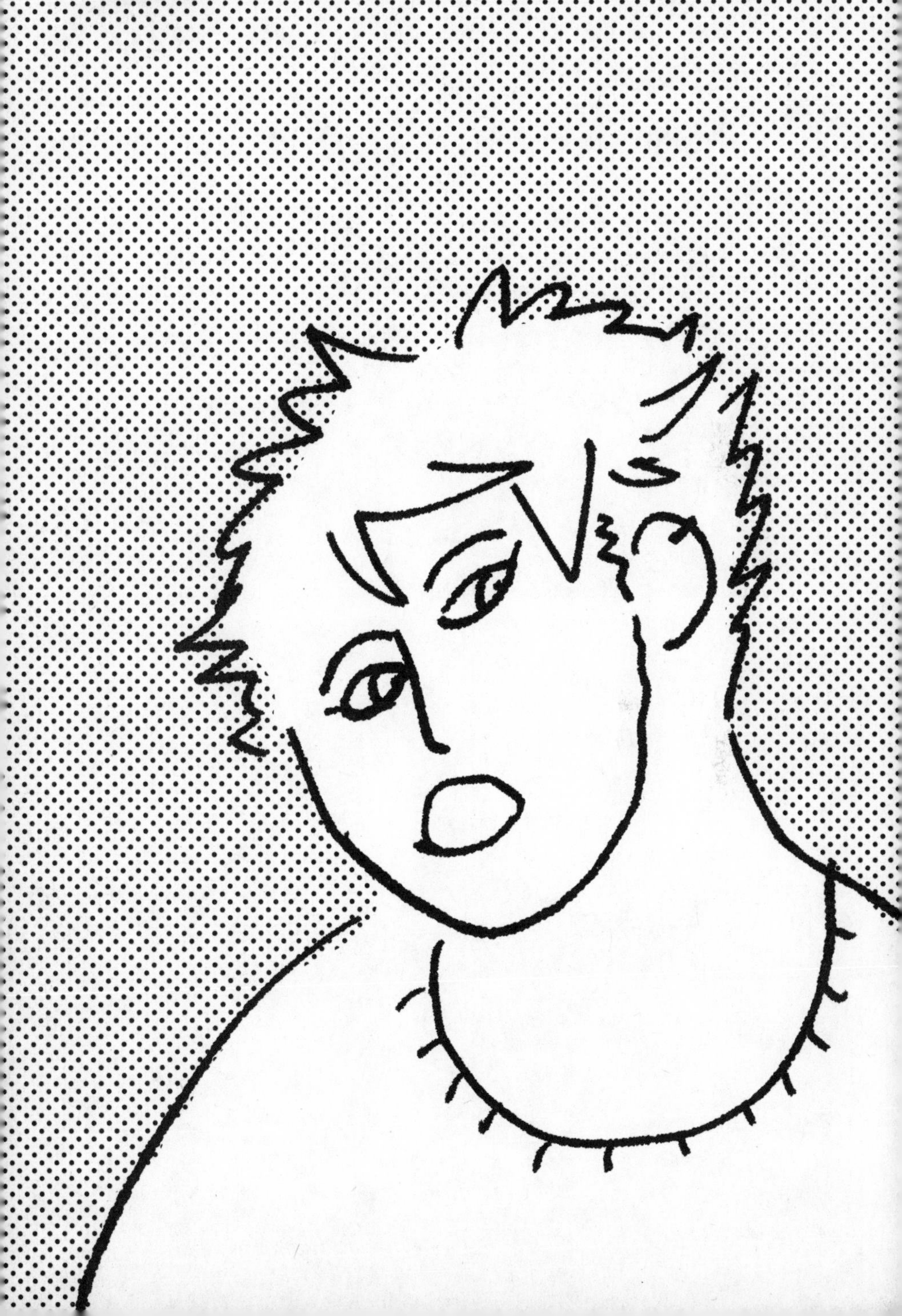

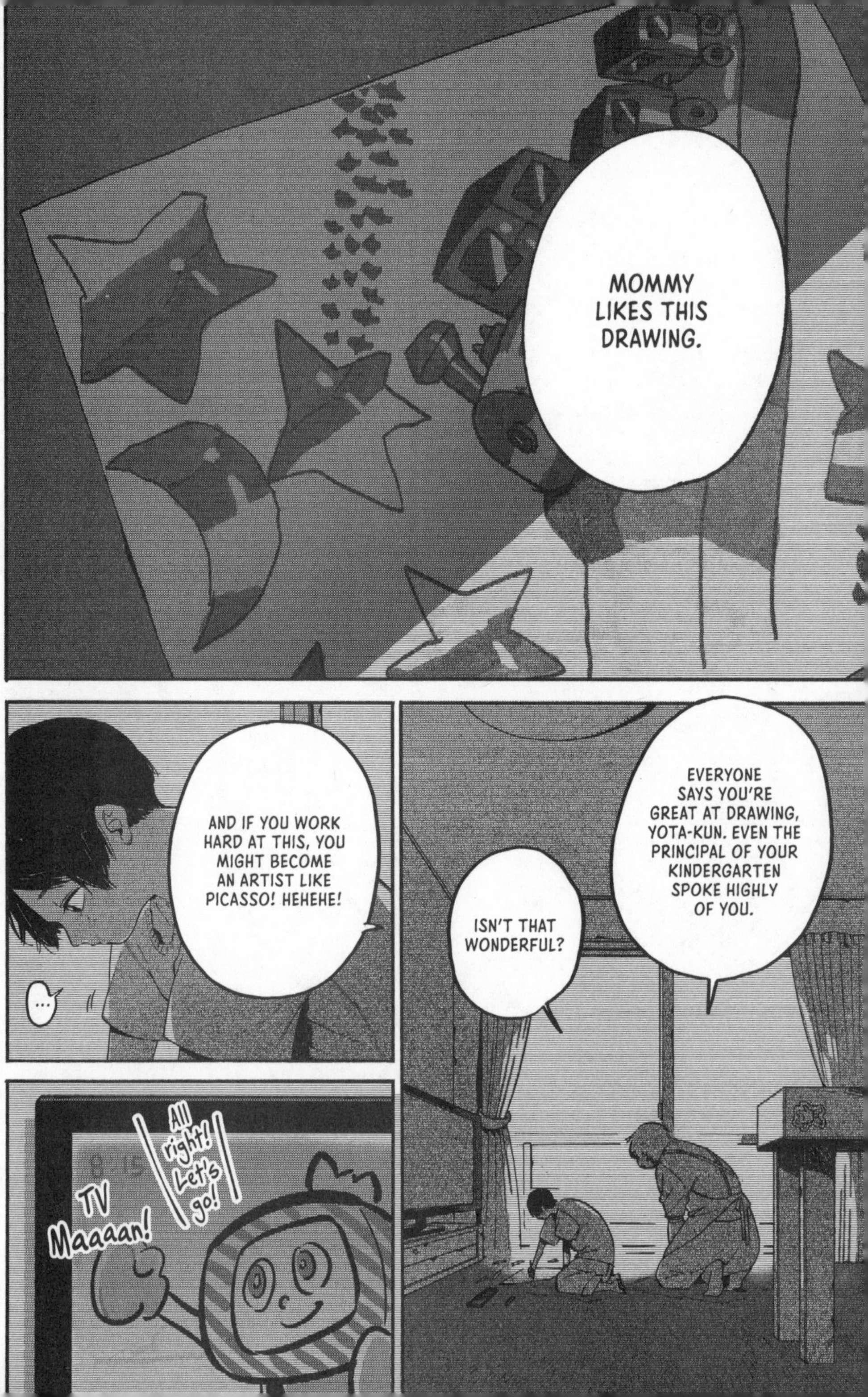
MOMMY LIKES THIS DRAWING.
EVERYONE SAYS YOU'RE GREAT AT DRAWING, YOTA-KUN. EVEN THE PRINCIPAL OF YOUR KINDERGARTEN SPOKE HIGHLY OF YOU.
ISN'T THAT WONDERFUL?
AND IF YOU WORK HARD AT THIS, YOU MIGHT BECOME AN ARTIST LIKE PICASSO! HEHEHE!
...
All right! Let's go!
TV Maaaan!

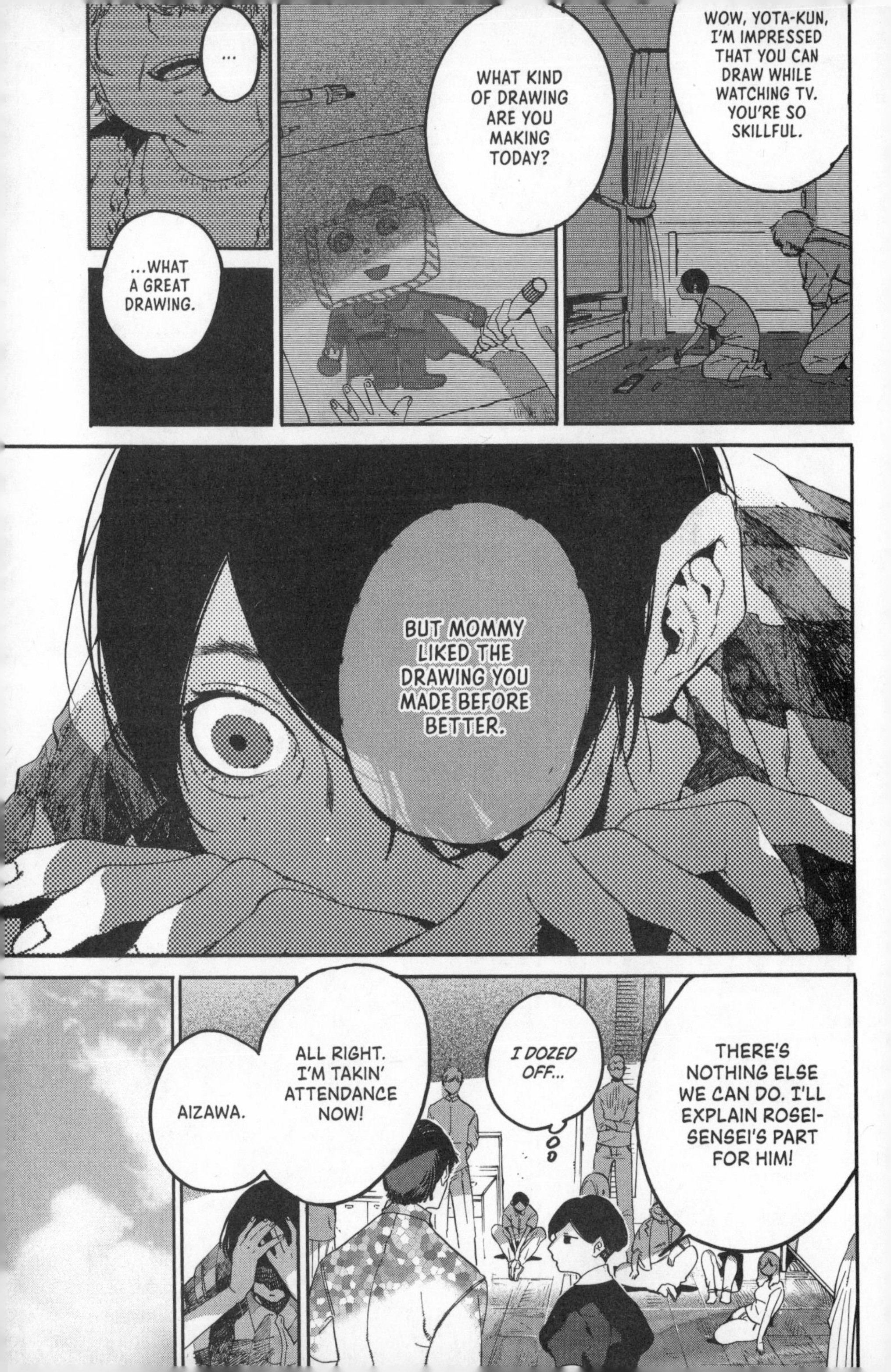

WOW, YOTA-KUN, I'M IMPRESSED THAT YOU CAN DRAW WHILE WATCHING TV. YOU'RE SO SKILLFUL.
WHAT KIND OF DRAWING ARE YOU MAKING TODAY?
...
...WHAT A GREAT DRAWING.
BUT MOMMY LIKED THE DRAWING YOU MADE BEFORE BETTER.
THERE'S NOTHING ELSE WE CAN DO. I'LL EXPLAIN ROSEI-SENSEI'S PART FOR HIM!
I DOZED OFF...
ALL RIGHT. I'M TAKIN' ATTENDANCE NOW!
AIZAWA.

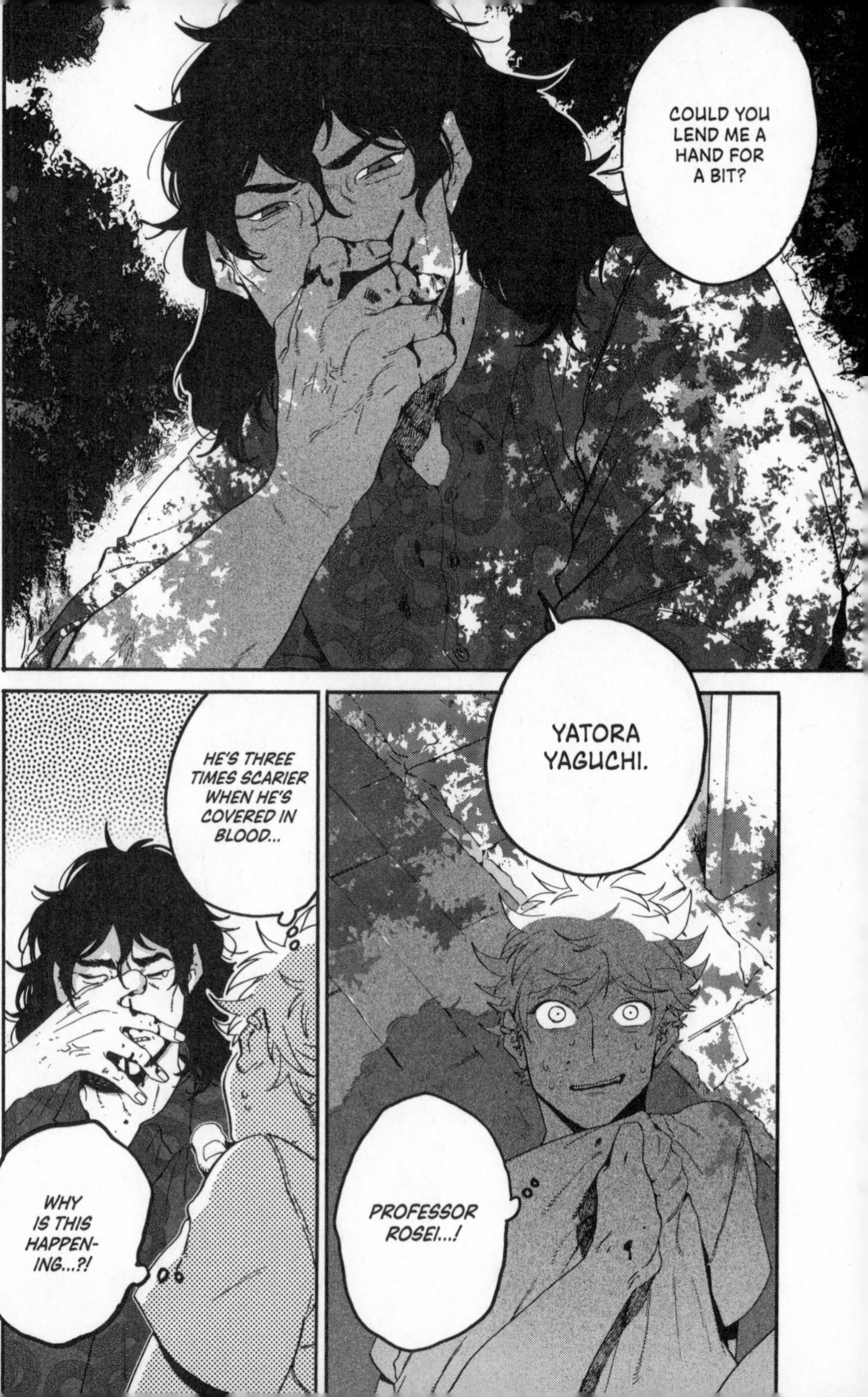
COULD YOU LEND ME A HAND FOR A BIT?
YATORA YAGUCHI.
PROFESSOR ROSEI...!
HE'S THREE TIMES SCARIER WHEN HE'S COVERED IN BLOOD...
WHY IS THIS HAPPEN-ING...?!

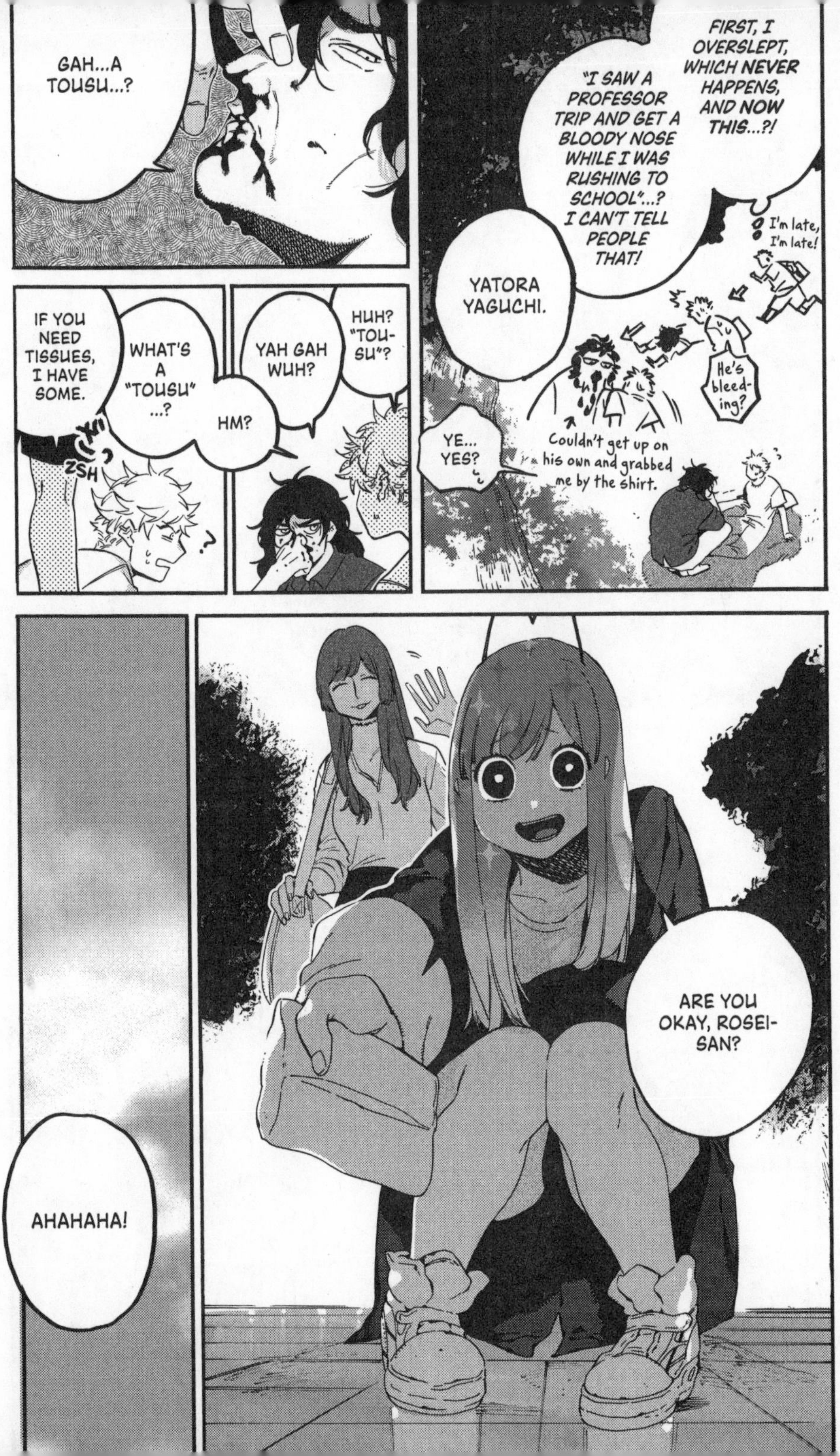
FIRST, I OVERSLEPT, WHICH NEVER HAPPENS, AND NOW THIS...?!
"I SAW A PROFESSOR TRIP AND GET A BLOODY NOSE WHILE I WAS RUSHING TO SCHOOL"...? I CAN'T TELL PEOPLE THAT!
I'm late, I'm late!
He's bleed-ing?
YATORA YAGUCHI.
YE... YES?
Couldn't get up on his own and grabbed me by the shirt.
GAH...A TOUSU...?
HUH? "TOU-SU"?
YAH GAH WUH?
HM?
WHAT'S A "TOUSU" ...?
IF YOU NEED TISSUES, I HAVE SOME.
ZSH
ARE YOU OKAY, ROSEI-SAN?
AHAHAHA!

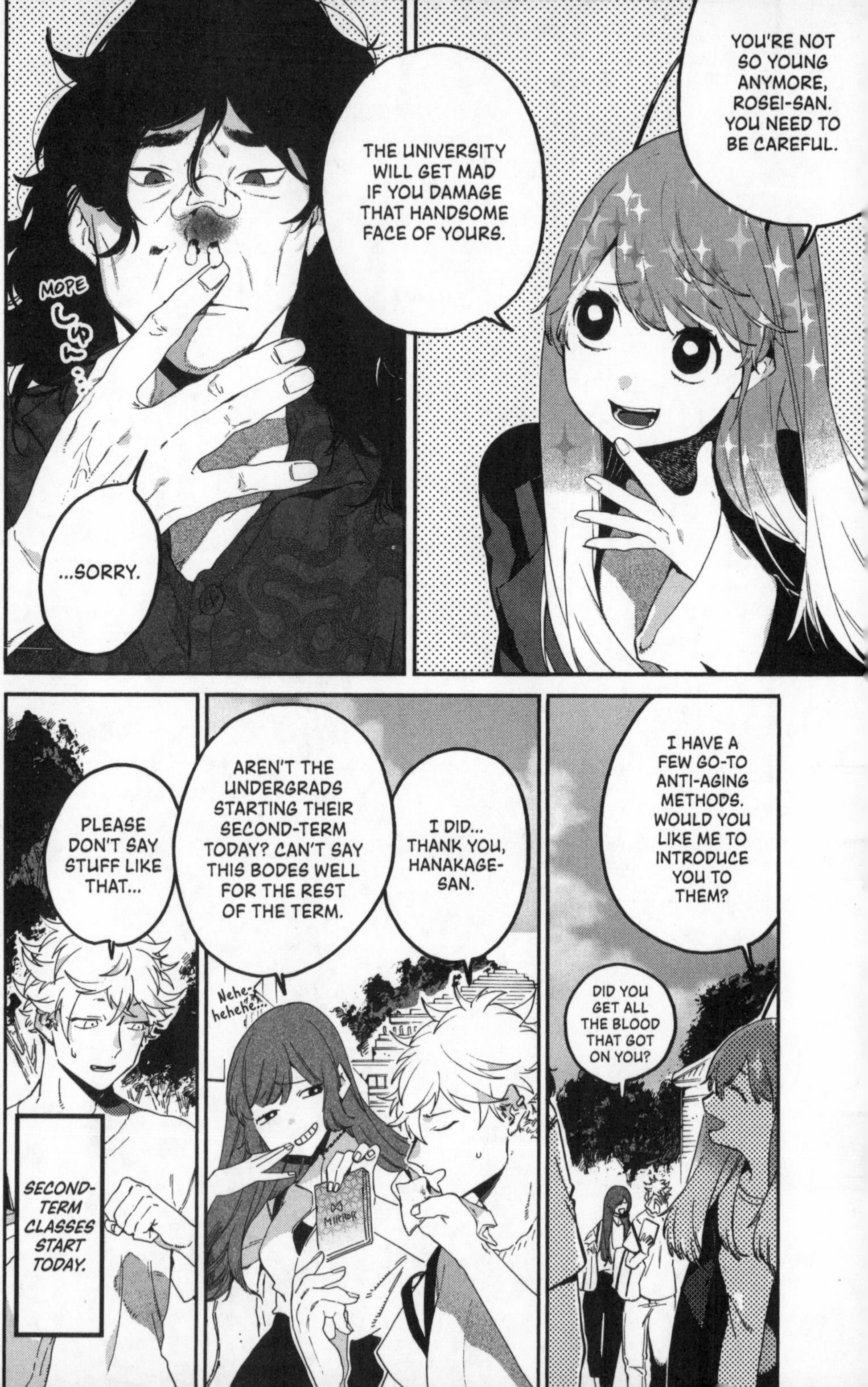
YOU'RE NOT SO YOUNG ANYMORE, ROSEI-SAN. YOU NEED TO BE CAREFUL.
THE UNIVERSITY WILL GET MAD IF YOU DAMAGE THAT HANDSOME FACE OF YOURS.
MOPE
しゅん…
...SORRY.
I HAVE A FEW GO-TO ANTI-AGING METHODS. WOULD YOU LIKE ME TO INTRODUCE YOU TO THEM?
DID YOU GET ALL THE BLOOD THAT GOT ON YOU?
I DID... THANK YOU, HANAKAGE-SAN.
Nehe-hehehe...
AREN'T THE UNDERGRADS STARTING THEIR SECOND-TERM TODAY? CAN'T SAY THIS BODES WELL FOR THE REST OF THE TERM.
PLEASE DON'T SAY STUFF LIKE THAT...
SECOND-TERM CLASSES START TODAY.

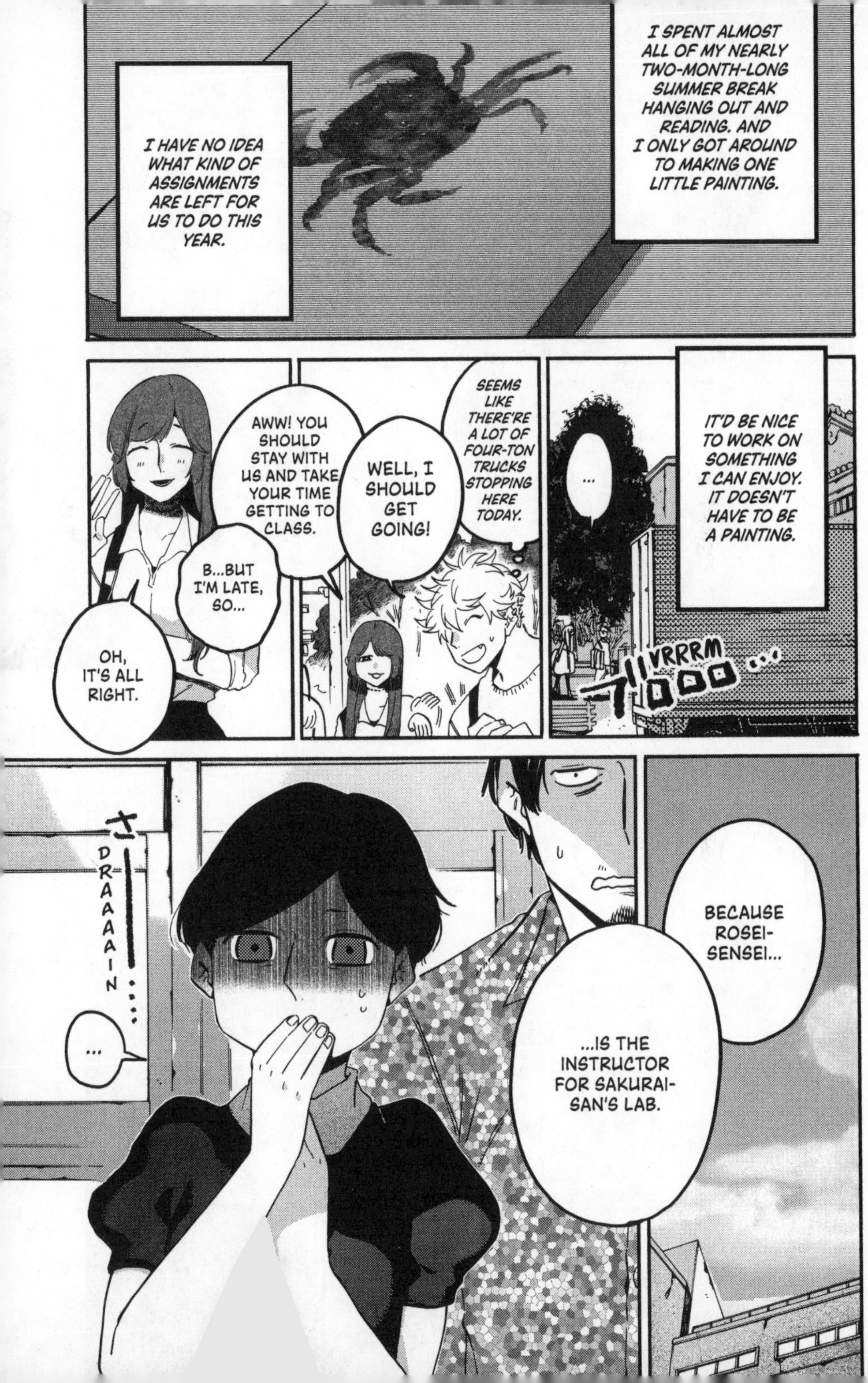
I SPENT ALMOST ALL OF MY NEARLY TWO-MONTH-LONG SUMMER BREAK HANGING OUT AND READING. AND I ONLY GOT AROUND TO MAKING ONE LITTLE PAINTING.
I HAVE NO IDEA WHAT KIND OF ASSIGNMENTS ARE LEFT FOR US TO DO THIS YEAR.
IT'D BE NICE TO WORK ON SOMETHING I CAN ENJOY. IT DOESN'T HAVE TO BE A PAINTING.
...
VRRRM
SEEMS LIKE THERE'RE A LOT OF FOUR-TON TRUCKS STOPPING HERE TODAY.
WELL, I SHOULD GET GOING!
AWW! YOU SHOULD STAY WITH US AND TAKE YOUR TIME GETTING TO CLASS.
B...BUT I'M LATE, SO...
OH, IT'S ALL RIGHT.
BECAUSE ROSEI-SENSEI...
...IS THE INSTRUCTOR FOR SAKURAI-SAN'S LAB.
DRAAAAIN
...

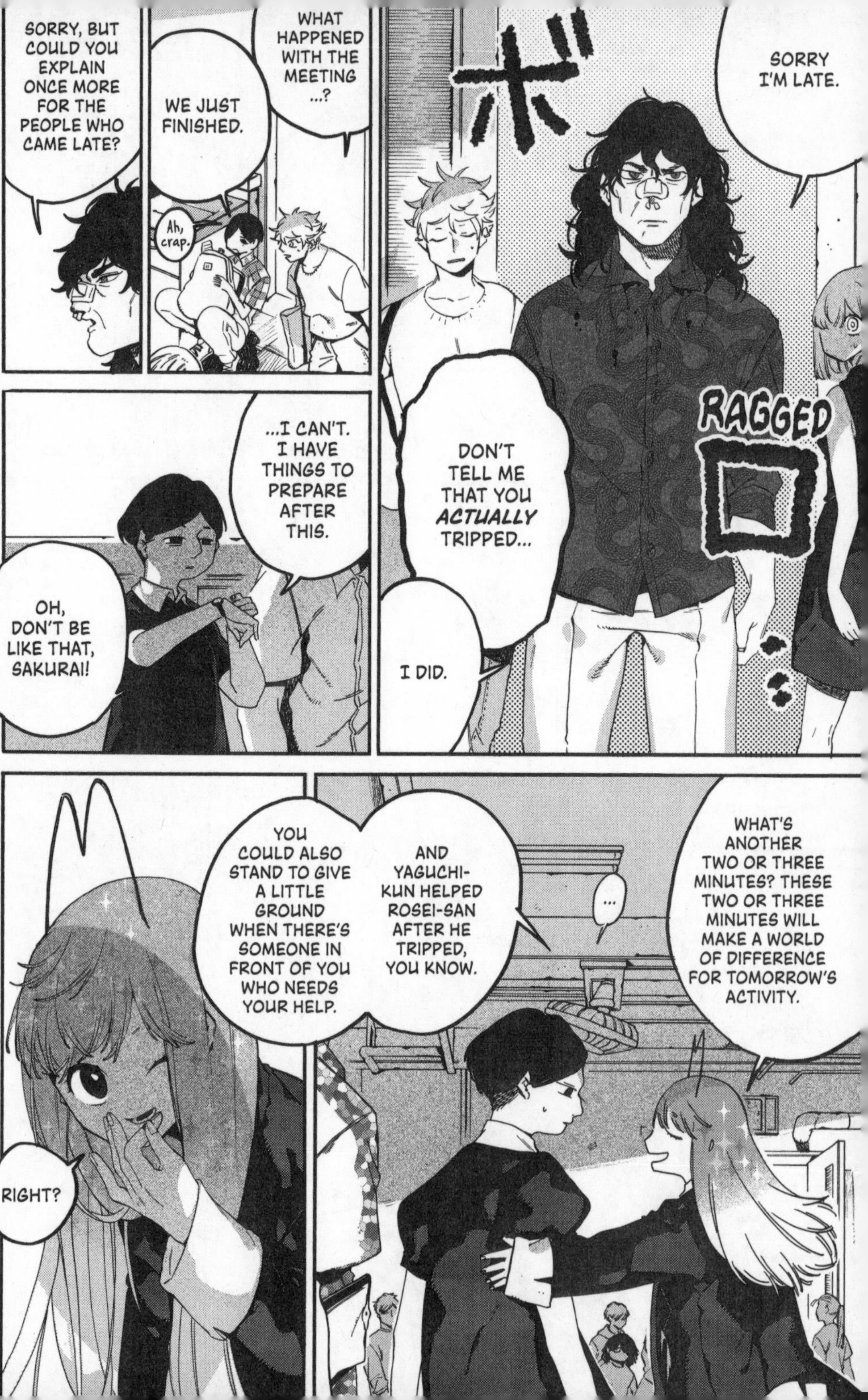

SORRY I'M LATE.
ボ
RAGGED
DON'T TELL ME THAT YOU *ACTUALLY* TRIPPED...
I DID.
WHAT HAPPENED WITH THE MEETING ...?
WE JUST FINISHED.
Ah, crap.
SORRY, BUT COULD YOU EXPLAIN ONCE MORE FOR THE PEOPLE WHO CAME LATE?
...I CAN'T. I HAVE THINGS TO PREPARE AFTER THIS.
OH, DON'T BE LIKE THAT, SAKURAI!
WHAT'S ANOTHER TWO OR THREE MINUTES? THESE TWO OR THREE MINUTES WILL MAKE A WORLD OF DIFFERENCE FOR TOMORROW'S ACTIVITY.
...
AND YAGUCHI-KUN HELPED ROSEI-SAN AFTER HE TRIPPED, YOU KNOW.
YOU COULD ALSO STAND TO GIVE A LITTLE GROUND WHEN THERE'S SOMEONE IN FRONT OF YOU WHO NEEDS YOUR HELP.
RIGHT?

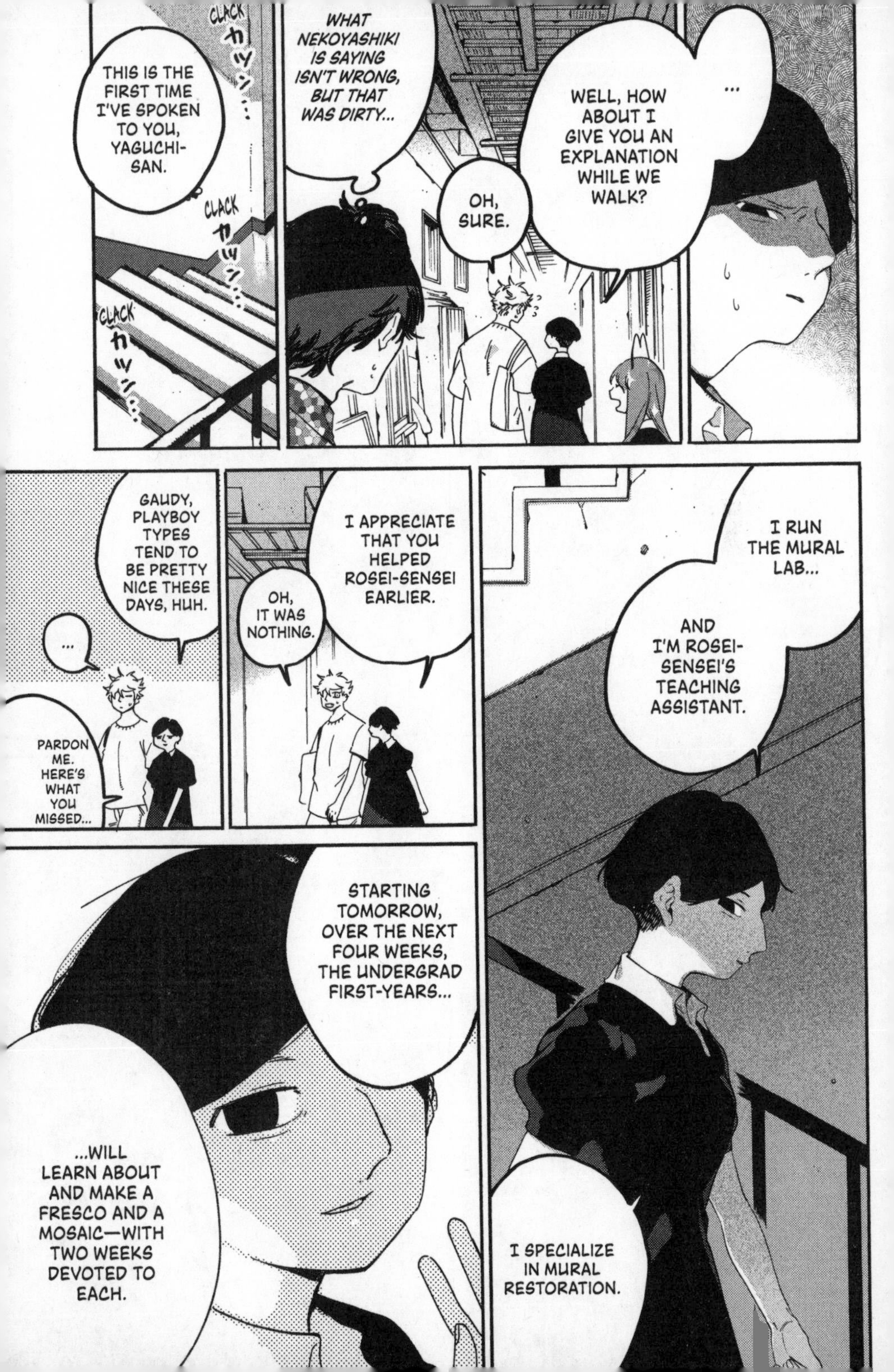
...
WELL, HOW ABOUT I GIVE YOU AN EXPLANATION WHILE WE WALK?
OH, SURE.
WHAT NEKOYASHIKI IS SAYING ISN'T WRONG, BUT THAT WAS DIRTY...
CLACK
THIS IS THE FIRST TIME I'VE SPOKEN TO YOU, YAGUCHI-SAN.
CLACK
CLACK
I RUN THE MURAL LAB...
AND I'M ROSEI-SENSEI'S TEACHING ASSISTANT.
I SPECIALIZE IN MURAL RESTORATION.
I APPRECIATE THAT YOU HELPED ROSEI-SENSEI EARLIER.
OH, IT WAS NOTHING.
GAUDY, PLAYBOY TYPES TEND TO BE PRETTY NICE THESE DAYS, HUH.
...
PARDON ME. HERE'S WHAT YOU MISSED...
STARTING TOMORROW, OVER THE NEXT FOUR WEEKS, THE UNDERGRAD FIRST-YEARS...
...WILL LEARN ABOUT AND MAKE A FRESCO AND A MOSAIC—WITH TWO WEEKS DEVOTED TO EACH.

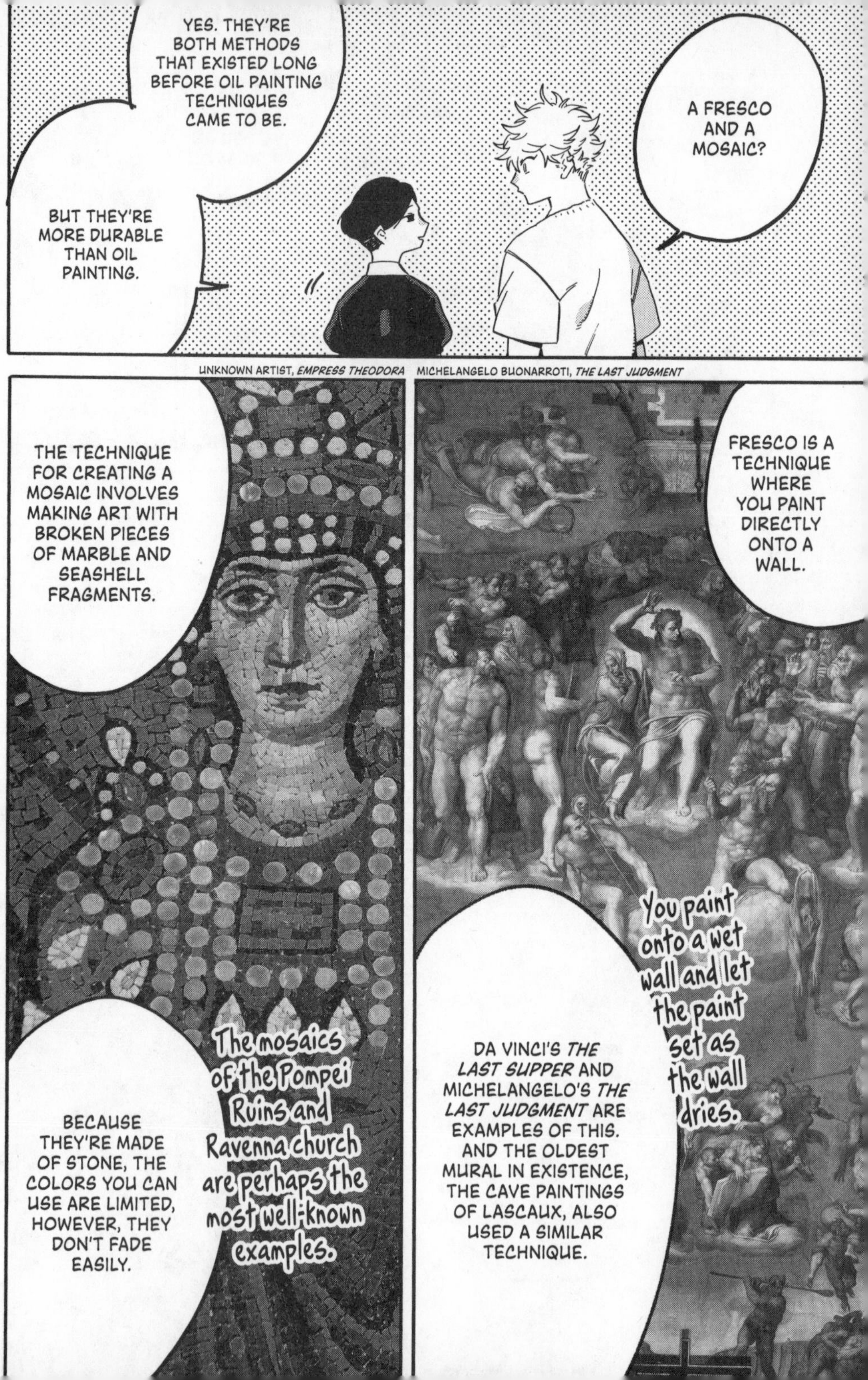
A FRESCO AND A MOSAIC?
YES. THEY'RE BOTH METHODS THAT EXISTED LONG BEFORE OIL PAINTING TECHNIQUES CAME TO BE.
BUT THEY'RE MORE DURABLE THAN OIL PAINTING.
MICHELANGELO BUONARROTI, *THE LAST JUDGMENT*
FRESCO IS A TECHNIQUE WHERE YOU PAINT DIRECTLY ONTO A WALL.
You paint onto a wet wall and let the paint set as the wall dries.
DA VINCI'S *THE LAST SUPPER* AND MICHELANGELO'S *THE LAST JUDGMENT* ARE EXAMPLES OF THIS. AND THE OLDEST MURAL IN EXISTENCE, THE CAVE PAINTINGS OF LASCAUX, ALSO USED A SIMILAR TECHNIQUE.
UNKNOWN ARTIST, *EMPRESS THEODORA*
THE TECHNIQUE FOR CREATING A MOSAIC INVOLVES MAKING ART WITH BROKEN PIECES OF MARBLE AND SEASHELL FRAGMENTS.
The mosaics of the Pompei Ruins and Ravenna church are perhaps the most well-known examples.
BECAUSE THEY'RE MADE OF STONE, THE COLORS YOU CAN USE ARE LIMITED, HOWEVER, THEY DON'T FADE EASILY.

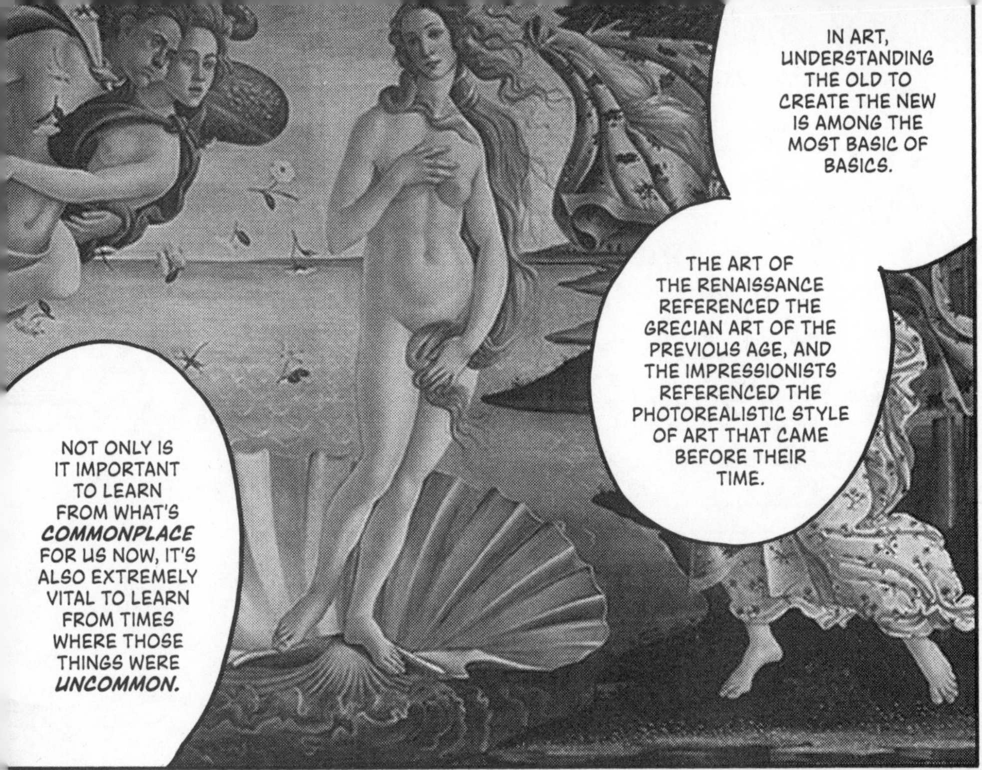
IN ART, UNDERSTANDING THE OLD TO CREATE THE NEW IS AMONG THE MOST BASIC OF BASICS.
THE ART OF THE RENAISSANCE REFERENCED THE GRECIAN ART OF THE PREVIOUS AGE, AND THE IMPRESSIONISTS REFERENCED THE PHOTOREALISTIC STYLE OF ART THAT CAME BEFORE THEIR TIME.
NOT ONLY IS IT IMPORTANT TO LEARN FROM WHAT'S *COMMONPLACE* FOR US NOW, IT'S ALSO EXTREMELY VITAL TO LEARN FROM TIMES WHERE THOSE THINGS WERE *UNCOMMON.*

SANDRO BOTTICELLI, *THE BIRTH OF VENUS*

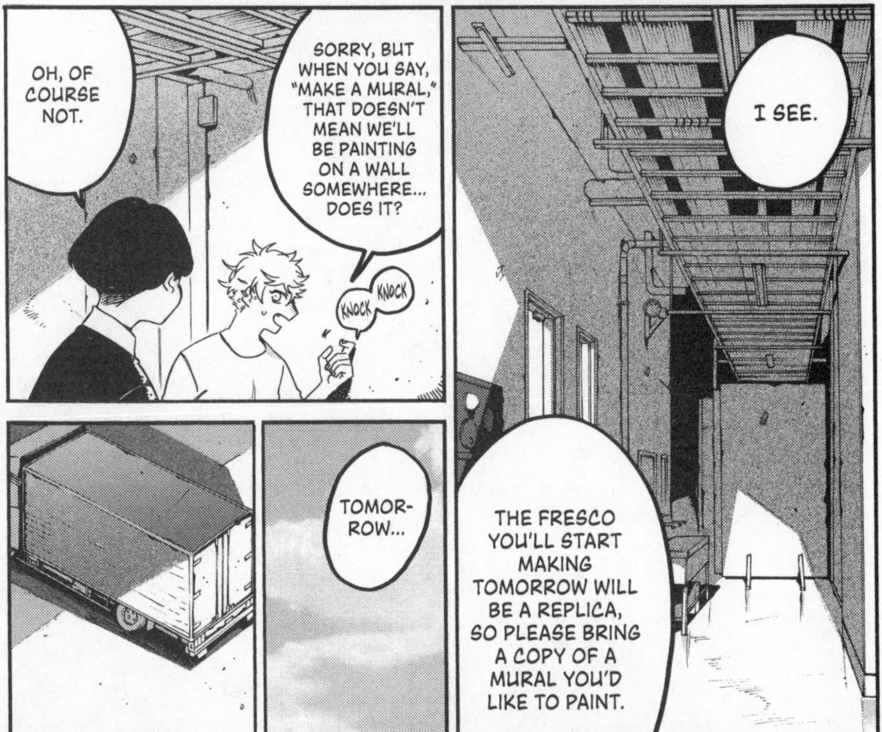
I SEE.
THE FRESCO YOU'LL START MAKING TOMORROW WILL BE A REPLICA, SO PLEASE BRING A COPY OF A MURAL YOU'D LIKE TO PAINT.
SORRY, BUT WHEN YOU SAY, "MAKE A MURAL," THAT DOESN'T MEAN WE'LL BE PAINTING ON A WALL SOMEWHERE... DOES IT?
OH, OF COURSE NOT.
KNOCK KNOCK
TOMOR-ROW...

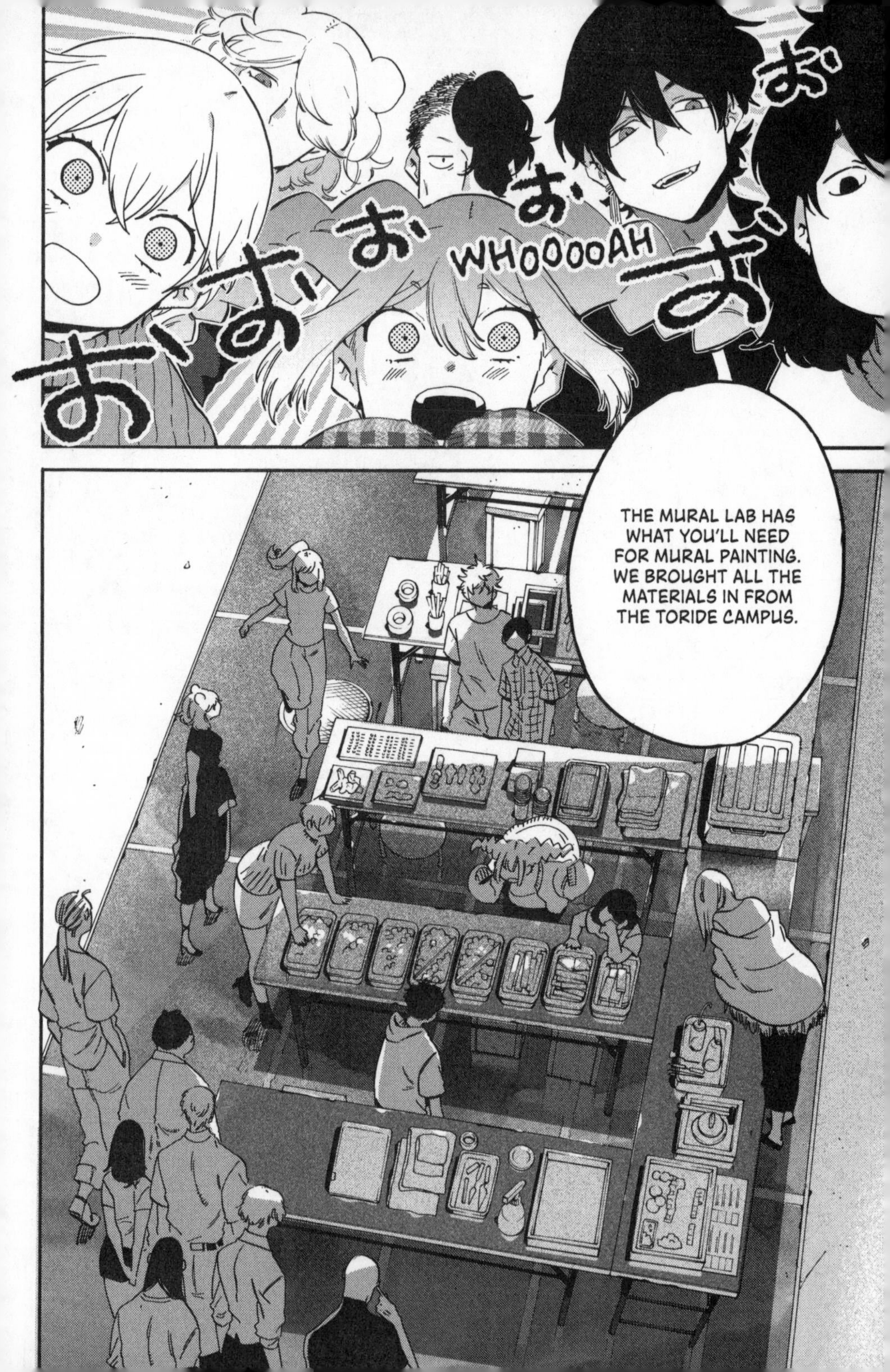
おおおおおお
WHOOOOAH
THE MURAL LAB HAS WHAT YOU'LL NEED FOR MURAL PAINTING. WE BROUGHT ALL THE MATERIALS IN FROM THE TORIDE CAMPUS.

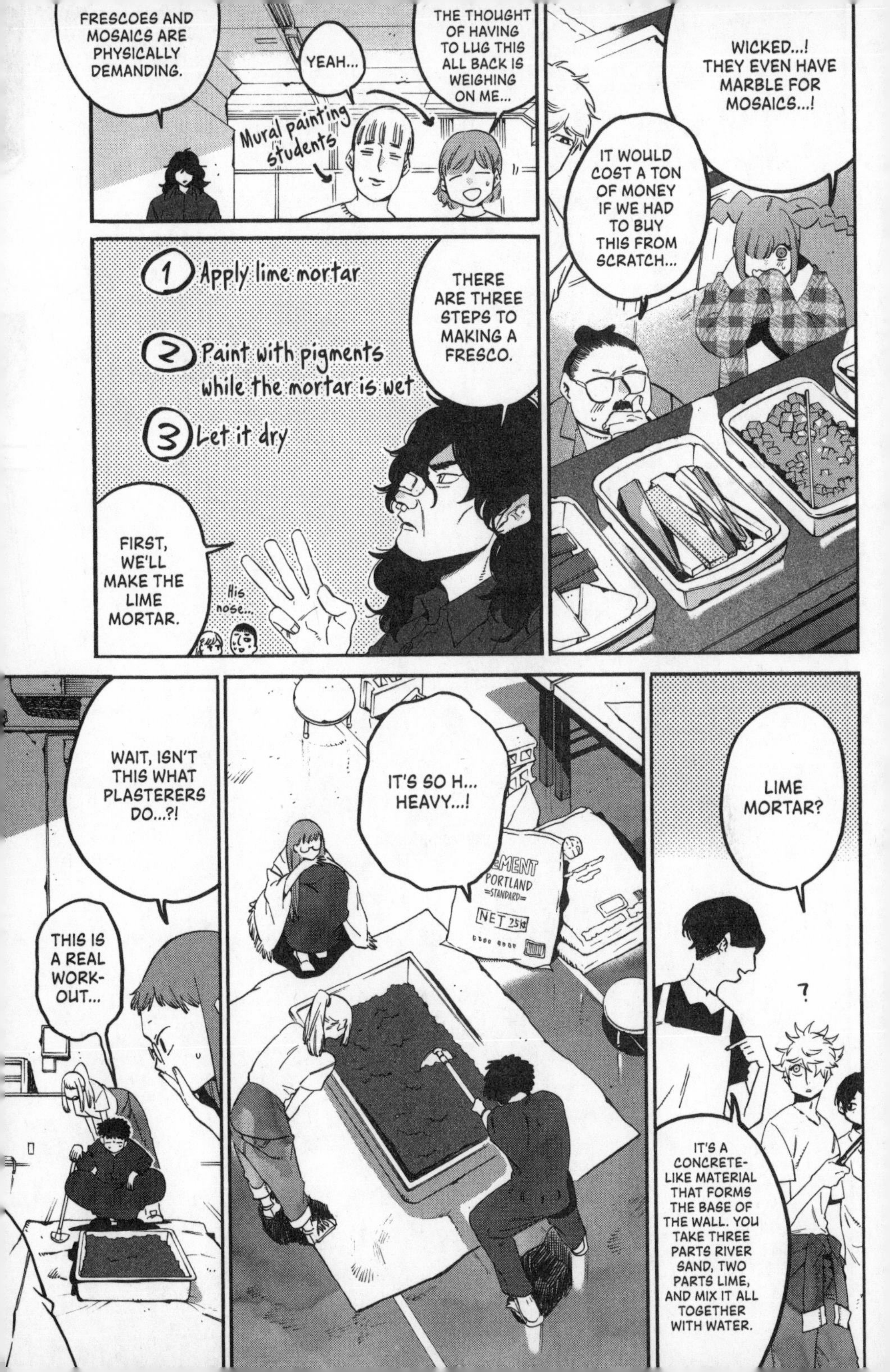
WICKED...! THEY EVEN HAVE MARBLE FOR MOSAICS...!
IT WOULD COST A TON OF MONEY IF WE HAD TO BUY THIS FROM SCRATCH...
THE THOUGHT OF HAVING TO LUG THIS ALL BACK IS WEIGHING ON ME...
YEAH...
FRESCOES AND MOSAICS ARE PHYSICALLY DEMANDING.
Mural painting students
THERE ARE THREE STEPS TO MAKING A FRESCO.
1 Apply lime mortar
2 Paint with pigments while the mortar is wet
3 Let it dry
FIRST, WE'LL MAKE THE LIME MORTAR.
His nose...
LIME MORTAR?
?
IT'S A CONCRETE-LIKE MATERIAL THAT FORMS THE BASE OF THE WALL. YOU TAKE THREE PARTS RIVER SAND, TWO PARTS LIME, AND MIX IT ALL TOGETHER WITH WATER.
IT'S SO H... HEAVY...!
PORTLAND
STANDARD
NET 25kg
WAIT, ISN'T THIS WHAT PLASTERERS DO...?!
THIS IS A REAL WORK-OUT...

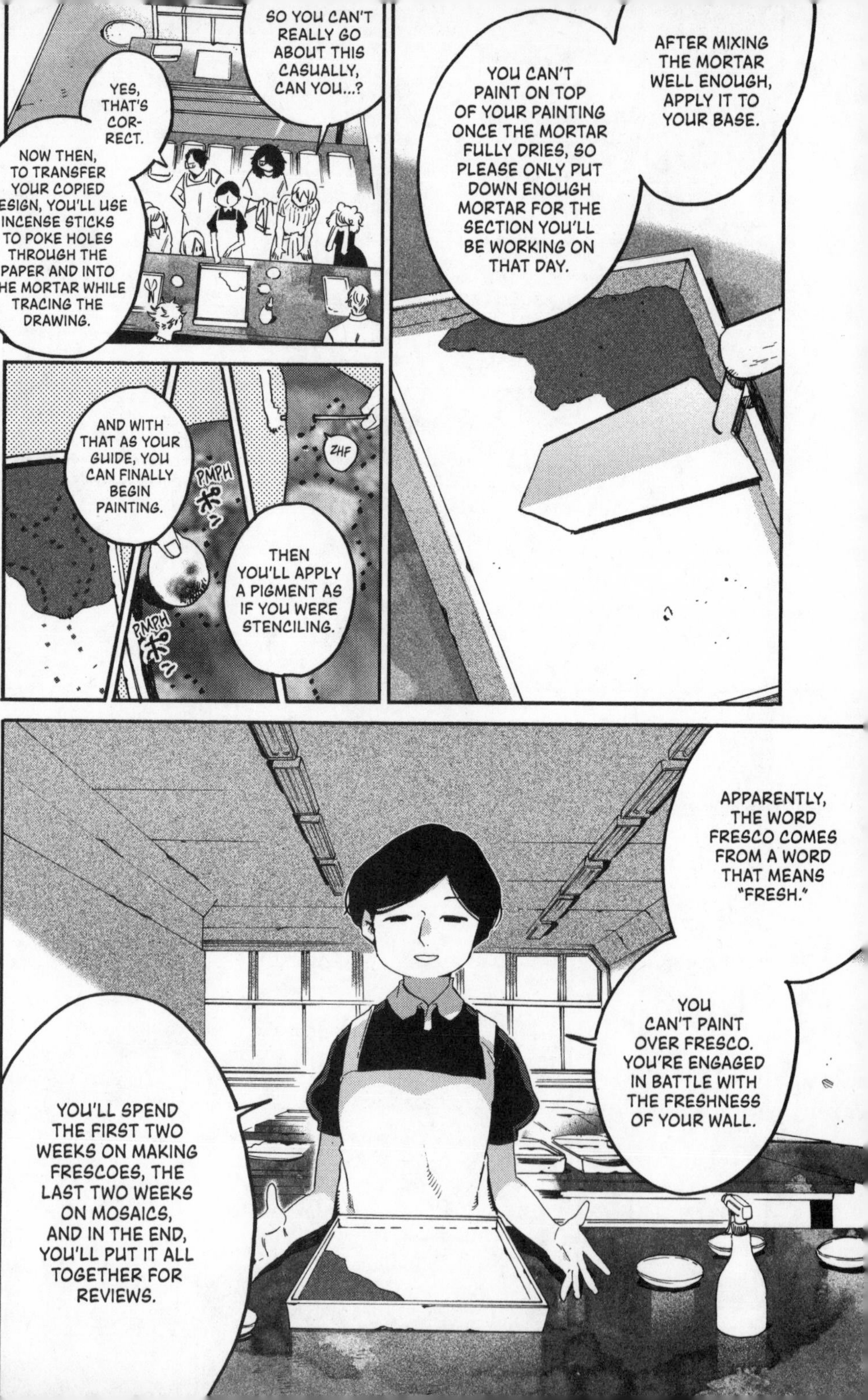
AFTER MIXING THE MORTAR WELL ENOUGH, APPLY IT TO YOUR BASE.
YOU CAN'T PAINT ON TOP OF YOUR PAINTING ONCE THE MORTAR FULLY DRIES, SO PLEASE ONLY PUT DOWN ENOUGH MORTAR FOR THE SECTION YOU'LL BE WORKING ON THAT DAY.
SO YOU CAN'T REALLY GO ABOUT THIS CASUALLY, CAN YOU...?
YES, THAT'S COR-RECT.
NOW THEN, TO TRANSFER YOUR COPIED DESIGN, YOU'LL USE INCENSE STICKS TO POKE HOLES THROUGH THE PAPER AND INTO THE MORTAR WHILE TRACING THE DRAWING.
ZHF
AND WITH THAT AS YOUR GUIDE, YOU CAN FINALLY BEGIN PAINTING.
PMPH
THEN YOU'LL APPLY A PIGMENT AS IF YOU WERE STENCILING.
PMPH
APPARENTLY, THE WORD FRESCO COMES FROM A WORD THAT MEANS "FRESH."
YOU CAN'T PAINT OVER FRESCO. YOU'RE ENGAGED IN BATTLE WITH THE FRESHNESS OF YOUR WALL.
YOU'LL SPEND THE FIRST TWO WEEKS ON MAKING FRESCOES, THE LAST TWO WEEKS ON MOSAICS, AND IN THE END, YOU'LL PUT IT ALL TOGETHER FOR REVIEWS.

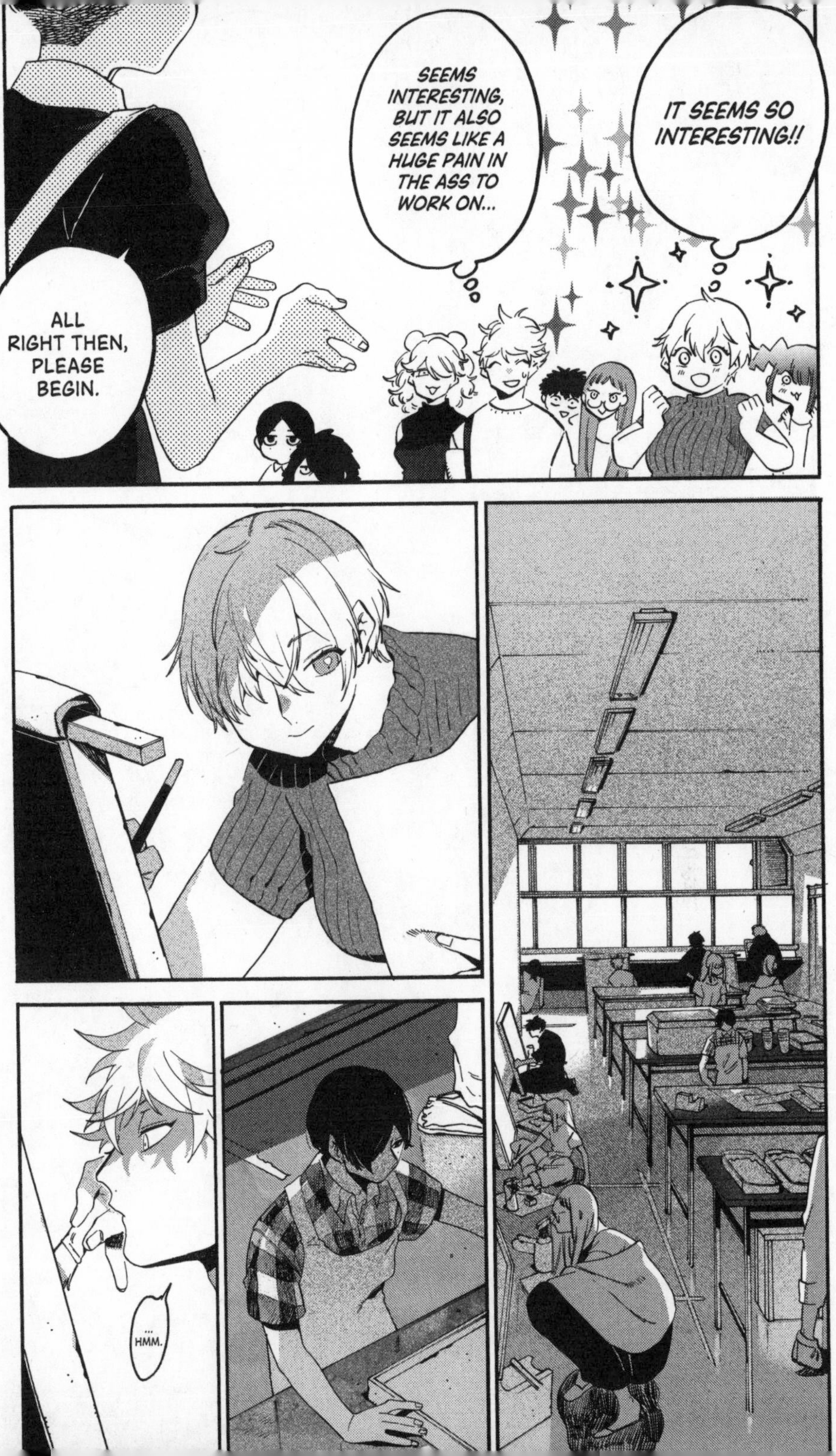

IT SEEMS SO INTERESTING!!
SEEMS INTERESTING, BUT IT ALSO SEEMS LIKE A HUGE PAIN IN THE ASS TO WORK ON...
ALL RIGHT THEN, PLEASE BEGIN.
... HMM.

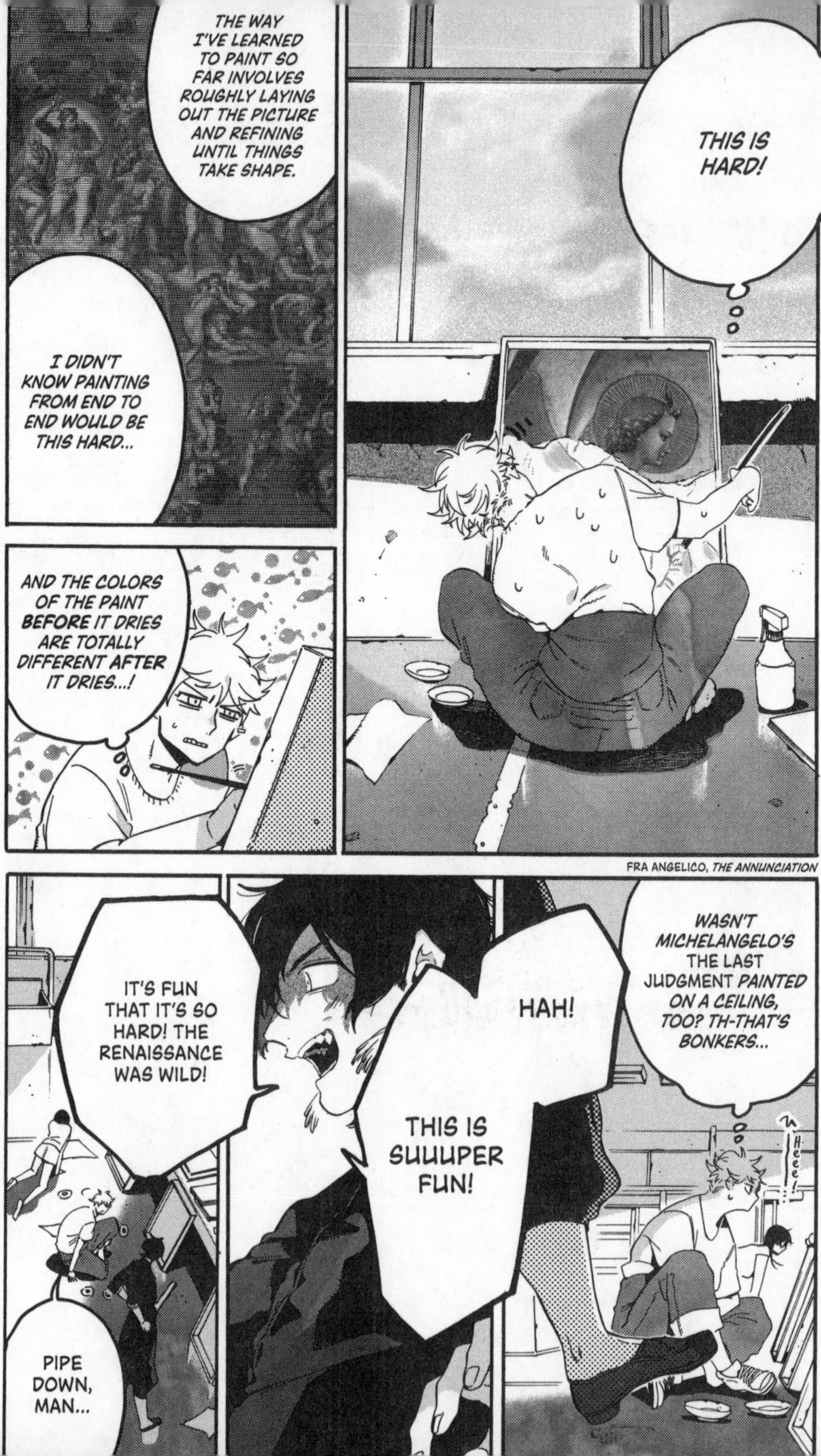
THIS IS HARD!
THE WAY I'VE LEARNED TO PAINT SO FAR INVOLVES ROUGHLY LAYING OUT THE PICTURE AND REFINING UNTIL THINGS TAKE SHAPE.
I DIDN'T KNOW PAINTING FROM END TO END WOULD BE THIS HARD...
AND THE COLORS OF THE PAINT **BEFORE** IT DRIES ARE TOTALLY DIFFERENT **AFTER** IT DRIES...!
WASN'T MICHELANGELO'S THE LAST JUDGMENT PAINTED ON A CEILING, TOO? TH-THAT'S BONKERS...
Heee...!
HAH!
THIS IS SUUUPER FUN!
IT'S FUN THAT IT'S SO HARD! THE RENAISSANCE WAS WILD!
PIPE DOWN, MAN...

FRA ANGELICO, *THE ANNUNCIATION*

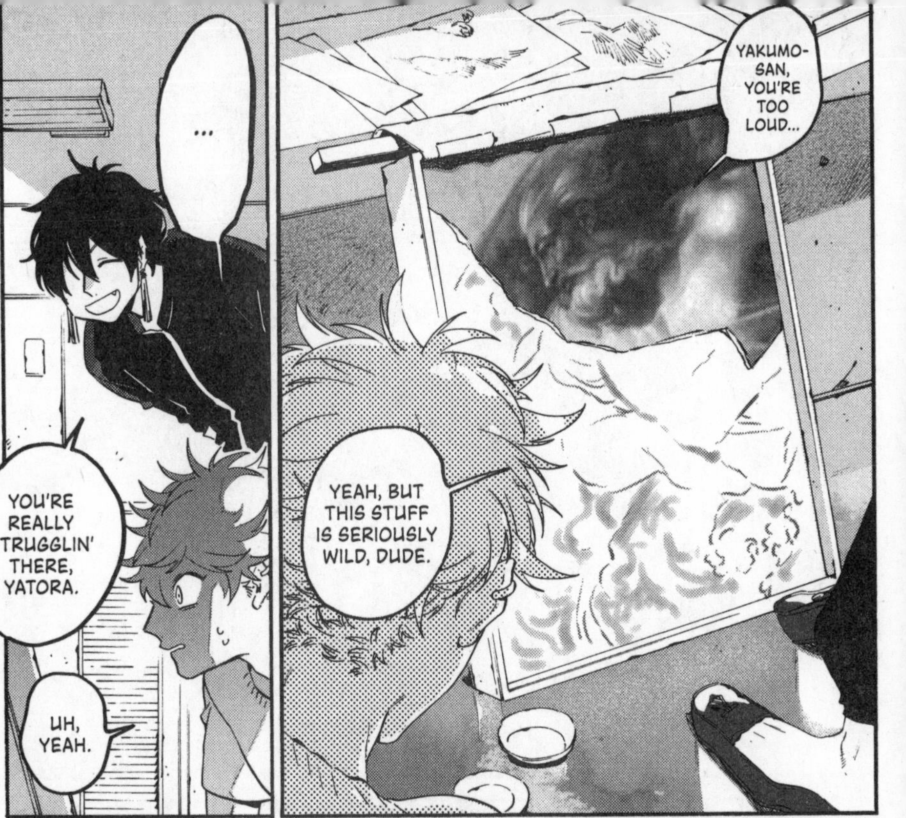
YAKUMO-SAN, YOU'RE TOO LOUD...
YEAH, BUT THIS STUFF IS SERIOUSLY WILD, DUDE.
...
YOU'RE REALLY STRUGGLIN' THERE, YATORA.
UH, YEAH.

MICHELANGELO BUONARROTI, *THE CREATION OF ADAM*

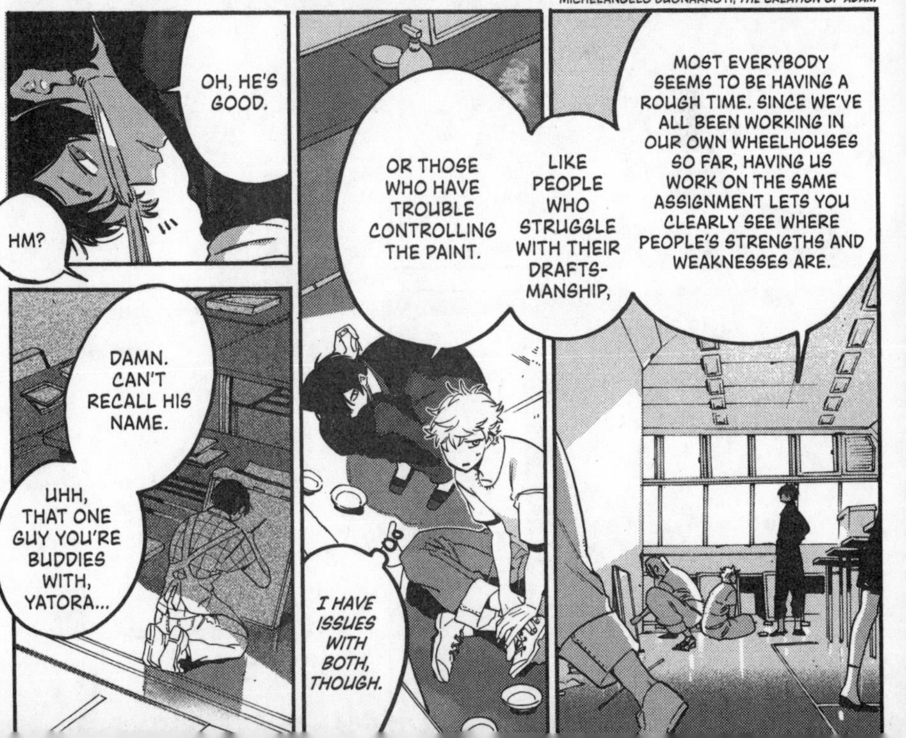
MOST EVERYBODY SEEMS TO BE HAVING A ROUGH TIME. SINCE WE'VE ALL BEEN WORKING IN OUR OWN WHEELHOUSES SO FAR, HAVING US WORK ON THE SAME ASSIGNMENT LETS YOU CLEARLY SEE WHERE PEOPLE'S STRENGTHS AND WEAKNESSES ARE.
LIKE PEOPLE WHO STRUGGLE WITH THEIR DRAFTS-MANSHIP,
OR THOSE WHO HAVE TROUBLE CONTROLLING THE PAINT.
I HAVE ISSUES WITH BOTH, THOUGH.
OH, HE'S GOOD.
HM?
DAMN. CAN'T RECALL HIS NAME.
UHH, THAT ONE GUY YOU'RE BUDDIES WITH, YATORA...

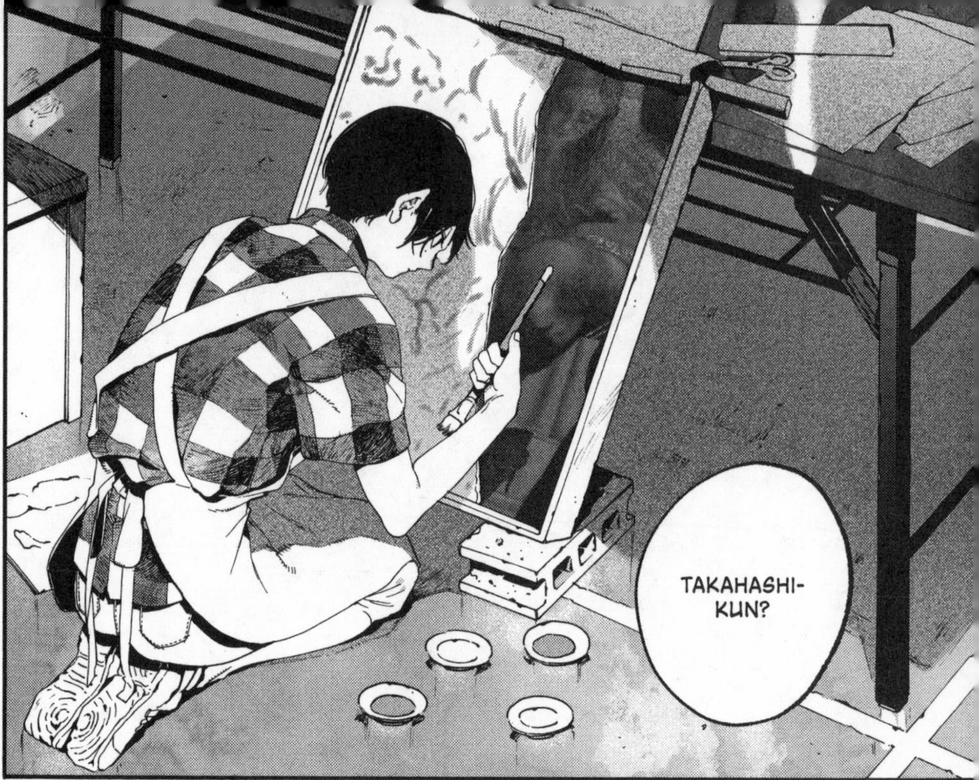
TAKAHASHI-KUN?

RAPHAEL SANZIO, *THE SCHOOL OF ATHENS*

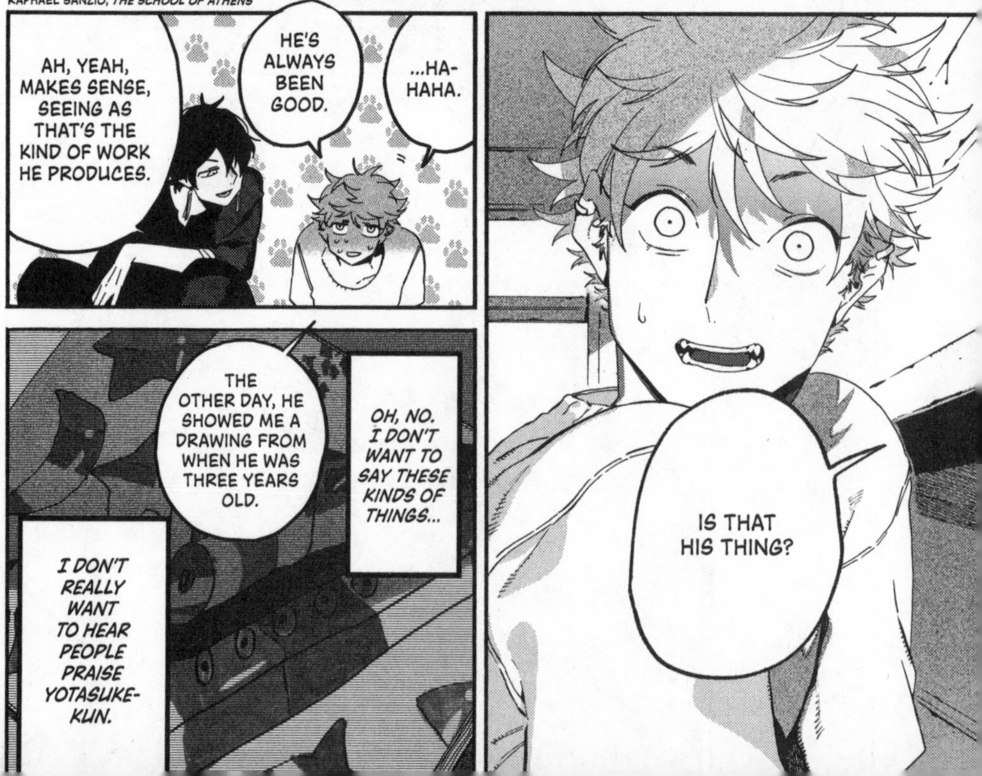
IS THAT HIS THING?
...HA-HAHA.
HE'S ALWAYS BEEN GOOD.
AH, YEAH, MAKES SENSE, SEEING AS THAT'S THE KIND OF WORK HE PRODUCES.
OH, NO. I DON'T WANT TO SAY THESE KINDS OF THINGS...
THE OTHER DAY, HE SHOWED ME A DRAWING FROM WHEN HE WAS THREE YEARS OLD.
I DON'T REALLY WANT TO HEAR PEOPLE PRAISE YOTASUKE-KUN.

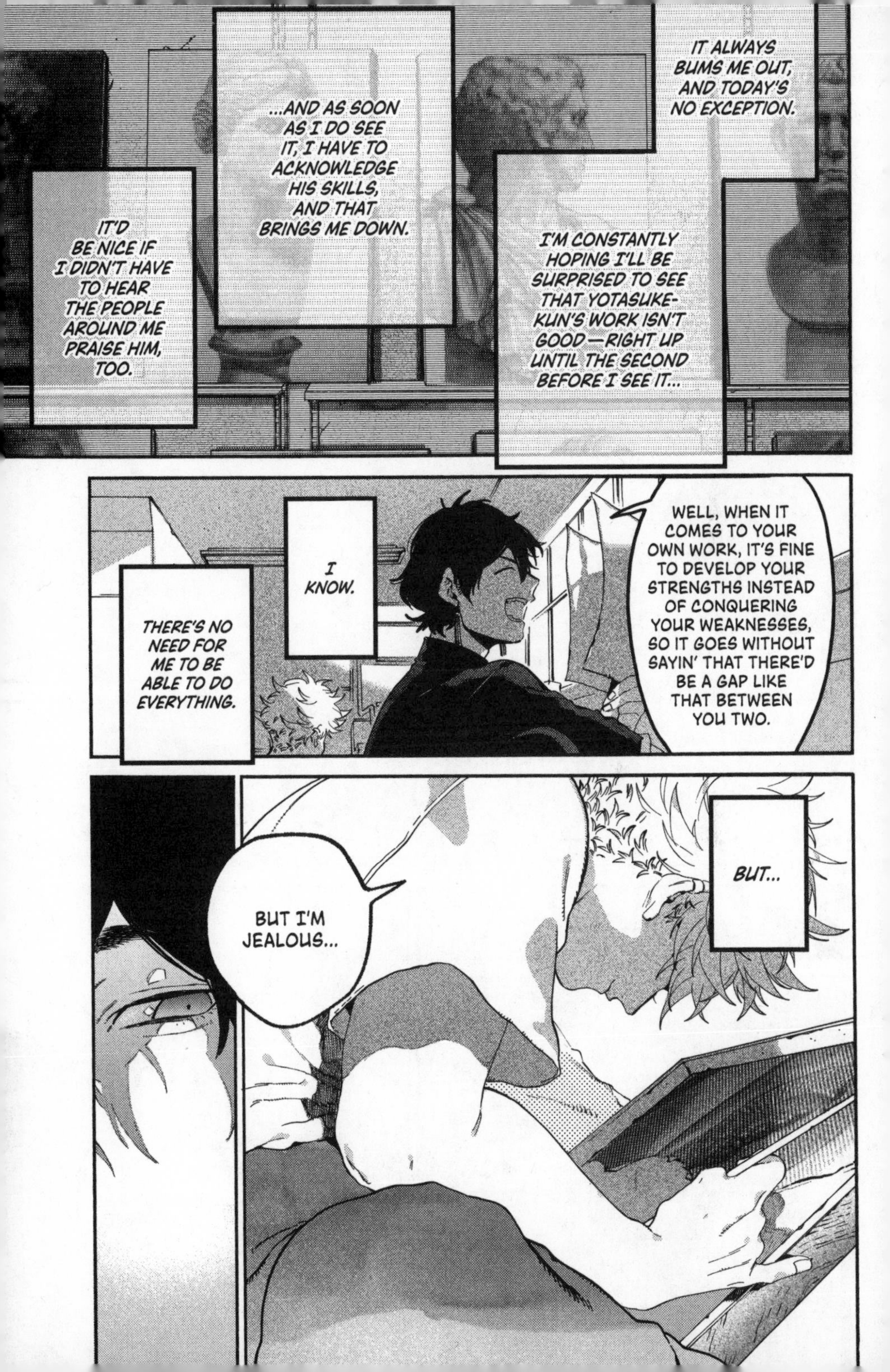
IT ALWAYS BUMS ME OUT, AND TODAY'S NO EXCEPTION.
I'M CONSTANTLY HOPING I'LL BE SURPRISED TO SEE THAT YOTASUKE-KUN'S WORK ISN'T GOOD—RIGHT UP UNTIL THE SECOND BEFORE I SEE IT...
...AND AS SOON AS I DO SEE IT, I HAVE TO ACKNOWLEDGE HIS SKILLS, AND THAT BRINGS ME DOWN.
IT'D BE NICE IF I DIDN'T HAVE TO HEAR THE PEOPLE AROUND ME PRAISE HIM, TOO.
WELL, WHEN IT COMES TO YOUR OWN WORK, IT'S FINE TO DEVELOP YOUR STRENGTHS INSTEAD OF CONQUERING YOUR WEAKNESSES, SO IT GOES WITHOUT SAYIN' THAT THERE'D BE A GAP LIKE THAT BETWEEN YOU TWO.
I KNOW.
THERE'S NO NEED FOR ME TO BE ABLE TO DO EVERYTHING.
BUT...
BUT I'M JEALOUS...

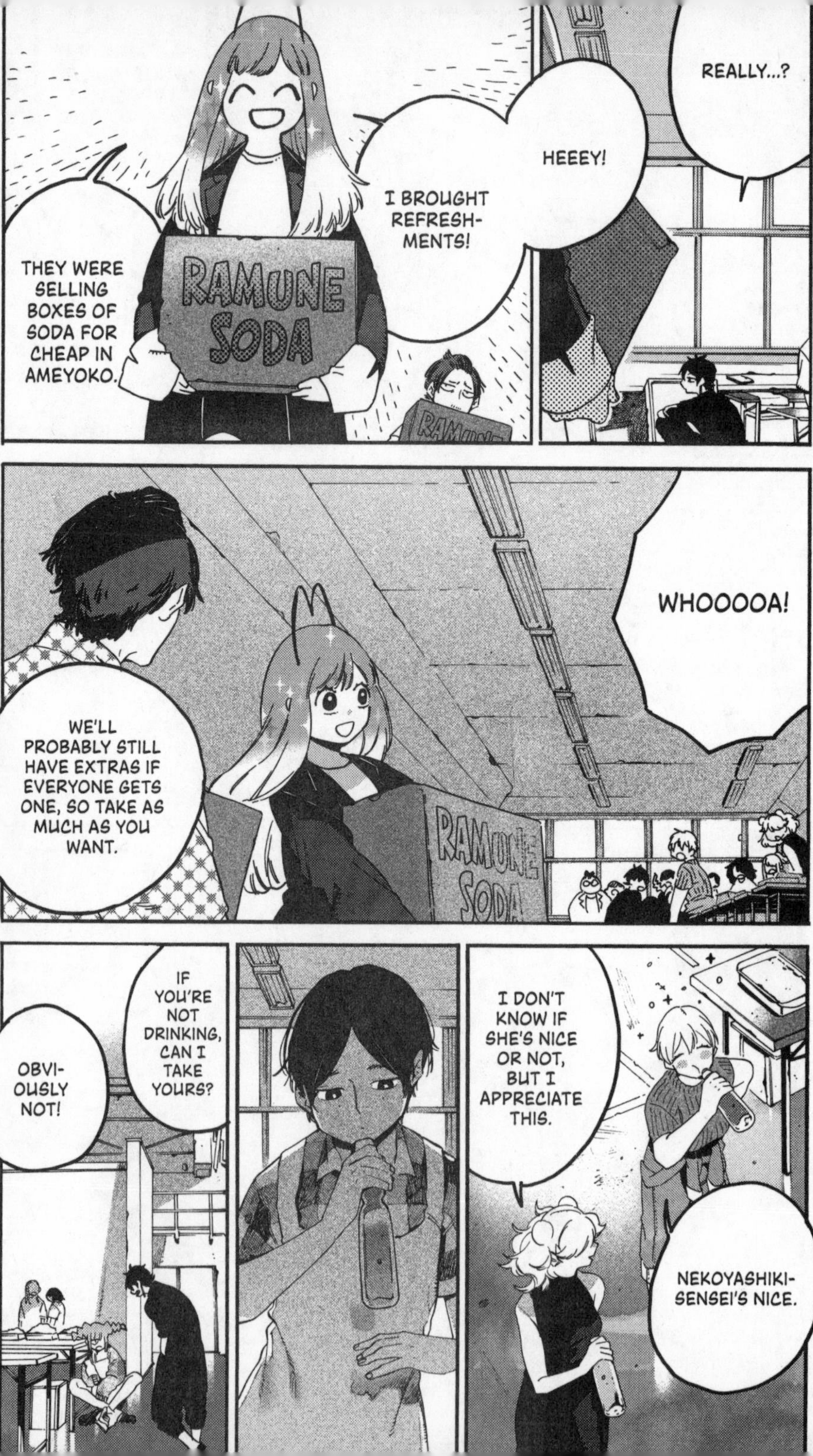
REALLY...?
HEEEY!
I BROUGHT REFRESH-MENTS!
THEY WERE SELLING BOXES OF SODA FOR CHEAP IN AMEYOKO.
RAMUNE SODA
WHOOOOA!
WE'LL PROBABLY STILL HAVE EXTRAS IF EVERYONE GETS ONE, SO TAKE AS MUCH AS YOU WANT.
NEKOYASHIKI-SENSEI'S NICE.
I DON'T KNOW IF SHE'S NICE OR NOT, BUT I APPRECIATE THIS.
IF YOU'RE NOT DRINKING, CAN I TAKE YOURS?
OBVI-OUSLY NOT!

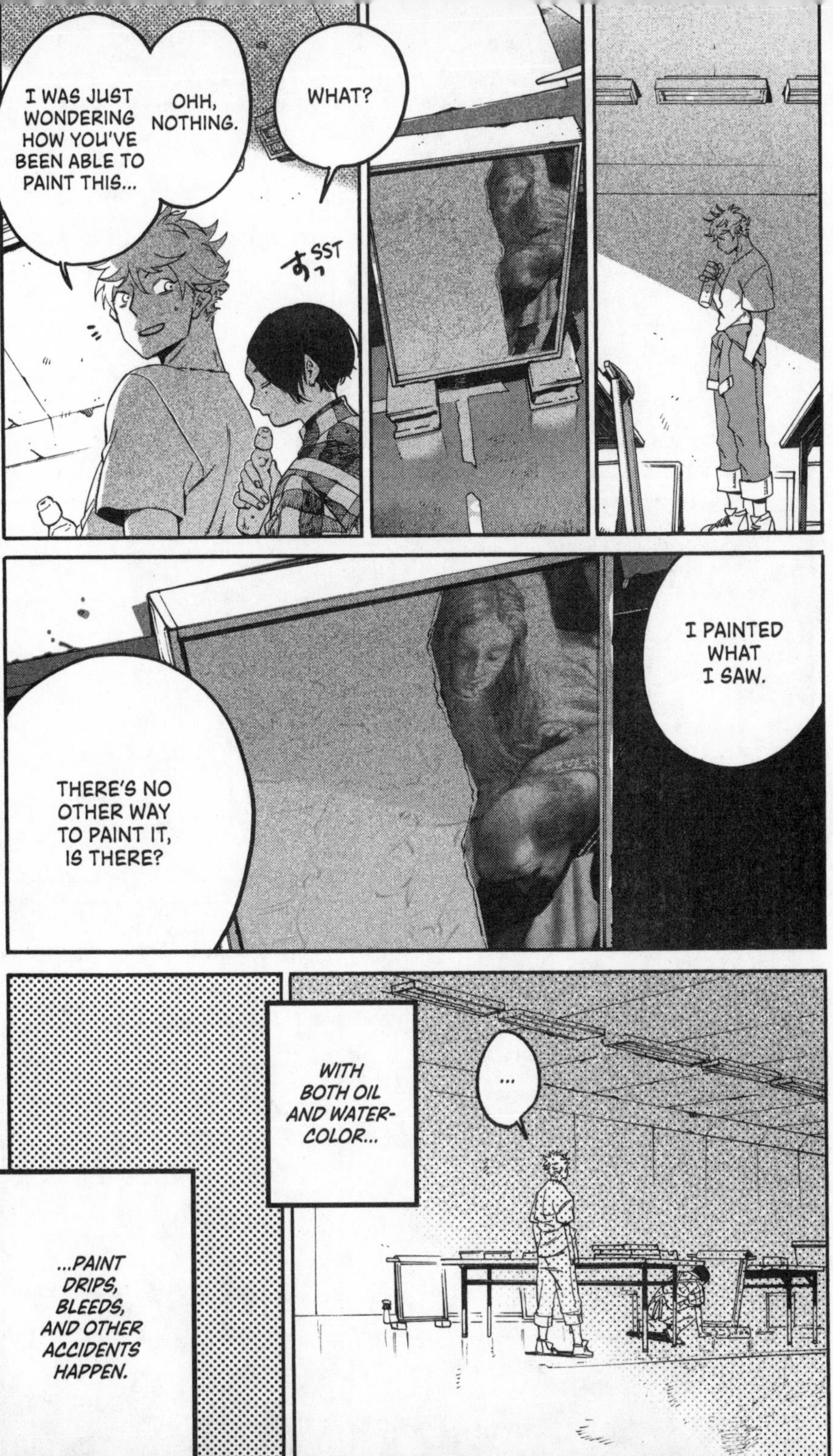
WHAT?
OHH, NOTHING.
I WAS JUST WONDERING HOW YOU'VE BEEN ABLE TO PAINT THIS...
すっ SST
I PAINTED WHAT I SAW.
THERE'S NO OTHER WAY TO PAINT IT, IS THERE?
...
WITH BOTH OIL AND WATER-COLOR...
...PAINT DRIPS, BLEEDS, AND OTHER ACCIDENTS HAPPEN.

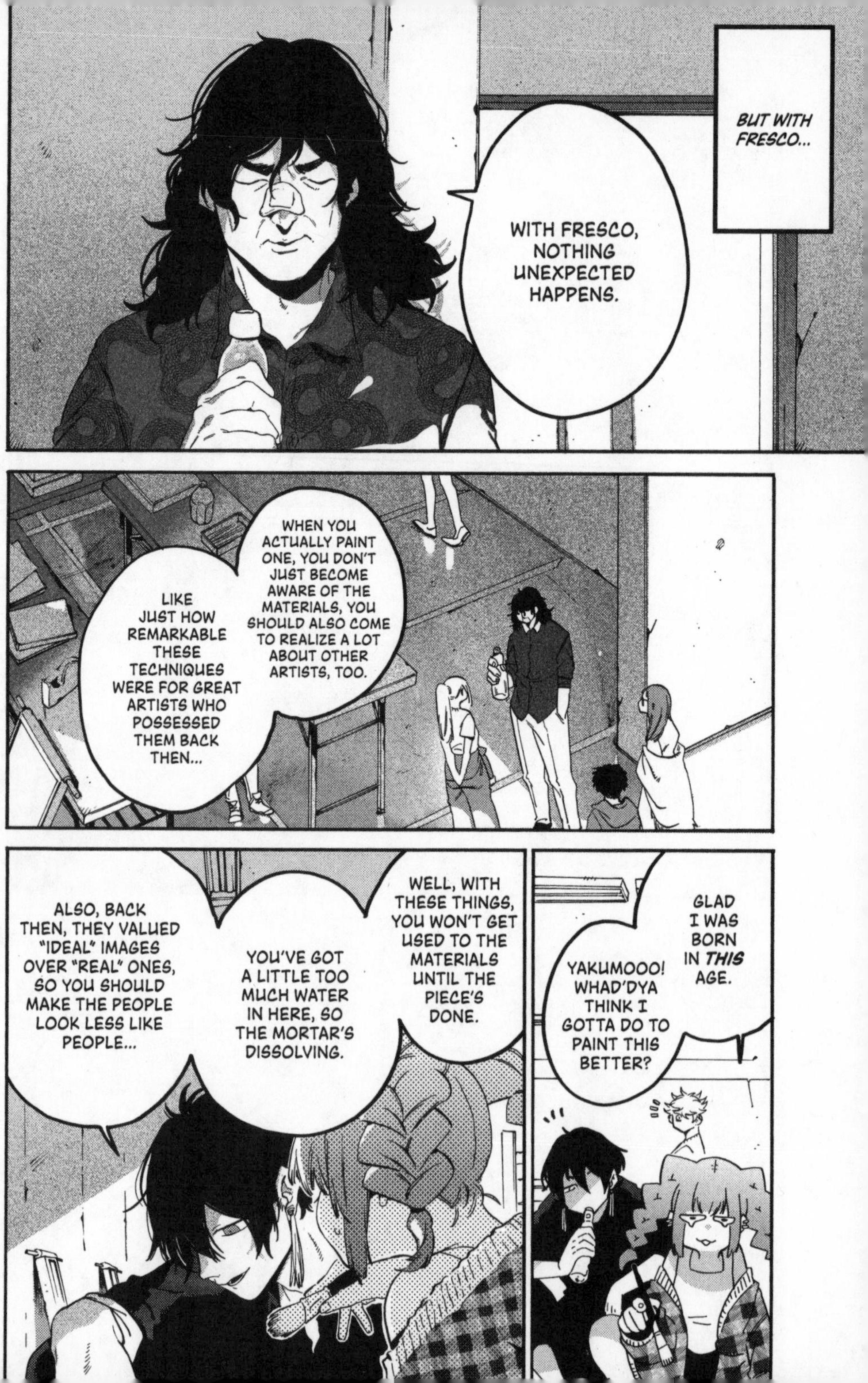
BUT WITH FRESCO...
WITH FRESCO, NOTHING UNEXPECTED HAPPENS.
WHEN YOU ACTUALLY PAINT ONE, YOU DON'T JUST BECOME AWARE OF THE MATERIALS, YOU SHOULD ALSO COME TO REALIZE A LOT ABOUT OTHER ARTISTS, TOO.
LIKE JUST HOW REMARKABLE THESE TECHNIQUES WERE FOR GREAT ARTISTS WHO POSSESSED THEM BACK THEN...
GLAD I WAS BORN IN *THIS* AGE.
YAKUMOOO! WHAD'DYA THINK I GOTTA DO TO PAINT THIS BETTER?
WELL, WITH THESE THINGS, YOU WON'T GET USED TO THE MATERIALS UNTIL THE PIECE'S DONE.
YOU'VE GOT A LITTLE TOO MUCH WATER IN HERE, SO THE MORTAR'S DISSOLVING.
ALSO, BACK THEN, THEY VALUED "IDEAL" IMAGES OVER "REAL" ONES, SO YOU SHOULD MAKE THE PEOPLE LOOK LESS LIKE PEOPLE...

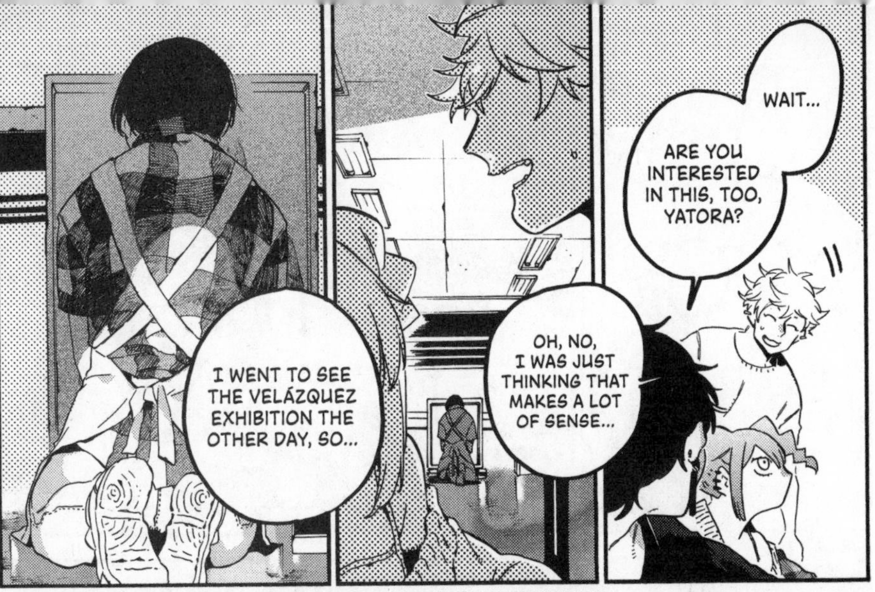
WAIT...
ARE YOU INTERESTED IN THIS, TOO, YATORA?
OH, NO, I WAS JUST THINKING THAT MAKES A LOT OF SENSE...
I WENT TO SEE THE VELÁZQUEZ EXHIBITION THE OTHER DAY, SO...

(LEFT AND MIDDLE) ELÍAS GARCÍA MARTINEZ, *ECCE HOMO*; UNKNOWN ARTIST, *NARCISSUS* (UNCOVERED IN POMPEII).

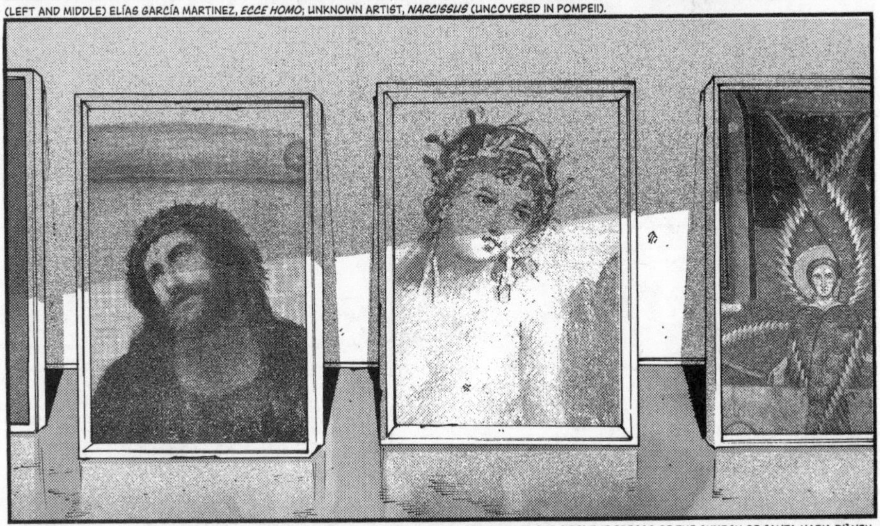

(RIGHT) UNKNOWN ARTIST, DETAIL OF SERAPHIM (RIGHT SIDE) THE FRESCO OF THE CHURCH OF SANTA MARIA D'ÀNEU.

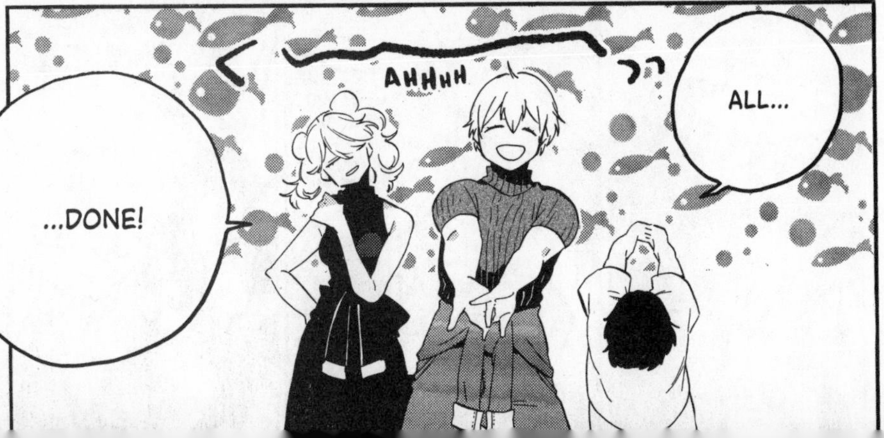
ALL...
AHHHH
...DONE!

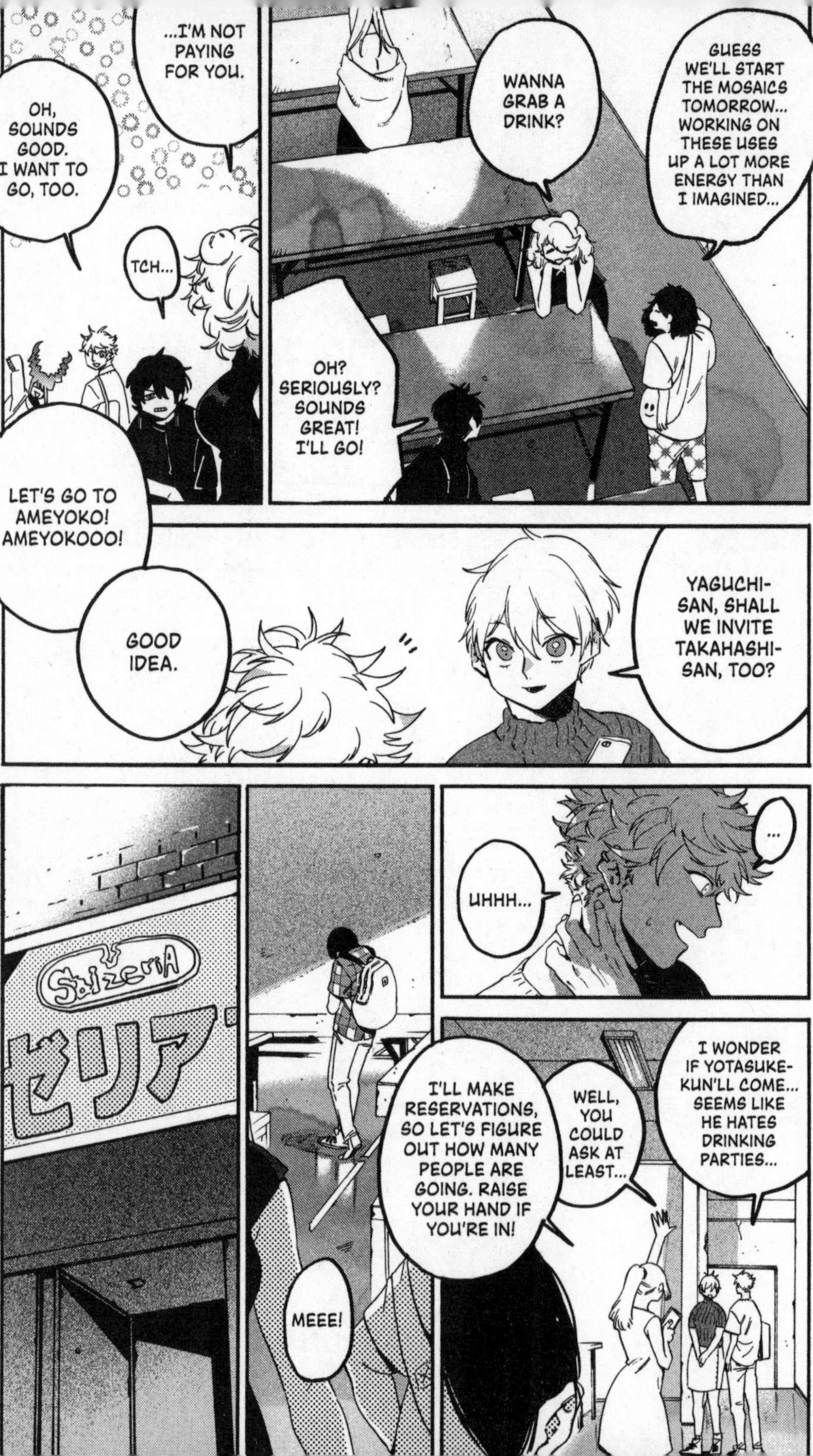
GUESS WE'LL START THE MOSAICS TOMORROW... WORKING ON THESE USES UP A LOT MORE ENERGY THAN I IMAGINED...
WANNA GRAB A DRINK?
OH? SERIOUSLY? SOUNDS GREAT! I'LL GO!
...I'M NOT PAYING FOR YOU.
OH, SOUNDS GOOD. I WANT TO GO, TOO.
TCH...
LET'S GO TO AMEYOKO! AMEYOKOOO!
YAGUCHI-SAN, SHALL WE INVITE TAKAHASHI-SAN, TOO?
GOOD IDEA.
...
UHHH...
I WONDER IF YOTASUKE-KUN'LL COME... SEEMS LIKE HE HATES DRINKING PARTIES...
WELL, YOU COULD ASK AT LEAST...
I'LL MAKE RESERVATIONS, SO LET'S FIGURE OUT HOW MANY PEOPLE ARE GOING. RAISE YOUR HAND IF YOU'RE IN!
MEEE!
Saizeria
ゼリア

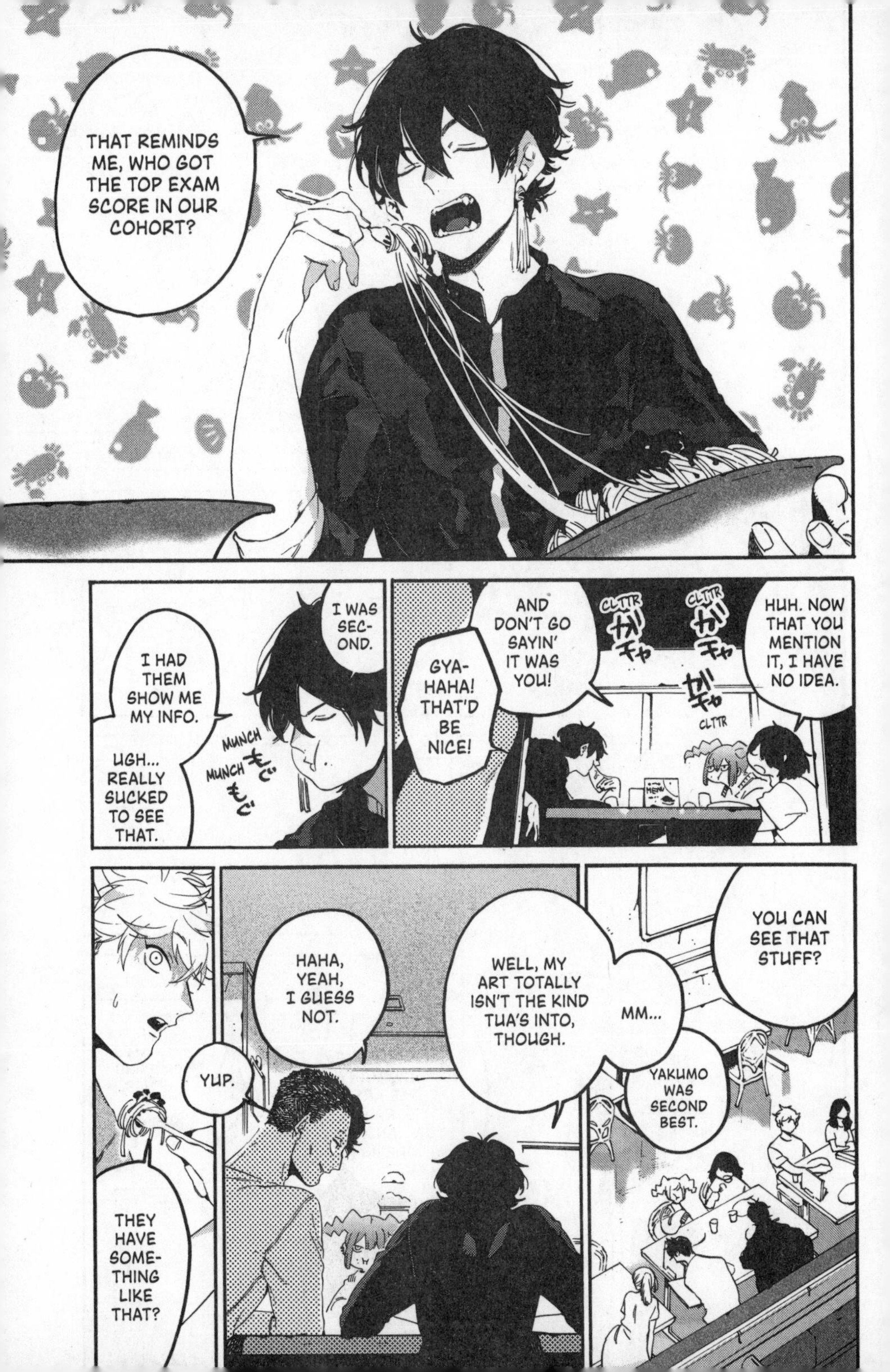
THAT REMINDS ME, WHO GOT THE TOP EXAM SCORE IN OUR COHORT?
HUH. NOW THAT YOU MENTION IT, I HAVE NO IDEA.
CLTTR ガチャ
CLTTR ガチャ
ガチャ CLTTR
AND DON'T GO SAYIN' IT WAS YOU!
GYA-HAHA! THAT'D BE NICE!
I WAS SEC-OND.
I HAD THEM SHOW ME MY INFO.
MUNCH もぐ MUNCH もぐ
UGH... REALLY SUCKED TO SEE THAT.
YOU CAN SEE THAT STUFF?
MM...
YAKUMO WAS SECOND BEST.
WELL, MY ART TOTALLY ISN'T THE KIND TUA'S INTO, THOUGH.
HAHA, YEAH, I GUESS NOT.
YUP.
THEY HAVE SOME-THING LIKE THAT?

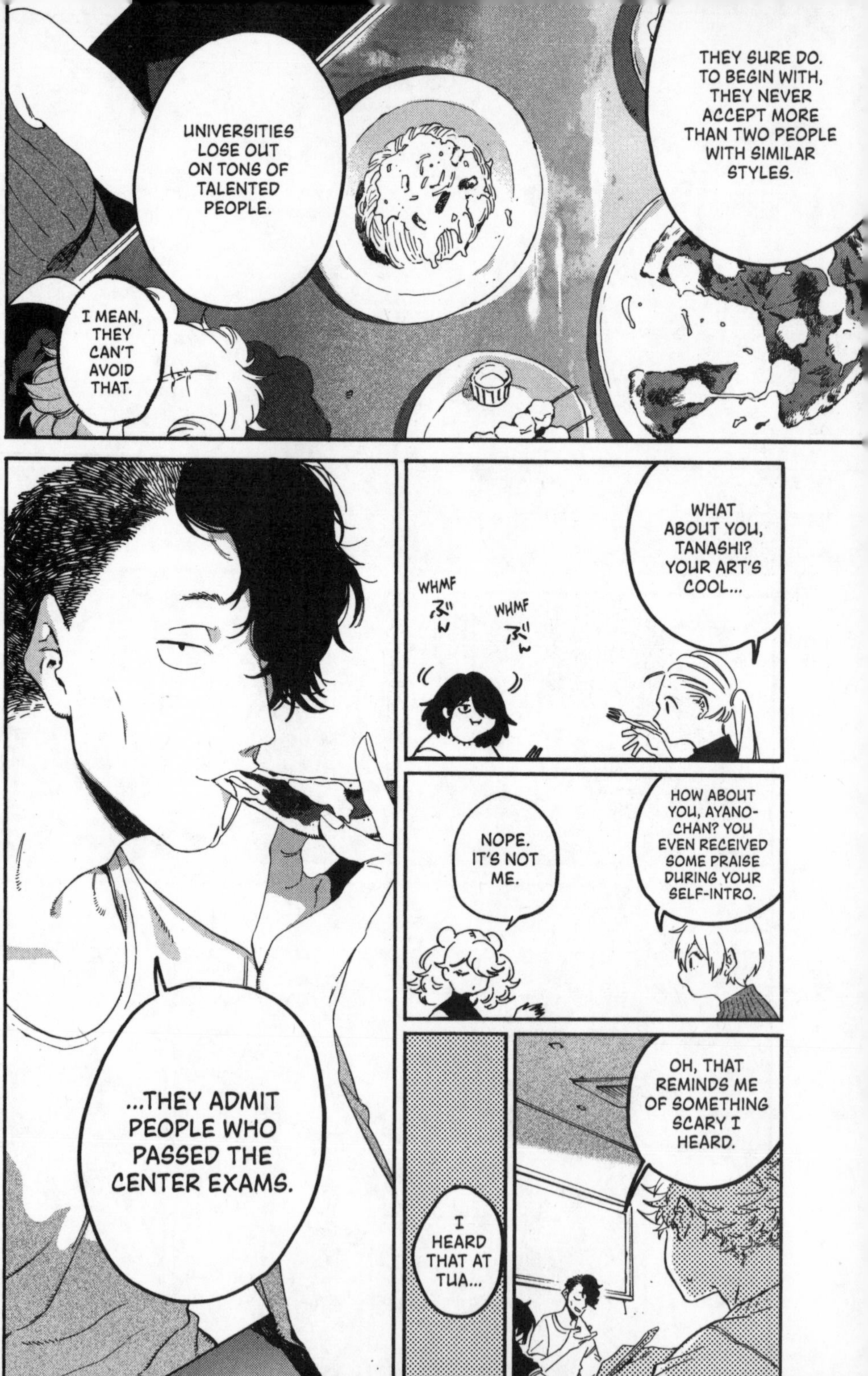
THEY SURE DO. TO BEGIN WITH, THEY NEVER ACCEPT MORE THAN TWO PEOPLE WITH SIMILAR STYLES.
UNIVERSITIES LOSE OUT ON TONS OF TALENTED PEOPLE.
I MEAN, THEY CAN'T AVOID THAT.
WHAT ABOUT YOU, TANASHI? YOUR ART'S COOL...
WHMF ぶん
WHMF ぶん
HOW ABOUT YOU, AYANO-CHAN? YOU EVEN RECEIVED SOME PRAISE DURING YOUR SELF-INTRO.
NOPE. IT'S NOT ME.
OH, THAT REMINDS ME OF SOMETHING SCARY I HEARD.
I HEARD THAT AT TUA...
...THEY ADMIT PEOPLE WHO PASSED THE CENTER EXAMS.

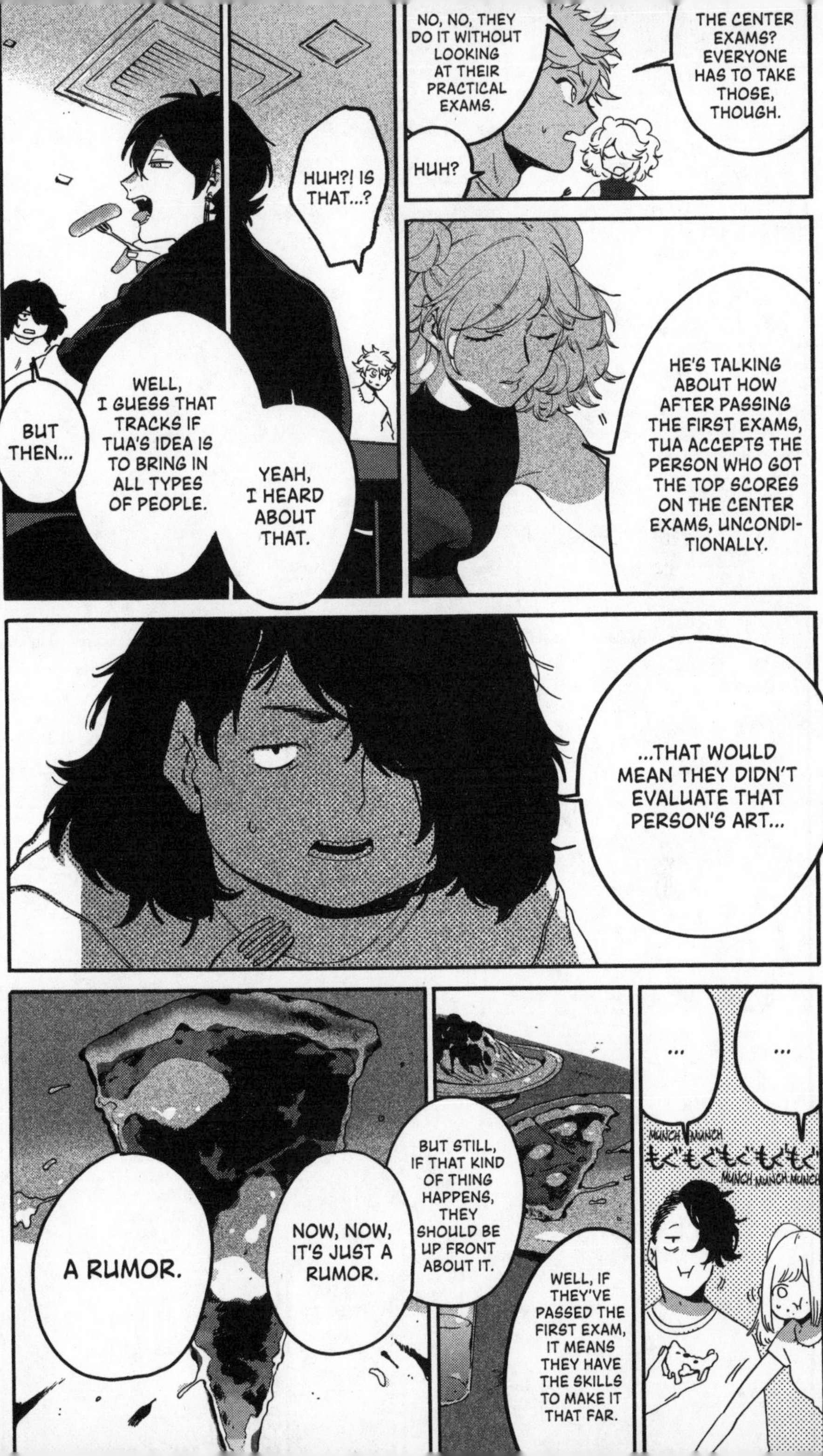
THE CENTER EXAMS? EVERYONE HAS TO TAKE THOSE, THOUGH.
NO, NO, THEY DO IT WITHOUT LOOKING AT THEIR PRACTICAL EXAMS.
HUH?
HE'S TALKING ABOUT HOW AFTER PASSING THE FIRST EXAMS, TUA ACCEPTS THE PERSON WHO GOT THE TOP SCORES ON THE CENTER EXAMS, UNCONDITIONALLY.
HUH?! IS THAT...?
YEAH, I HEARD ABOUT THAT.
WELL, I GUESS THAT TRACKS IF TUA'S IDEA IS TO BRING IN ALL TYPES OF PEOPLE.
BUT THEN...
...THAT WOULD MEAN THEY DIDN'T EVALUATE THAT PERSON'S ART...
...
...
MUNCH MUNCH
もぐもぐもぐもぐもぐ
MUNCH MUNCH MUNCH
BUT STILL, IF THAT KIND OF THING HAPPENS, THEY SHOULD BE UP FRONT ABOUT IT.
WELL, IF THEY'VE PASSED THE FIRST EXAM, IT MEANS THEY HAVE THE SKILLS TO MAKE IT THAT FAR.
NOW, NOW, IT'S JUST A RUMOR.
A RUMOR.

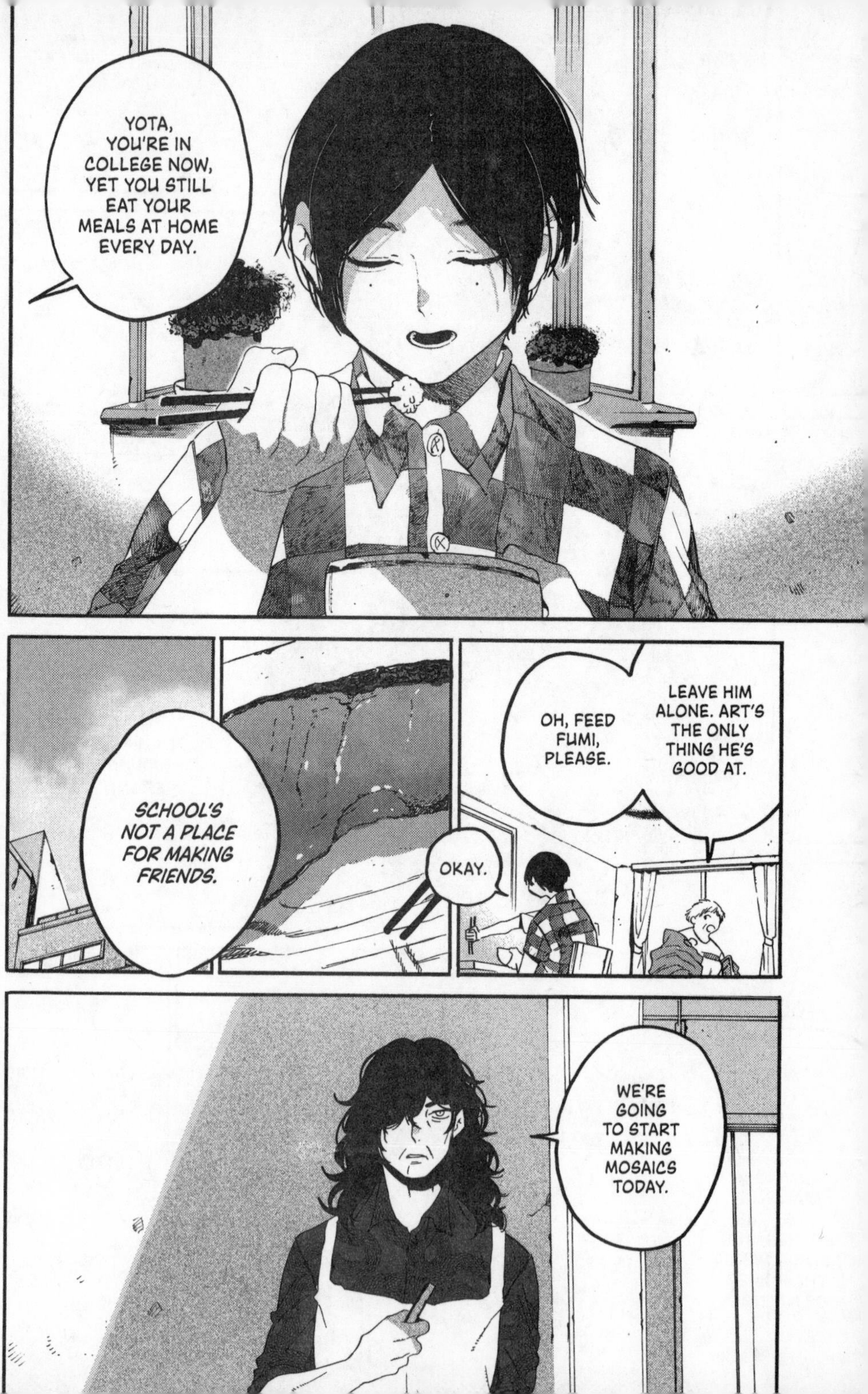
YOTA, YOU'RE IN COLLEGE NOW, YET YOU STILL EAT YOUR MEALS AT HOME EVERY DAY.
LEAVE HIM ALONE. ART'S THE ONLY THING HE'S GOOD AT.
OH, FEED FUMI, PLEASE.
OKAY.
SCHOOL'S NOT A PLACE FOR MAKING FRIENDS.
WE'RE GOING TO START MAKING MOSAICS TODAY.

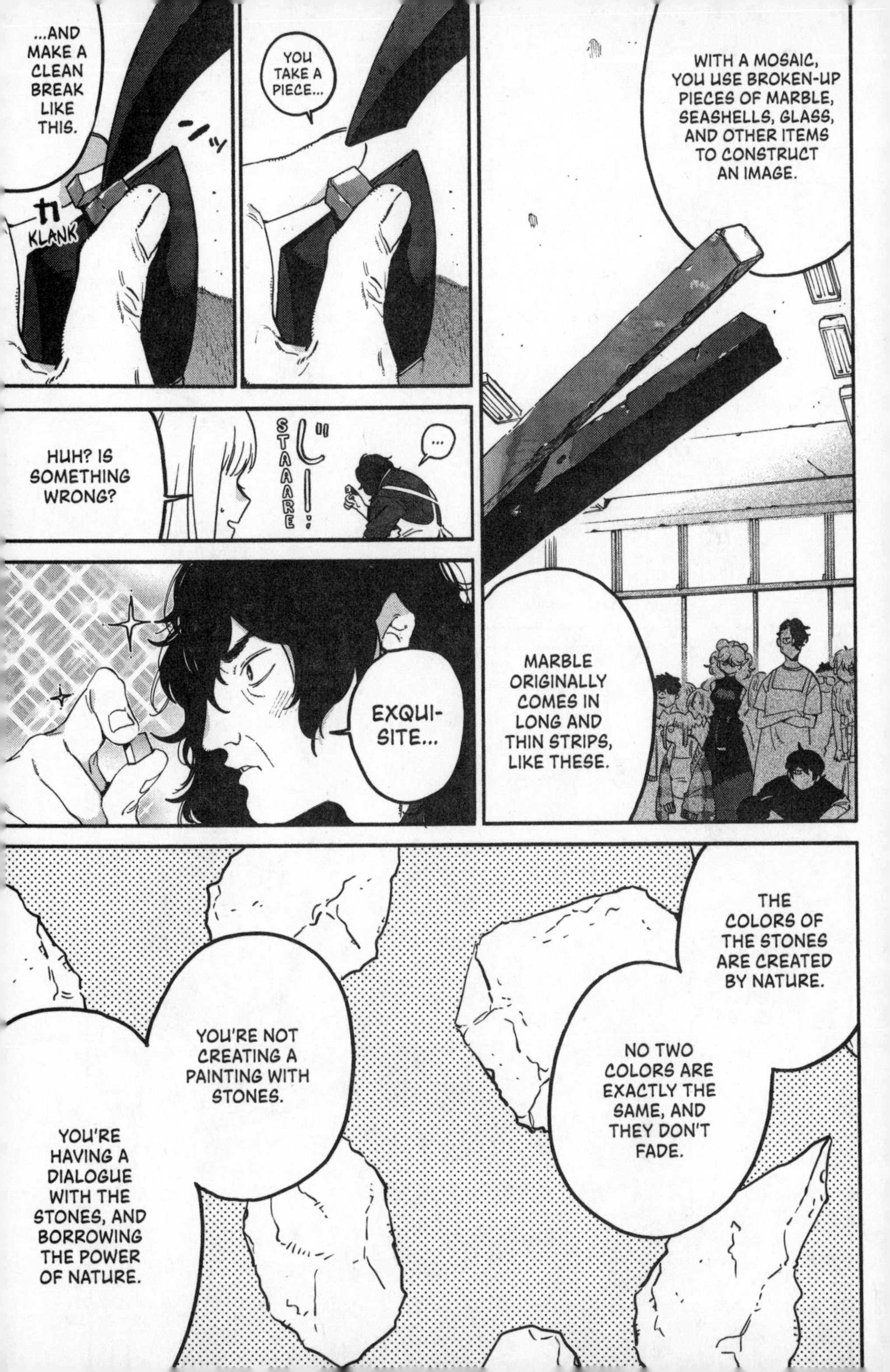
WITH A MOSAIC, YOU USE BROKEN-UP PIECES OF MARBLE, SEASHELLS, GLASS, AND OTHER ITEMS TO CONSTRUCT AN IMAGE.
MARBLE ORIGINALLY COMES IN LONG AND THIN STRIPS, LIKE THESE.
YOU TAKE A PIECE...
...AND MAKE A CLEAN BREAK LIKE THIS.
KLANK
HUH? IS SOMETHING WRONG?
じー
STAAARE
...
EXQUI-SITE...
THE COLORS OF THE STONES ARE CREATED BY NATURE.
NO TWO COLORS ARE EXACTLY THE SAME, AND THEY DON'T FADE.
YOU'RE NOT CREATING A PAINTING WITH STONES.
YOU'RE HAVING A DIALOGUE WITH THE STONES, AND BORROWING THE POWER OF NATURE.

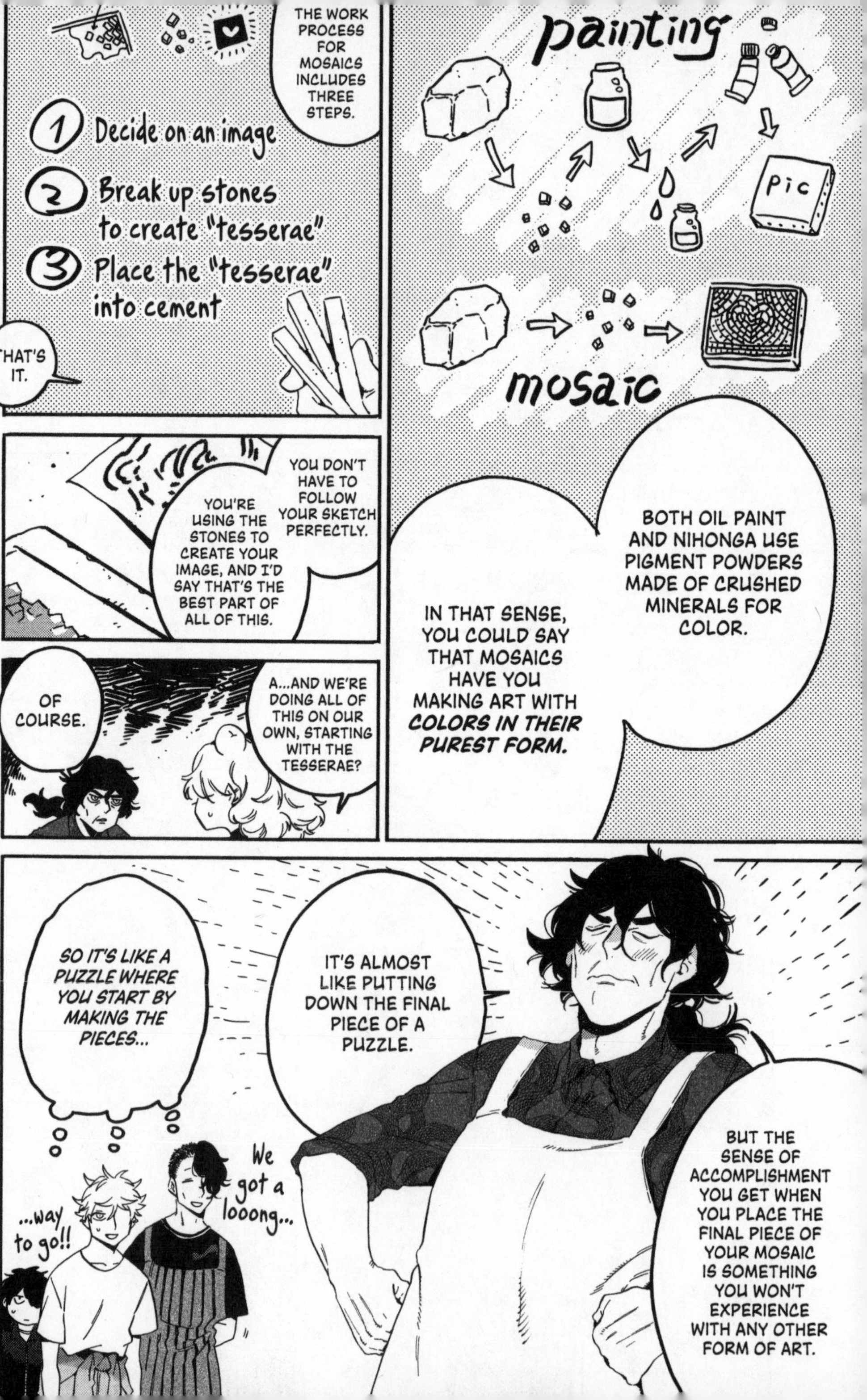
painting
Pic
mosaic
BOTH OIL PAINT AND NIHONGA USE PIGMENT POWDERS MADE OF CRUSHED MINERALS FOR COLOR.
IN THAT SENSE, YOU COULD SAY THAT MOSAICS HAVE YOU MAKING ART WITH *COLORS IN THEIR PUREST FORM.*
THE WORK PROCESS FOR MOSAICS INCLUDES THREE STEPS.
1 Decide on an image
2 Break up stones to create "tesserae"
3 Place the "tesserae" into cement
THAT'S IT.
YOU DON'T HAVE TO FOLLOW YOUR SKETCH PERFECTLY.
YOU'RE USING THE STONES TO CREATE YOUR IMAGE, AND I'D SAY THAT'S THE BEST PART OF ALL OF THIS.
A...AND WE'RE DOING ALL OF THIS ON OUR OWN, STARTING WITH THE TESSERAE?
OF COURSE.
BUT THE SENSE OF ACCOMPLISHMENT YOU GET WHEN YOU PLACE THE FINAL PIECE OF YOUR MOSAIC IS SOMETHING YOU WON'T EXPERIENCE WITH ANY OTHER FORM OF ART.
IT'S ALMOST LIKE PUTTING DOWN THE FINAL PIECE OF A PUZZLE.
SO IT'S LIKE A PUZZLE WHERE YOU START BY MAKING THE PIECES...
We got a looong...
...way to go!!

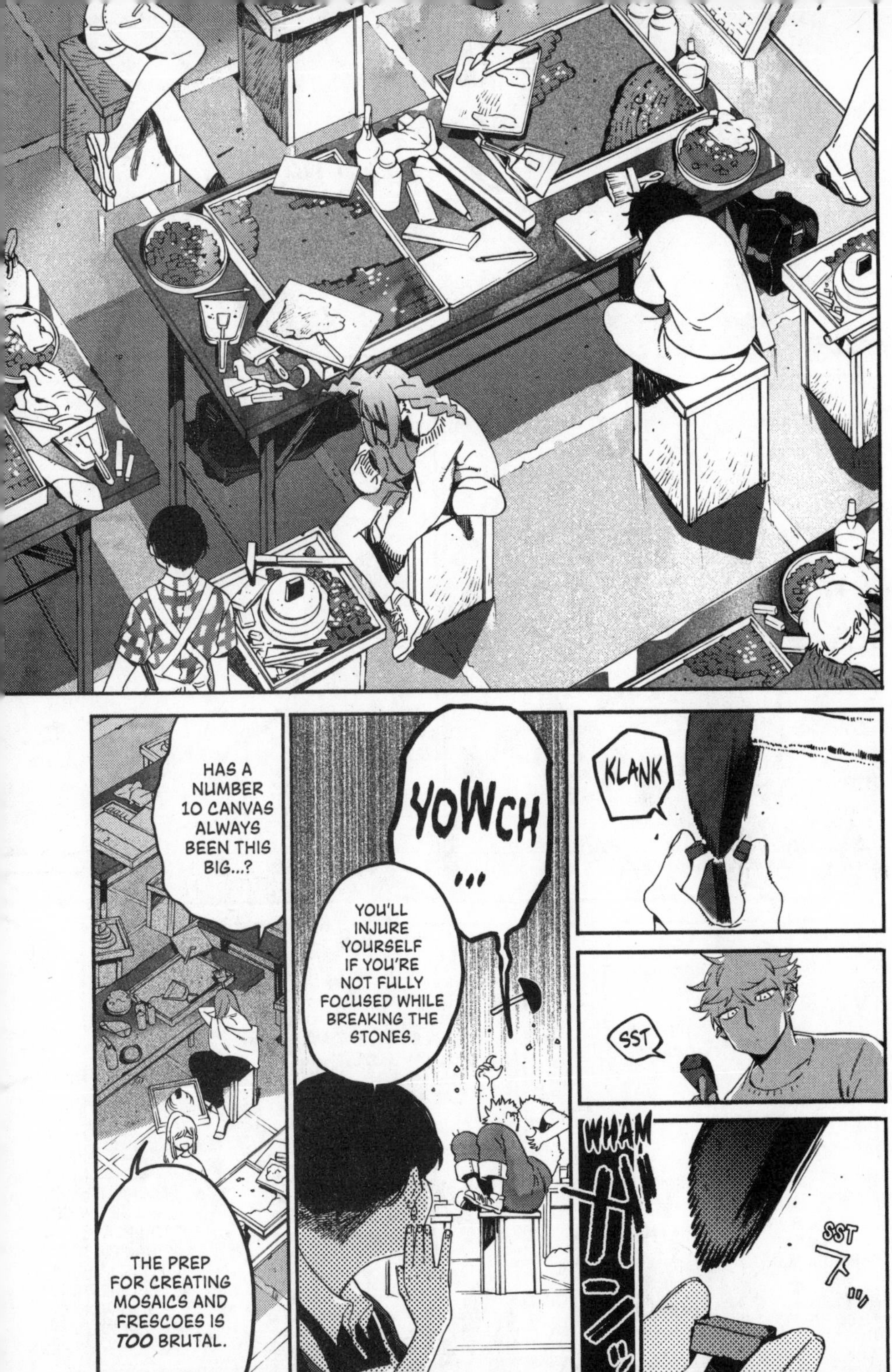

KLANK
SST
WHAM
SST
YOWCH
...
YOU'LL INJURE YOURSELF IF YOU'RE NOT FULLY FOCUSED WHILE BREAKING THE STONES.
HAS A NUMBER 10 CANVAS ALWAYS BEEN THIS BIG...?
THE PREP FOR CREATING MOSAICS AND FRESCOES IS *TOO* BRUTAL.

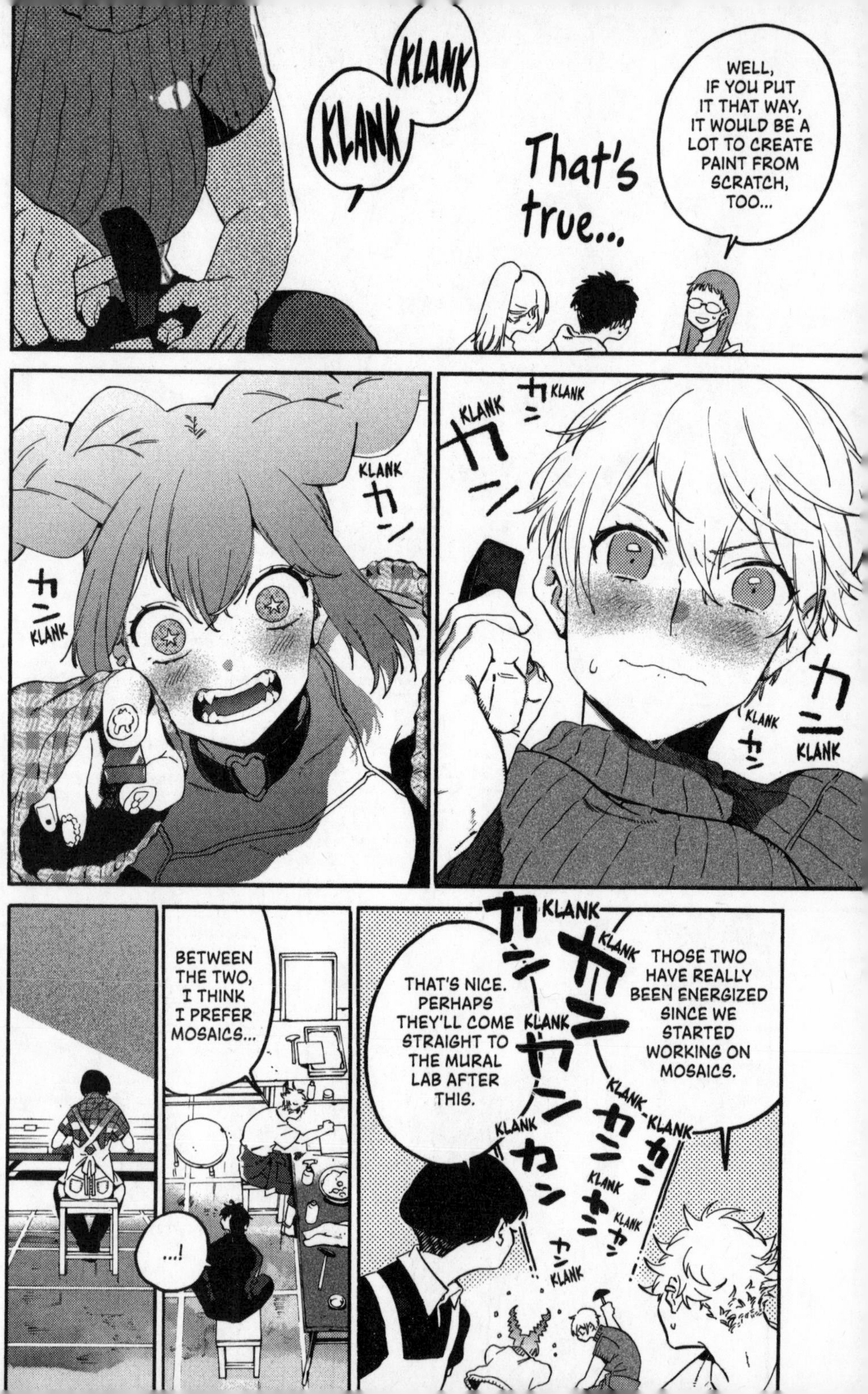
WELL, IF YOU PUT IT THAT WAY, IT WOULD BE A LOT TO CREATE PAINT FROM SCRATCH, TOO...
That's true...
KLANK
KLANK
KLANK
KLANK
KLANK
KLANK
KLANK
KLANK
THOSE TWO HAVE REALLY BEEN ENERGIZED SINCE WE STARTED WORKING ON MOSAICS.
THAT'S NICE. PERHAPS THEY'LL COME STRAIGHT TO THE MURAL LAB AFTER THIS.
KLANK
KLANK
KLANK
KLANK-KLANK
KLANK
KLANK
KLANK
KLANK
BETWEEN THE TWO, I THINK I PREFER MOSAICS...
...!

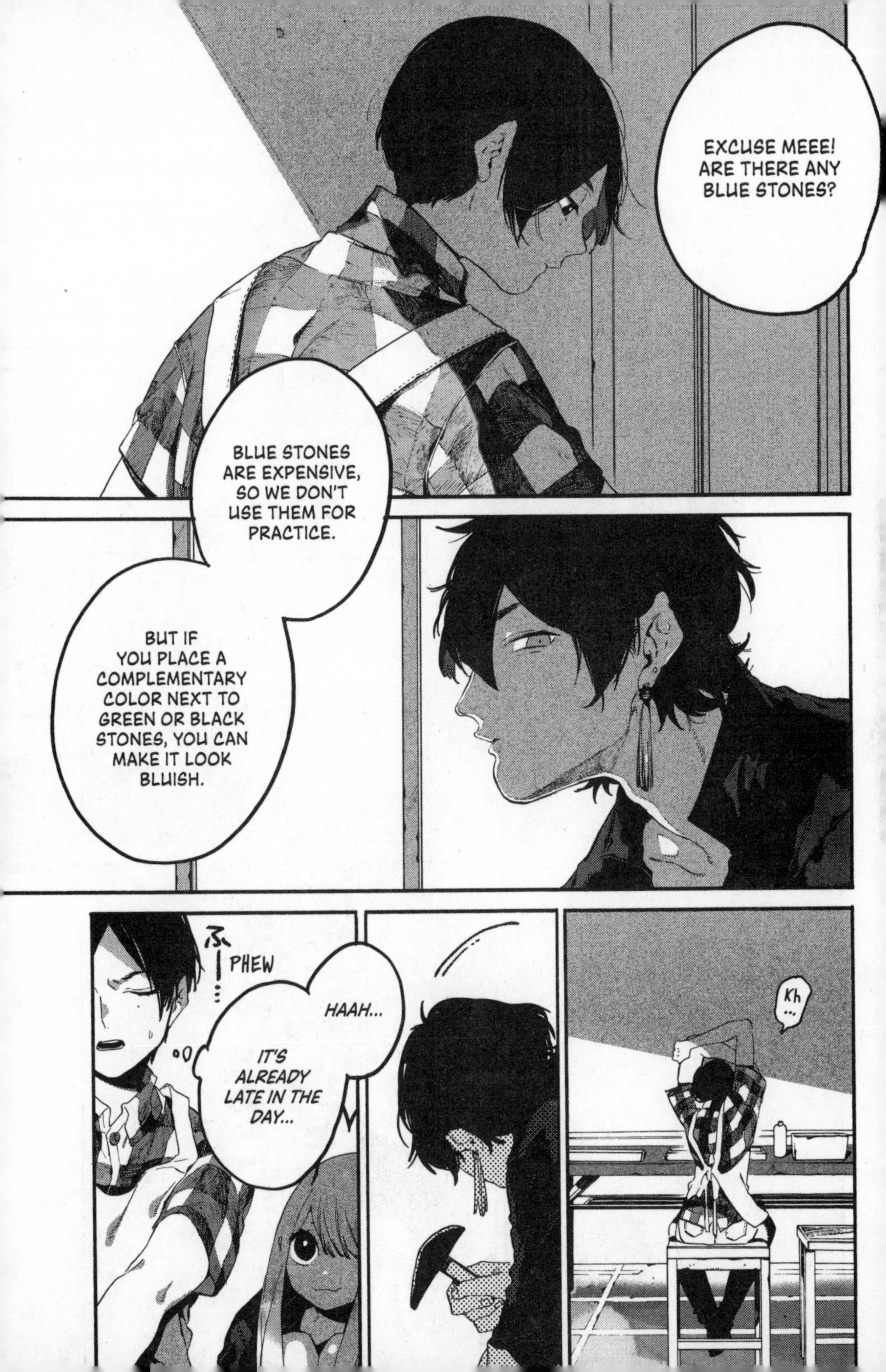
EXCUSE MEEE! ARE THERE ANY BLUE STONES?
BLUE STONES ARE EXPENSIVE, SO WE DON'T USE THEM FOR PRACTICE.
BUT IF YOU PLACE A COMPLEMENTARY COLOR NEXT TO GREEN OR BLACK STONES, YOU CAN MAKE IT LOOK BLUISH.
Kh...
HAAH...
IT'S ALREADY LATE IN THE DAY...
ふ―…
PHEW

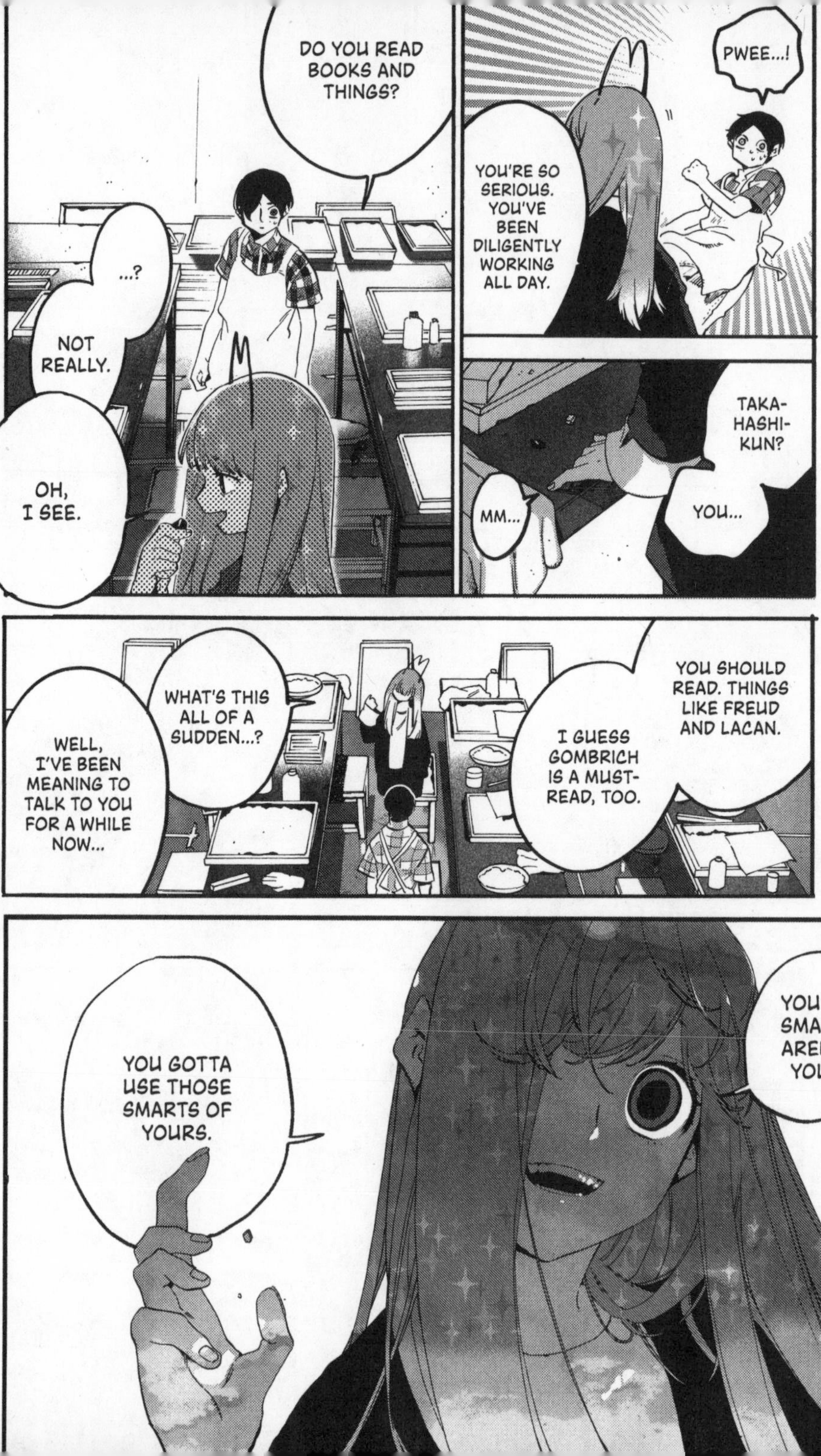
PWEE...!
YOU'RE SO SERIOUS. YOU'VE BEEN DILIGENTLY WORKING ALL DAY.
TAKA-HASHI-KUN?
YOU...
MM...
DO YOU READ BOOKS AND THINGS?
...?
NOT REALLY.
OH, I SEE.
YOU SHOULD READ. THINGS LIKE FREUD AND LACAN.
I GUESS GOMBRICH IS A MUST-READ, TOO.
WHAT'S THIS ALL OF A SUDDEN...?
WELL, I'VE BEEN MEANING TO TALK TO YOU FOR A WHILE NOW...
YOU'RE SMART, AREN'T YOU?
YOU GOTTA USE THOSE SMARTS OF YOURS.

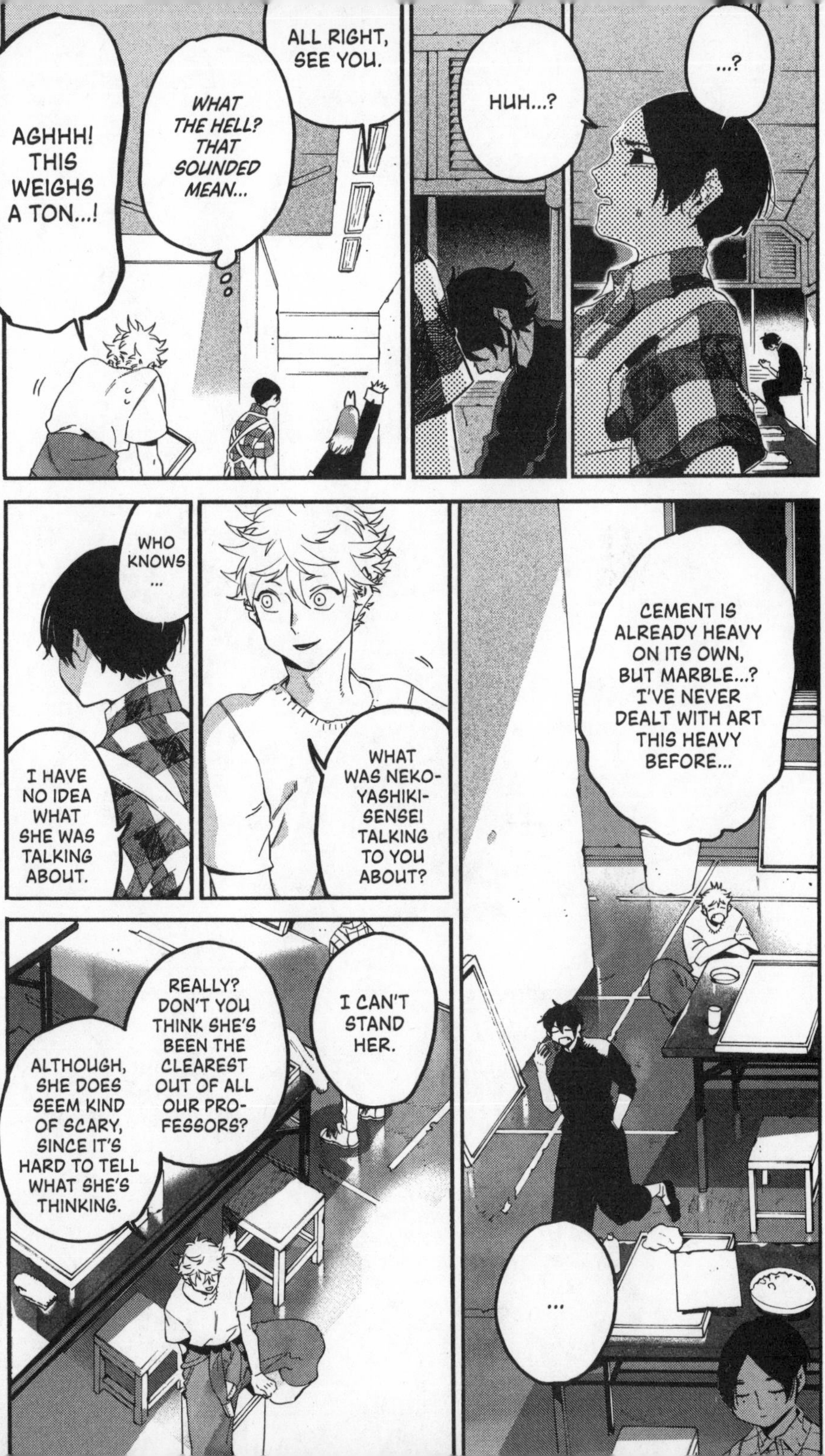
...?
HUH...?
ALL RIGHT, SEE YOU.
WHAT THE HELL? THAT SOUNDED MEAN...
AGHHH! THIS WEIGHS A TON...!
CEMENT IS ALREADY HEAVY ON ITS OWN, BUT MARBLE...? I'VE NEVER DEALT WITH ART THIS HEAVY BEFORE...
...
WHAT WAS NEKO-YASHIKI-SENSEI TALKING TO YOU ABOUT?
WHO KNOWS...
I HAVE NO IDEA WHAT SHE WAS TALKING ABOUT.
I CAN'T STAND HER.
REALLY? DON'T YOU THINK SHE'S BEEN THE CLEAREST OUT OF ALL OUR PRO-FESSORS?
ALTHOUGH, SHE DOES SEEM KIND OF SCARY, SINCE IT'S HARD TO TELL WHAT SHE'S THINKING.

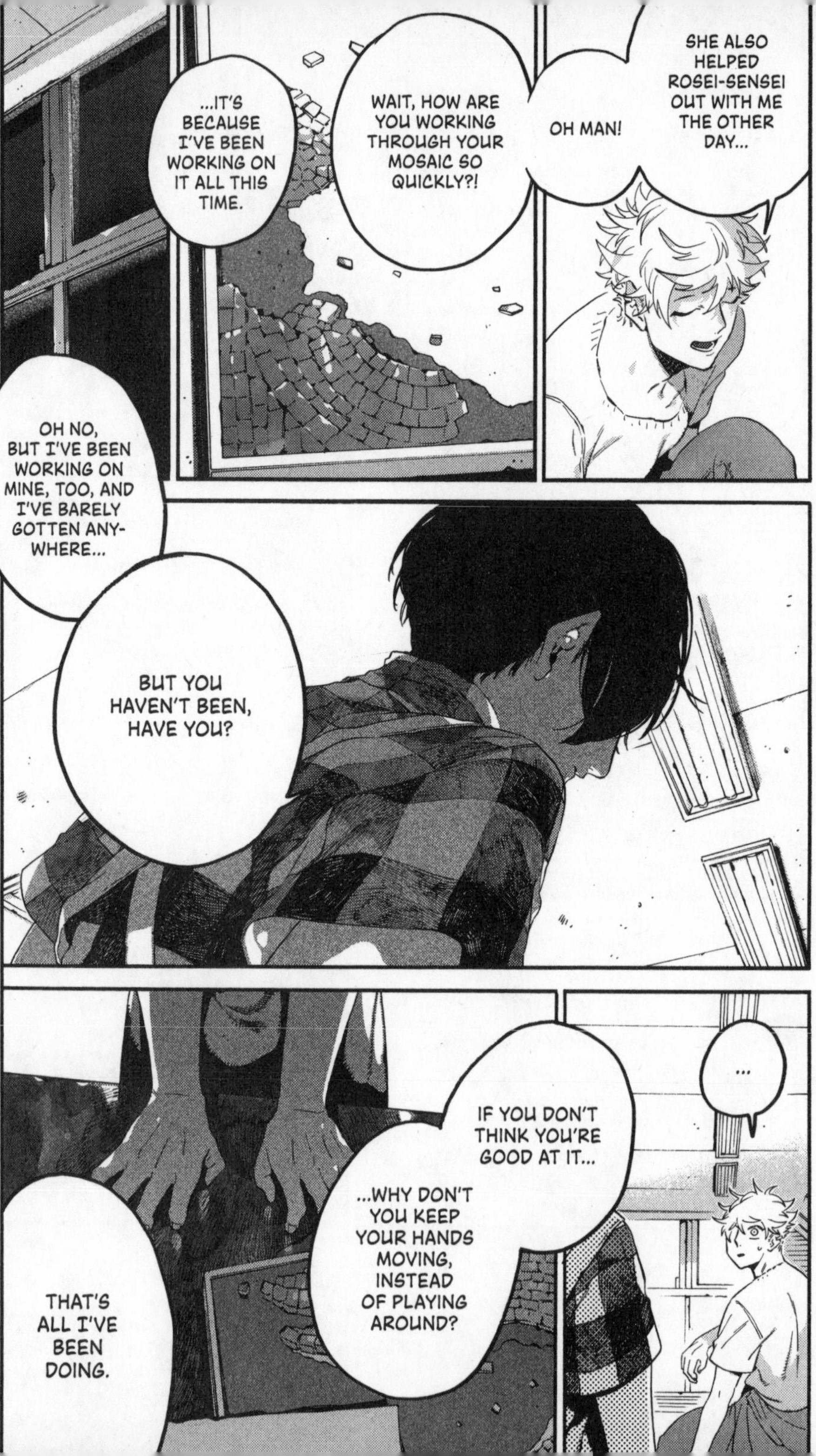
SHE ALSO HELPED ROSEI-SENSEI OUT WITH ME THE OTHER DAY...
OH MAN!
WAIT, HOW ARE YOU WORKING THROUGH YOUR MOSAIC SO QUICKLY?!
...IT'S BECAUSE I'VE BEEN WORKING ON IT ALL THIS TIME.
OH NO, BUT I'VE BEEN WORKING ON MINE, TOO, AND I'VE BARELY GOTTEN ANY-WHERE...
BUT YOU HAVEN'T BEEN, HAVE YOU?
...
IF YOU DON'T THINK YOU'RE GOOD AT IT...
...WHY DON'T YOU KEEP YOUR HANDS MOVING, INSTEAD OF PLAYING AROUND?
THAT'S ALL I'VE BEEN DOING.

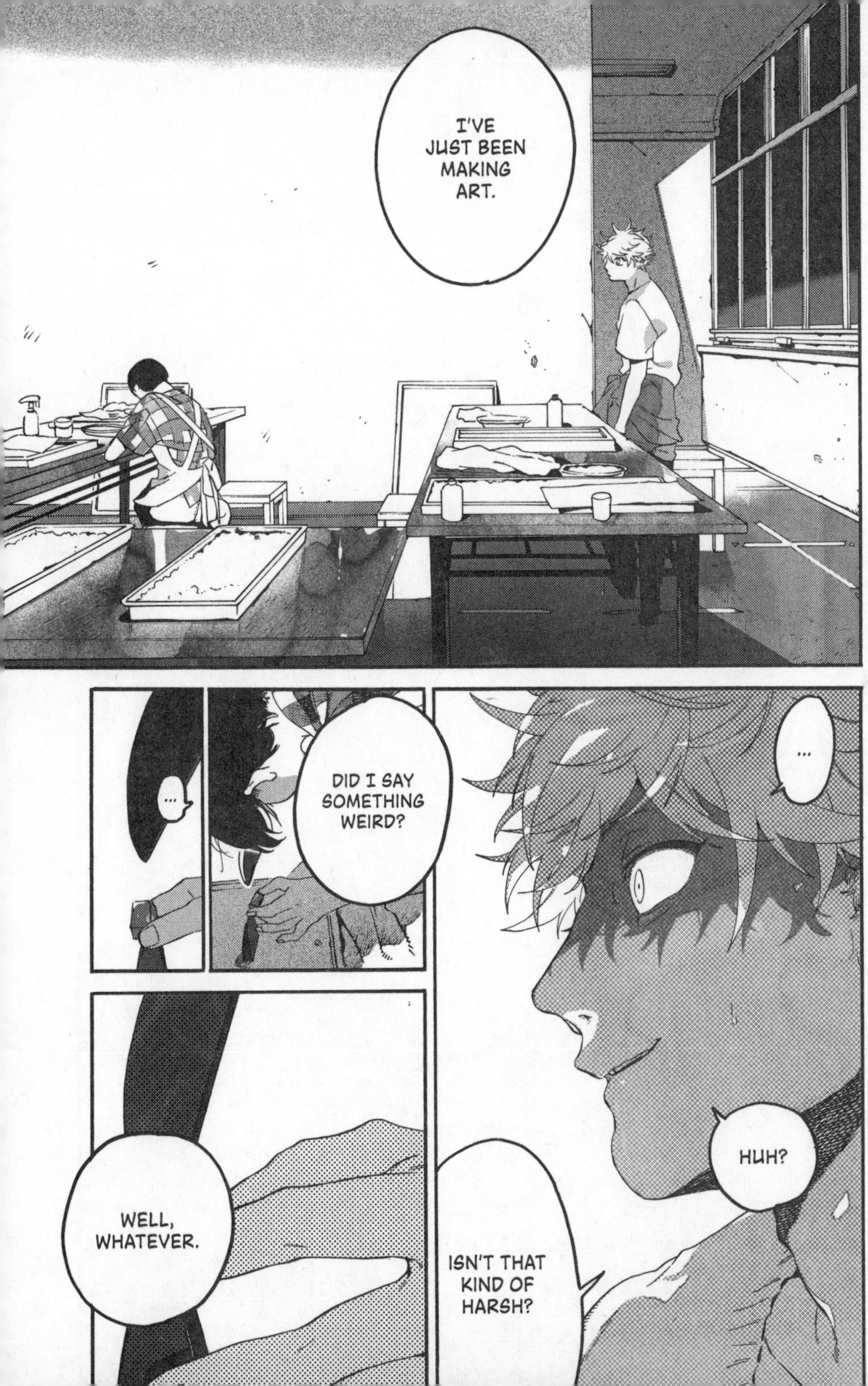
I'VE JUST BEEN MAKING ART.
...
HUH?
ISN'T THAT KIND OF HARSH?
DID I SAY SOMETHING WEIRD?
...
WELL, WHATEVER.

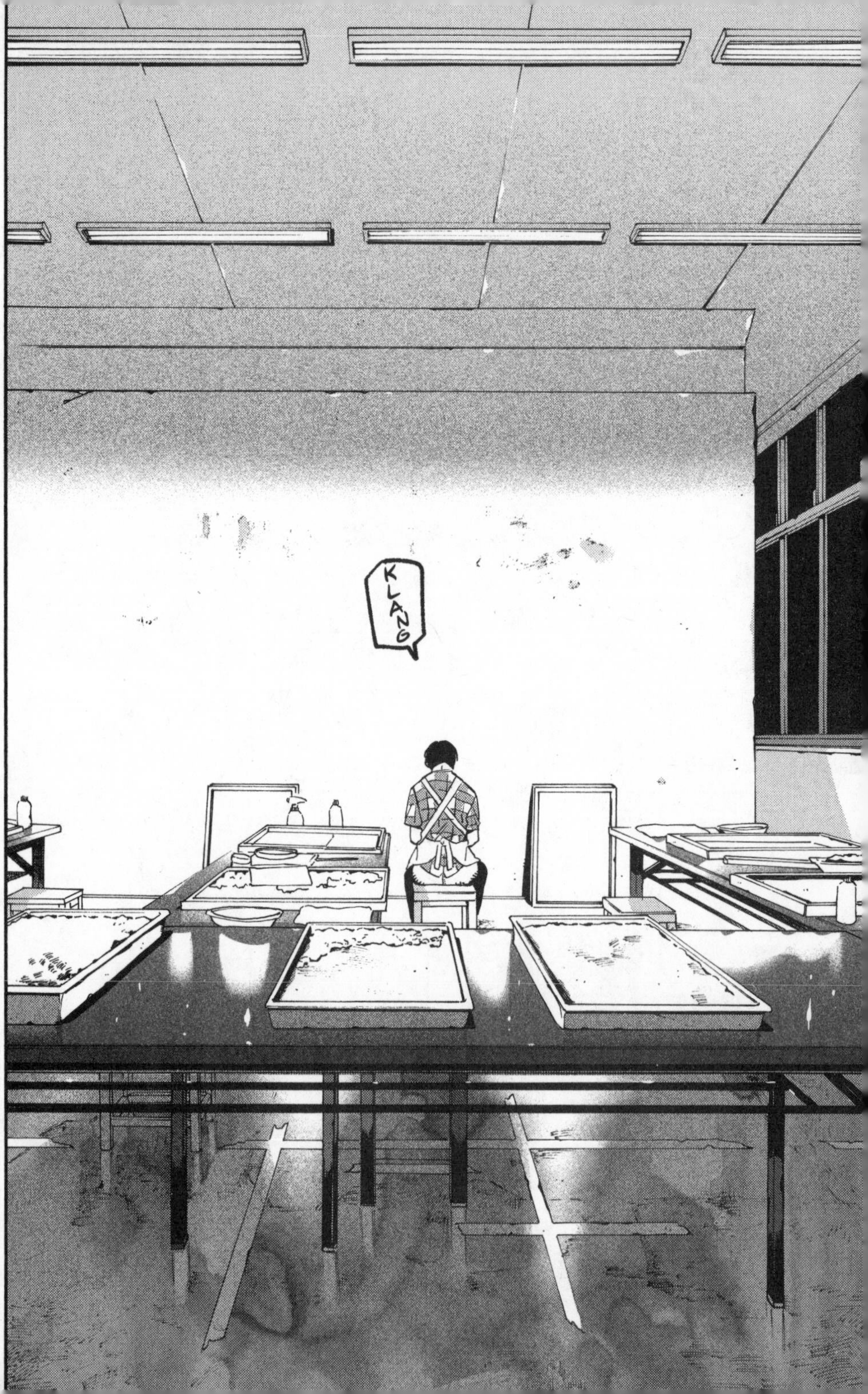
KLANG

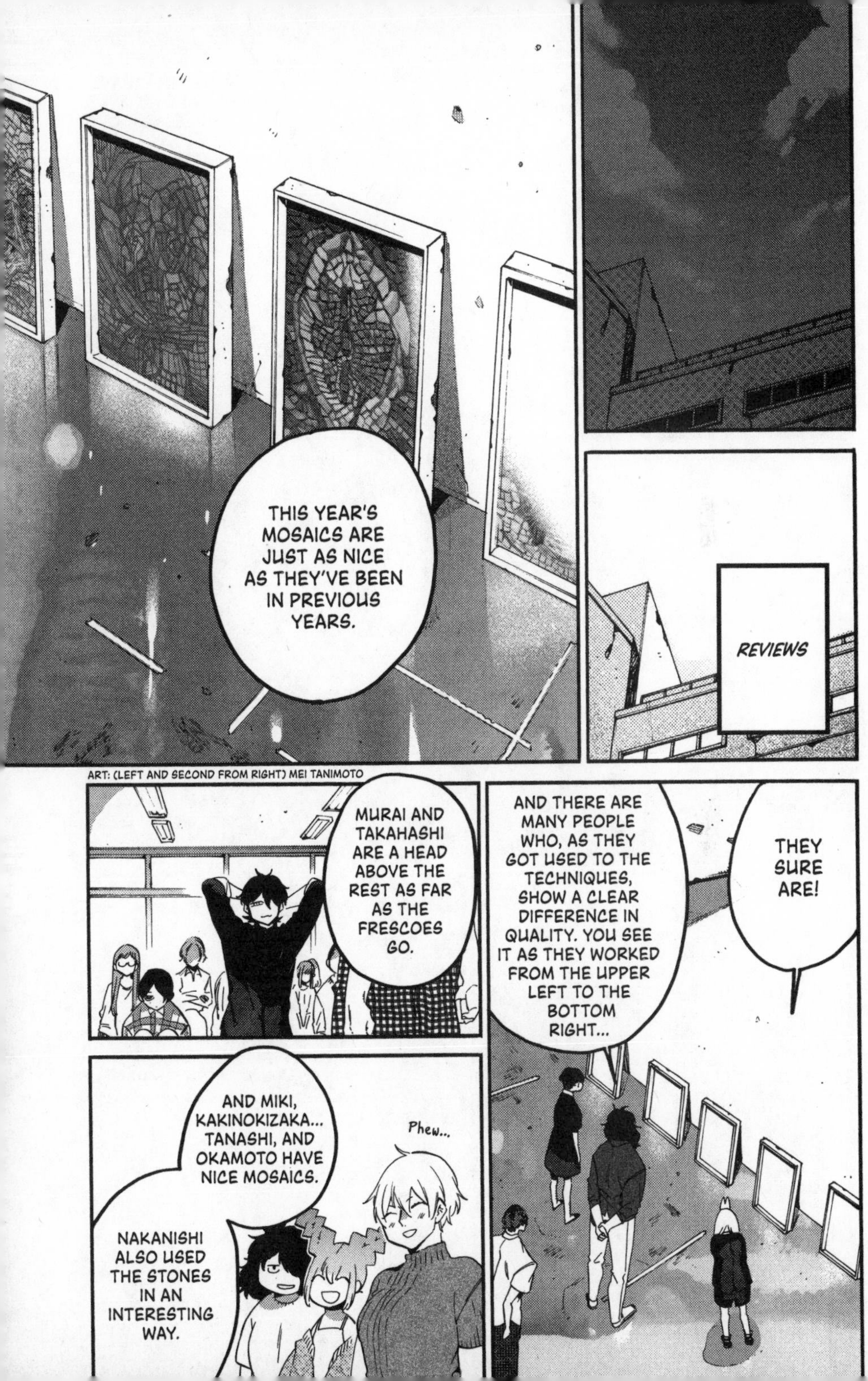
REVIEWS
THIS YEAR'S MOSAICS ARE JUST AS NICE AS THEY'VE BEEN IN PREVIOUS YEARS.
ART: (LEFT AND SECOND FROM RIGHT) MEI TANIMOTO
THEY SURE ARE!
AND THERE ARE MANY PEOPLE WHO, AS THEY GOT USED TO THE TECHNIQUES, SHOW A CLEAR DIFFERENCE IN QUALITY. YOU SEE IT AS THEY WORKED FROM THE UPPER LEFT TO THE BOTTOM RIGHT...
MURAI AND TAKAHASHI ARE A HEAD ABOVE THE REST AS FAR AS THE FRESCOES GO.
AND MIKI, KAKINOKIZAKA... TANASHI, AND OKAMOTO HAVE NICE MOSAICS.
Phew...
NAKANISHI ALSO USED THE STONES IN AN INTERESTING WAY.

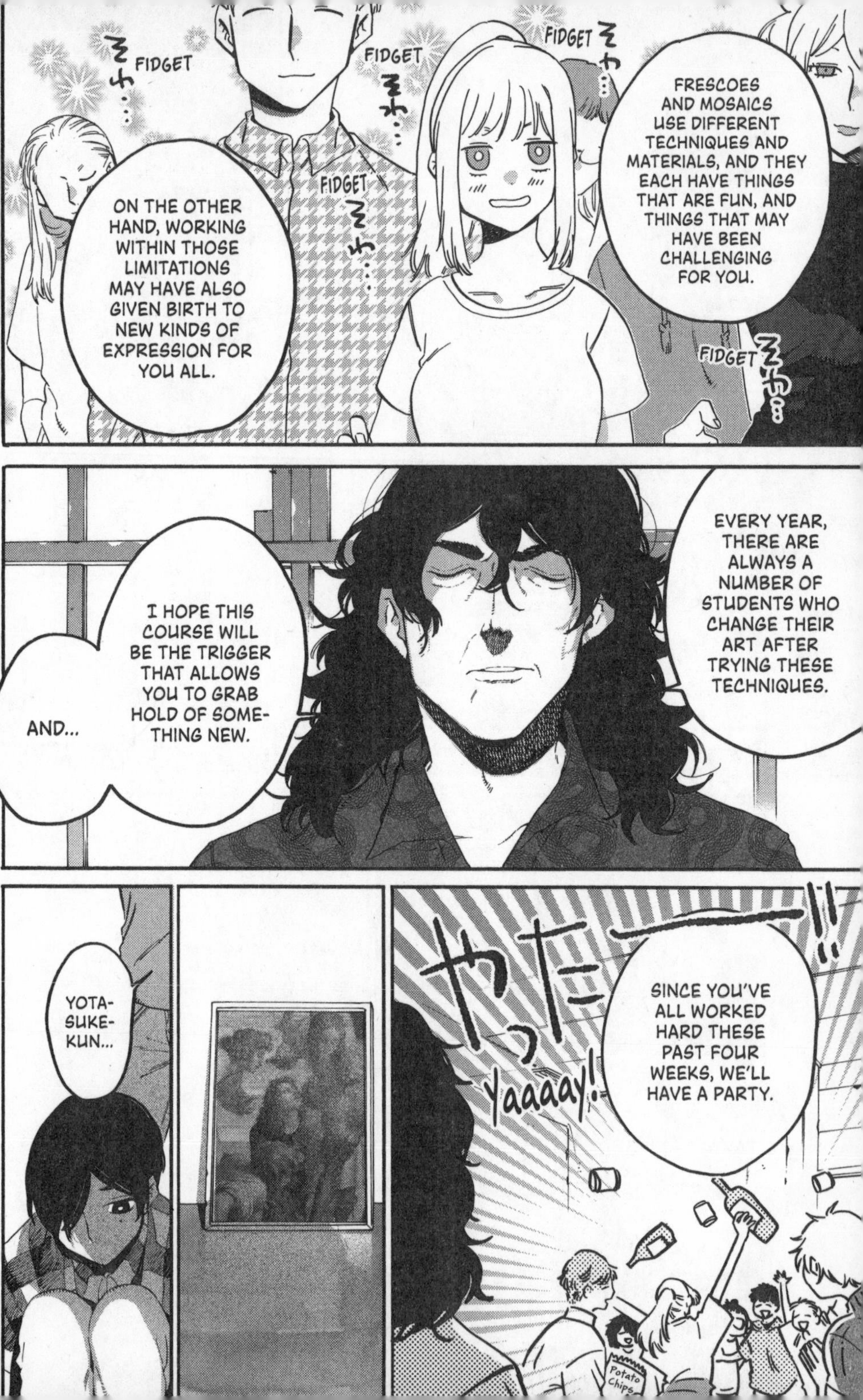
FRESCOES AND MOSAICS USE DIFFERENT TECHNIQUES AND MATERIALS, AND THEY EACH HAVE THINGS THAT ARE FUN, AND THINGS THAT MAY HAVE BEEN CHALLENGING FOR YOU.
FIDGET ざわ…
FIDGET ざわ…
FIDGET ざわ…
FIDGET ざわ…
FIDGET ざわ…
ON THE OTHER HAND, WORKING WITHIN THOSE LIMITATIONS MAY HAVE ALSO GIVEN BIRTH TO NEW KINDS OF EXPRESSION FOR YOU ALL.
EVERY YEAR, THERE ARE ALWAYS A NUMBER OF STUDENTS WHO CHANGE THEIR ART AFTER TRYING THESE TECHNIQUES.
I HOPE THIS COURSE WILL BE THE TRIGGER THAT ALLOWS YOU TO GRAB HOLD OF SOME-THING NEW.
AND...
SINCE YOU'VE ALL WORKED HARD THESE PAST FOUR WEEKS, WE'LL HAVE A PARTY.
やったーー!!
Yaaaay!
Potato Chips
YOTA-SUKE-KUN...

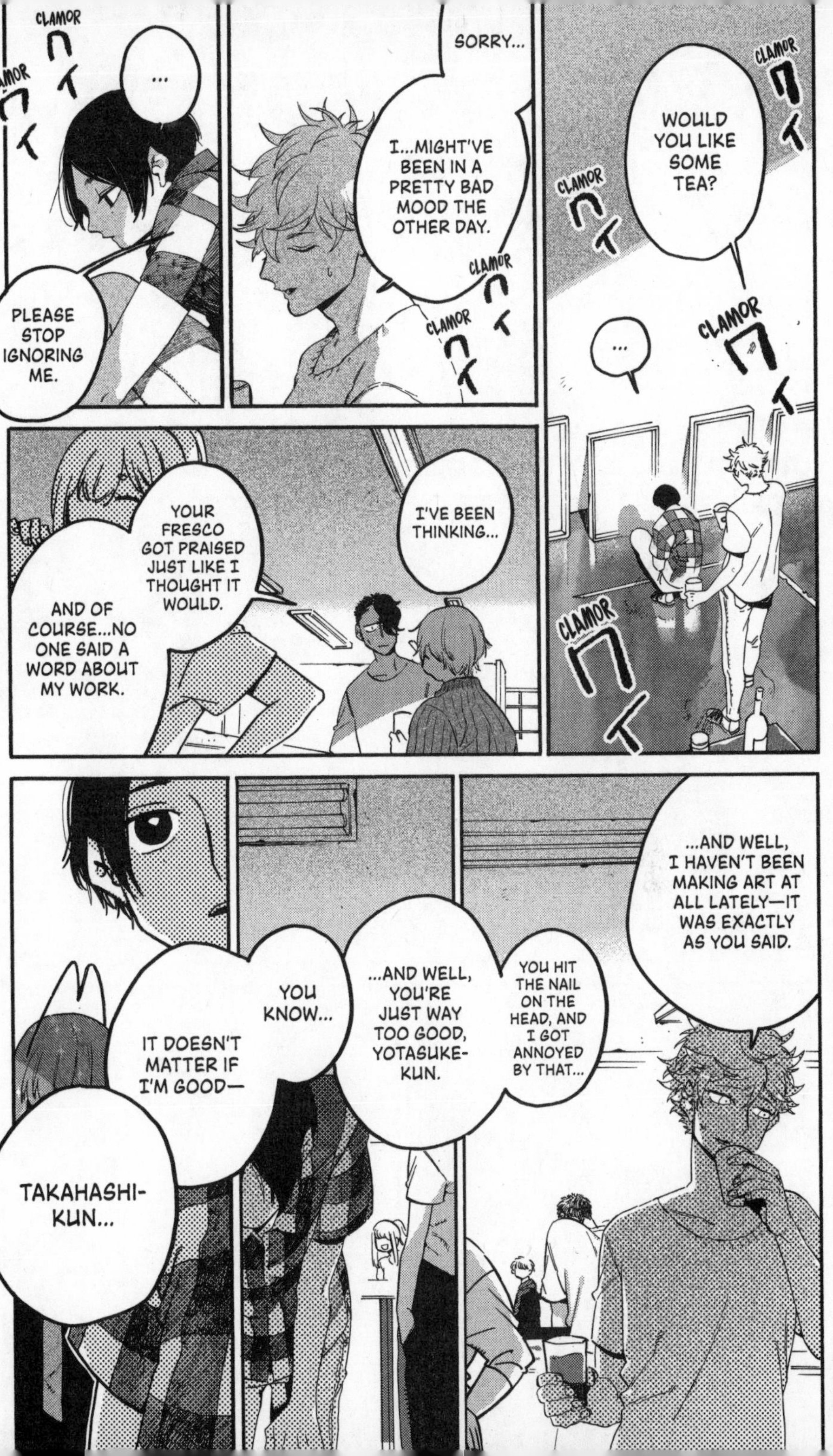
CLAMOR
WOULD YOU LIKE SOME TEA?
CLAMOR
CLAMOR
...
CLAMOR
SORRY...
I...MIGHT'VE BEEN IN A PRETTY BAD MOOD THE OTHER DAY.
CLAMOR
CLAMOR
CLAMOR
CLAMOR
...
PLEASE STOP IGNORING ME.
I'VE BEEN THINKING...
YOUR FRESCO GOT PRAISED JUST LIKE I THOUGHT IT WOULD.
AND OF COURSE...NO ONE SAID A WORD ABOUT MY WORK.
...AND WELL, I HAVEN'T BEEN MAKING ART AT ALL LATELY—IT WAS EXACTLY AS YOU SAID.
YOU HIT THE NAIL ON THE HEAD, AND I GOT ANNOYED BY THAT...
...AND WELL, YOU'RE JUST WAY TOO GOOD, YOTASUKE-KUN.
YOU KNOW...
IT DOESN'T MATTER IF I'M GOOD—
TAKAHASHI-KUN...

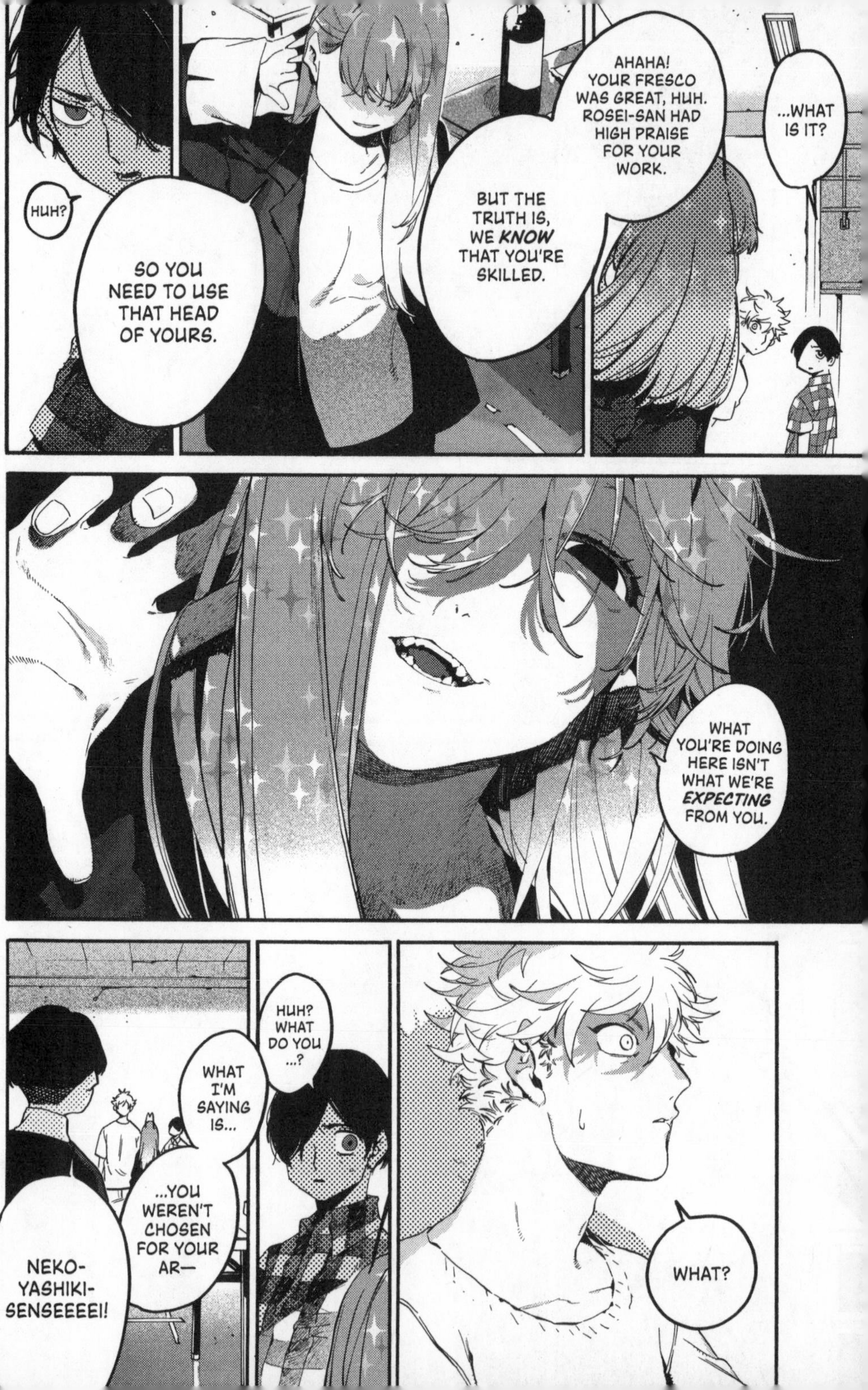
...WHAT IS IT?
AHAHA! YOUR FRESCO WAS GREAT, HUH. ROSEI-SAN HAD HIGH PRAISE FOR YOUR WORK.
BUT THE TRUTH IS, WE *KNOW* THAT YOU'RE SKILLED.
SO YOU NEED TO USE THAT HEAD OF YOURS.
HUH?
WHAT YOU'RE DOING HERE ISN'T WHAT WE'RE *EXPECTING* FROM YOU.
WHAT?
HUH? WHAT DO YOU ...?
WHAT I'M SAYING IS...
...YOU WEREN'T CHOSEN FOR YOUR AR—
NEKO-YASHIKI-SENSEEEEI!

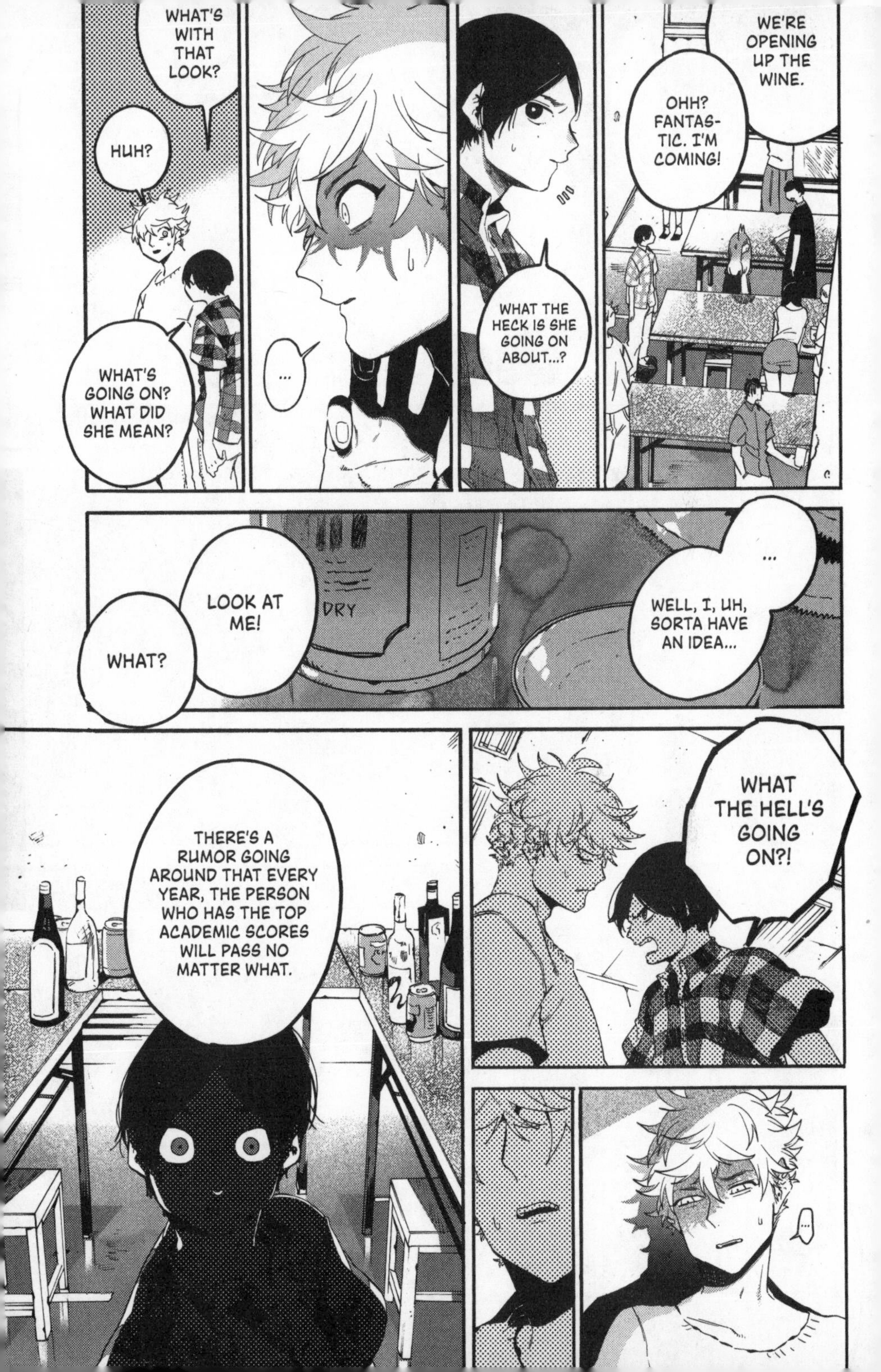
WE'RE OPENING UP THE WINE.
OHH? FANTASTIC. I'M COMING!
WHAT THE HECK IS SHE GOING ON ABOUT...?
...
WHAT'S WITH THAT LOOK?
HUH?
WHAT'S GOING ON? WHAT DID SHE MEAN?
...
WELL, I, UH, SORTA HAVE AN IDEA...
DRY
LOOK AT ME!
WHAT?
WHAT THE HELL'S GOING ON?!
...
THERE'S A RUMOR GOING AROUND THAT EVERY YEAR, THE PERSON WHO HAS THE TOP ACADEMIC SCORES WILL PASS NO MATTER WHAT.

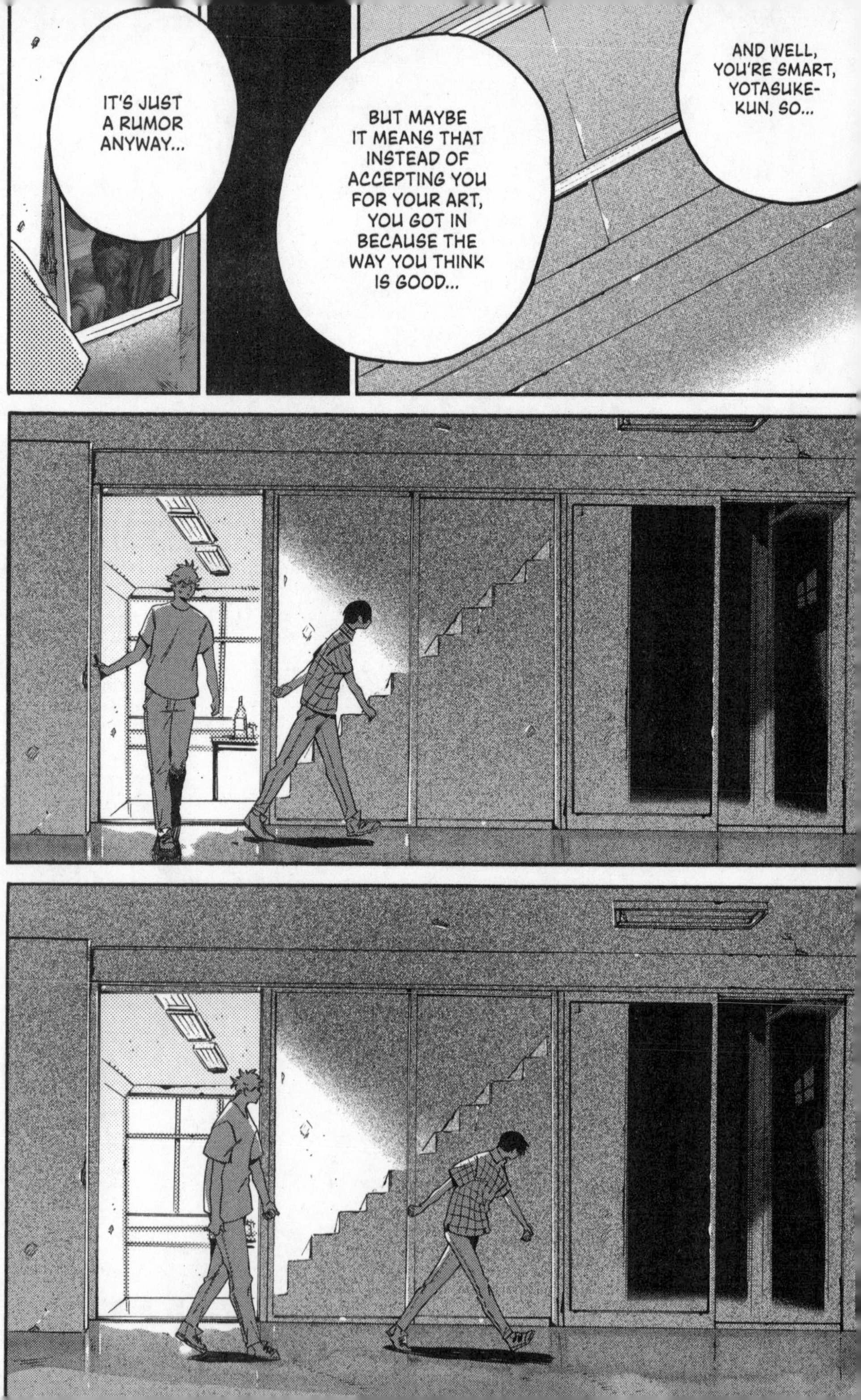
AND WELL, YOU'RE SMART, YOTASUKE-KUN, SO...
BUT MAYBE IT MEANS THAT INSTEAD OF ACCEPTING YOU FOR YOUR ART, YOU GOT IN BECAUSE THE WAY YOU THINK IS GOOD...
IT'S JUST A RUMOR ANYWAY...

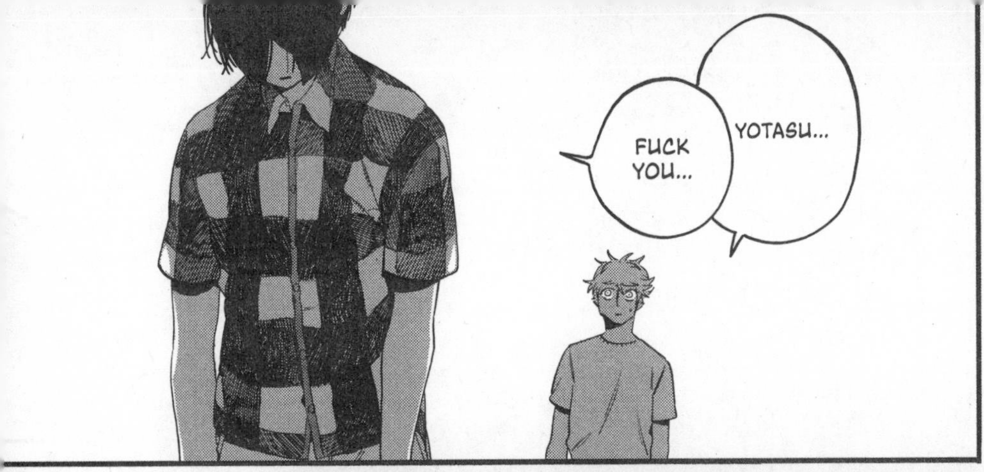
YOTASU...
FUCK YOU...

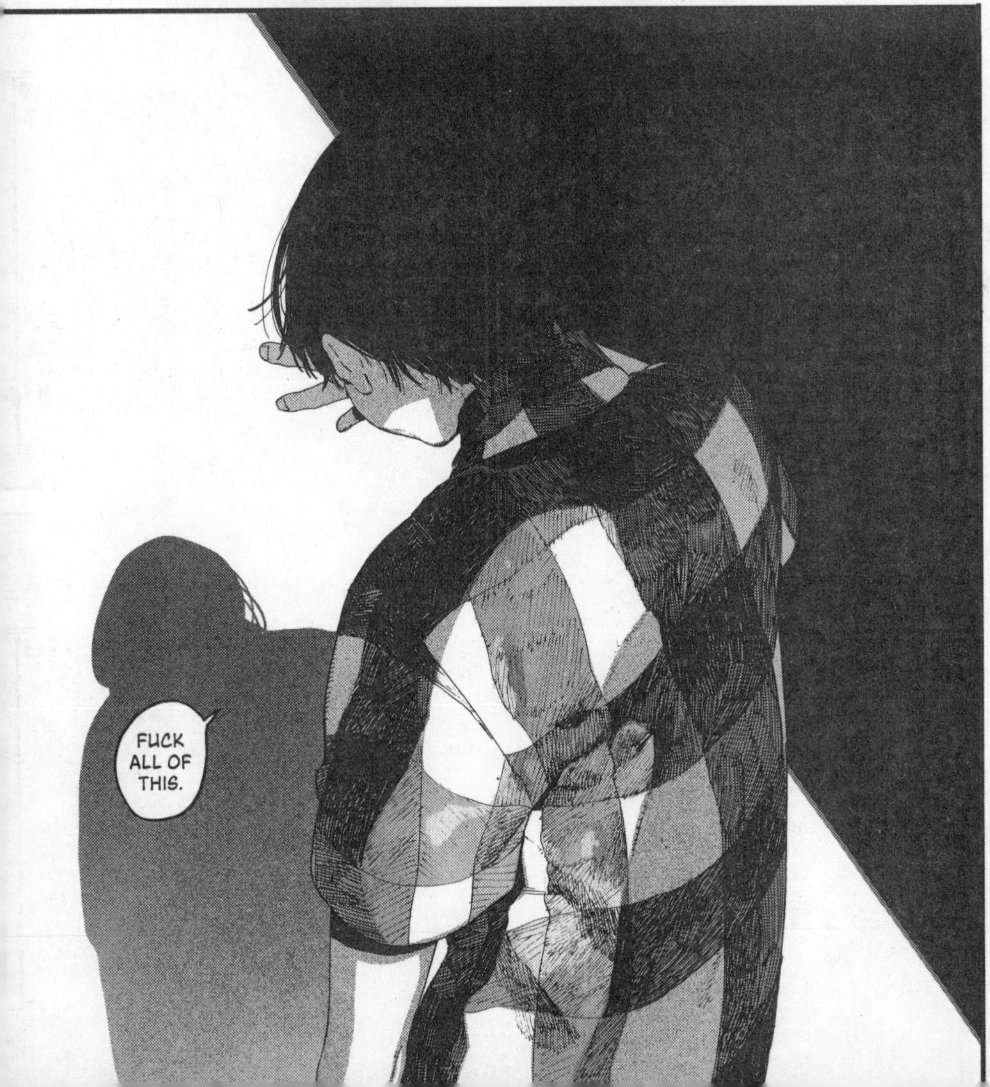
FUCK ALL OF THIS.

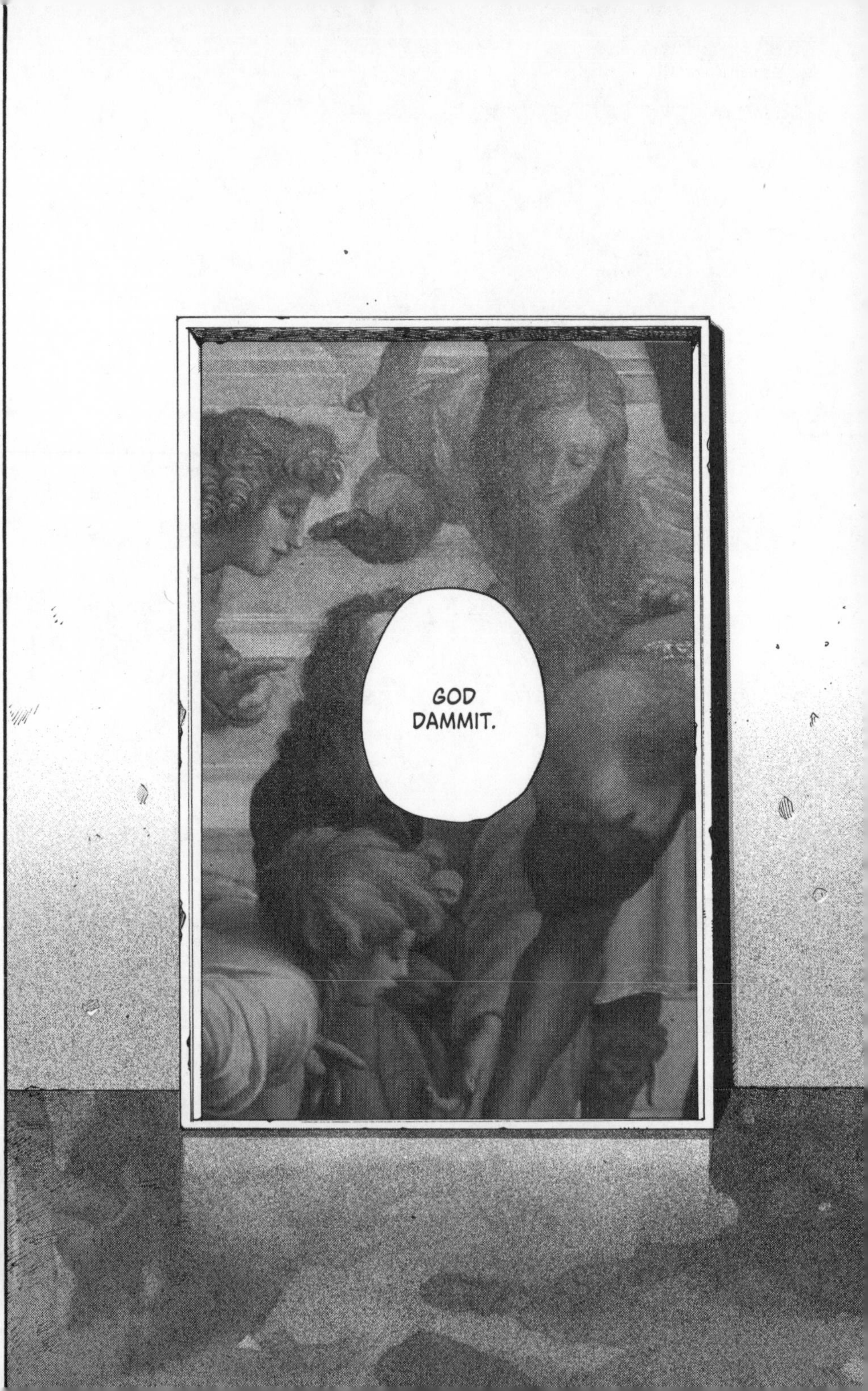
GOD DAMMIT.

STROKE 37

ARMOR-CLAD VENUS

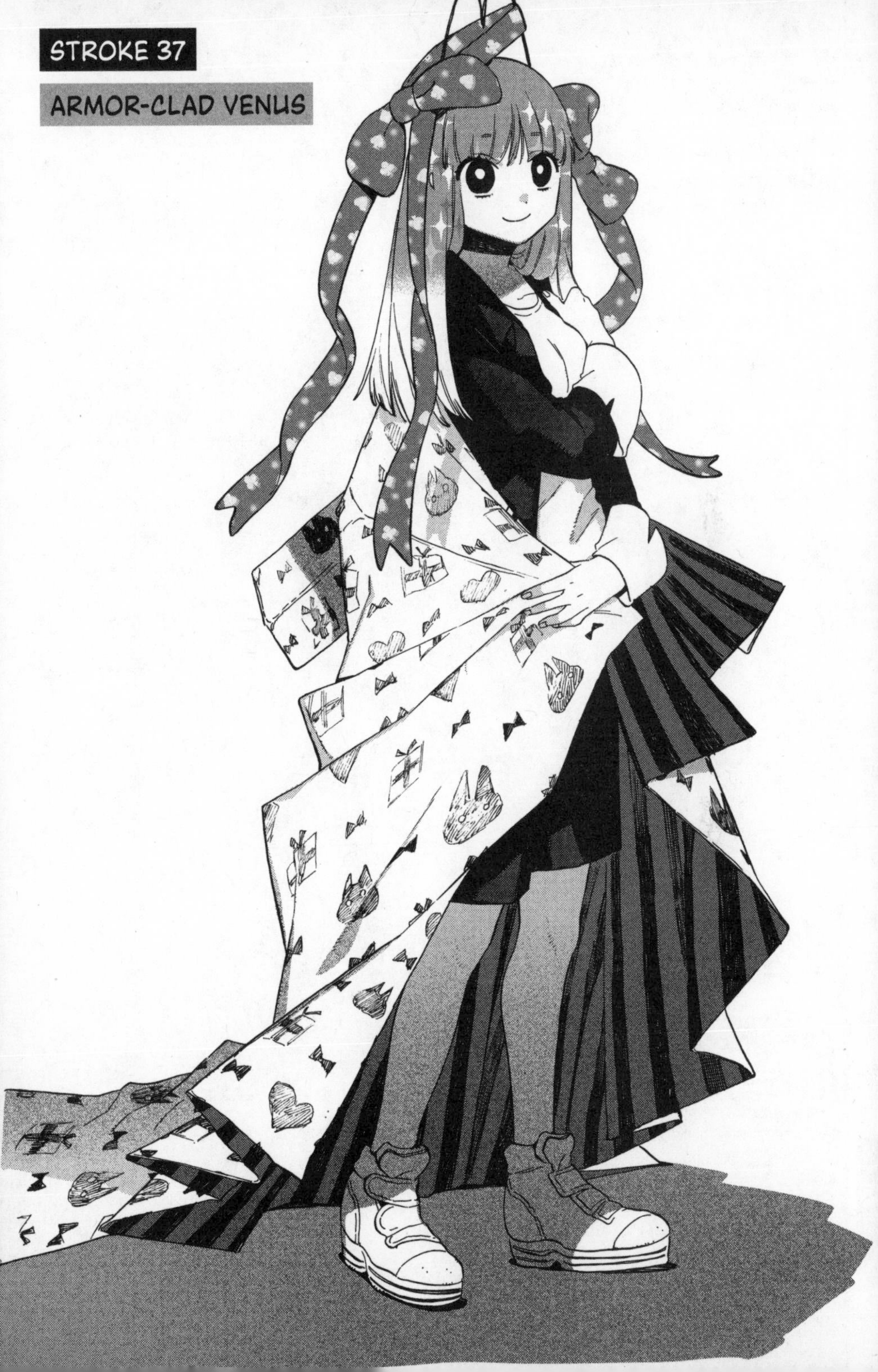

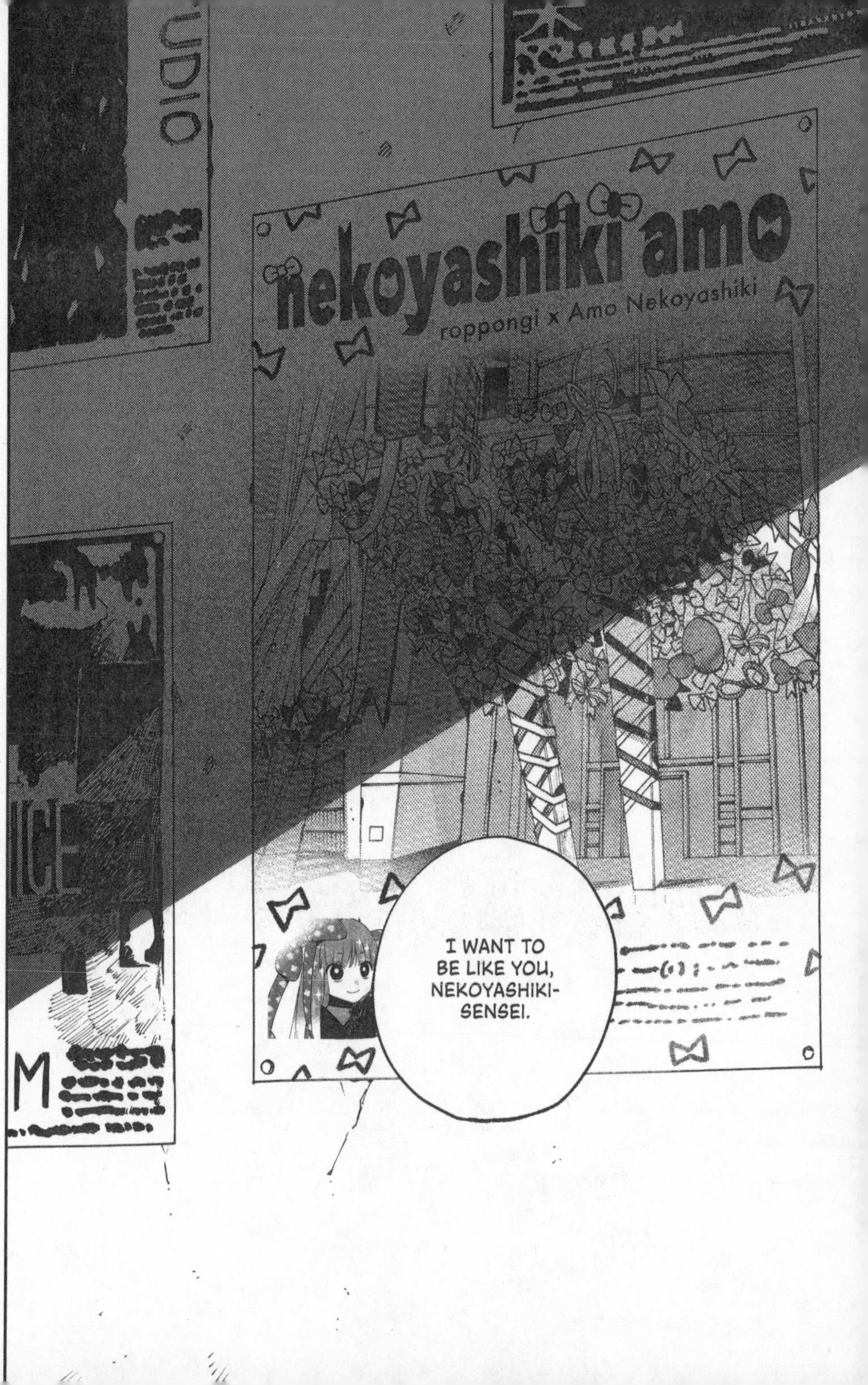
UDIO
nekoyashiki amo
roppongi x Amo Nekoyashiki
I WANT TO BE LIKE YOU, NEKOYASHIKI-SENSEI.

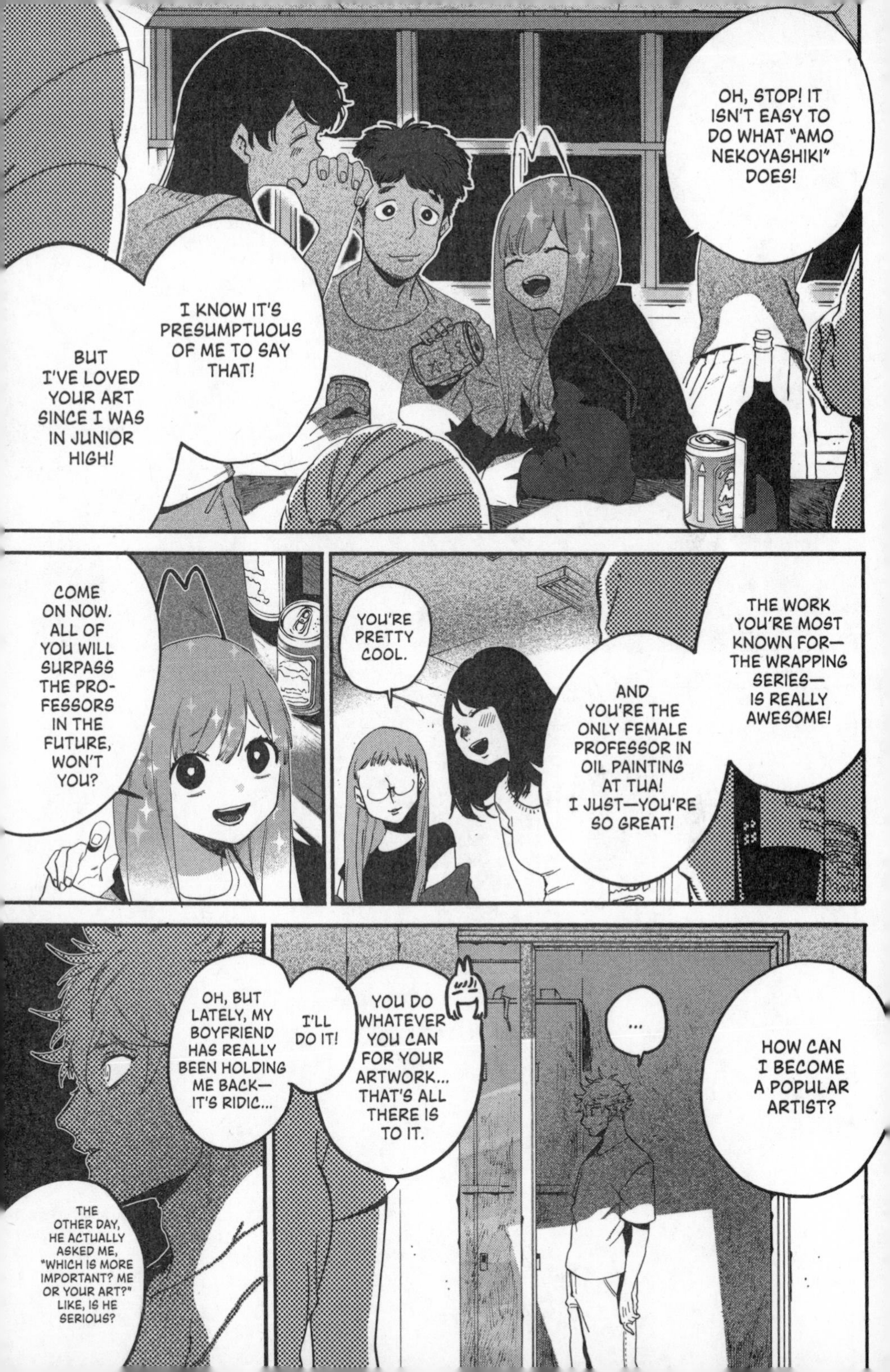
OH, STOP! IT ISN'T EASY TO DO WHAT "AMO NEKOYASHIKI" DOES!
I KNOW IT'S PRESUMPTUOUS OF ME TO SAY THAT!
BUT I'VE LOVED YOUR ART SINCE I WAS IN JUNIOR HIGH!
THE WORK YOU'RE MOST KNOWN FOR—THE WRAPPING SERIES—IS REALLY AWESOME!
AND YOU'RE THE ONLY FEMALE PROFESSOR IN OIL PAINTING AT TUA! I JUST—YOU'RE SO GREAT!
YOU'RE PRETTY COOL.
COME ON NOW. ALL OF YOU WILL SURPASS THE PRO-FESSORS IN THE FUTURE, WON'T YOU?
HOW CAN I BECOME A POPULAR ARTIST?
...
YOU DO WHATEVER YOU CAN FOR YOUR ARTWORK... THAT'S ALL THERE IS TO IT.
I'LL DO IT!
OH, BUT LATELY, MY BOYFRIEND HAS REALLY BEEN HOLDING ME BACK—IT'S RIDIC...
THE OTHER DAY, HE ACTUALLY ASKED ME, "WHICH IS MORE IMPORTANT? ME OR YOUR ART?" LIKE, IS HE SERIOUS?

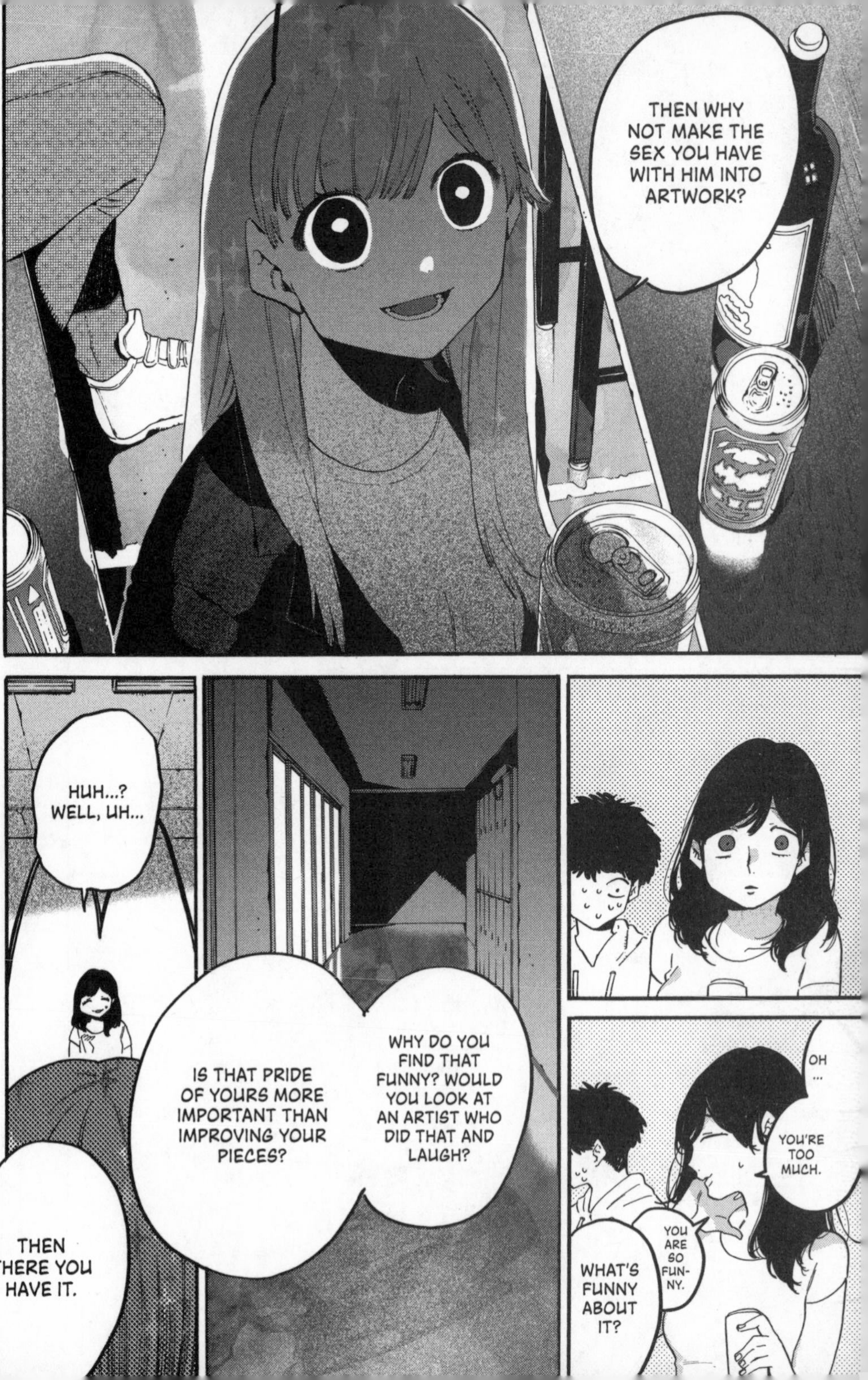
THEN WHY NOT MAKE THE SEX YOU HAVE WITH HIM INTO ARTWORK?
HUH...? WELL, UH...
OH ...
YOU'RE TOO MUCH.
YOU ARE SO FUN-NY.
WHAT'S FUNNY ABOUT IT?
WHY DO YOU FIND THAT FUNNY? WOULD YOU LOOK AT AN ARTIST WHO DID THAT AND LAUGH?
IS THAT PRIDE OF YOURS MORE IMPORTANT THAN IMPROVING YOUR PIECES?
THEN THERE YOU HAVE IT.

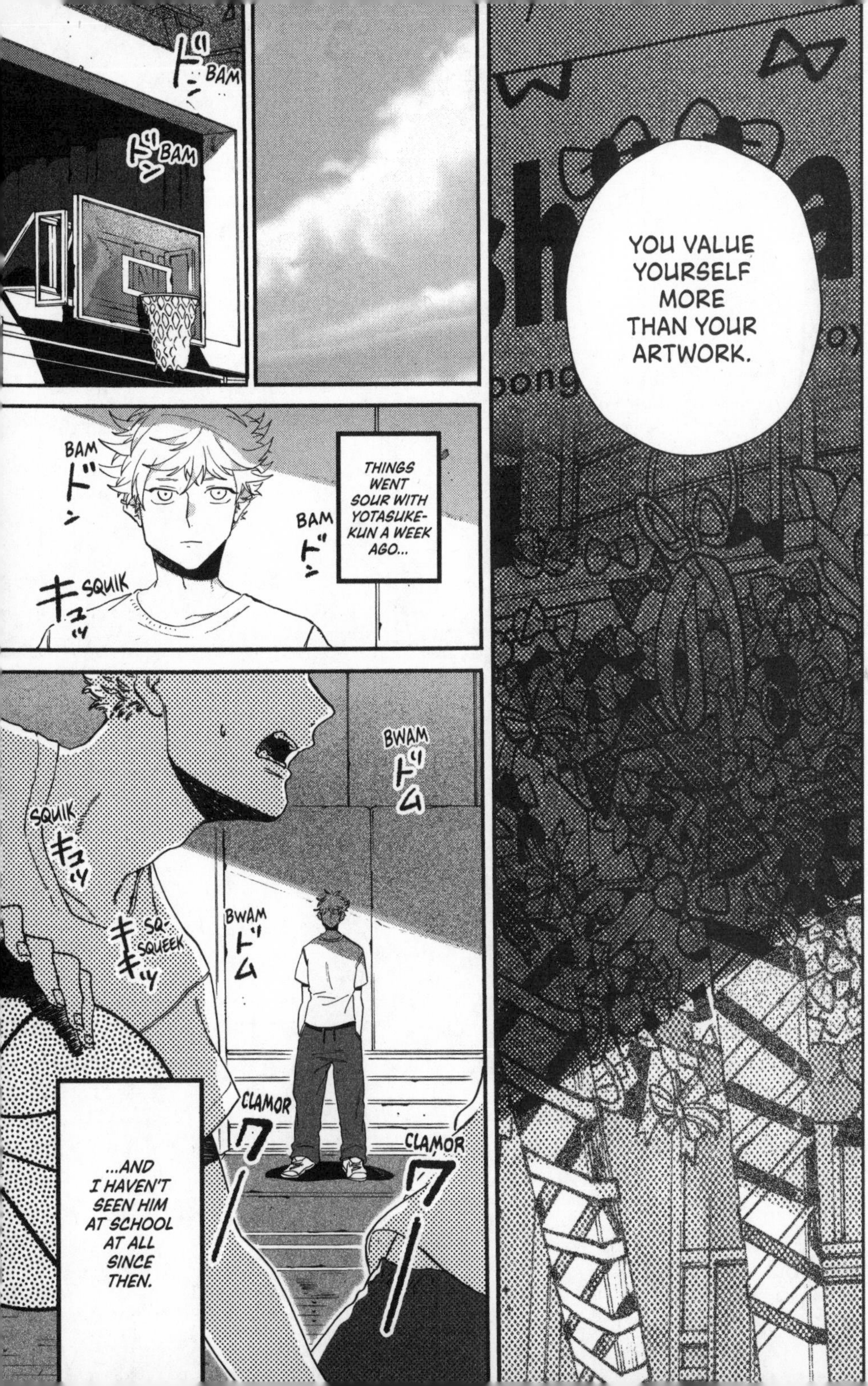

YOU VALUE YOURSELF MORE THAN YOUR ARTWORK.
ドッ BAM
ドッ BAM
THINGS WENT SOUR WITH YOTASUKE-KUN A WEEK AGO...
BAM ドン
BAM ドン
キュッ SQUIK
BWAM ドム
SQUIK キュッ
SQ-SQUEEK キキッ
BWAM ドム
CLAMOR ワ
CLAMOR ワ
...AND I HAVEN'T SEEN HIM AT SCHOOL AT ALL SINCE THEN.

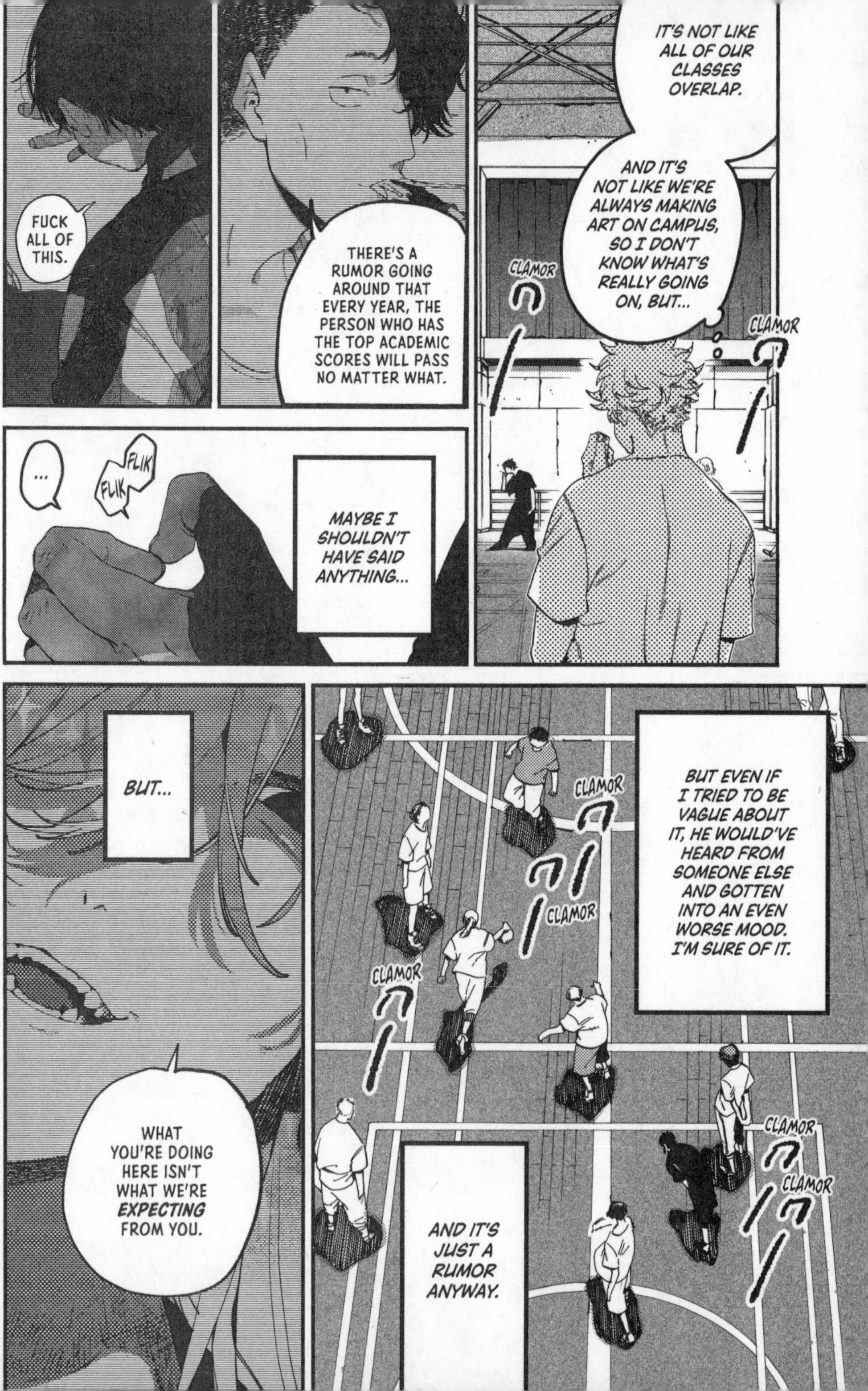
IT'S NOT LIKE ALL OF OUR CLASSES OVERLAP.
AND IT'S NOT LIKE WE'RE ALWAYS MAKING ART ON CAMPUS, SO I DON'T KNOW WHAT'S REALLY GOING ON, BUT...
CLAMOR
CLAMOR
THERE'S A RUMOR GOING AROUND THAT EVERY YEAR, THE PERSON WHO HAS THE TOP ACADEMIC SCORES WILL PASS NO MATTER WHAT.
FUCK ALL OF THIS.
MAYBE I SHOULDN'T HAVE SAID ANYTHING...
FLIK
FLIK
...
BUT EVEN IF I TRIED TO BE VAGUE ABOUT IT, HE WOULD'VE HEARD FROM SOMEONE ELSE AND GOTTEN INTO AN EVEN WORSE MOOD. I'M SURE OF IT.
CLAMOR
CLAMOR
CLAMOR
CLAMOR
CLAMOR
AND IT'S JUST A RUMOR ANYWAY.
BUT...
WHAT YOU'RE DOING HERE ISN'T WHAT WE'RE *EXPECTING* FROM YOU.

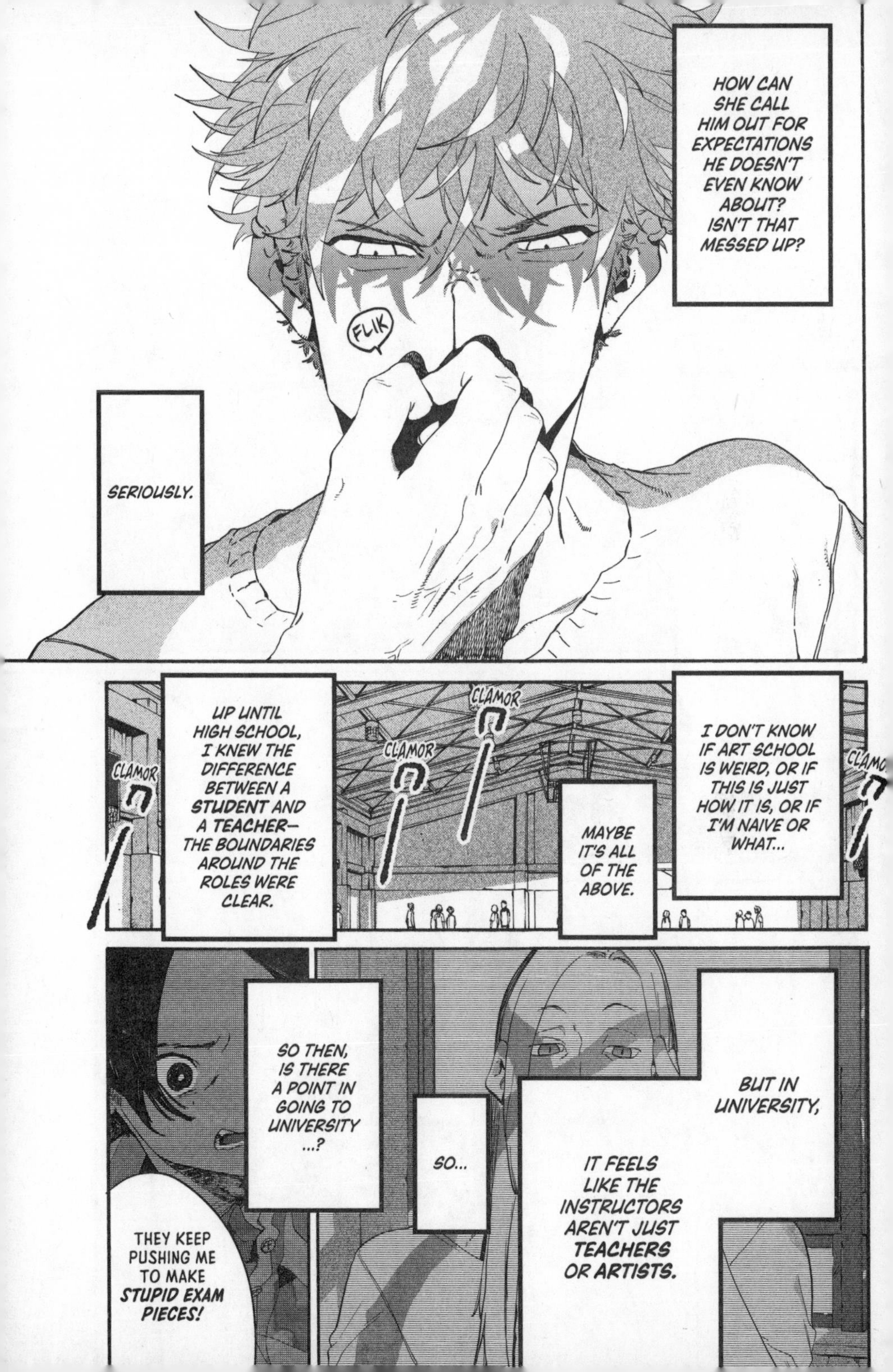
HOW CAN SHE CALL HIM OUT FOR EXPECTATIONS HE DOESN'T EVEN KNOW ABOUT? ISN'T THAT MESSED UP?
FLIK
SERIOUSLY.
I DON'T KNOW IF ART SCHOOL IS WEIRD, OR IF THIS IS JUST HOW IT IS, OR IF I'M NAIVE OR WHAT...
MAYBE IT'S ALL OF THE ABOVE.
CLAMOR
CLAMOR
UP UNTIL HIGH SCHOOL, I KNEW THE DIFFERENCE BETWEEN A STUDENT AND A TEACHER— THE BOUNDARIES AROUND THE ROLES WERE CLEAR.
CLAMOR
BUT IN UNIVERSITY,
IT FEELS LIKE THE INSTRUCTORS AREN'T JUST TEACHERS OR ARTISTS.
SO...
SO THEN, IS THERE A POINT IN GOING TO UNIVERSITY ...?
THEY KEEP PUSHING ME TO MAKE STUPID EXAM PIECES!

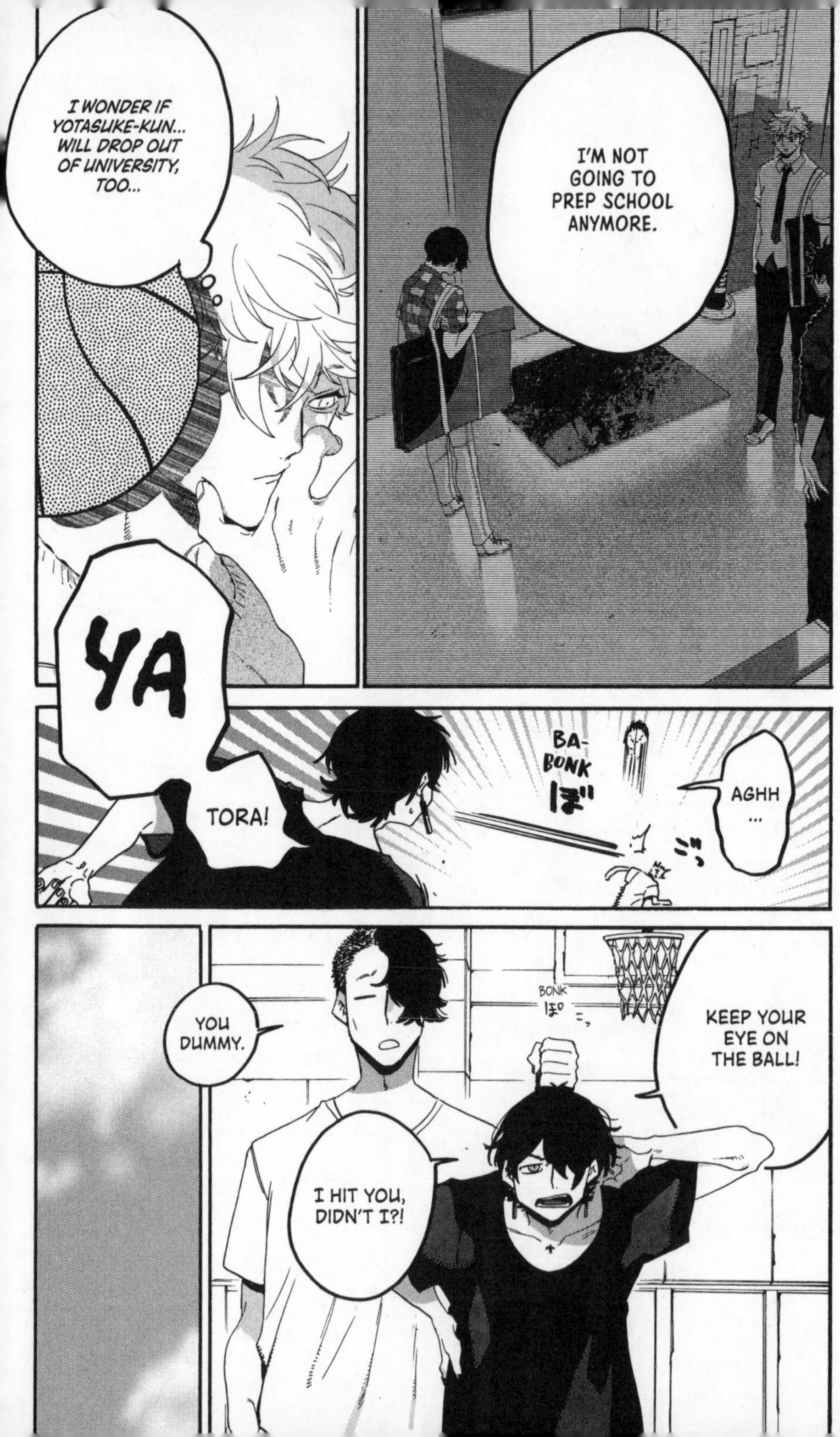
I'M NOT GOING TO PREP SCHOOL ANYMORE.
I WONDER IF YOTASUKE-KUN... WILL DROP OUT OF UNIVERSITY, TOO...
YA
TORA!
AGHH ...
BA-BONK
ぼ
KEEP YOUR EYE ON THE BALL!
BONK
ぽ
YOU DUMMY.
I HIT YOU, DIDN'T I?!

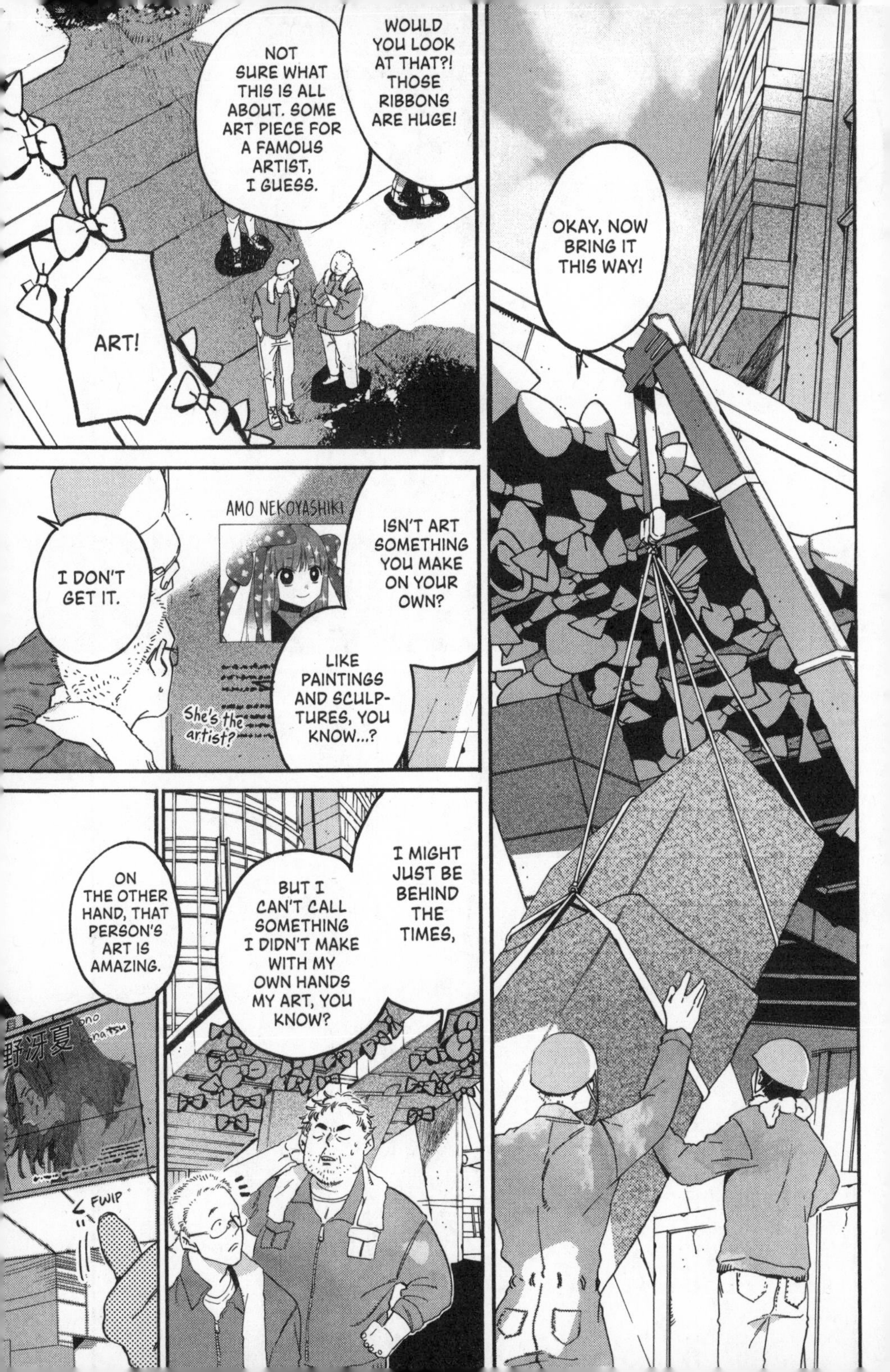
OKAY, NOW BRING IT THIS WAY!
WOULD YOU LOOK AT THAT?! THOSE RIBBONS ARE HUGE!
NOT SURE WHAT THIS IS ALL ABOUT. SOME ART PIECE FOR A FAMOUS ARTIST, I GUESS.
ART!
ISN'T ART SOMETHING YOU MAKE ON YOUR OWN?
AMO NEKOYASHIKI
LIKE PAINTINGS AND SCULP-TURES, YOU KNOW...?
I DON'T GET IT.
She's the artist?
I MIGHT JUST BE BEHIND THE TIMES,
BUT I CAN'T CALL SOMETHING I DIDN'T MAKE WITH MY OWN HANDS MY ART, YOU KNOW?
ON THE OTHER HAND, THAT PERSON'S ART IS AMAZING.
野冴夏
FWIP

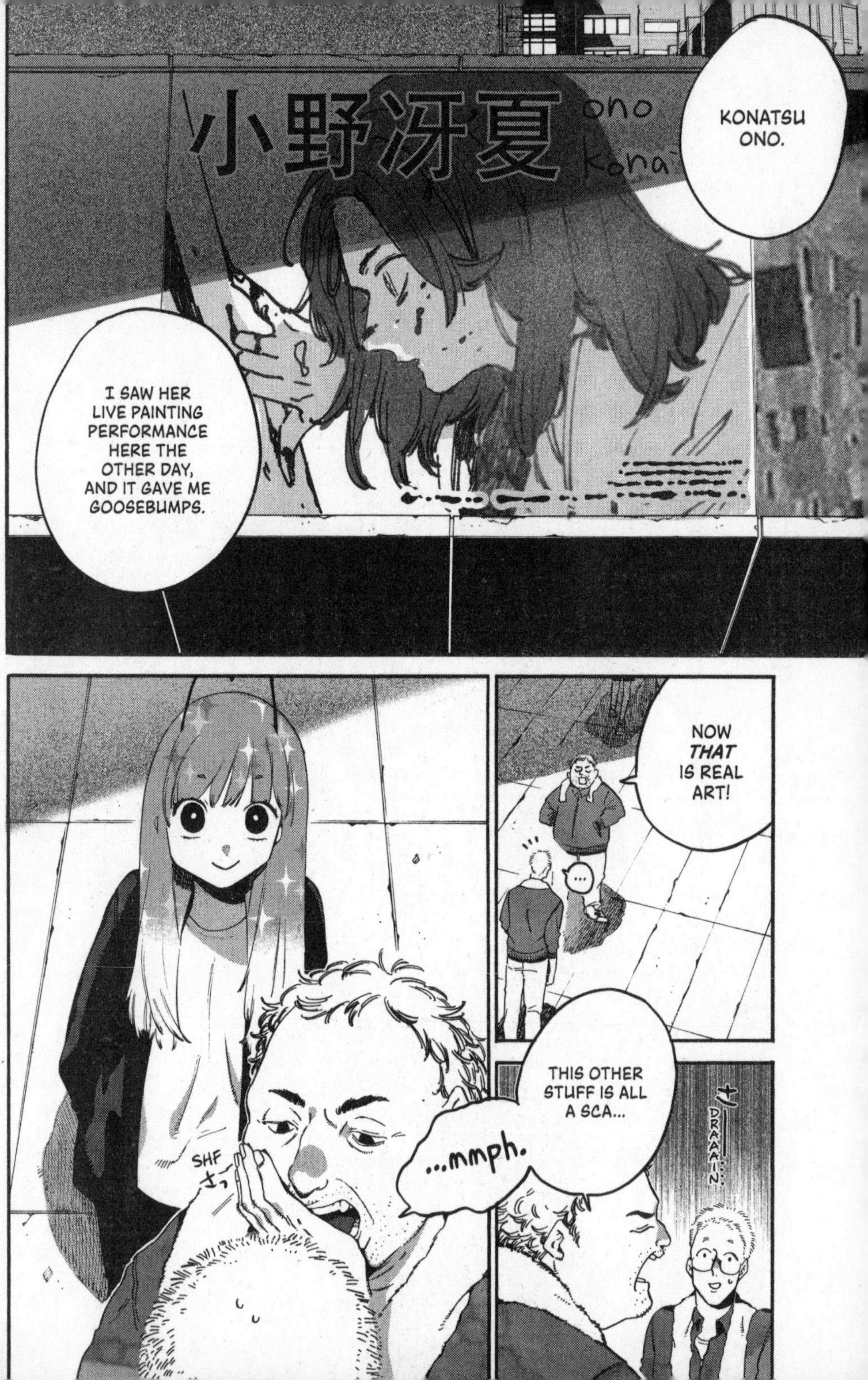
小野冴夏
ono
kona
KONATSU ONO.
I SAW HER LIVE PAINTING PERFORMANCE HERE THE OTHER DAY, AND IT GAVE ME GOOSEBUMPS.
NOW *THAT* IS REAL ART!
...
THIS OTHER STUFF IS ALL A SCA...
さー
DRAAAIN...
...mmph.
SHF
さっ

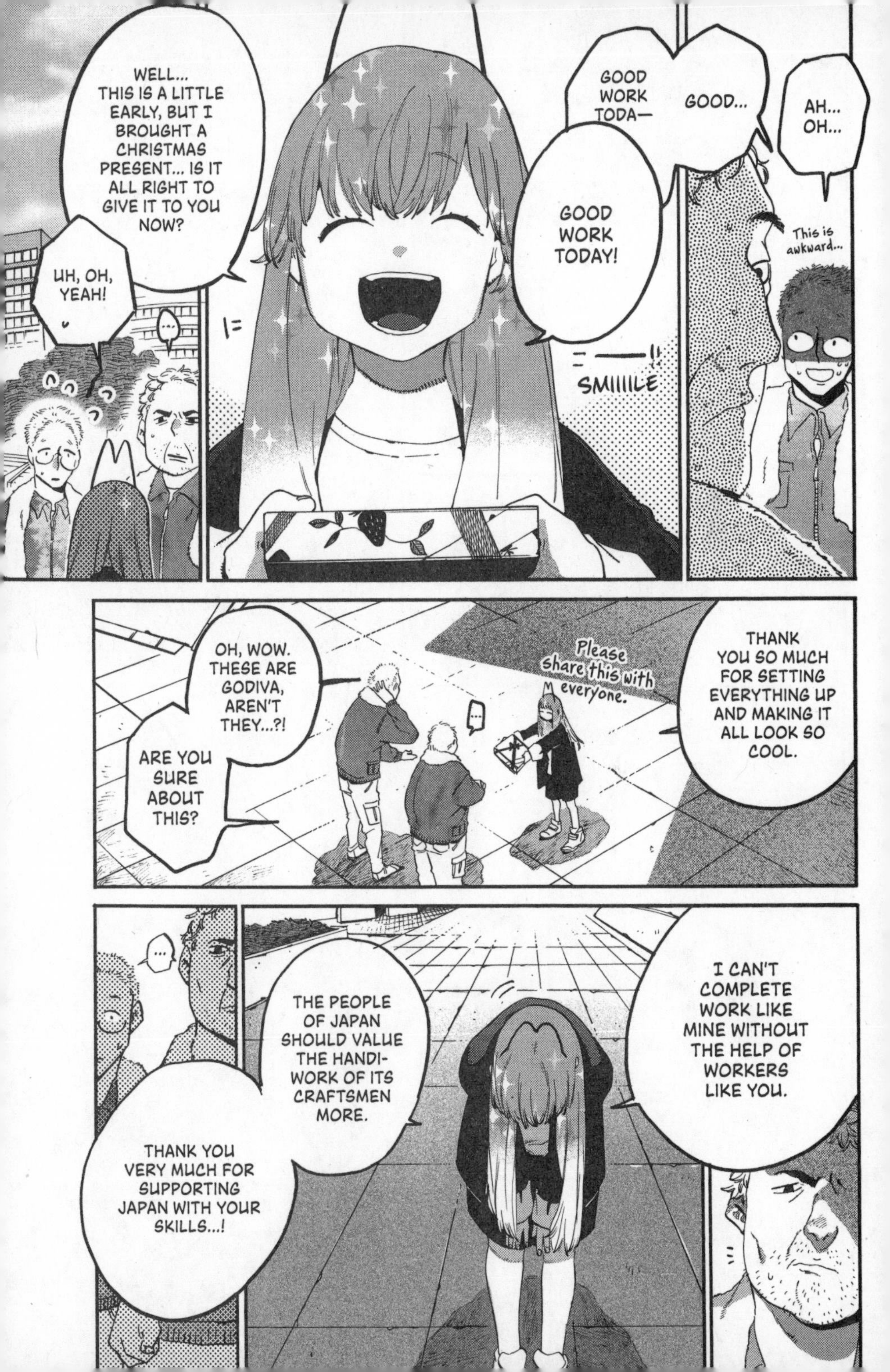
GOOD WORK TODA—
GOOD...
AH... OH...
GOOD WORK TODAY!
SMIIIILE
This is awkward...
WELL... THIS IS A LITTLE EARLY, BUT I BROUGHT A CHRISTMAS PRESENT... IS IT ALL RIGHT TO GIVE IT TO YOU NOW?
UH, OH, YEAH!
...
THANK YOU SO MUCH FOR SETTING EVERYTHING UP AND MAKING IT ALL LOOK SO COOL.
Please share this with everyone.
...
OH, WOW. THESE ARE GODIVA, AREN'T THEY...?!
ARE YOU SURE ABOUT THIS?
I CAN'T COMPLETE WORK LIKE MINE WITHOUT THE HELP OF WORKERS LIKE YOU.
THE PEOPLE OF JAPAN SHOULD VALUE THE HANDI-WORK OF ITS CRAFTSMEN MORE.
THANK YOU VERY MUCH FOR SUPPORTING JAPAN WITH YOUR SKILLS...!
...

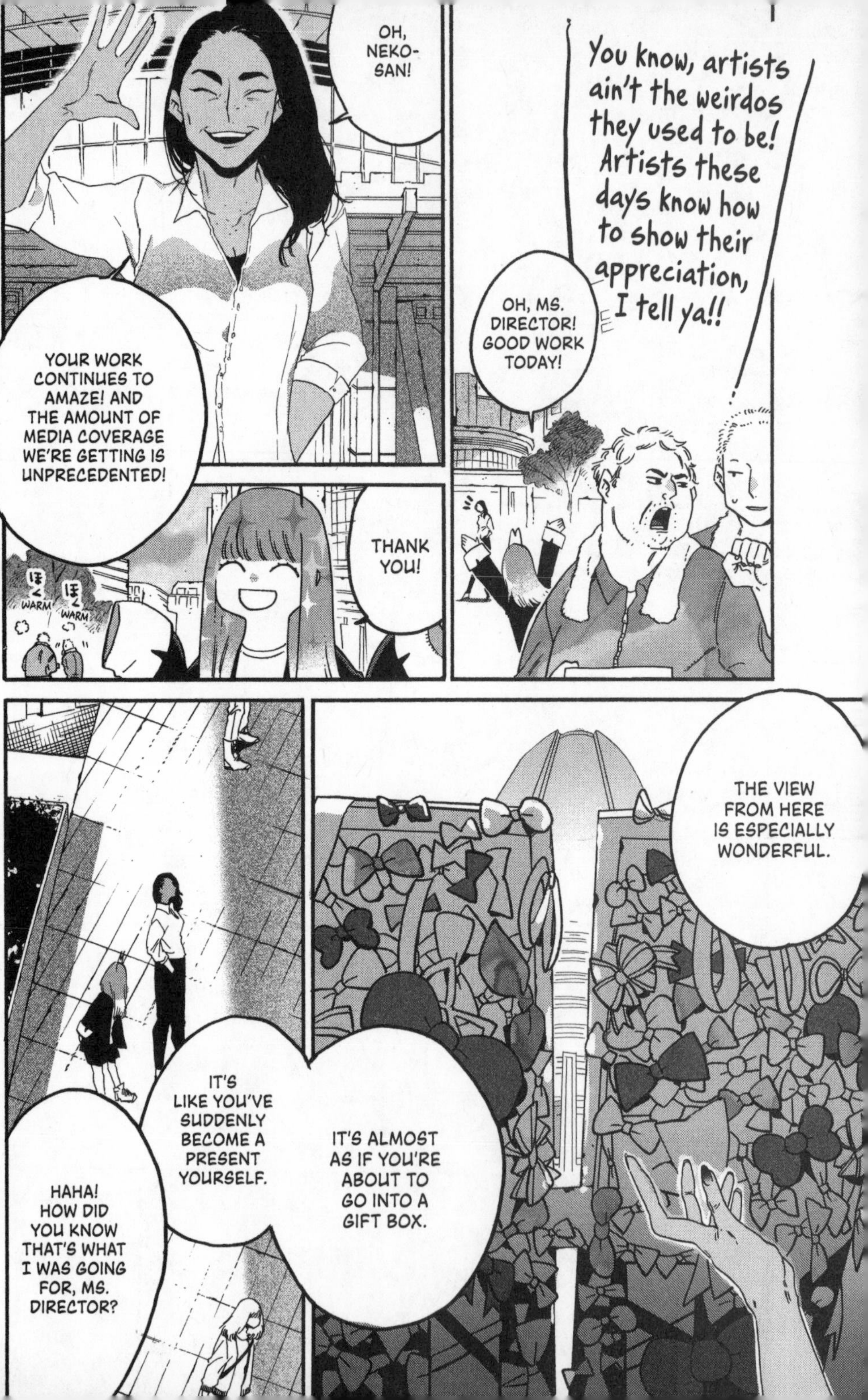
You know, artists ain't the weirdos they used to be! Artists these days know how to show their appreciation, I tell ya!!
OH, MS. DIRECTOR! GOOD WORK TODAY!
OH, NEKO-SAN!
YOUR WORK CONTINUES TO AMAZE! AND THE AMOUNT OF MEDIA COVERAGE WE'RE GETTING IS UNPRECEDENTED!
THANK YOU!
ほく WARM
ほく WARM
THE VIEW FROM HERE IS ESPECIALLY WONDERFUL.
IT'S ALMOST AS IF YOU'RE ABOUT TO GO INTO A GIFT BOX.
IT'S LIKE YOU'VE SUDDENLY BECOME A PRESENT YOURSELF.
HAHA! HOW DID YOU KNOW THAT'S WHAT I WAS GOING FOR, MS. DIRECTOR?

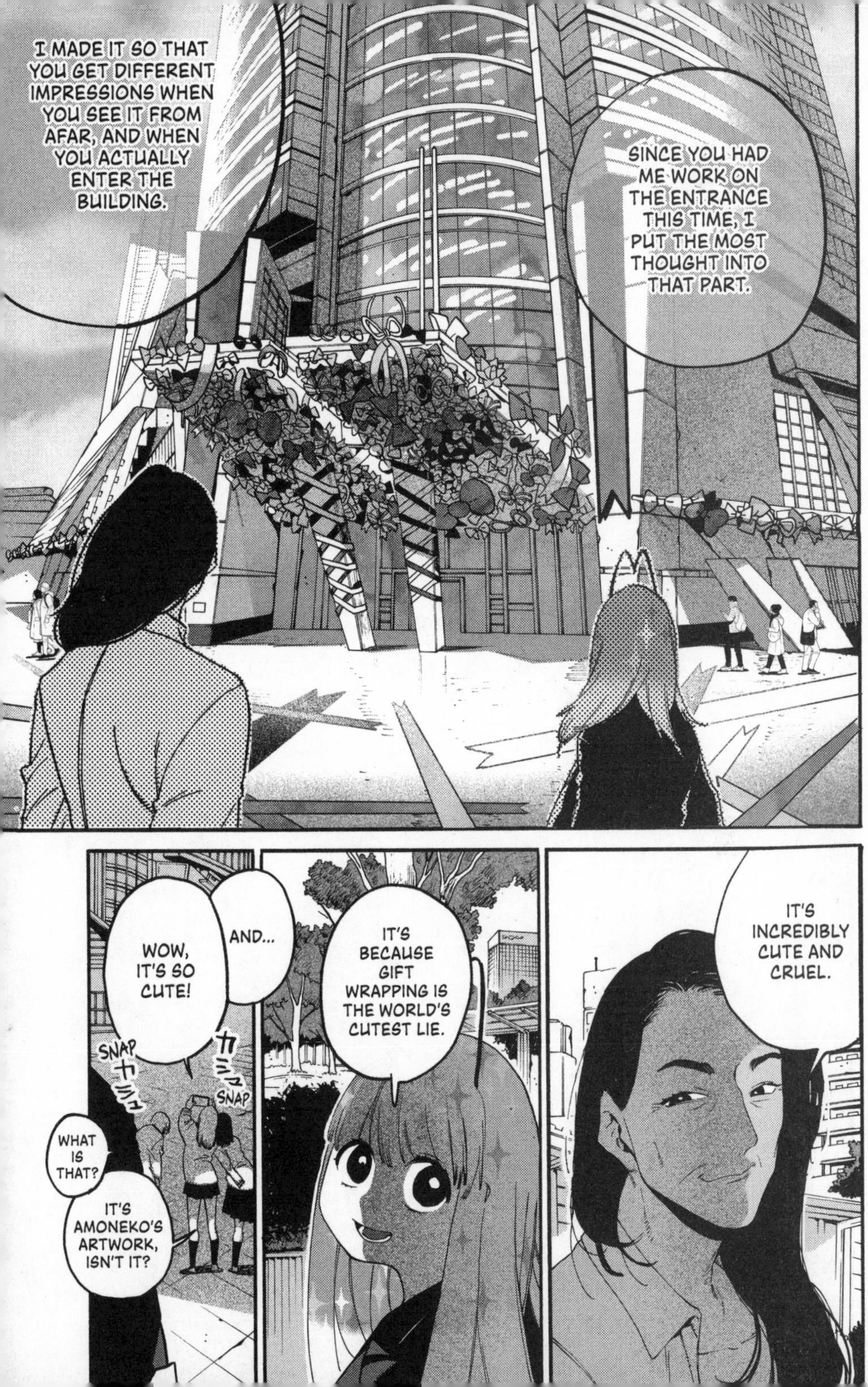
SINCE YOU HAD ME WORK ON THE ENTRANCE THIS TIME, I PUT THE MOST THOUGHT INTO THAT PART.
I MADE IT SO THAT YOU GET DIFFERENT IMPRESSIONS WHEN YOU SEE IT FROM AFAR, AND WHEN YOU ACTUALLY ENTER THE BUILDING.
IT'S INCREDIBLY CUTE AND CRUEL.
IT'S BECAUSE GIFT WRAPPING IS THE WORLD'S CUTEST LIE.
AND...
WOW, IT'S SO CUTE!
SNAP
SNAP
WHAT IS THAT?
IT'S AMONEKO'S ARTWORK, ISN'T IT?

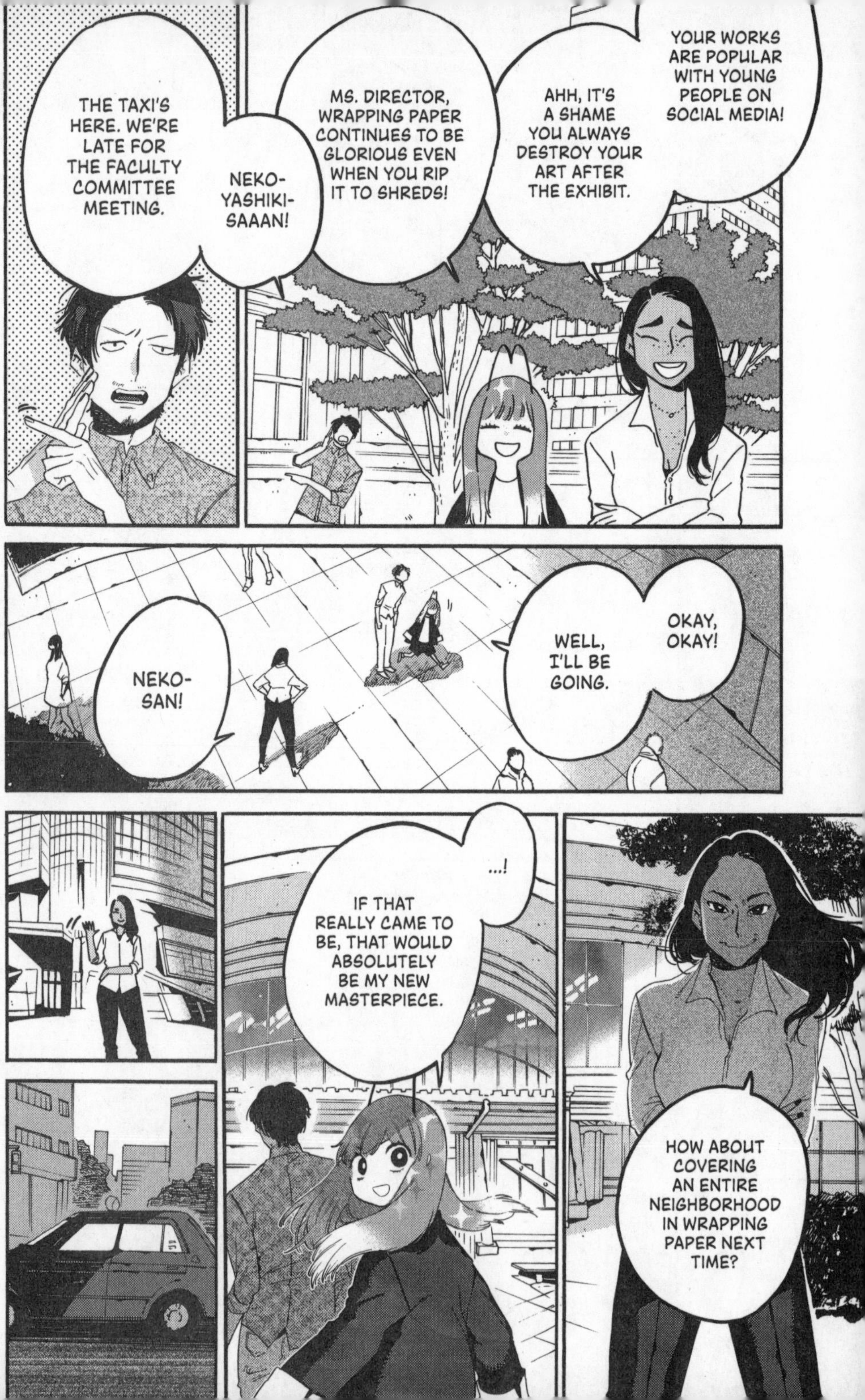
YOUR WORKS ARE POPULAR WITH YOUNG PEOPLE ON SOCIAL MEDIA!
AHH, IT'S A SHAME YOU ALWAYS DESTROY YOUR ART AFTER THE EXHIBIT.
MS. DIRECTOR, WRAPPING PAPER CONTINUES TO BE GLORIOUS EVEN WHEN YOU RIP IT TO SHREDS!
NEKO-YASHIKI-SAAAN!
THE TAXI'S HERE. WE'RE LATE FOR THE FACULTY COMMITTEE MEETING.
OKAY, OKAY!
WELL, I'LL BE GOING.
NEKO-SAN!
HOW ABOUT COVERING AN ENTIRE NEIGHBORHOOD IN WRAPPING PAPER NEXT TIME?
...!
IF THAT REALLY CAME TO BE, THAT WOULD ABSOLUTELY BE MY NEW MASTERPIECE.

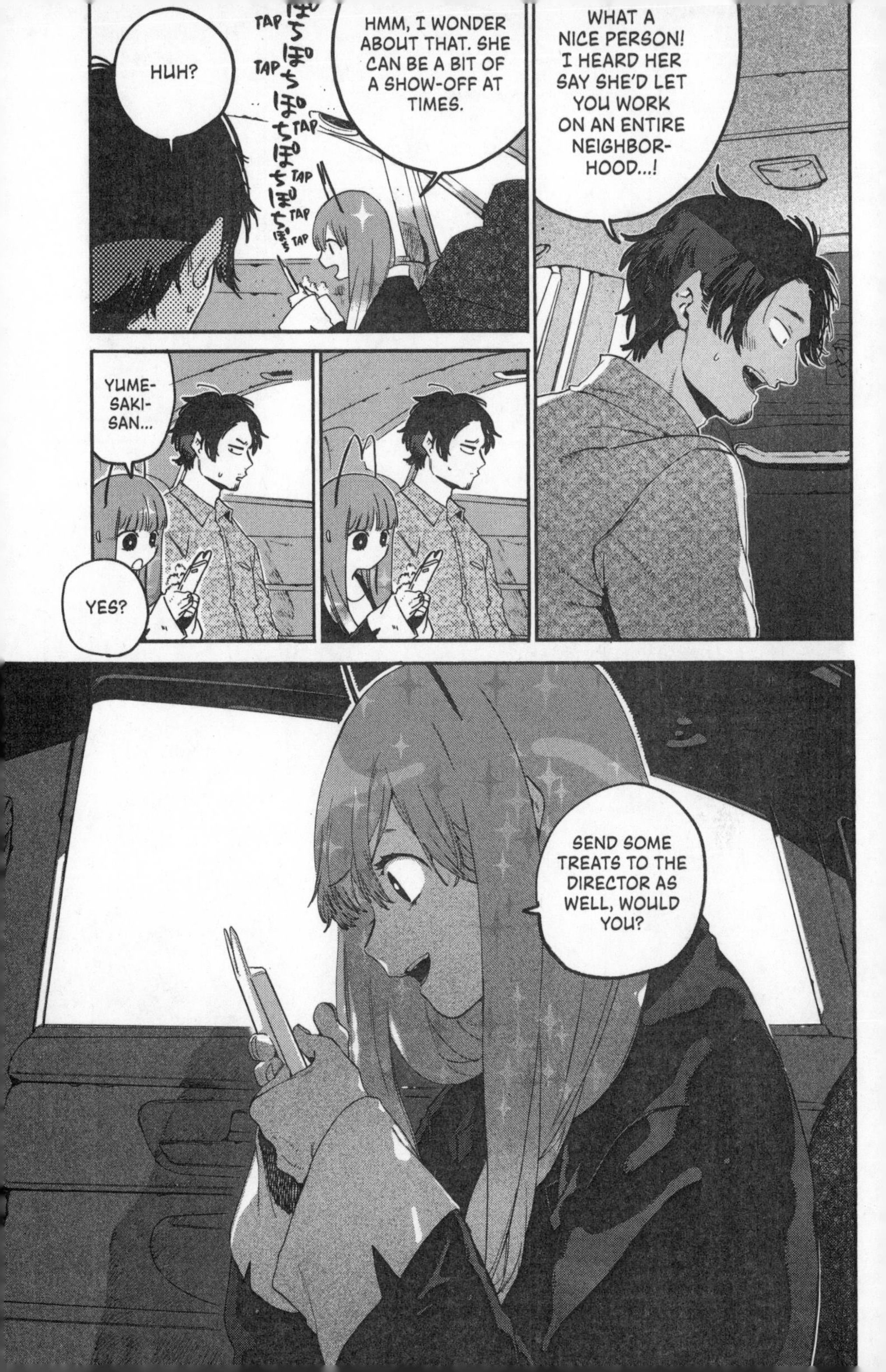

WHAT A NICE PERSON! I HEARD HER SAY SHE'D LET YOU WORK ON AN ENTIRE NEIGHBOR-HOOD...!
HMM, I WONDER ABOUT THAT. SHE CAN BE A BIT OF A SHOW-OFF AT TIMES.
TAP TAP TAP TAP TAP TAP TAP
HUH?
YUME-SAKI-SAN...
YES?
SEND SOME TREATS TO THE DIRECTOR AS WELL, WOULD YOU?

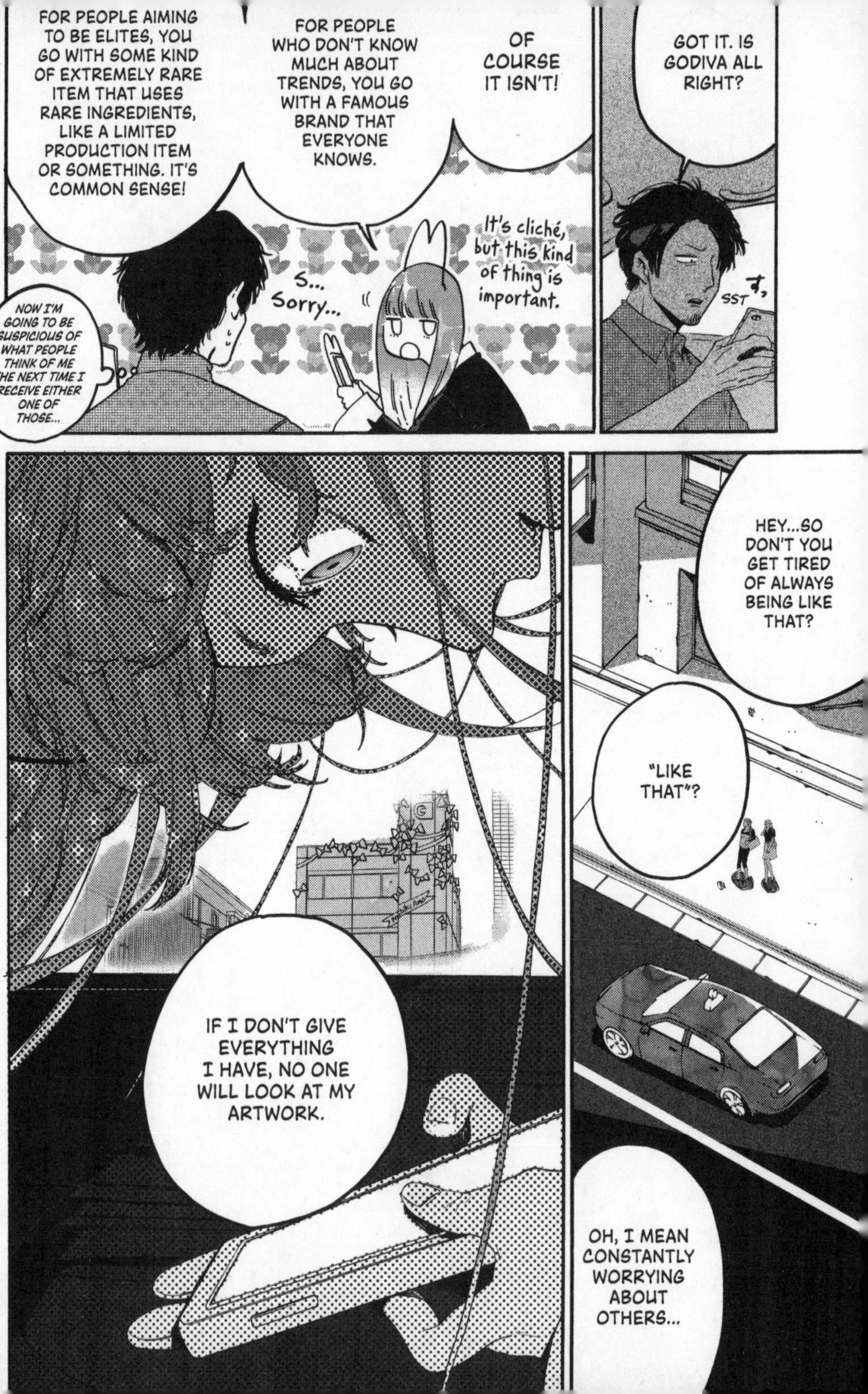
GOT IT. IS GODIVA ALL RIGHT?
SST
す,
OF COURSE IT ISN'T!
FOR PEOPLE WHO DON'T KNOW MUCH ABOUT TRENDS, YOU GO WITH A FAMOUS BRAND THAT EVERYONE KNOWS.
FOR PEOPLE AIMING TO BE ELITES, YOU GO WITH SOME KIND OF EXTREMELY RARE ITEM THAT USES RARE INGREDIENTS, LIKE A LIMITED PRODUCTION ITEM OR SOMETHING. IT'S COMMON SENSE!
It's cliché, but this kind of thing is important.
S... Sorry...
NOW I'M GOING TO BE SUSPICIOUS OF WHAT PEOPLE THINK OF ME THE NEXT TIME I RECEIVE EITHER ONE OF THOSE...
HEY...SO DON'T YOU GET TIRED OF ALWAYS BEING LIKE THAT?
"LIKE THAT"?
OH, I MEAN CONSTANTLY WORRYING ABOUT OTHERS...
IF I DON'T GIVE EVERYTHING I HAVE, NO ONE WILL LOOK AT MY ARTWORK.

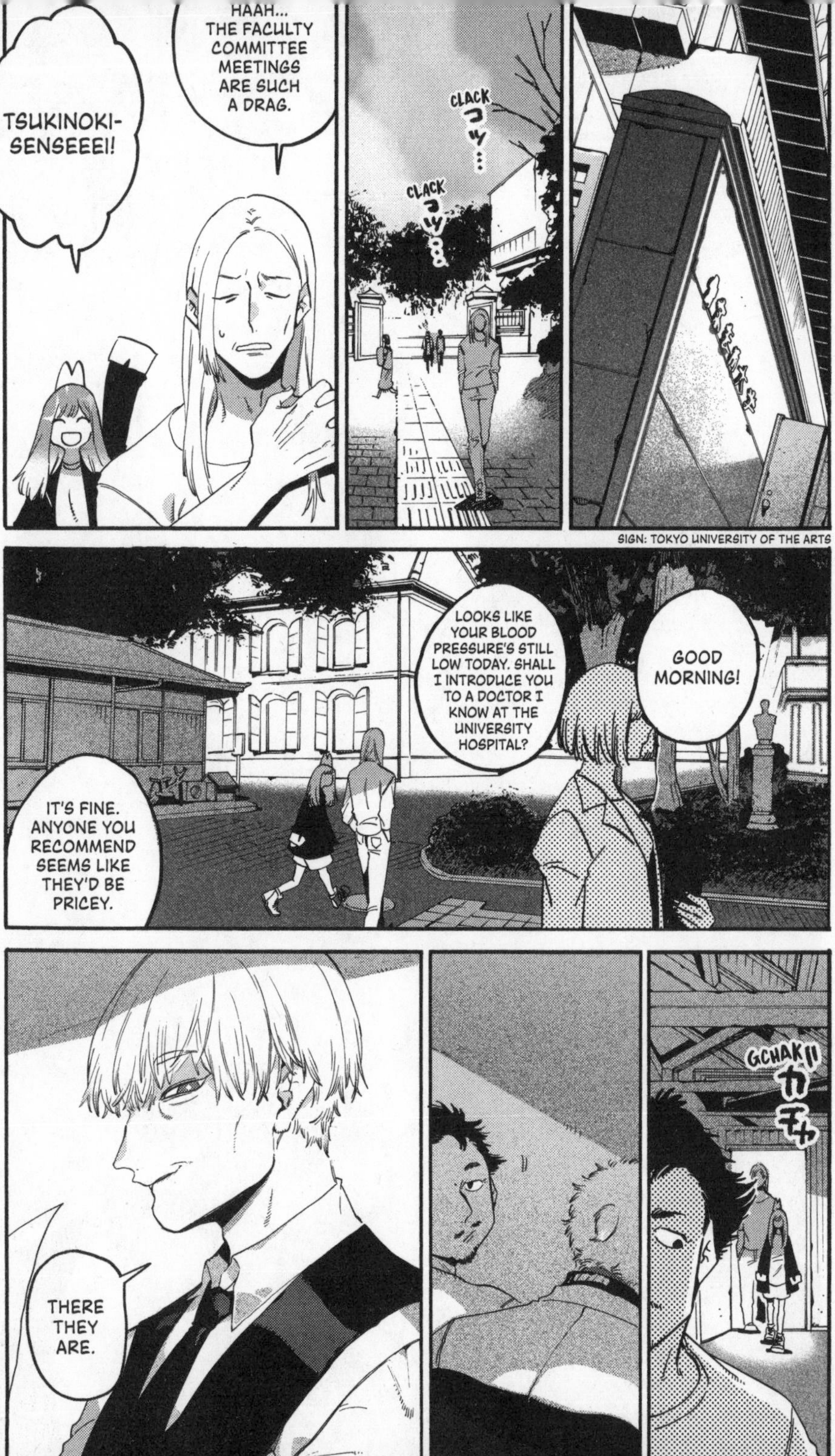
SIGN: TOKYO UNIVERSITY OF THE ARTS
CLACK コツ…
CLACK コツ…
HAAH... THE FACULTY COMMITTEE MEETINGS ARE SUCH A DRAG.
TSUKINOKI-SENSEEEI!
GOOD MORNING!
LOOKS LIKE YOUR BLOOD PRESSURE'S STILL LOW TODAY. SHALL I INTRODUCE YOU TO A DOCTOR I KNOW AT THE UNIVERSITY HOSPITAL?
IT'S FINE. ANYONE YOU RECOMMEND SEEMS LIKE THEY'D BE PRICEY.
GCHAK!! カチャ
THERE THEY ARE.

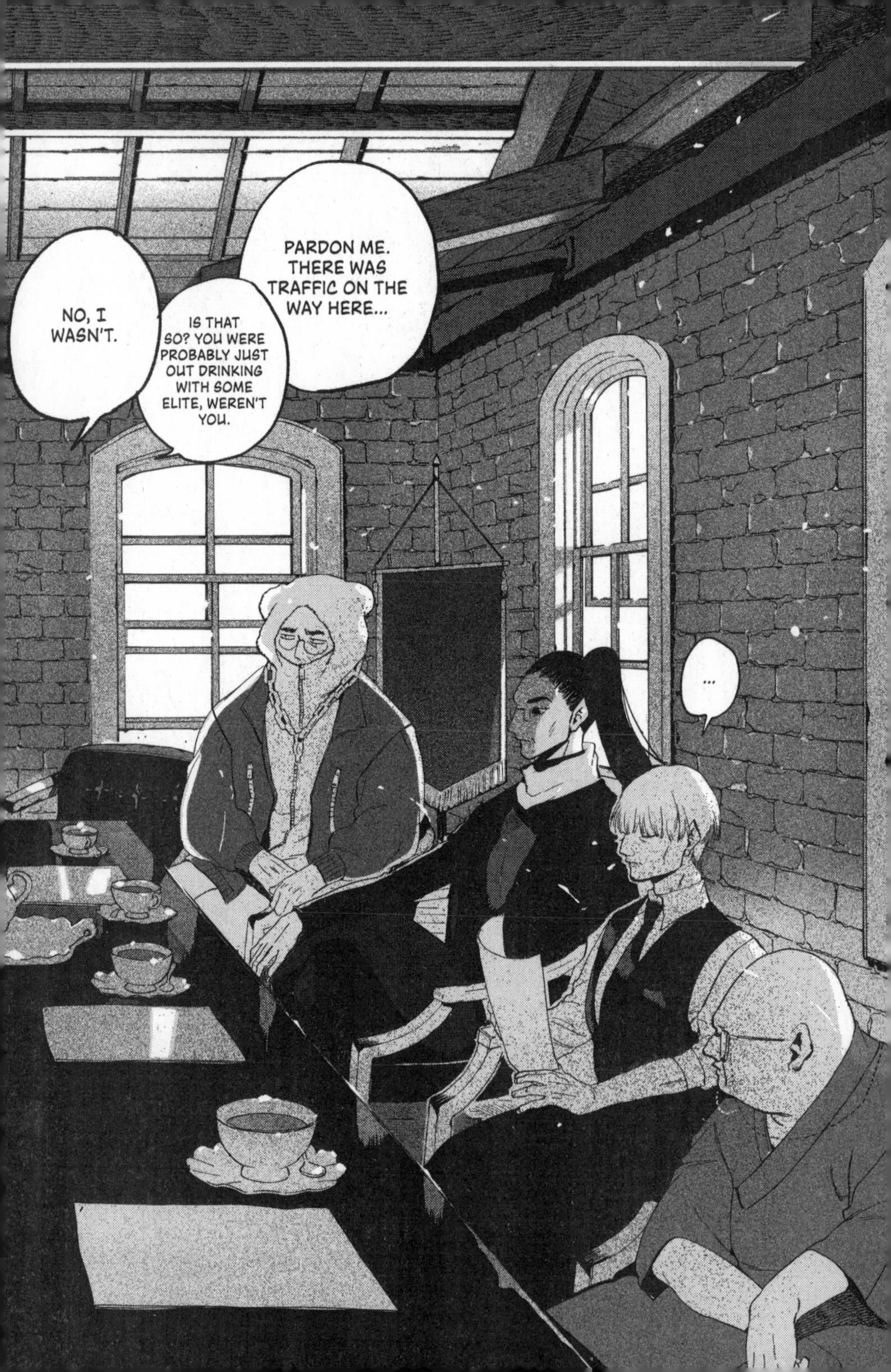
PARDON ME. THERE WAS TRAFFIC ON THE WAY HERE...
IS THAT SO? YOU WERE PROBABLY JUST OUT DRINKING WITH SOME ELITE, WEREN'T YOU.
NO, I WASN'T.
...

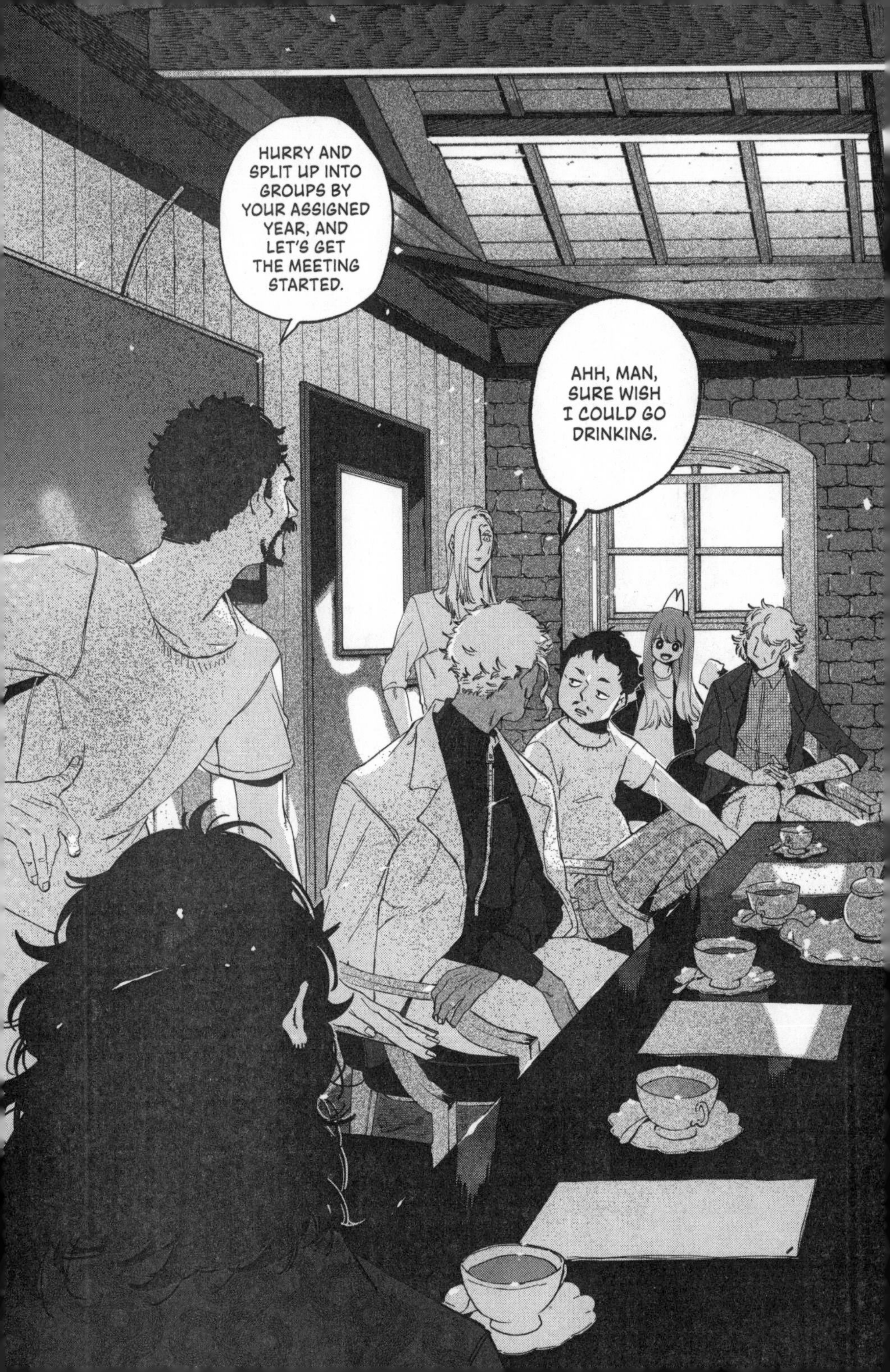
AHH, MAN, SURE WISH I COULD GO DRINKING.
HURRY AND SPLIT UP INTO GROUPS BY YOUR ASSIGNED YEAR, AND LET'S GET THE MEETING STARTED.

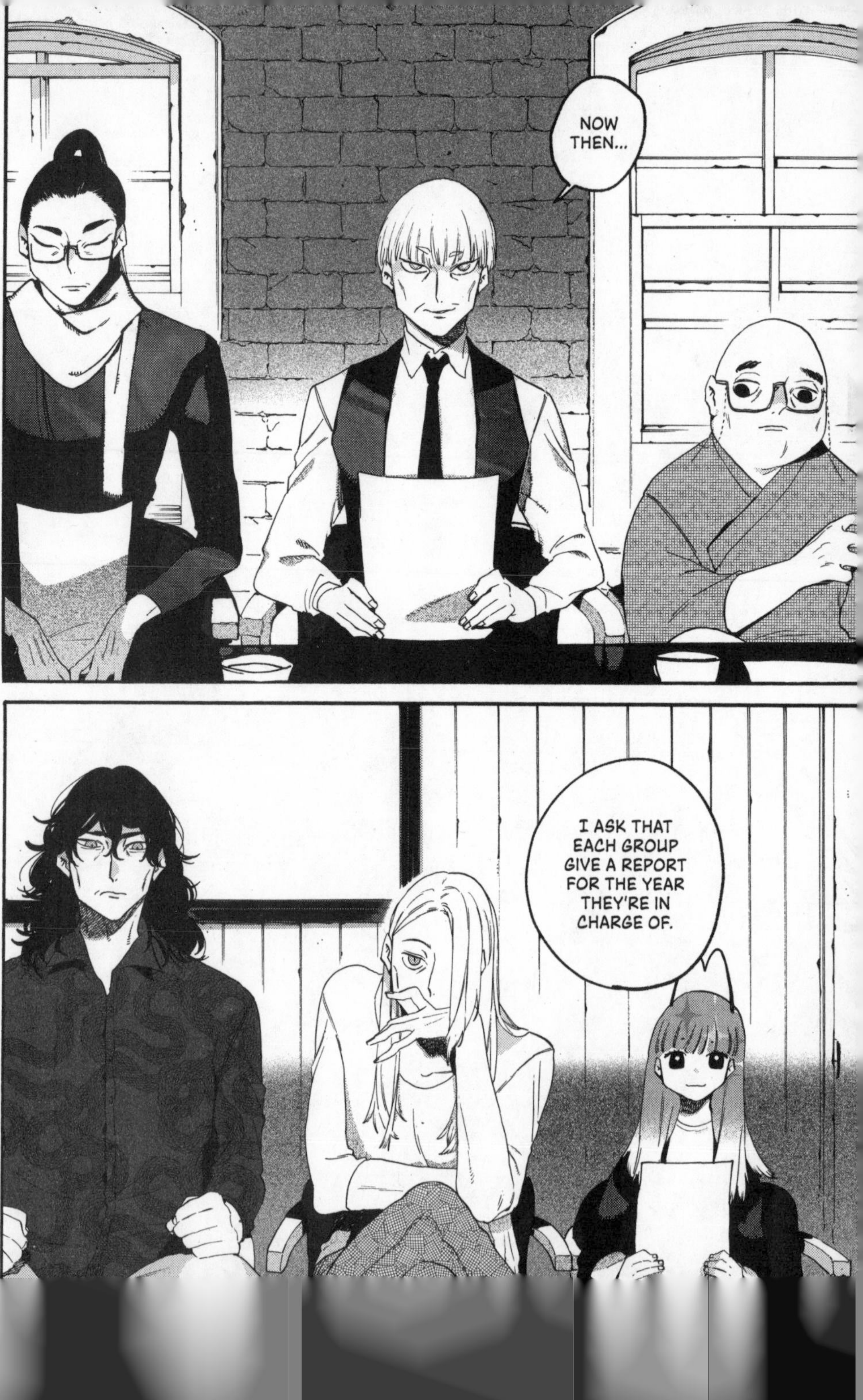
NOW THEN...
I ASK THAT EACH GROUP GIVE A REPORT FOR THE YEAR THEY'RE IN CHARGE OF.

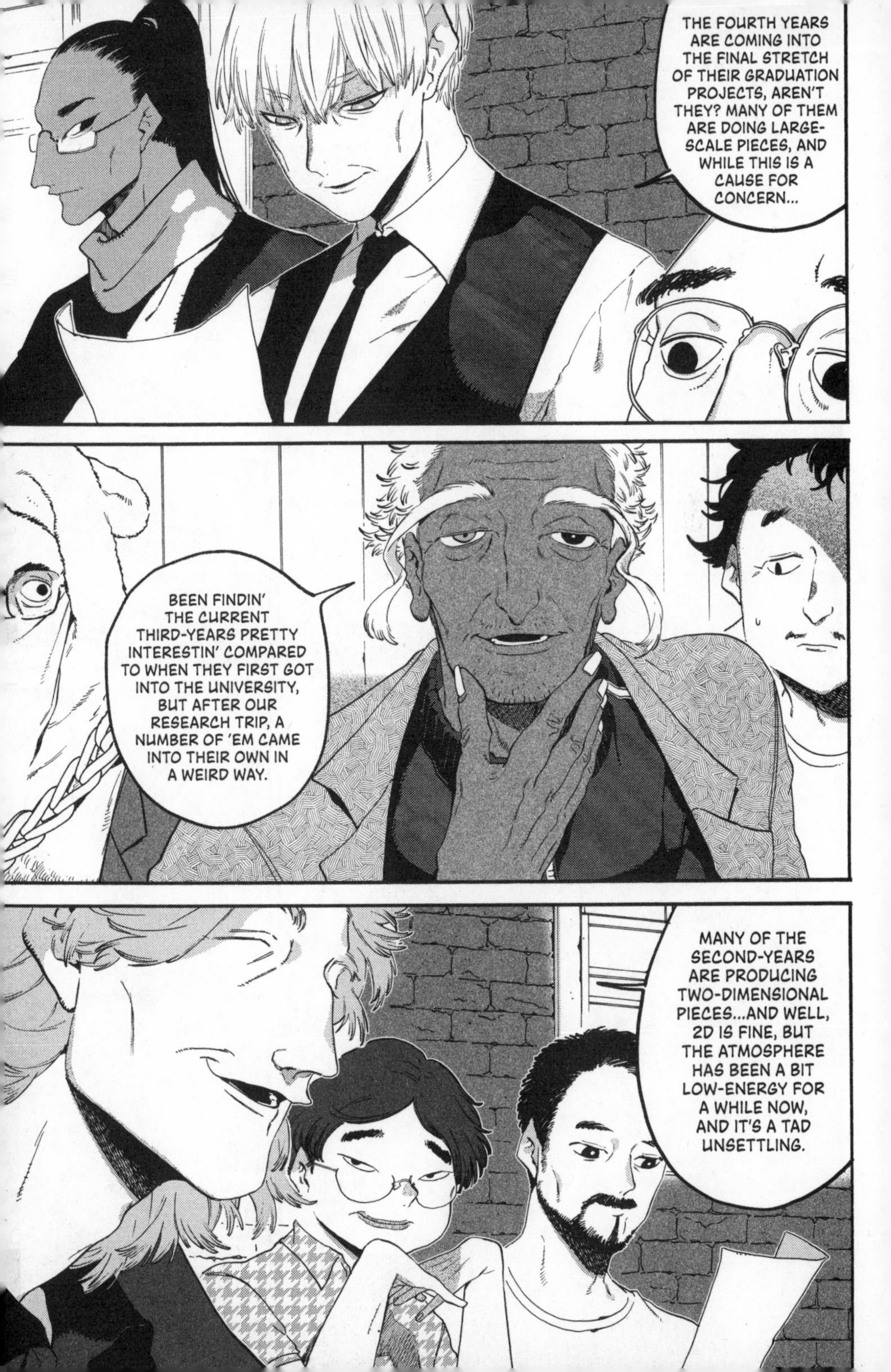
THE FOURTH YEARS ARE COMING INTO THE FINAL STRETCH OF THEIR GRADUATION PROJECTS, AREN'T THEY? MANY OF THEM ARE DOING LARGE-SCALE PIECES, AND WHILE THIS IS A CAUSE FOR CONCERN...
BEEN FINDIN' THE CURRENT THIRD-YEARS PRETTY INTERESTIN' COMPARED TO WHEN THEY FIRST GOT INTO THE UNIVERSITY, BUT AFTER OUR RESEARCH TRIP, A NUMBER OF 'EM CAME INTO THEIR OWN IN A WEIRD WAY.
MANY OF THE SECOND-YEARS ARE PRODUCING TWO-DIMENSIONAL PIECES...AND WELL, 2D IS FINE, BUT THE ATMOSPHERE HAS BEEN A BIT LOW-ENERGY FOR A WHILE NOW, AND IT'S A TAD UNSETTLING.

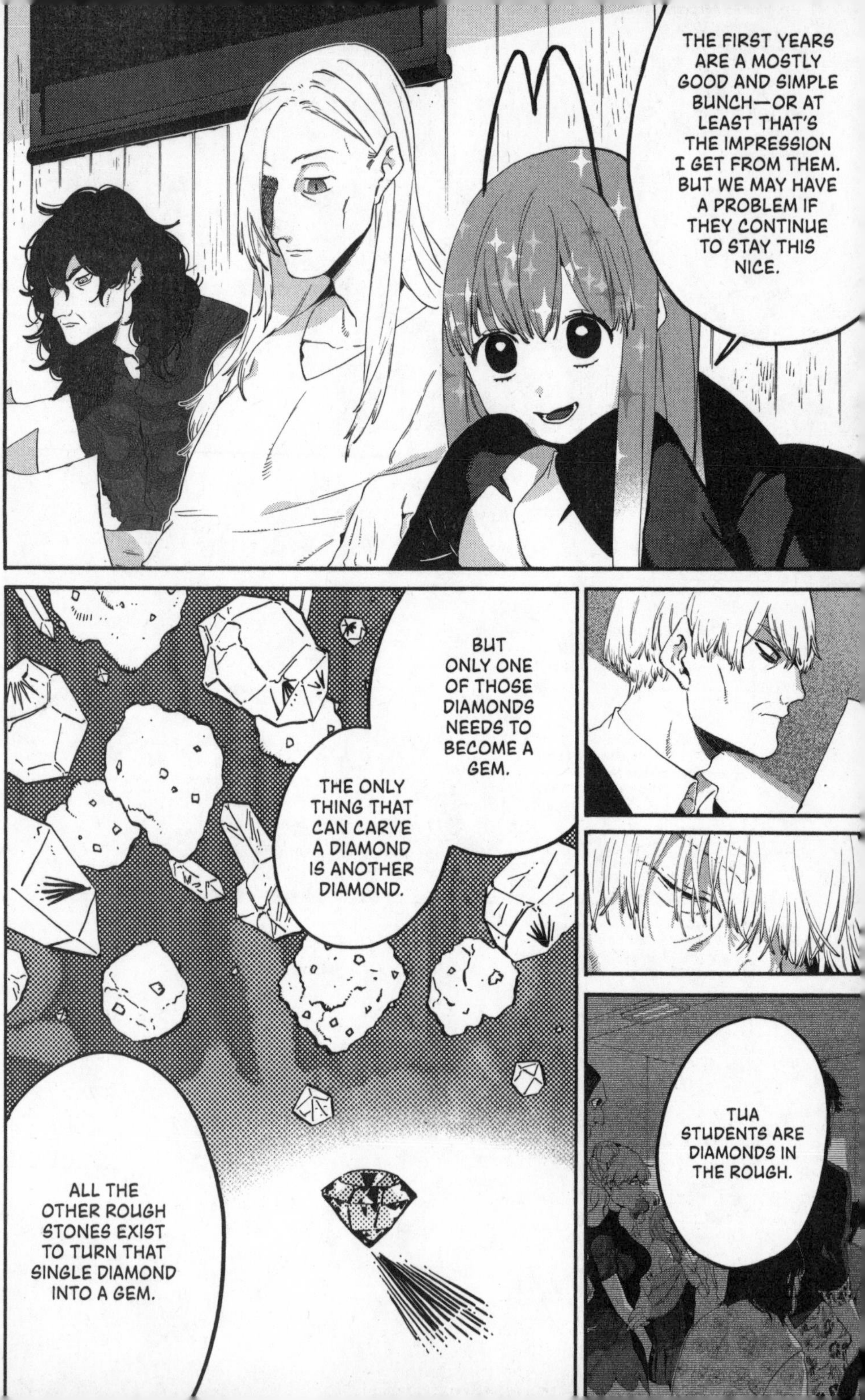
THE FIRST YEARS ARE A MOSTLY GOOD AND SIMPLE BUNCH—OR AT LEAST THAT'S THE IMPRESSION I GET FROM THEM. BUT WE MAY HAVE A PROBLEM IF THEY CONTINUE TO STAY THIS NICE.
TUA STUDENTS ARE DIAMONDS IN THE ROUGH.
BUT ONLY ONE OF THOSE DIAMONDS NEEDS TO BECOME A GEM.
THE ONLY THING THAT CAN CARVE A DIAMOND IS ANOTHER DIAMOND.
ALL THE OTHER ROUGH STONES EXIST TO TURN THAT SINGLE DIAMOND INTO A GEM.

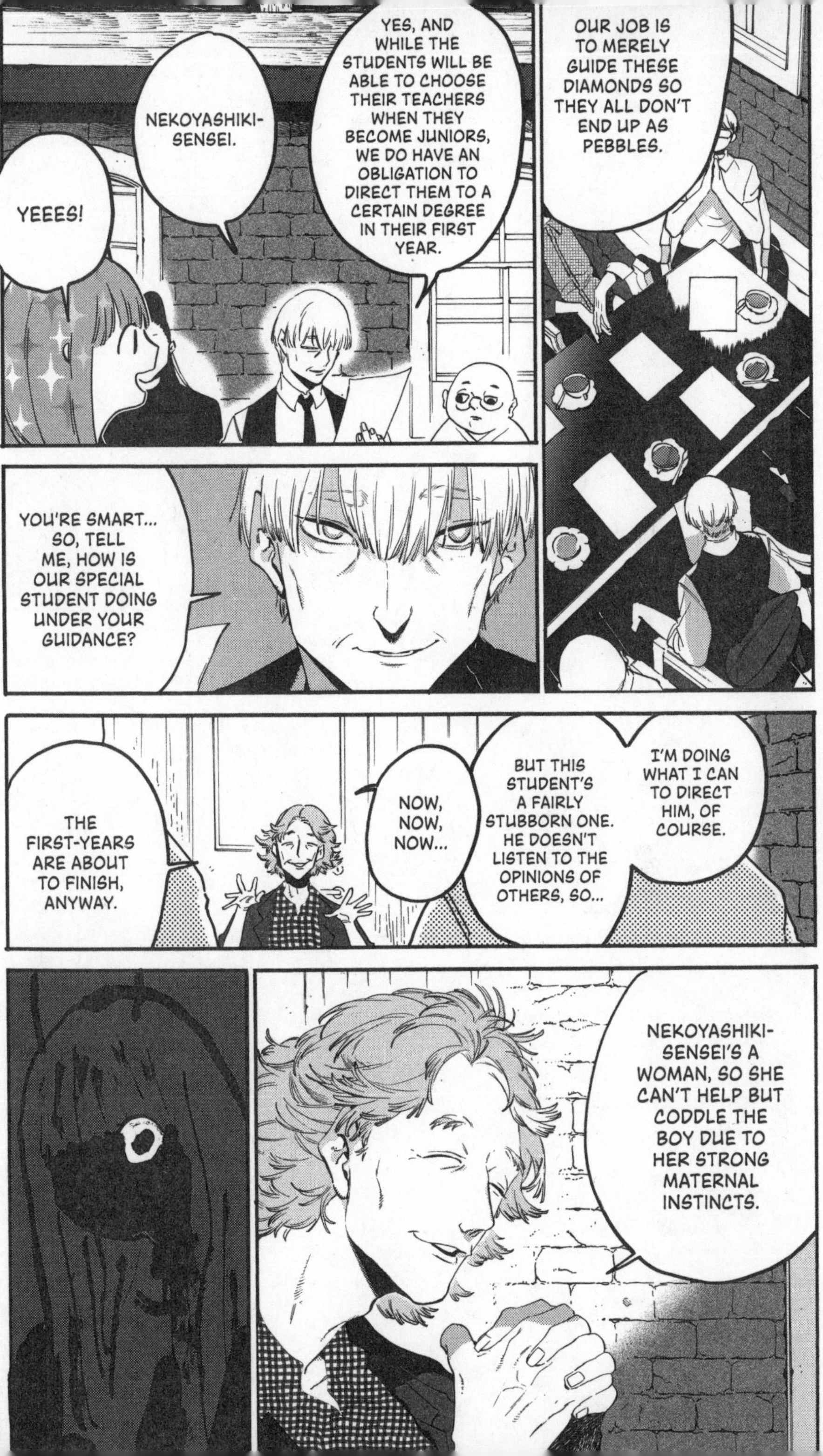
OUR JOB IS TO MERELY GUIDE THESE DIAMONDS SO THEY ALL DON'T END UP AS PEBBLES.
YES, AND WHILE THE STUDENTS WILL BE ABLE TO CHOOSE THEIR TEACHERS WHEN THEY BECOME JUNIORS, WE DO HAVE AN OBLIGATION TO DIRECT THEM TO A CERTAIN DEGREE IN THEIR FIRST YEAR.
NEKOYASHIKI-SENSEI.
YEEES!
YOU'RE SMART... SO, TELL ME, HOW IS OUR SPECIAL STUDENT DOING UNDER YOUR GUIDANCE?
I'M DOING WHAT I CAN TO DIRECT HIM, OF COURSE.
BUT THIS STUDENT'S A FAIRLY STUBBORN ONE. HE DOESN'T LISTEN TO THE OPINIONS OF OTHERS, SO...
NOW, NOW, NOW...
THE FIRST-YEARS ARE ABOUT TO FINISH, ANYWAY.
NEKOYASHIKI-SENSEI'S A WOMAN, SO SHE CAN'T HELP BUT CODDLE THE BOY DUE TO HER STRONG MATERNAL INSTINCTS.

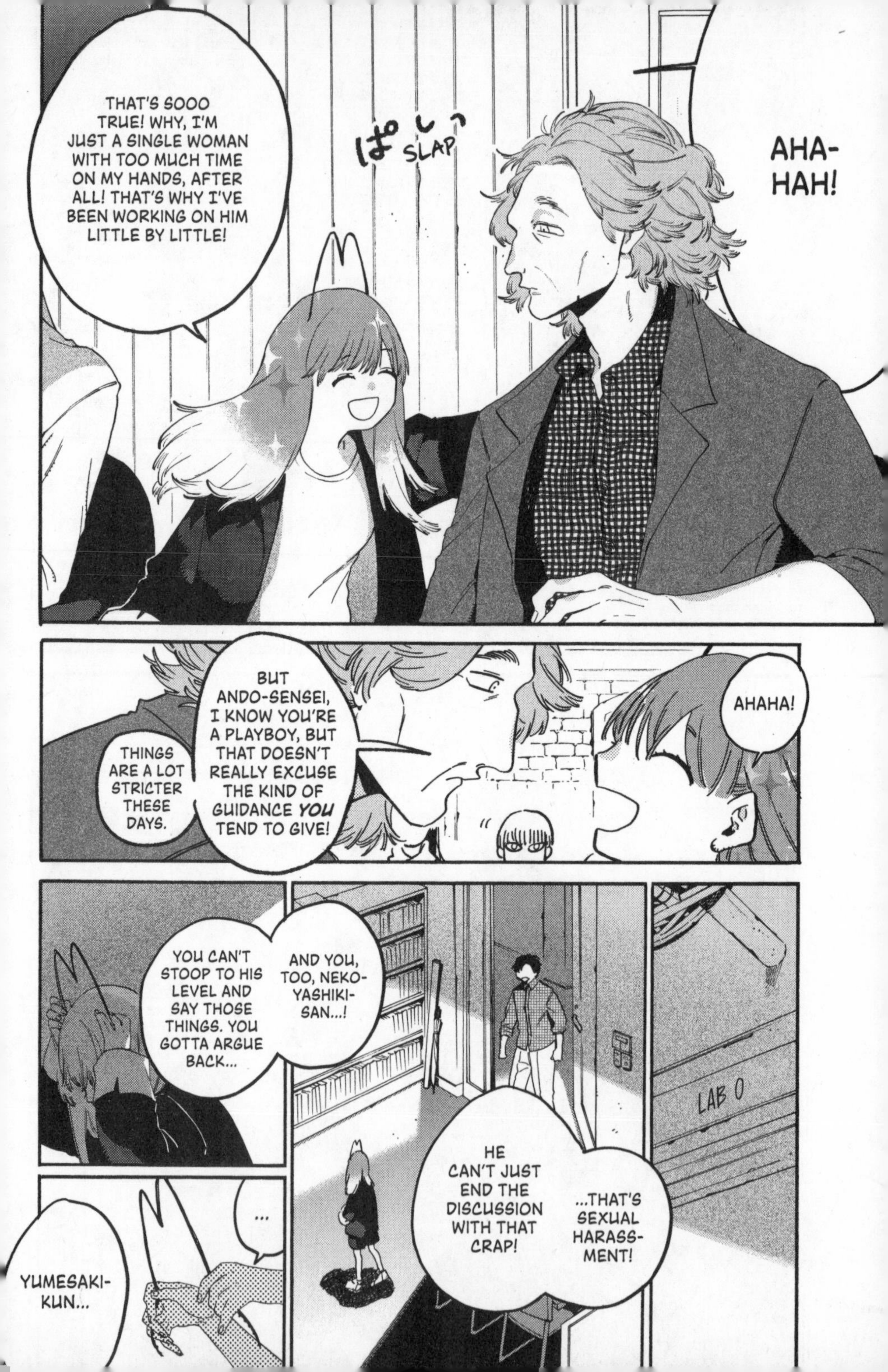
AHA-HAH!
ぱしっ SLAP
THAT'S SOOO TRUE! WHY, I'M JUST A SINGLE WOMAN WITH TOO MUCH TIME ON MY HANDS, AFTER ALL! THAT'S WHY I'VE BEEN WORKING ON HIM LITTLE BY LITTLE!
AHAHA!
BUT ANDO-SENSEI, I KNOW YOU'RE A PLAYBOY, BUT THAT DOESN'T REALLY EXCUSE THE KIND OF GUIDANCE *YOU* TEND TO GIVE!
THINGS ARE A LOT STRICTER THESE DAYS.
LAB 0
...THAT'S SEXUAL HARASS-MENT!
HE CAN'T JUST END THE DISCUSSION WITH THAT CRAP!
AND YOU, TOO, NEKO-YASHIKI-SAN...!
YOU CAN'T STOOP TO HIS LEVEL AND SAY THOSE THINGS. YOU GOTTA ARGUE BACK...
...
YUMESAKI-KUN...

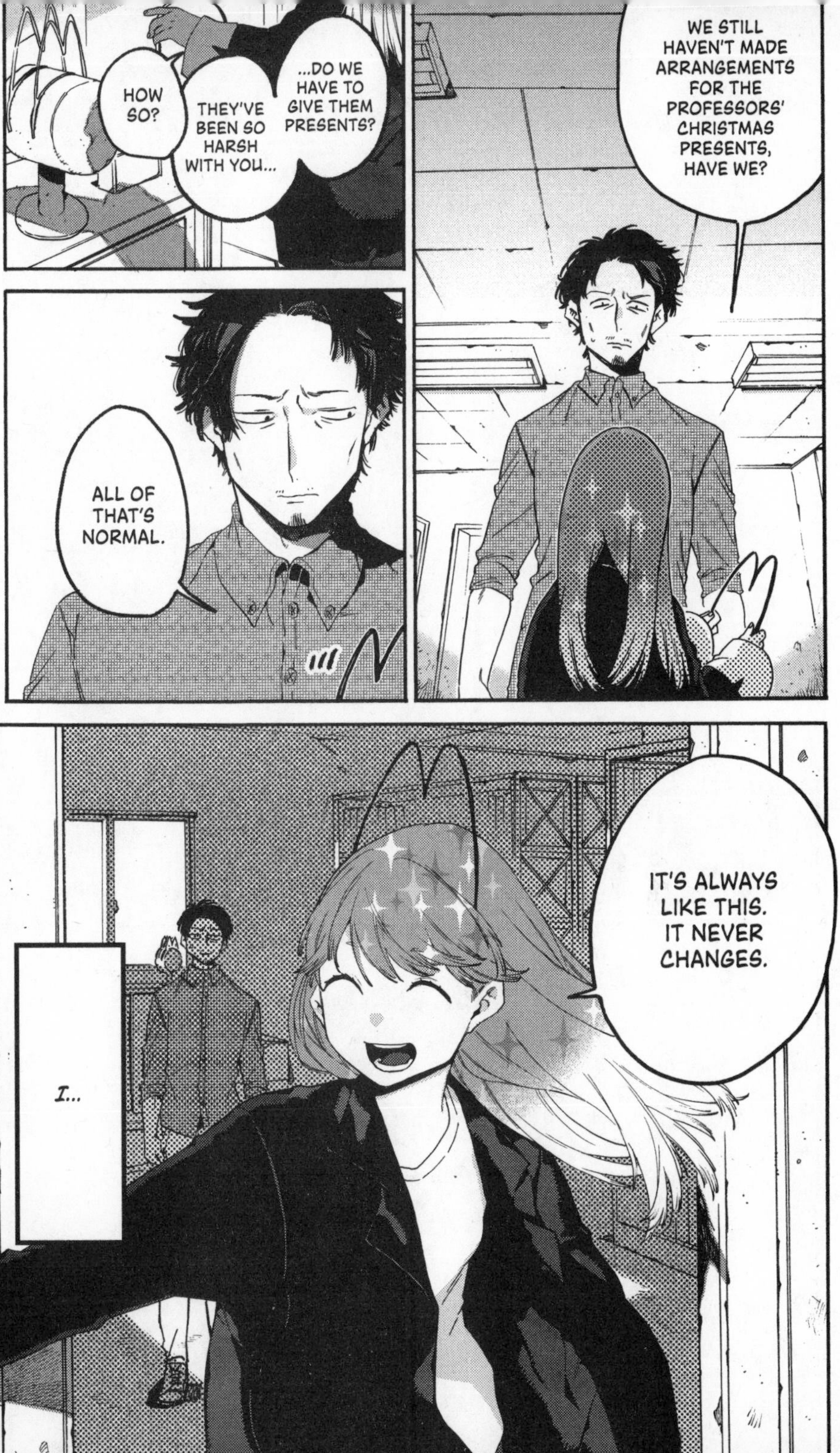
WE STILL HAVEN'T MADE ARRANGEMENTS FOR THE PROFESSORS' CHRISTMAS PRESENTS, HAVE WE?
...DO WE HAVE TO GIVE THEM PRESENTS?
THEY'VE BEEN SO HARSH WITH YOU...
HOW SO?
ALL OF THAT'S NORMAL.
IT'S ALWAYS LIKE THIS. IT NEVER CHANGES.
I...

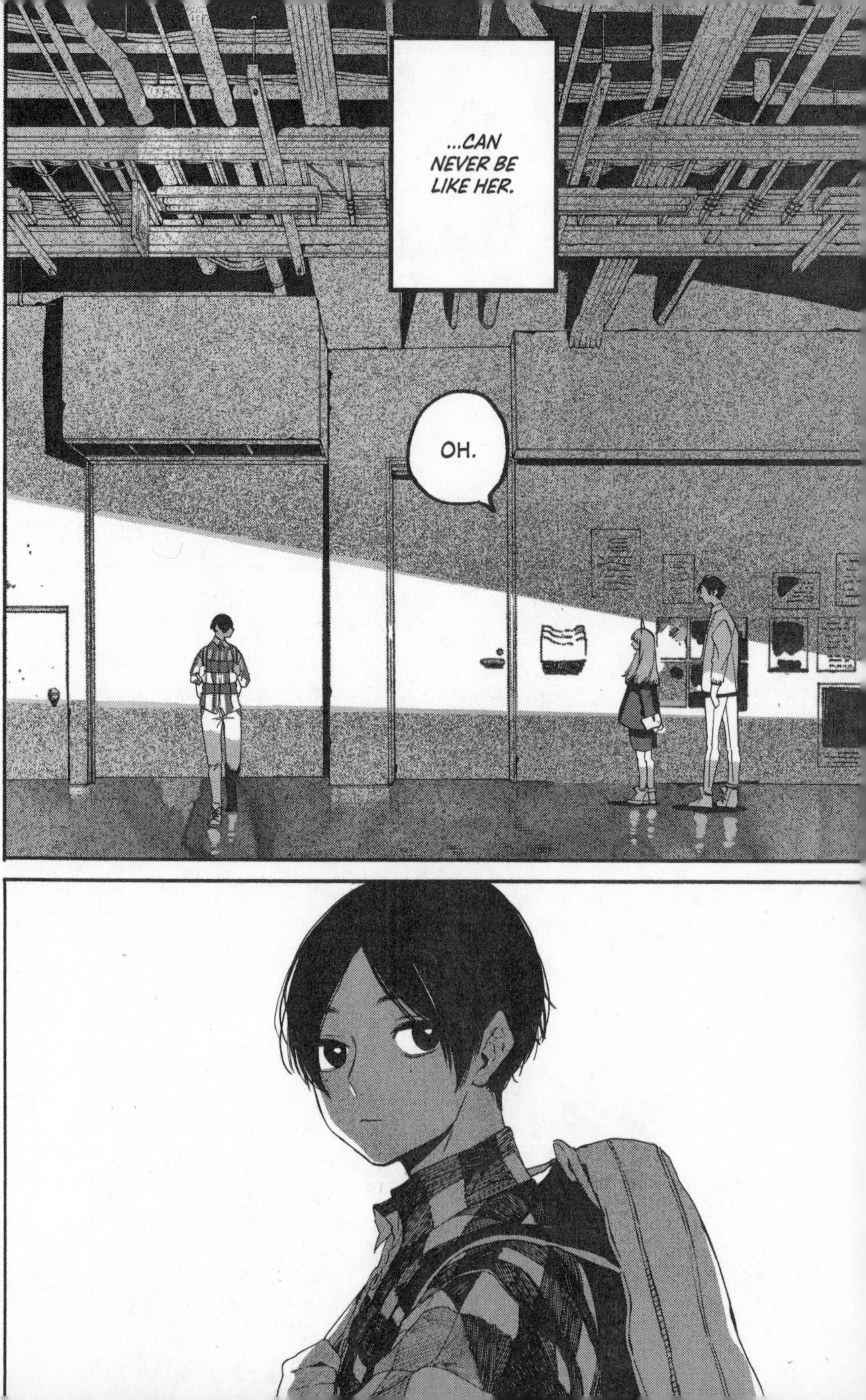
...CAN NEVER BE LIKE HER.
OH.

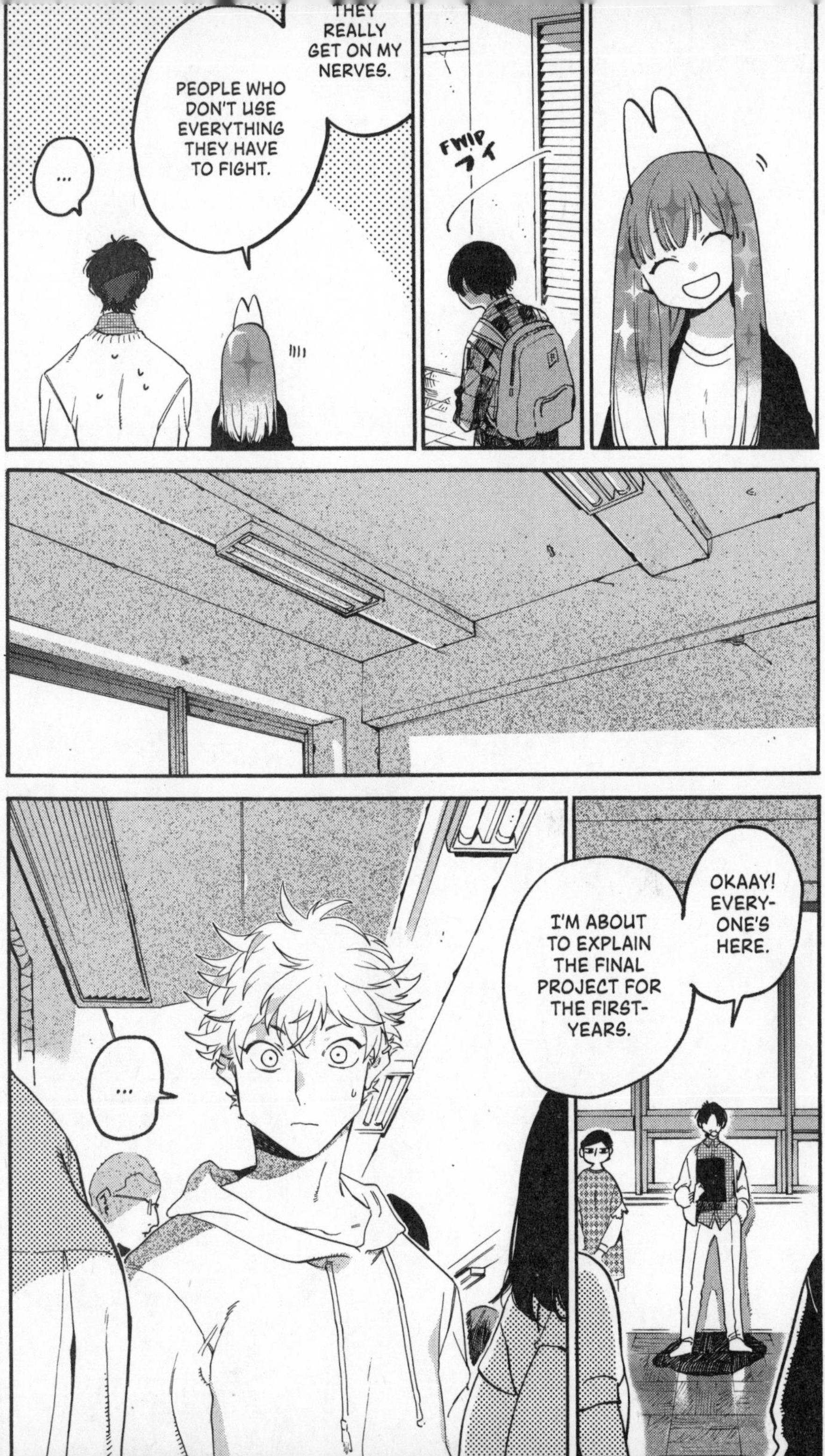
FWIP
THEY REALLY GET ON MY NERVES.
PEOPLE WHO DON'T USE EVERYTHING THEY HAVE TO FIGHT.
...
OKAAY! EVERY-ONE'S HERE.
I'M ABOUT TO EXPLAIN THE FINAL PROJECT FOR THE FIRST-YEARS.
...

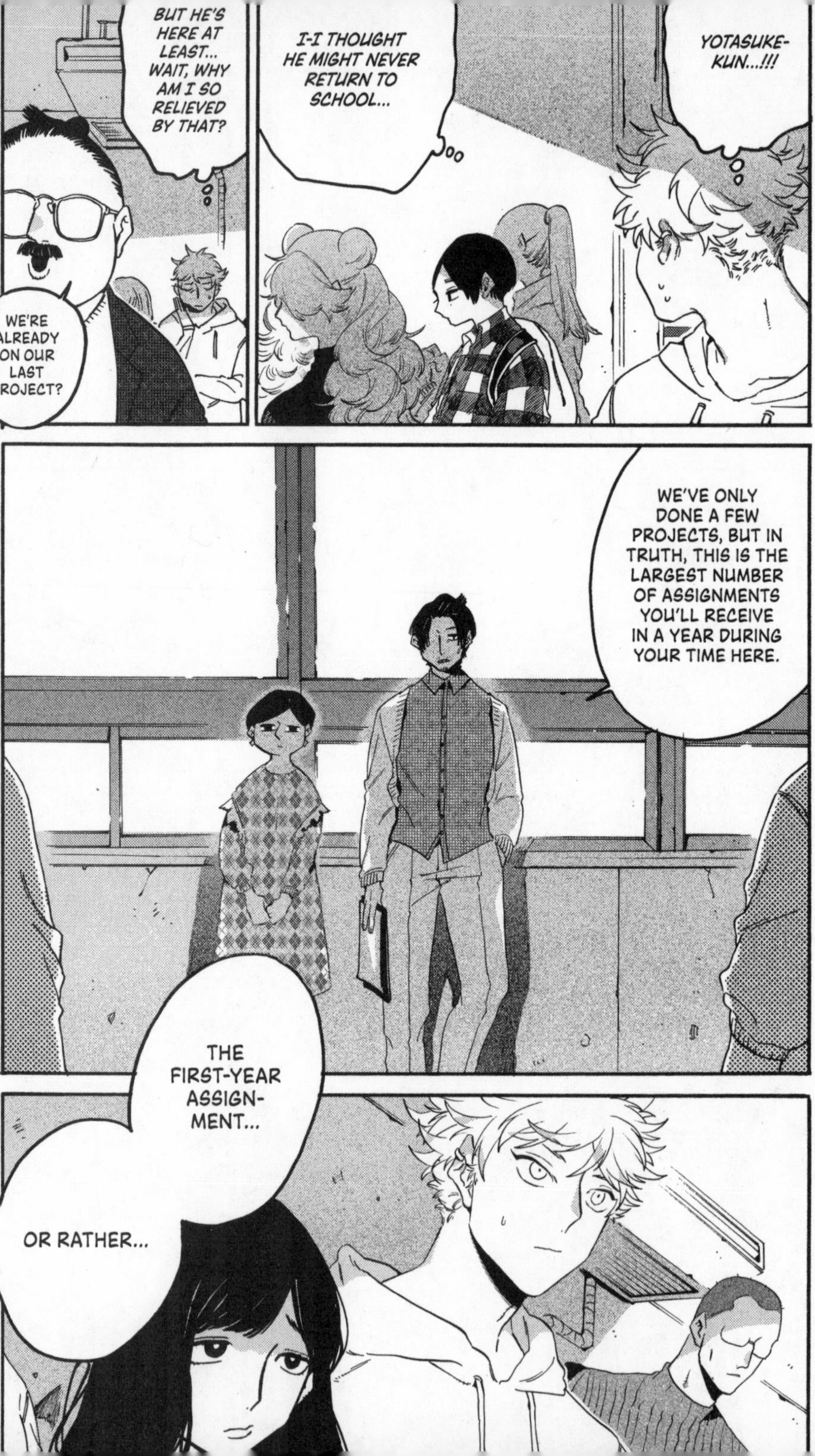
YOTASUKE-KUN...!!!
I-I THOUGHT HE MIGHT NEVER RETURN TO SCHOOL...
BUT HE'S HERE AT LEAST... WAIT, WHY AM I SO RELIEVED BY THAT?
WE'RE ALREADY ON OUR LAST PROJECT?
WE'VE ONLY DONE A FEW PROJECTS, BUT IN TRUTH, THIS IS THE LARGEST NUMBER OF ASSIGNMENTS YOU'LL RECEIVE IN A YEAR DURING YOUR TIME HERE.
THE FIRST-YEAR ASSIGNMENT...
OR RATHER...

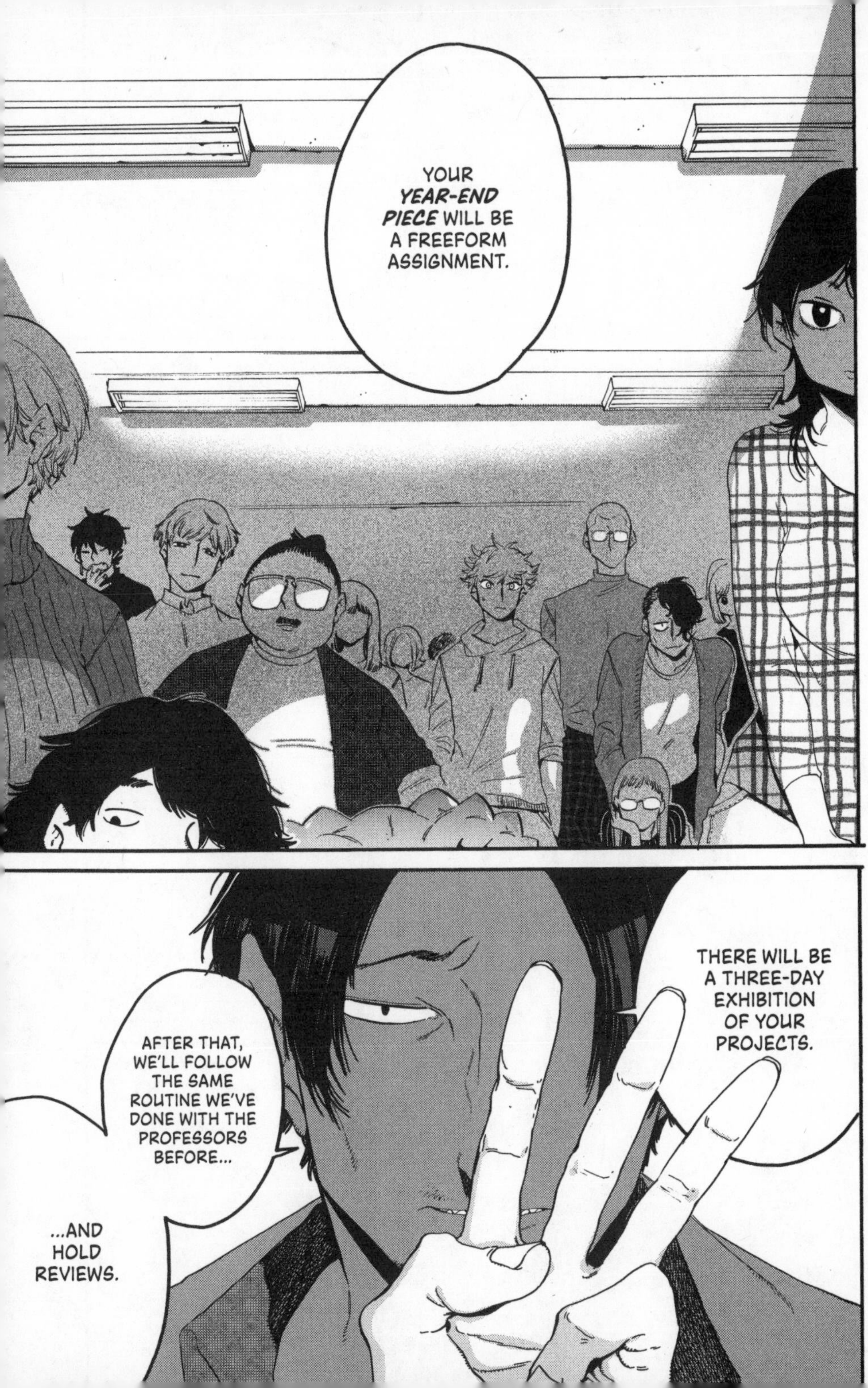
YOUR *YEAR-END PIECE* WILL BE A FREEFORM ASSIGNMENT.
THERE WILL BE A THREE-DAY EXHIBITION OF YOUR PROJECTS.
AFTER THAT, WE'LL FOLLOW THE SAME ROUTINE WE'VE DONE WITH THE PROFESSORS BEFORE...
...AND HOLD REVIEWS.

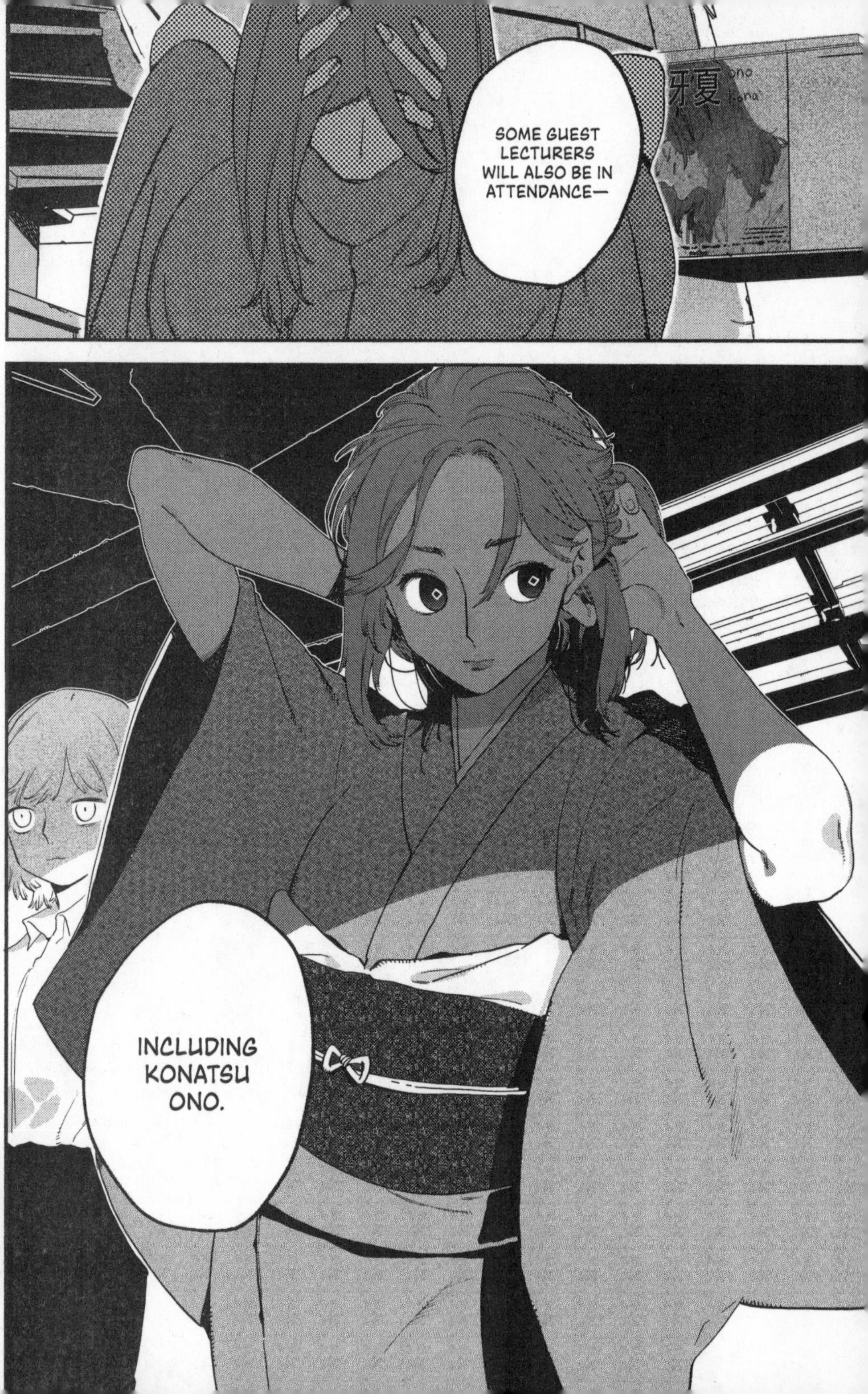
SOME GUEST LECTURERS WILL ALSO BE IN ATTENDANCE—
INCLUDING KONATSU ONO.

STROKE 37 END

STROKE 38 TALENT AND HARD WORK

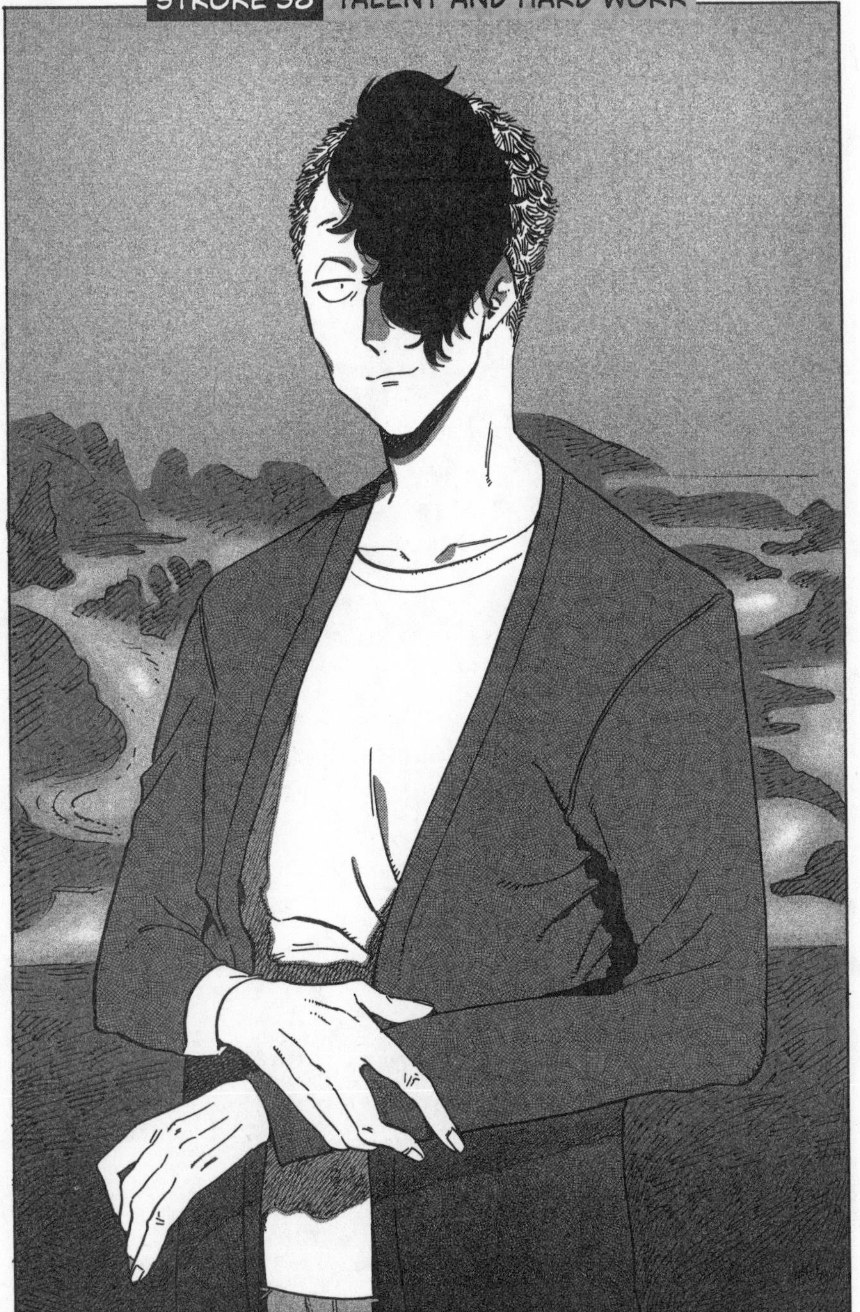

H.A.C.H.I.R.O

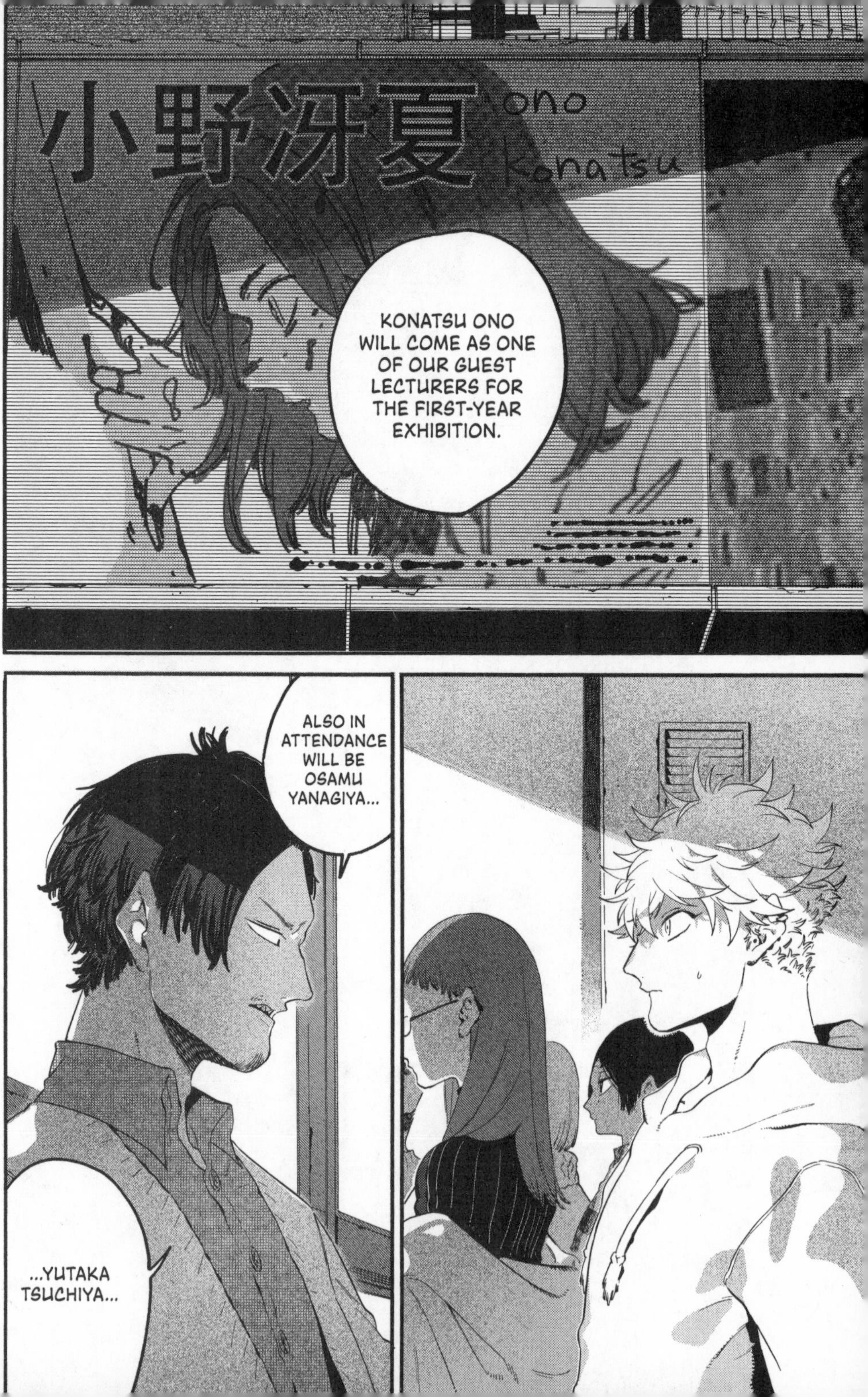
小野冴夏
ono konatsu
KONATSU ONO WILL COME AS ONE OF OUR GUEST LECTURERS FOR THE FIRST-YEAR EXHIBITION.
ALSO IN ATTENDANCE WILL BE OSAMU YANAGIYA...
...YUTAKA TSUCHIYA...

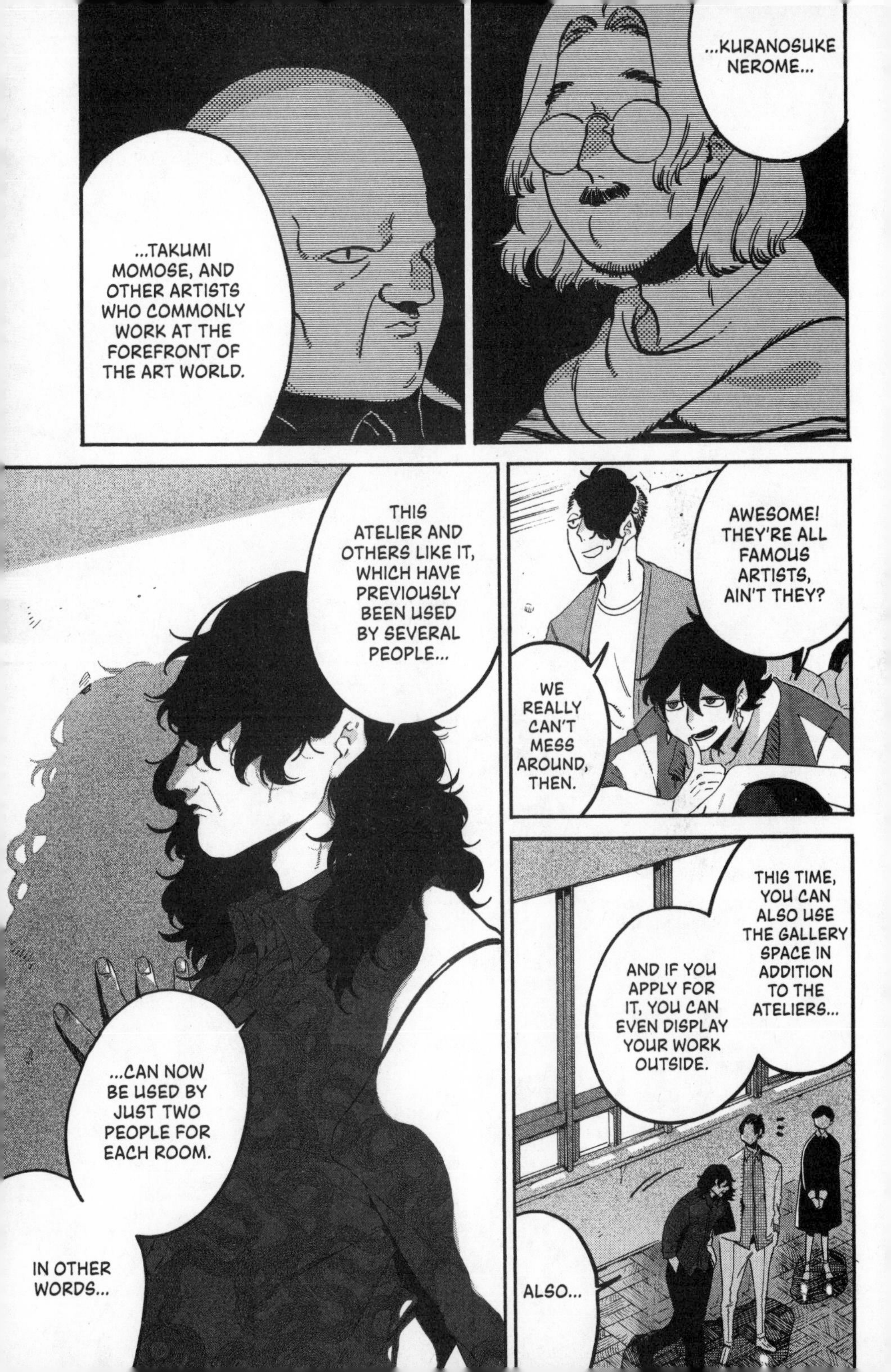
...KURANOSUKE NEROME...
...TAKUMI MOMOSE, AND OTHER ARTISTS WHO COMMONLY WORK AT THE FOREFRONT OF THE ART WORLD.
AWESOME! THEY'RE ALL FAMOUS ARTISTS, AIN'T THEY?
WE REALLY CAN'T MESS AROUND, THEN.
THIS TIME, YOU CAN ALSO USE THE GALLERY SPACE IN ADDITION TO THE ATELIERS...
AND IF YOU APPLY FOR IT, YOU CAN EVEN DISPLAY YOUR WORK OUTSIDE.
ALSO...
THIS ATELIER AND OTHERS LIKE IT, WHICH HAVE PREVIOUSLY BEEN USED BY SEVERAL PEOPLE...
...CAN NOW BE USED BY JUST TWO PEOPLE FOR EACH ROOM.
IN OTHER WORDS...

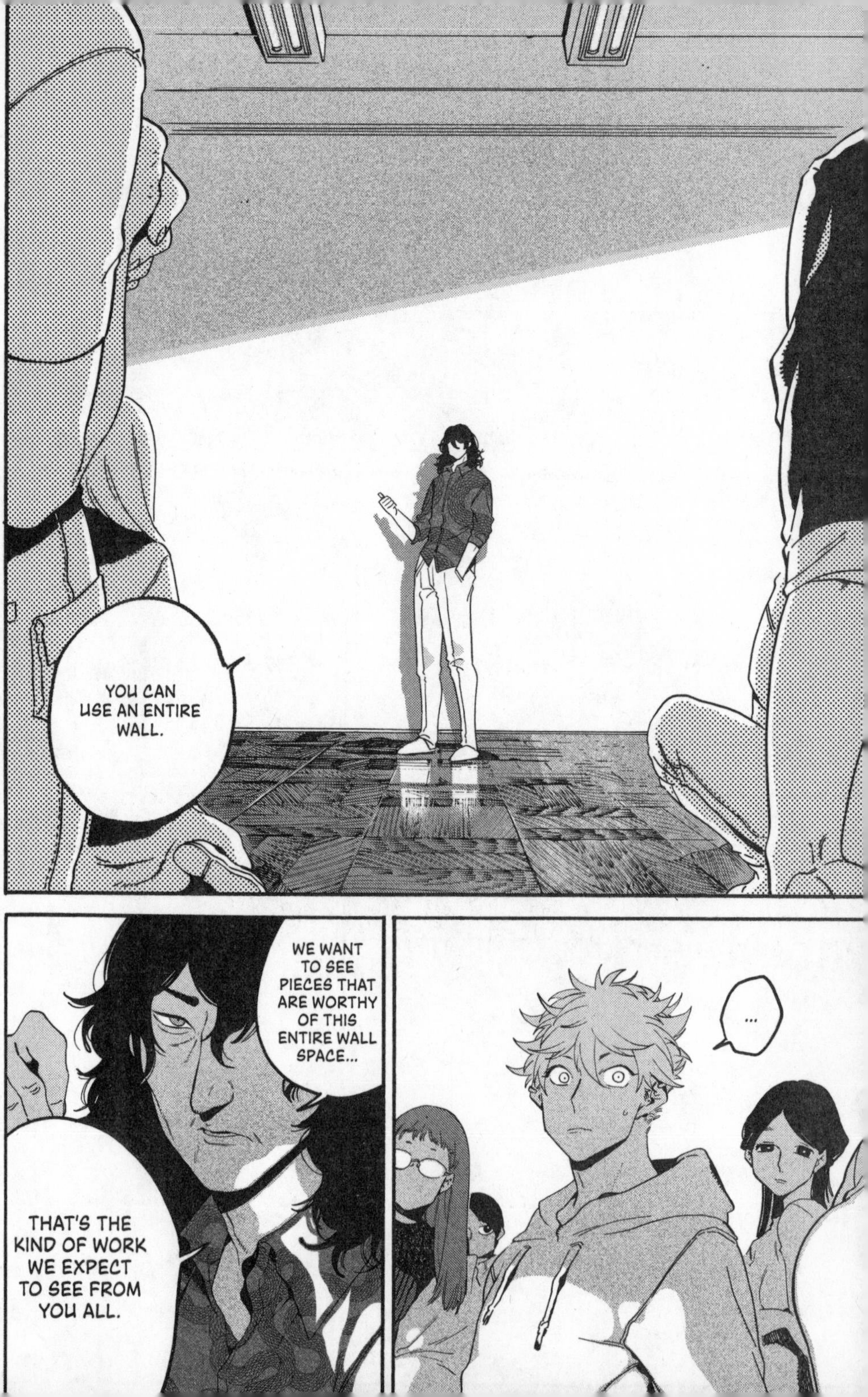
YOU CAN USE AN ENTIRE WALL.
...
WE WANT TO SEE PIECES THAT ARE WORTHY OF THIS ENTIRE WALL SPACE...
THAT'S THE KIND OF WORK WE EXPECT TO SEE FROM YOU ALL.

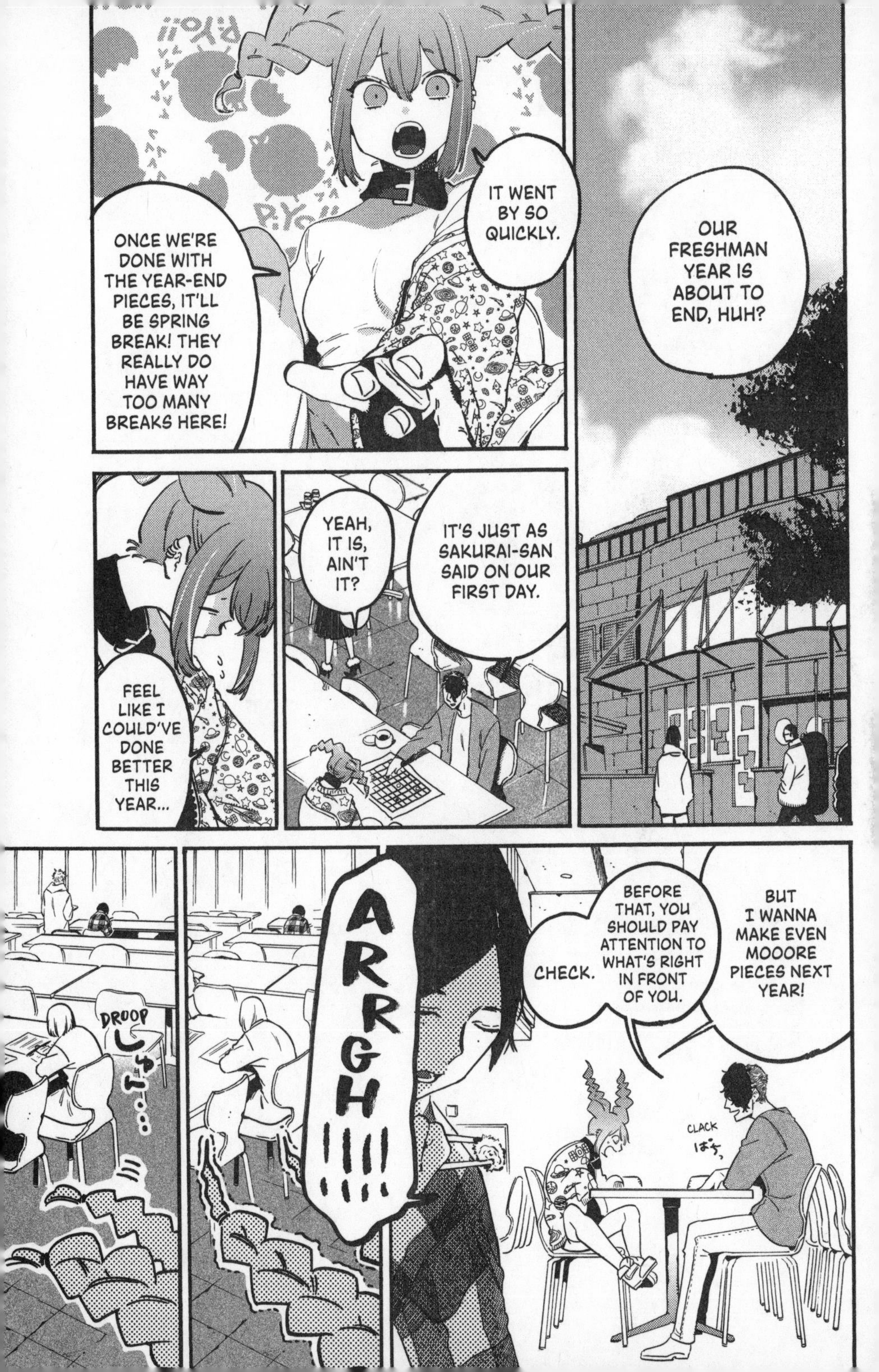

OUR FRESHMAN YEAR IS ABOUT TO END, HUH?
IT WENT BY SO QUICKLY.
ONCE WE'RE DONE WITH THE YEAR-END PIECES, IT'LL BE SPRING BREAK! THEY REALLY DO HAVE WAY TOO MANY BREAKS HERE!
IT'S JUST AS SAKURAI-SAN SAID ON OUR FIRST DAY.
YEAH, IT IS, AIN'T IT?
FEEL LIKE I COULD'VE DONE BETTER THIS YEAR...
BUT I WANNA MAKE EVEN MOOORE PIECES NEXT YEAR!
BEFORE THAT, YOU SHOULD PAY ATTENTION TO WHAT'S RIGHT IN FRONT OF YOU.
CHECK.
CLACK
ARRGH!!!!!
DROOP

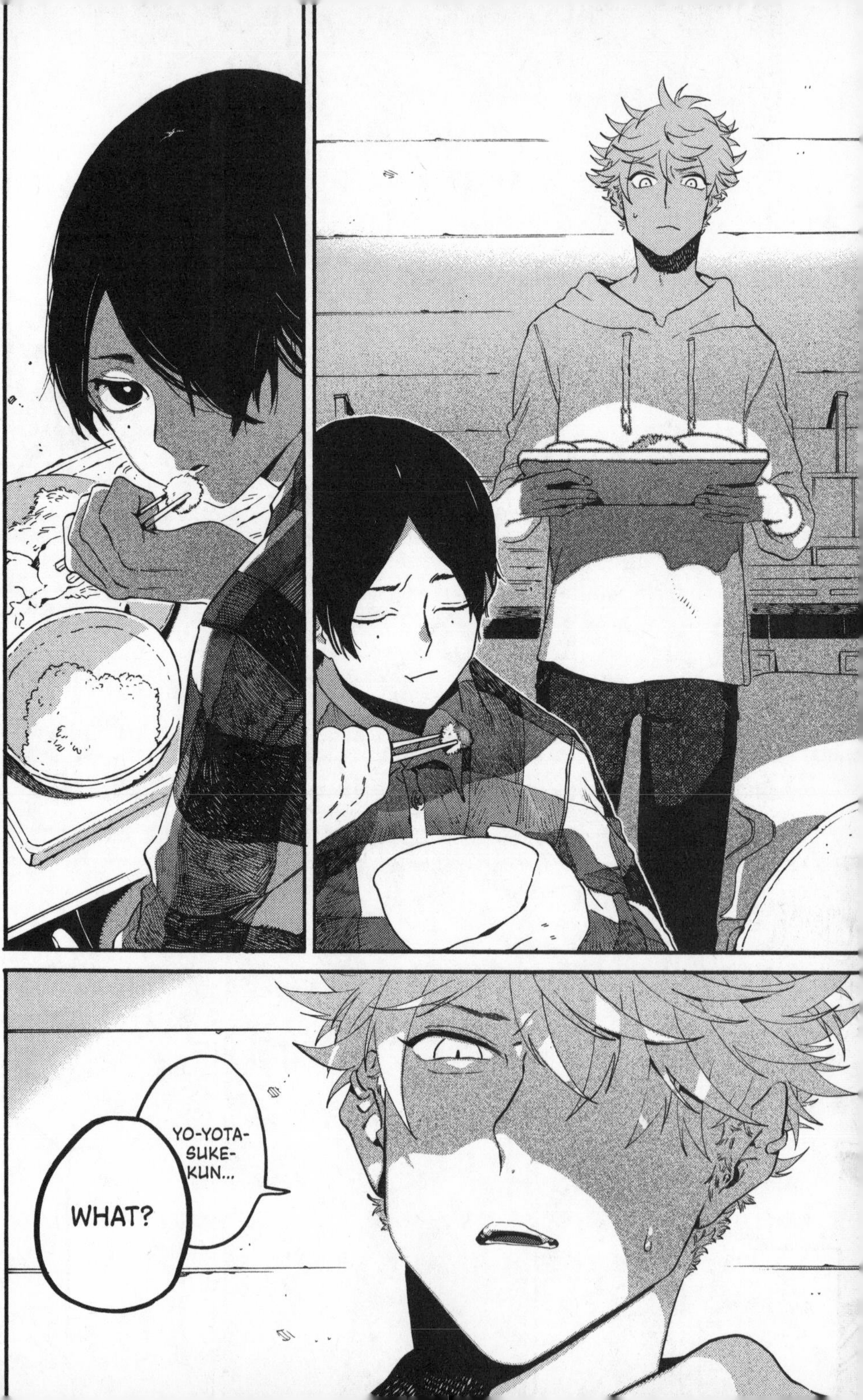

YO-YOTA-SUKE-KUN...
WHAT?

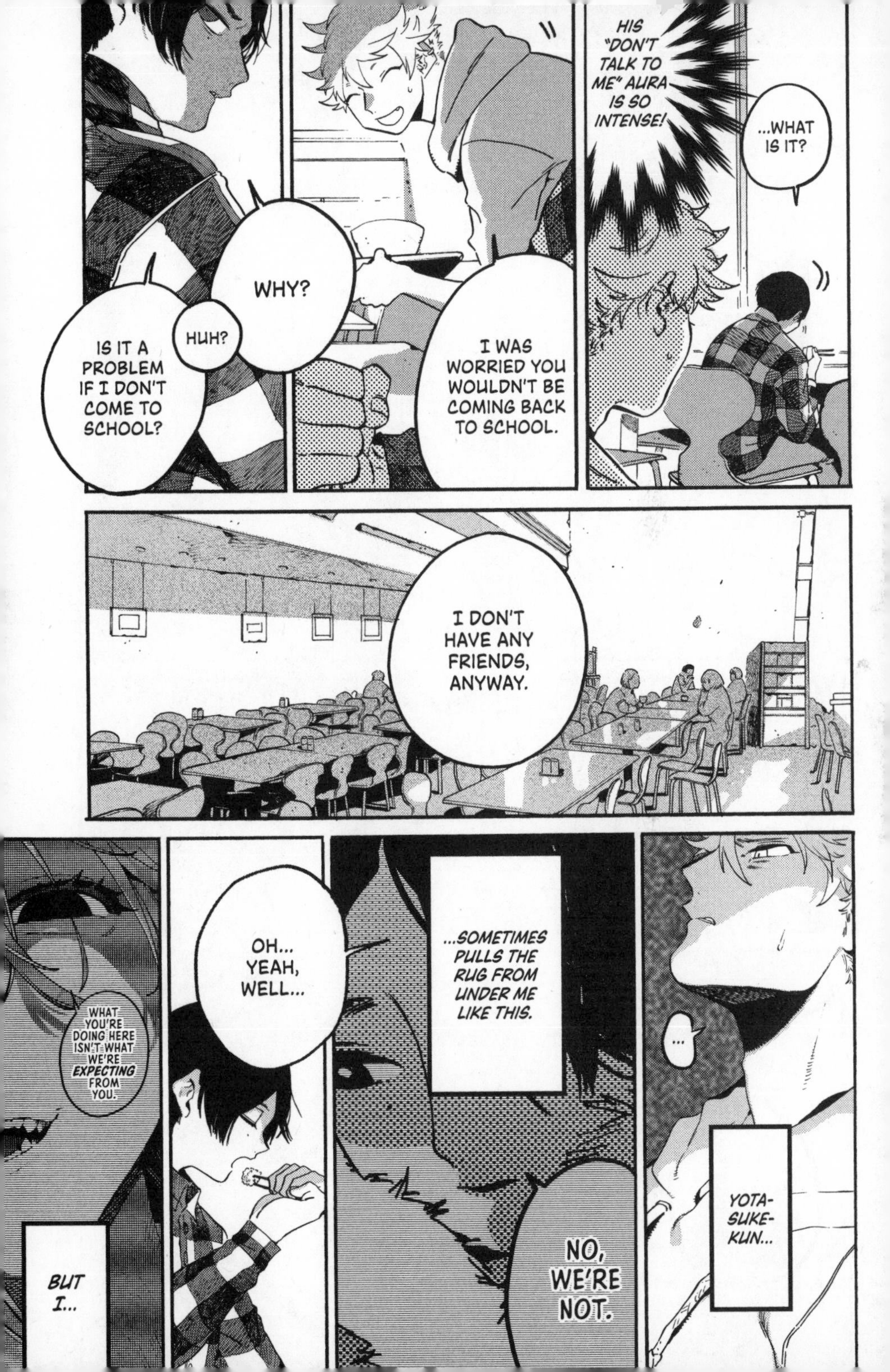
HIS "DON'T TALK TO ME" AURA IS SO INTENSE!
...WHAT IS IT?
I WAS WORRIED YOU WOULDN'T BE COMING BACK TO SCHOOL.
WHY?
HUH?
IS IT A PROBLEM IF I DON'T COME TO SCHOOL?
I DON'T HAVE ANY FRIENDS, ANYWAY.
...
YOTA-SUKE-KUN...
...SOMETIMES PULLS THE RUG FROM UNDER ME LIKE THIS.
NO, WE'RE NOT.
OH... YEAH, WELL...
WHAT YOU'RE DOING HERE ISN'T WHAT WE'RE EXPECTING FROM YOU.
BUT I...

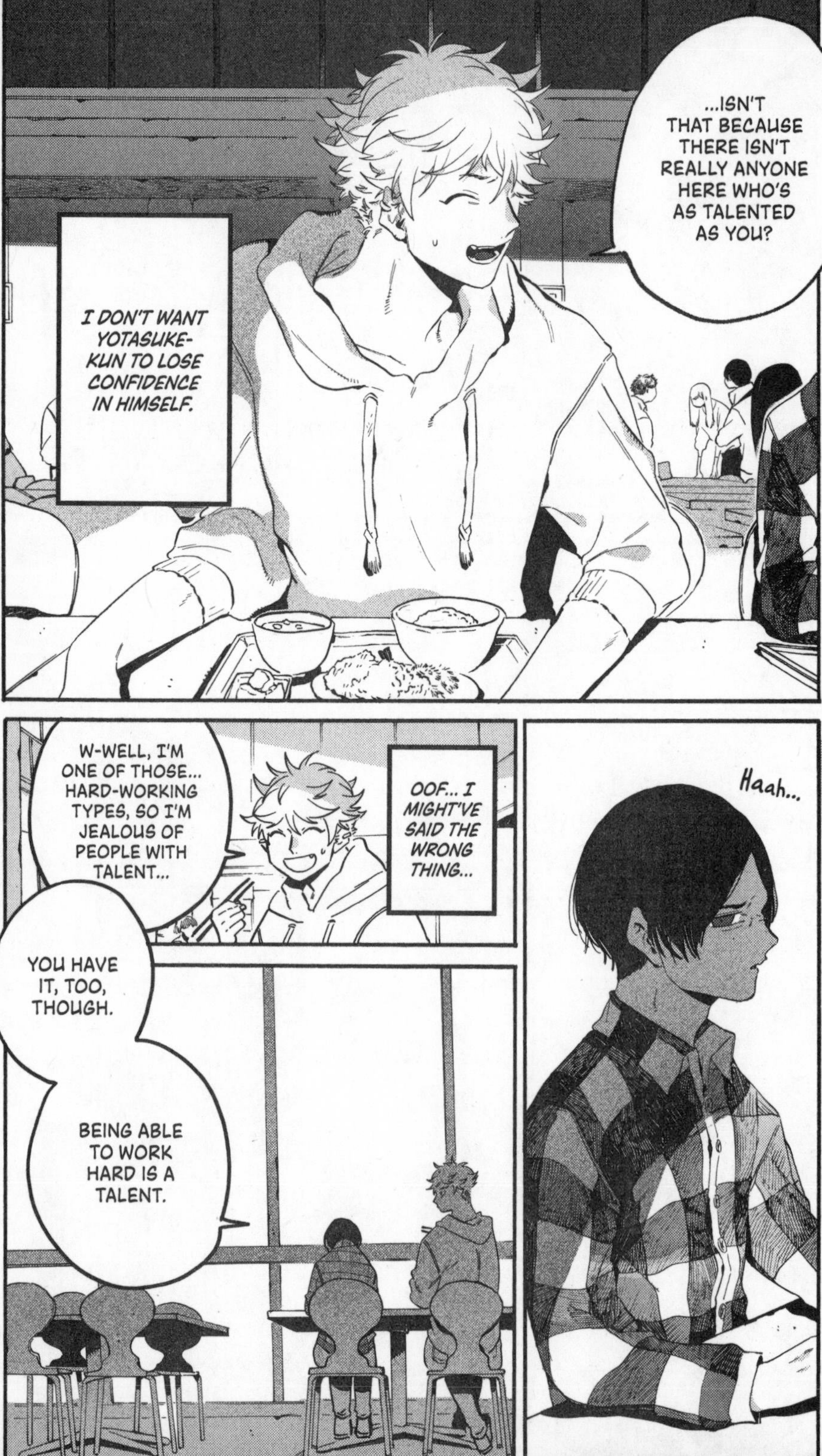
...ISN'T THAT BECAUSE THERE ISN'T REALLY ANYONE HERE WHO'S AS TALENTED AS YOU?
I DON'T WANT YOTASUKE-KUN TO LOSE CONFIDENCE IN HIMSELF.
Haah...
W-WELL, I'M ONE OF THOSE... HARD-WORKING TYPES, SO I'M JEALOUS OF PEOPLE WITH TALENT...
OOF... I MIGHT'VE SAID THE WRONG THING...
YOU HAVE IT, TOO, THOUGH.
BEING ABLE TO WORK HARD IS A TALENT.

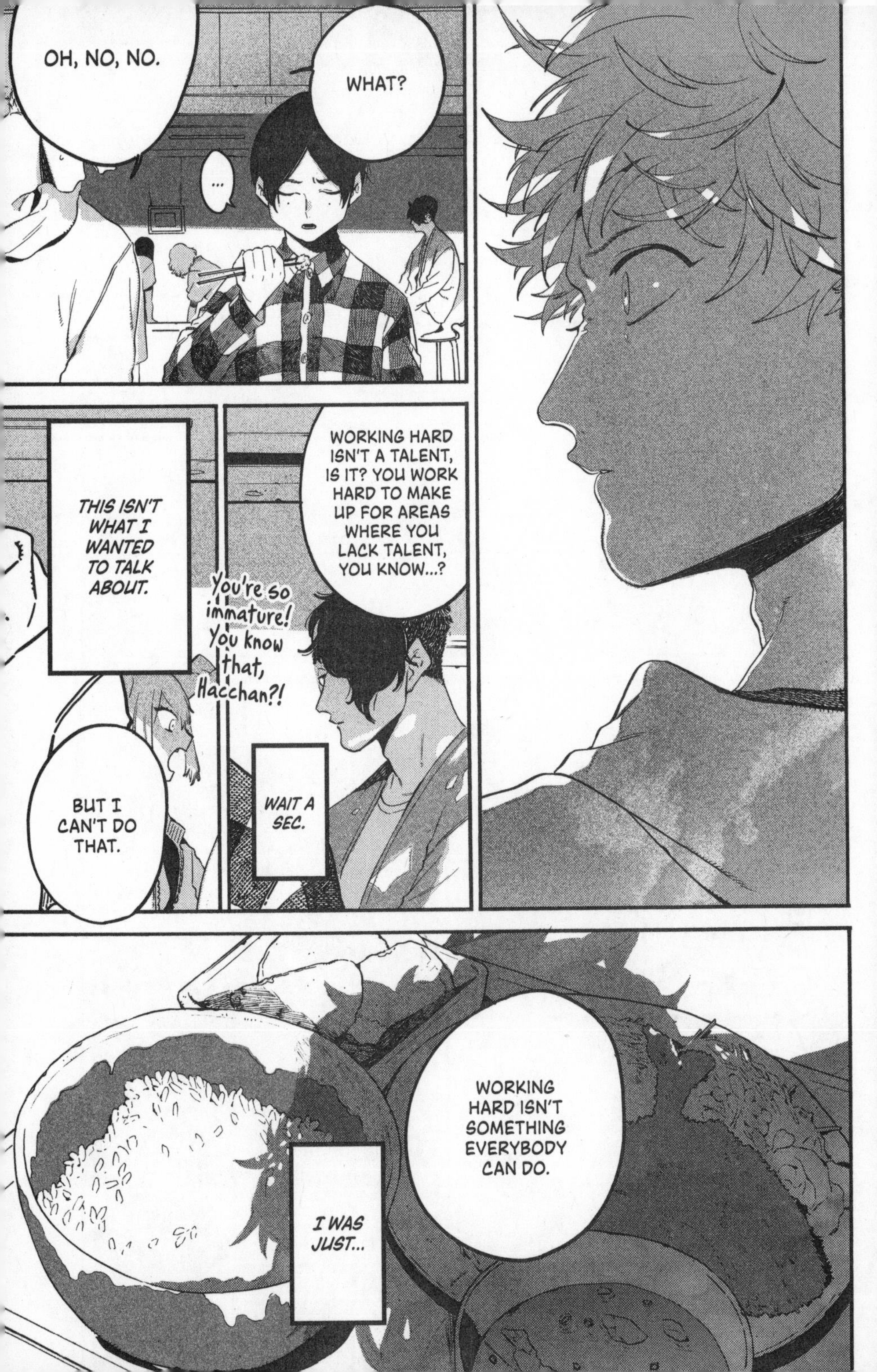
OH, NO, NO.
WHAT?
...
WORKING HARD ISN'T A TALENT, IS IT? YOU WORK HARD TO MAKE UP FOR AREAS WHERE YOU LACK TALENT, YOU KNOW...?
You're so immature! You know that, Hacchan?!
WAIT A SEC.
THIS ISN'T WHAT I WANTED TO TALK ABOUT.
BUT I CAN'T DO THAT.
WORKING HARD ISN'T SOMETHING EVERYBODY CAN DO.
I WAS JUST...

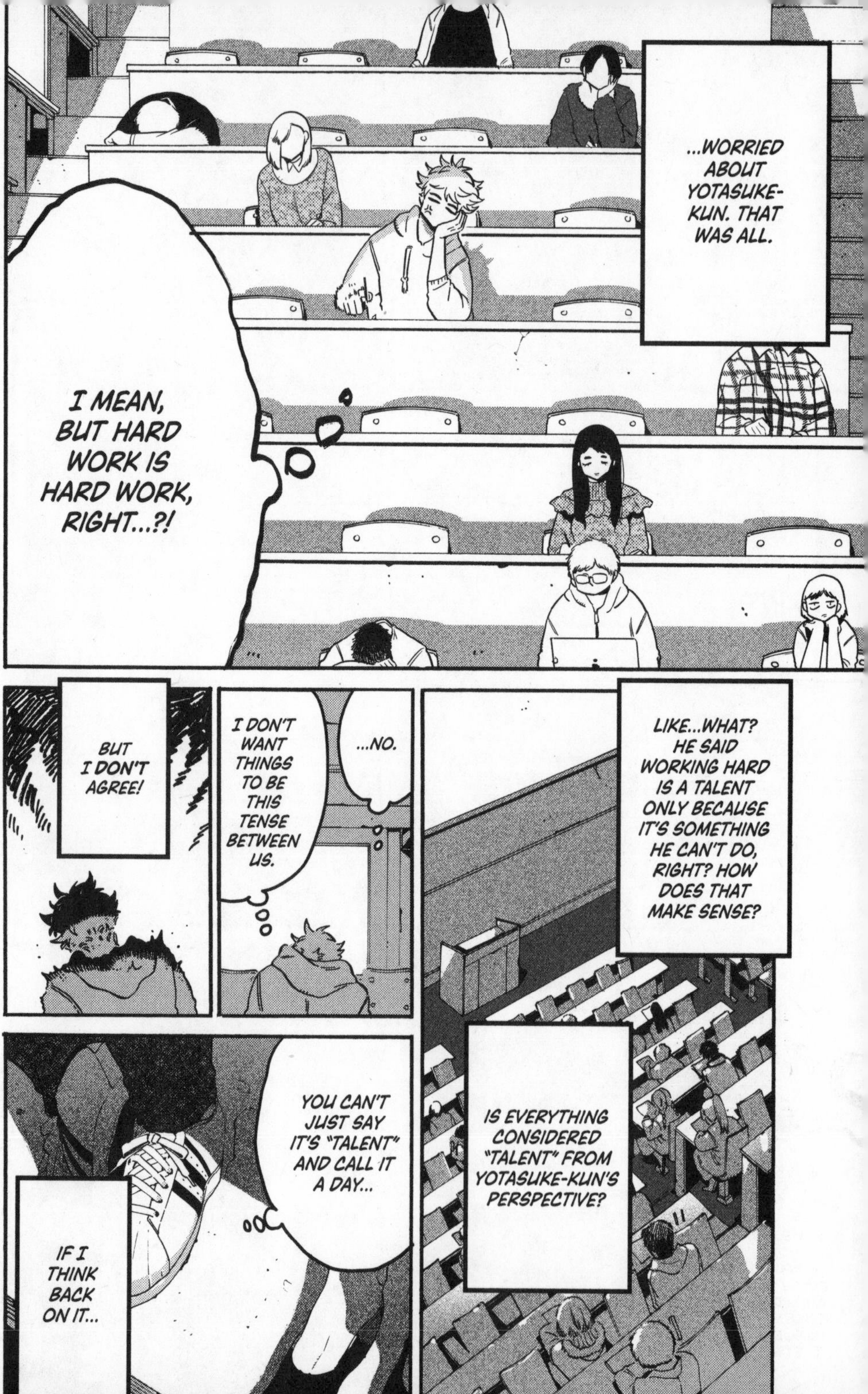
...WORRIED ABOUT YOTASUKE-KUN. THAT WAS ALL.
I MEAN, BUT HARD WORK IS HARD WORK, RIGHT...?!
LIKE...WHAT? HE SAID WORKING HARD IS A TALENT ONLY BECAUSE IT'S SOMETHING HE CAN'T DO, RIGHT? HOW DOES THAT MAKE SENSE?
IS EVERYTHING CONSIDERED "TALENT" FROM YOTASUKE-KUN'S PERSPECTIVE?
...NO.
I DON'T WANT THINGS TO BE THIS TENSE BETWEEN US.
BUT I DON'T AGREE!
YOU CAN'T JUST SAY IT'S "TALENT" AND CALL IT A DAY...
IF I THINK BACK ON IT...

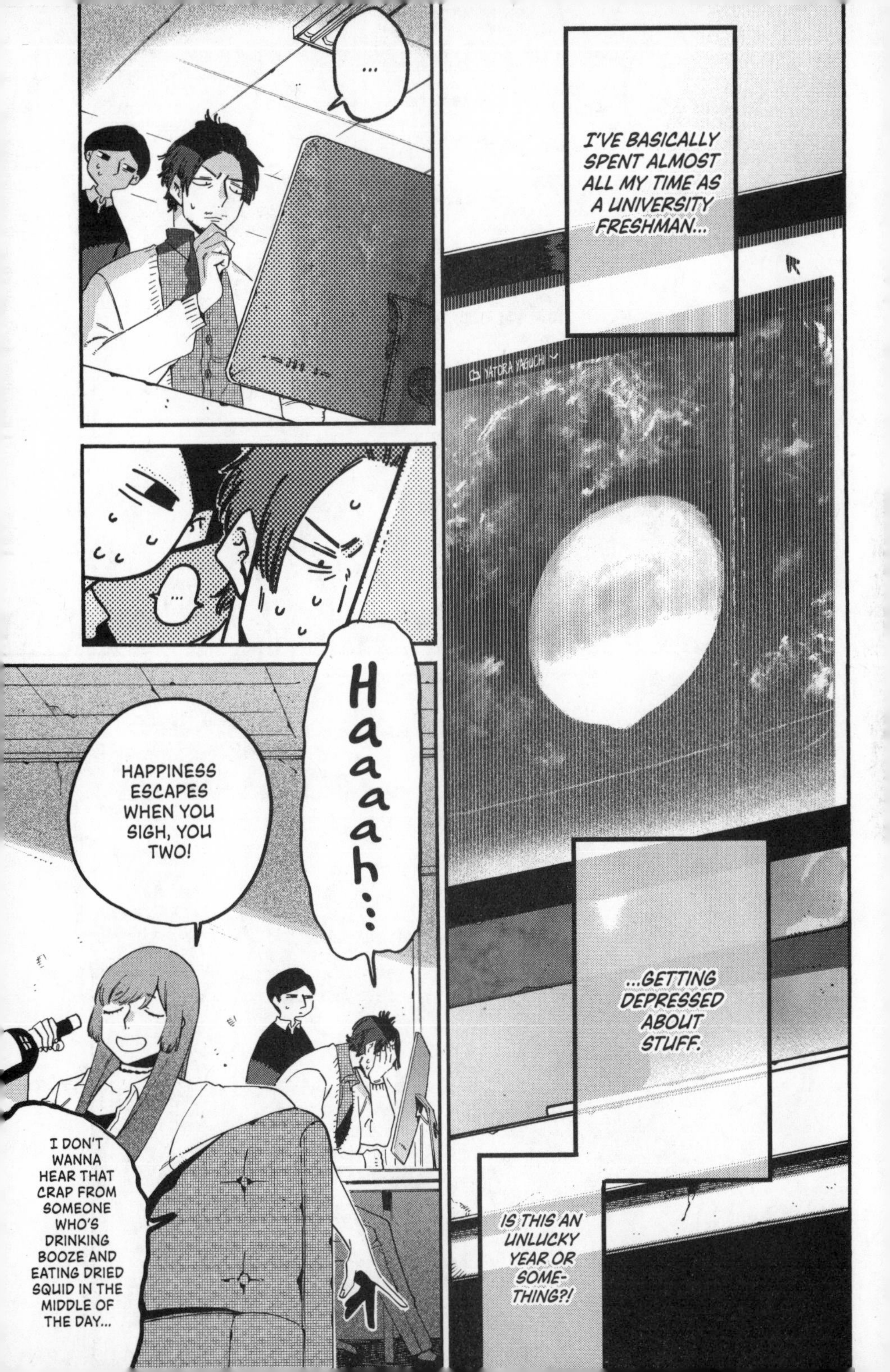
I'VE BASICALLY SPENT ALMOST ALL MY TIME AS A UNIVERSITY FRESHMAN...
YATORA YAGUCHI
...GETTING DEPRESSED ABOUT STUFF.
IS THIS AN UNLUCKY YEAR OR SOME-THING?!
...
...
Haaaah..
HAPPINESS ESCAPES WHEN YOU SIGH, YOU TWO!
I DON'T WANNA HEAR THAT CRAP FROM SOMEONE WHO'S DRINKING BOOZE AND EATING DRIED SQUID IN THE MIDDLE OF THE DAY...

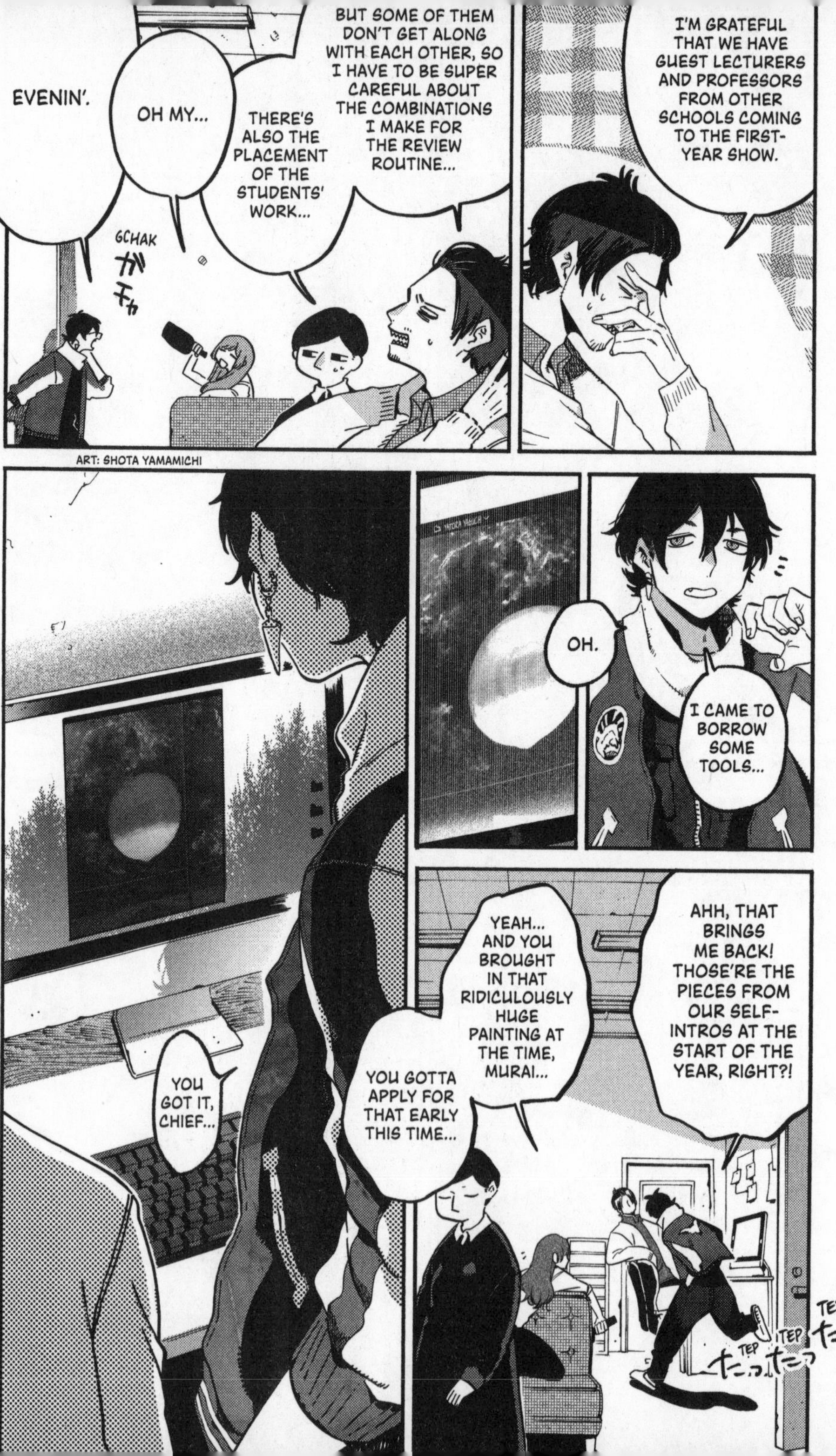
I'M GRATEFUL THAT WE HAVE GUEST LECTURERS AND PROFESSORS FROM OTHER SCHOOLS COMING TO THE FIRST-YEAR SHOW.
THERE'S ALSO THE PLACEMENT OF THE STUDENTS' WORK...
BUT SOME OF THEM DON'T GET ALONG WITH EACH OTHER, SO I HAVE TO BE SUPER CAREFUL ABOUT THE COMBINATIONS I MAKE FOR THE REVIEW ROUTINE...
OH MY...
EVENIN'.
GCHAK
ART: SHOTA YAMAMICHI
OH.
I CAME TO BORROW SOME TOOLS...
AHH, THAT BRINGS ME BACK! THOSE'RE THE PIECES FROM OUR SELF-INTROS AT THE START OF THE YEAR, RIGHT?!
YEAH... AND YOU BROUGHT IN THAT RIDICULOUSLY HUGE PAINTING AT THE TIME, MURAI...
YOU GOTTA APPLY FOR THAT EARLY THIS TIME...
TEP TEP TEP
YOU GOT IT, CHIEF...

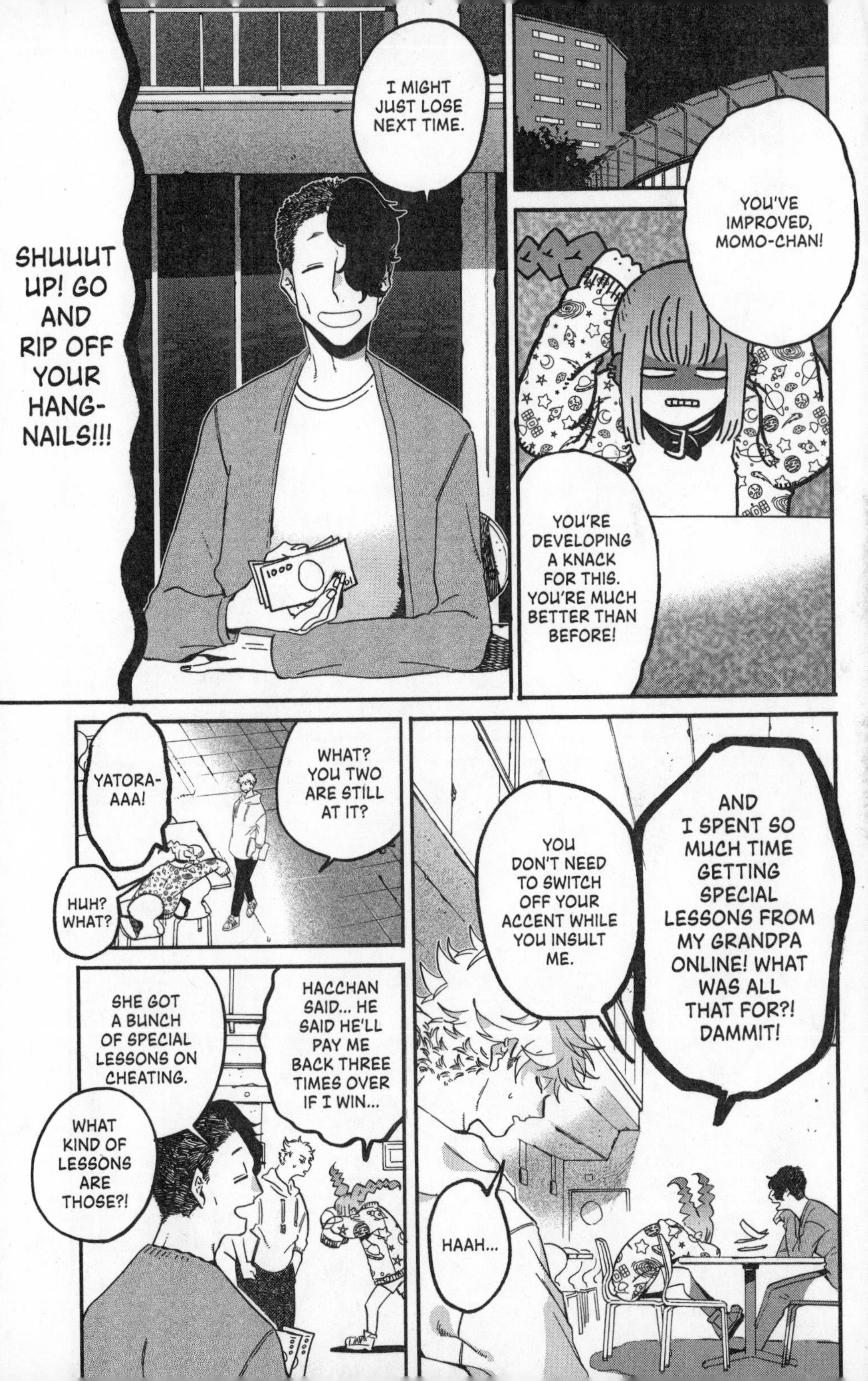
YOU'VE IMPROVED, MOMO-CHAN!
YOU'RE DEVELOPING A KNACK FOR THIS. YOU'RE MUCH BETTER THAN BEFORE!
I MIGHT JUST LOSE NEXT TIME.
SHUUUT UP! GO AND RIP OFF YOUR HANG-NAILS!!!
AND I SPENT SO MUCH TIME GETTING SPECIAL LESSONS FROM MY GRANDPA ONLINE! WHAT WAS ALL THAT FOR?! DAMMIT!
YOU DON'T NEED TO SWITCH OFF YOUR ACCENT WHILE YOU INSULT ME.
HAAH...
WHAT? YOU TWO ARE STILL AT IT?
YATORA-AAA!
HUH? WHAT?
HACCHAN SAID... HE SAID HE'LL PAY ME BACK THREE TIMES OVER IF I WIN...
SHE GOT A BUNCH OF SPECIAL LESSONS ON CHEATING.
WHAT KIND OF LESSONS ARE THOSE?!

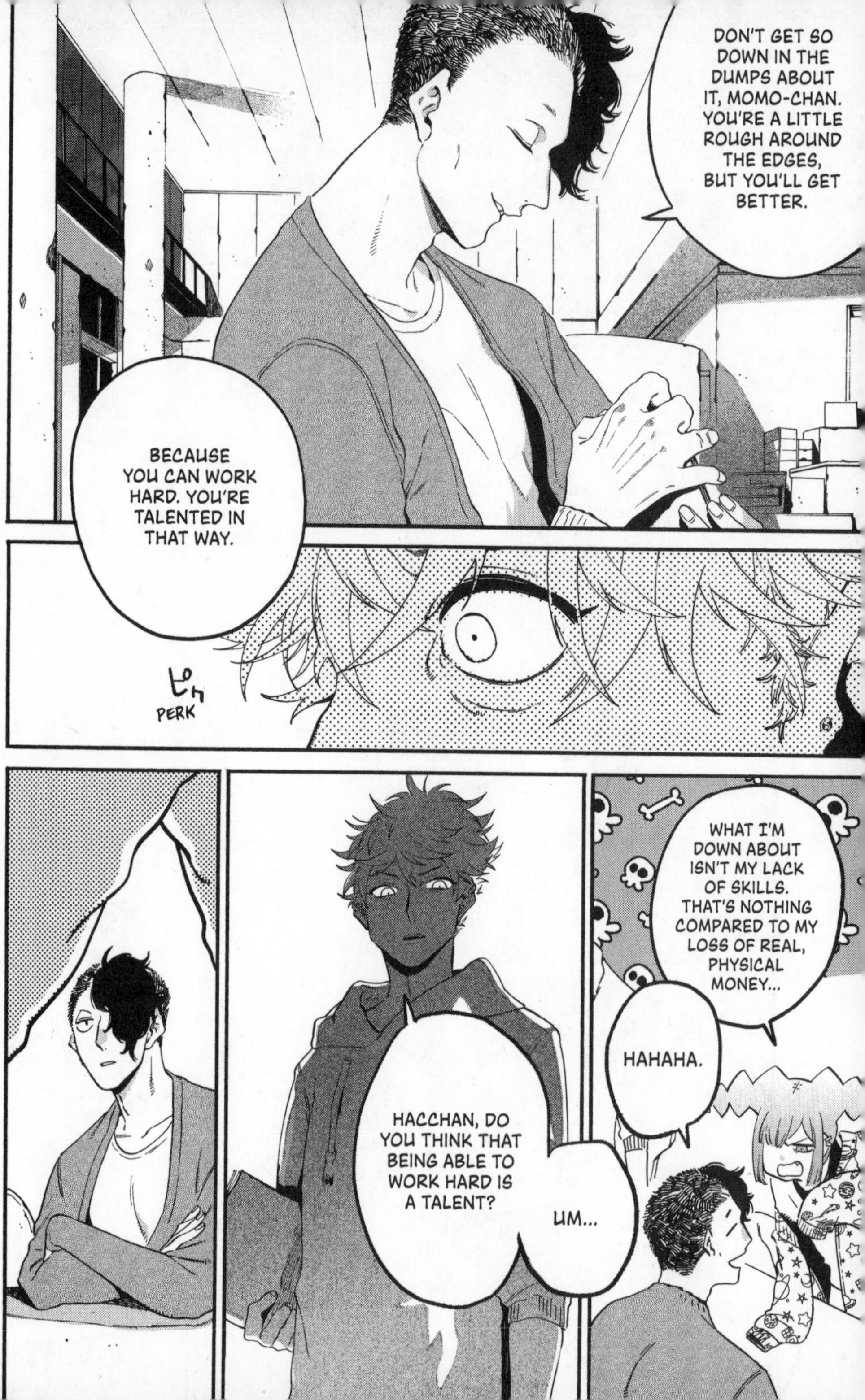
DON'T GET SO DOWN IN THE DUMPS ABOUT IT, MOMO-CHAN. YOU'RE A LITTLE ROUGH AROUND THE EDGES, BUT YOU'LL GET BETTER.
BECAUSE YOU CAN WORK HARD. YOU'RE TALENTED IN THAT WAY.
ピク
PERK
WHAT I'M DOWN ABOUT ISN'T MY LACK OF SKILLS. THAT'S NOTHING COMPARED TO MY LOSS OF REAL, PHYSICAL MONEY...
HAHAHA.
HACCHAN, DO YOU THINK THAT BEING ABLE TO WORK HARD IS A TALENT?
UM...

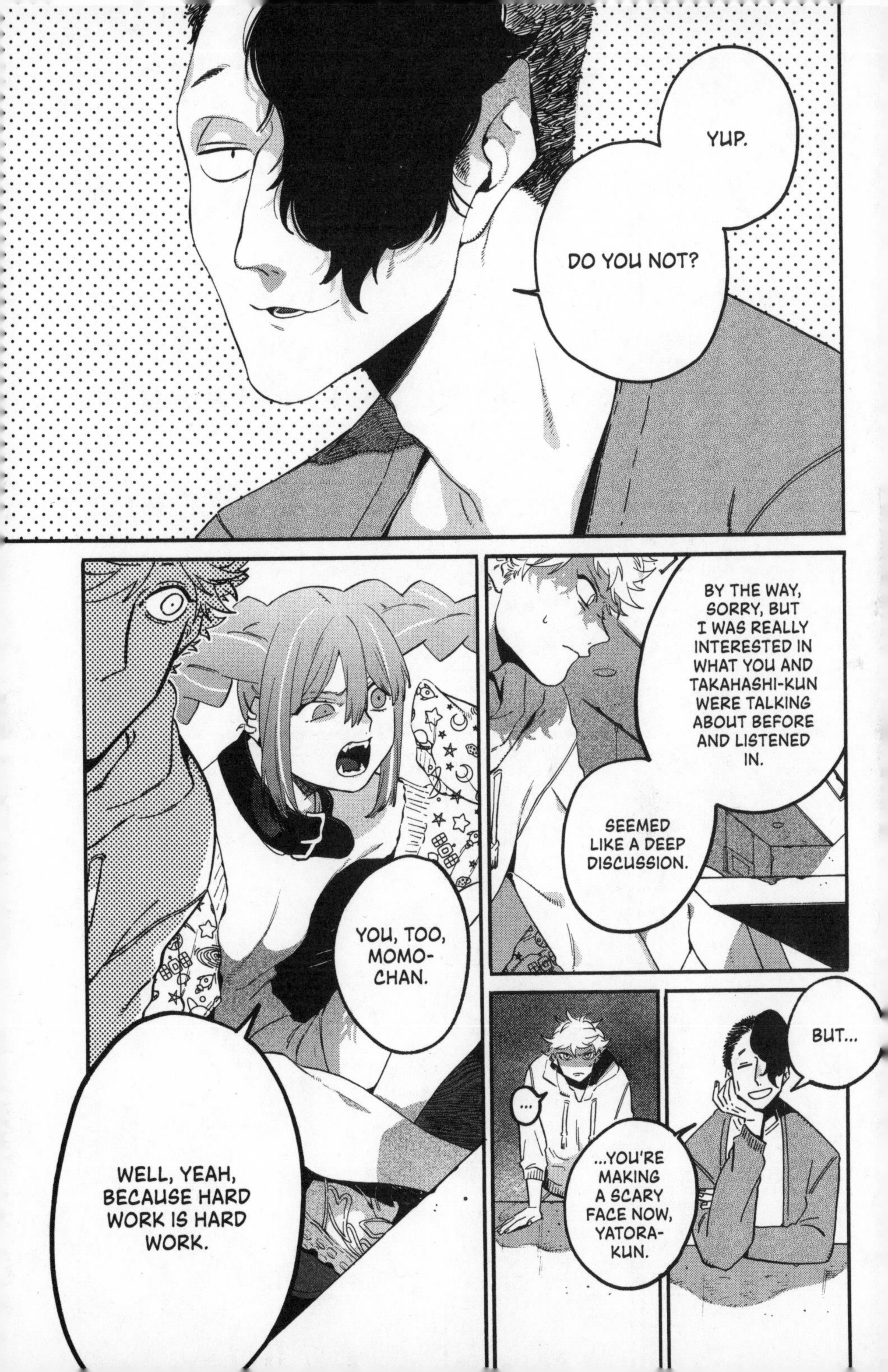
YUP.
DO YOU NOT?
BY THE WAY, SORRY, BUT I WAS REALLY INTERESTED IN WHAT YOU AND TAKAHASHI-KUN WERE TALKING ABOUT BEFORE AND LISTENED IN.
SEEMED LIKE A DEEP DISCUSSION.
BUT...
...YOU'RE MAKING A SCARY FACE NOW, YATORA-KUN.
...
YOU, TOO, MOMO-CHAN.
WELL, YEAH, BECAUSE HARD WORK IS HARD WORK.

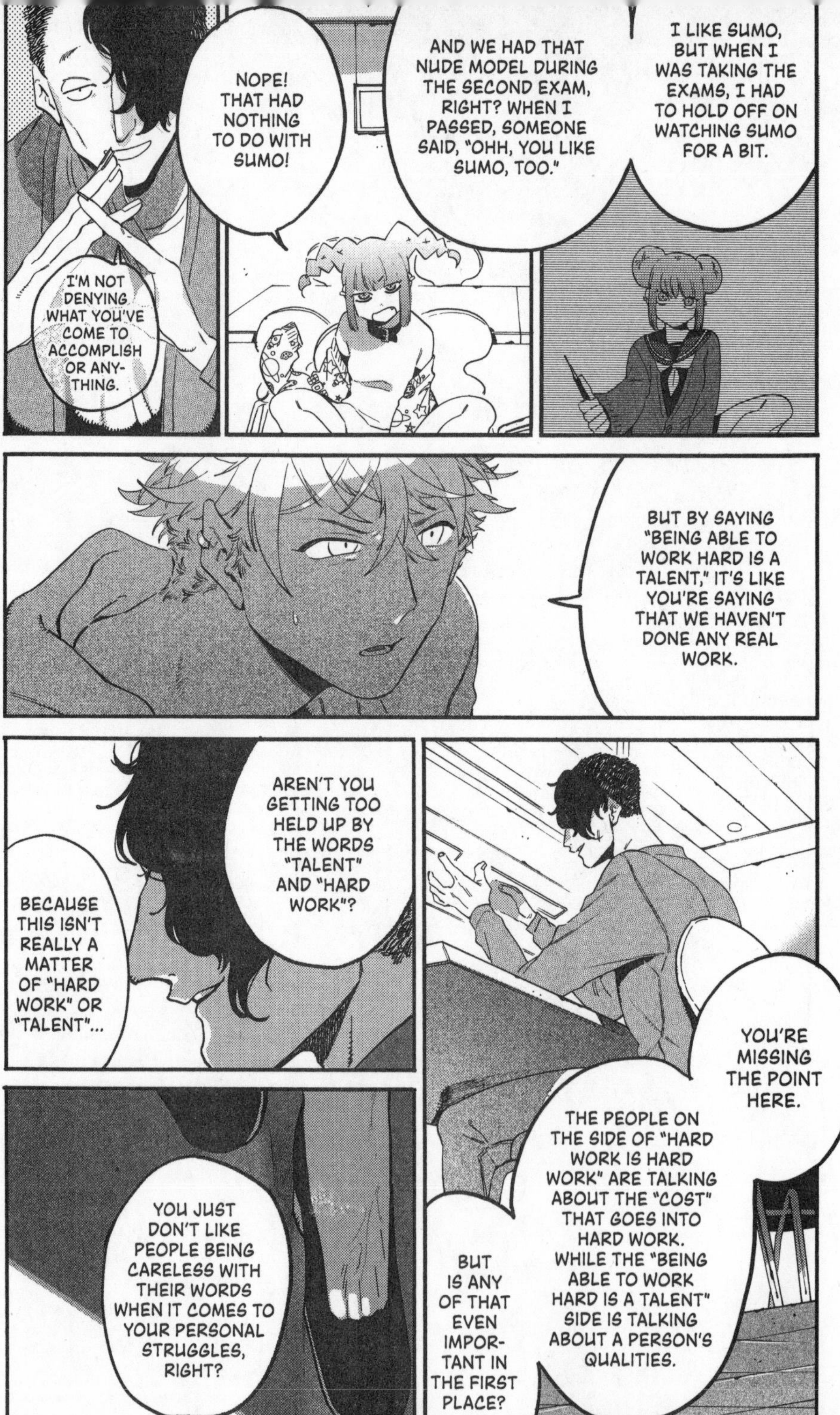
I LIKE SUMO, BUT WHEN I WAS TAKING THE EXAMS, I HAD TO HOLD OFF ON WATCHING SUMO FOR A BIT.
AND WE HAD THAT NUDE MODEL DURING THE SECOND EXAM, RIGHT? WHEN I PASSED, SOMEONE SAID, "OHH, YOU LIKE SUMO, TOO."
NOPE! THAT HAD NOTHING TO DO WITH SUMO!
I'M NOT DENYING WHAT YOU'VE COME TO ACCOMPLISH OR ANY-THING.
BUT BY SAYING "BEING ABLE TO WORK HARD IS A TALENT," IT'S LIKE YOU'RE SAYING THAT WE HAVEN'T DONE ANY REAL WORK.
YOU'RE MISSING THE POINT HERE.
THE PEOPLE ON THE SIDE OF "HARD WORK IS HARD WORK" ARE TALKING ABOUT THE "COST" THAT GOES INTO HARD WORK. WHILE THE "BEING ABLE TO WORK HARD IS A TALENT" SIDE IS TALKING ABOUT A PERSON'S QUALITIES.
BUT IS ANY OF THAT EVEN IMPOR-TANT IN THE FIRST PLACE?
AREN'T YOU GETTING TOO HELD UP BY THE WORDS "TALENT" AND "HARD WORK"?
BECAUSE THIS ISN'T REALLY A MATTER OF "HARD WORK" OR "TALENT"...
YOU JUST DON'T LIKE PEOPLE BEING CARELESS WITH THEIR WORDS WHEN IT COMES TO YOUR PERSONAL STRUGGLES, RIGHT?

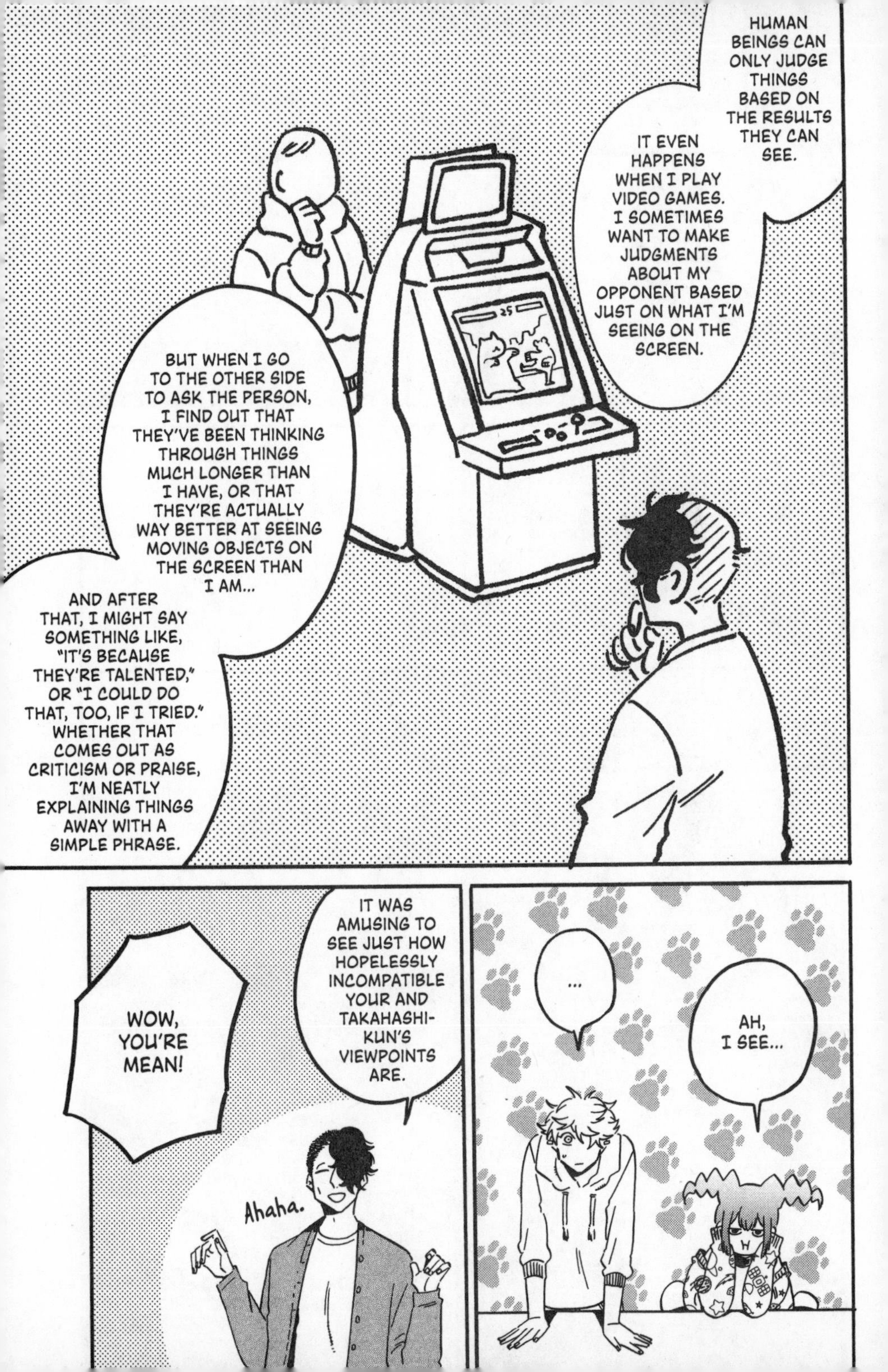
HUMAN BEINGS CAN ONLY JUDGE THINGS BASED ON THE RESULTS THEY CAN SEE.
IT EVEN HAPPENS WHEN I PLAY VIDEO GAMES. I SOMETIMES WANT TO MAKE JUDGMENTS ABOUT MY OPPONENT BASED JUST ON WHAT I'M SEEING ON THE SCREEN.
BUT WHEN I GO TO THE OTHER SIDE TO ASK THE PERSON, I FIND OUT THAT THEY'VE BEEN THINKING THROUGH THINGS MUCH LONGER THAN I HAVE, OR THAT THEY'RE ACTUALLY WAY BETTER AT SEEING MOVING OBJECTS ON THE SCREEN THAN I AM...
AND AFTER THAT, I MIGHT SAY SOMETHING LIKE, "IT'S BECAUSE THEY'RE TALENTED," OR "I COULD DO THAT, TOO, IF I TRIED." WHETHER THAT COMES OUT AS CRITICISM OR PRAISE, I'M NEATLY EXPLAINING THINGS AWAY WITH A SIMPLE PHRASE.
...
AH, I SEE...
IT WAS AMUSING TO SEE JUST HOW HOPELESSLY INCOMPATIBLE YOUR AND TAKAHASHI-KUN'S VIEWPOINTS ARE.
WOW, YOU'RE MEAN!
Ahaha.

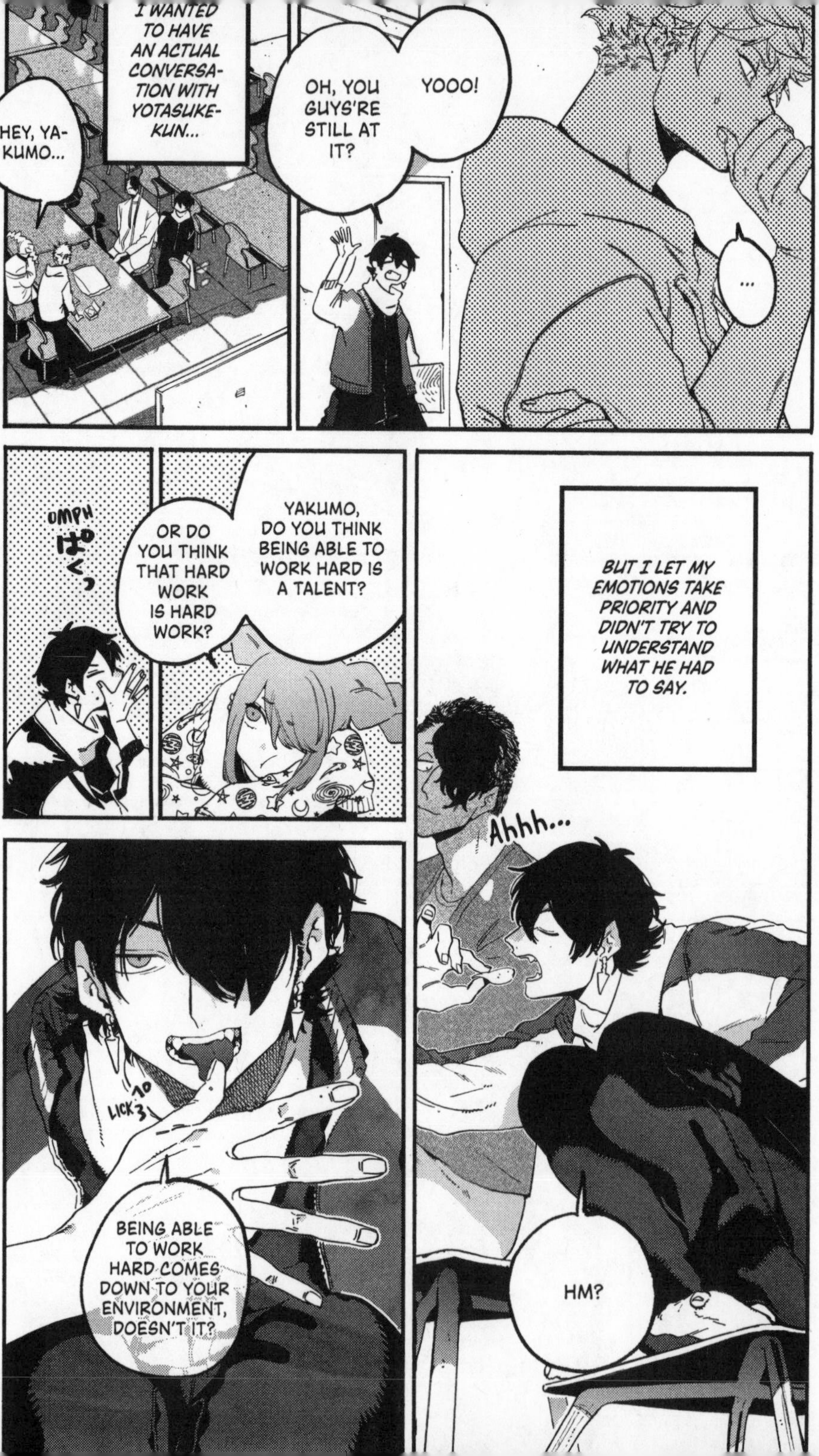
...
YOOO!
OH, YOU GUYS'RE STILL AT IT?
I WANTED TO HAVE AN ACTUAL CONVERSATION WITH YOTASUKE-KUN...
HEY, YA-KUMO...
BUT I LET MY EMOTIONS TAKE PRIORITY AND DIDN'T TRY TO UNDERSTAND WHAT HE HAD TO SAY.
Ahhh...
HM?
YAKUMO, DO YOU THINK BEING ABLE TO WORK HARD IS A TALENT?
OR DO YOU THINK THAT HARD WORK IS HARD WORK?
OMPH
ぱくっ
LICK
BEING ABLE TO WORK HARD COMES DOWN TO YOUR ENVIRONMENT, DOESN'T IT?

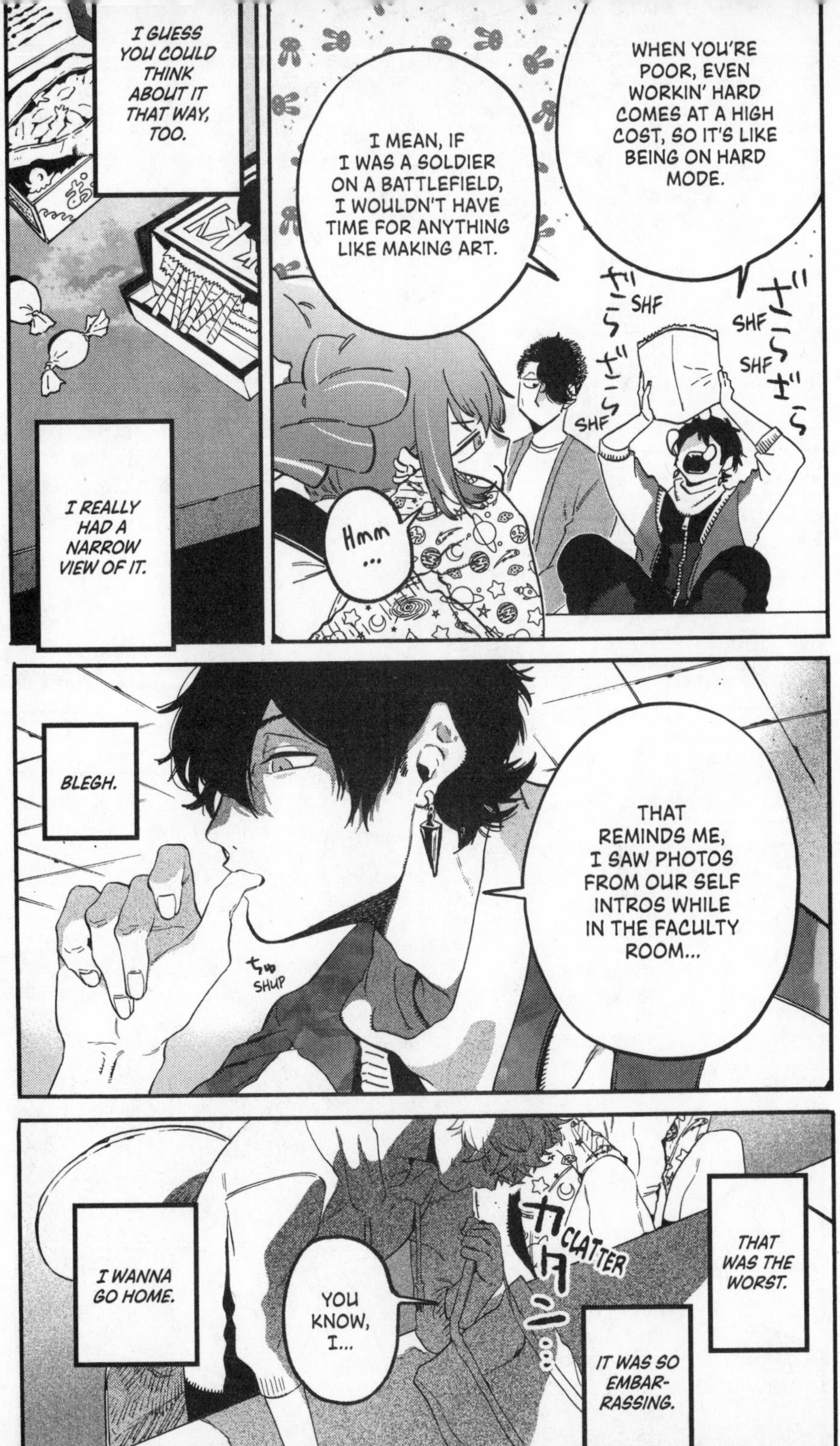

WHEN YOU'RE POOR, EVEN WORKIN' HARD COMES AT A HIGH COST, SO IT'S LIKE BEING ON HARD MODE.
I MEAN, IF I WAS A SOLDIER ON A BATTLEFIELD, I WOULDN'T HAVE TIME FOR ANYTHING LIKE MAKING ART.
SHF SHF SHF SHF
Hmm ...
I GUESS YOU COULD THINK ABOUT IT THAT WAY, TOO.
I REALLY HAD A NARROW VIEW OF IT.
THAT REMINDS ME, I SAW PHOTOS FROM OUR SELF INTROS WHILE IN THE FACULTY ROOM...
BLEGH.
SHUP
THAT WAS THE WORST.
IT WAS SO EMBARRASSING.
CLATTER
YOU KNOW, I...
I WANNA GO HOME.

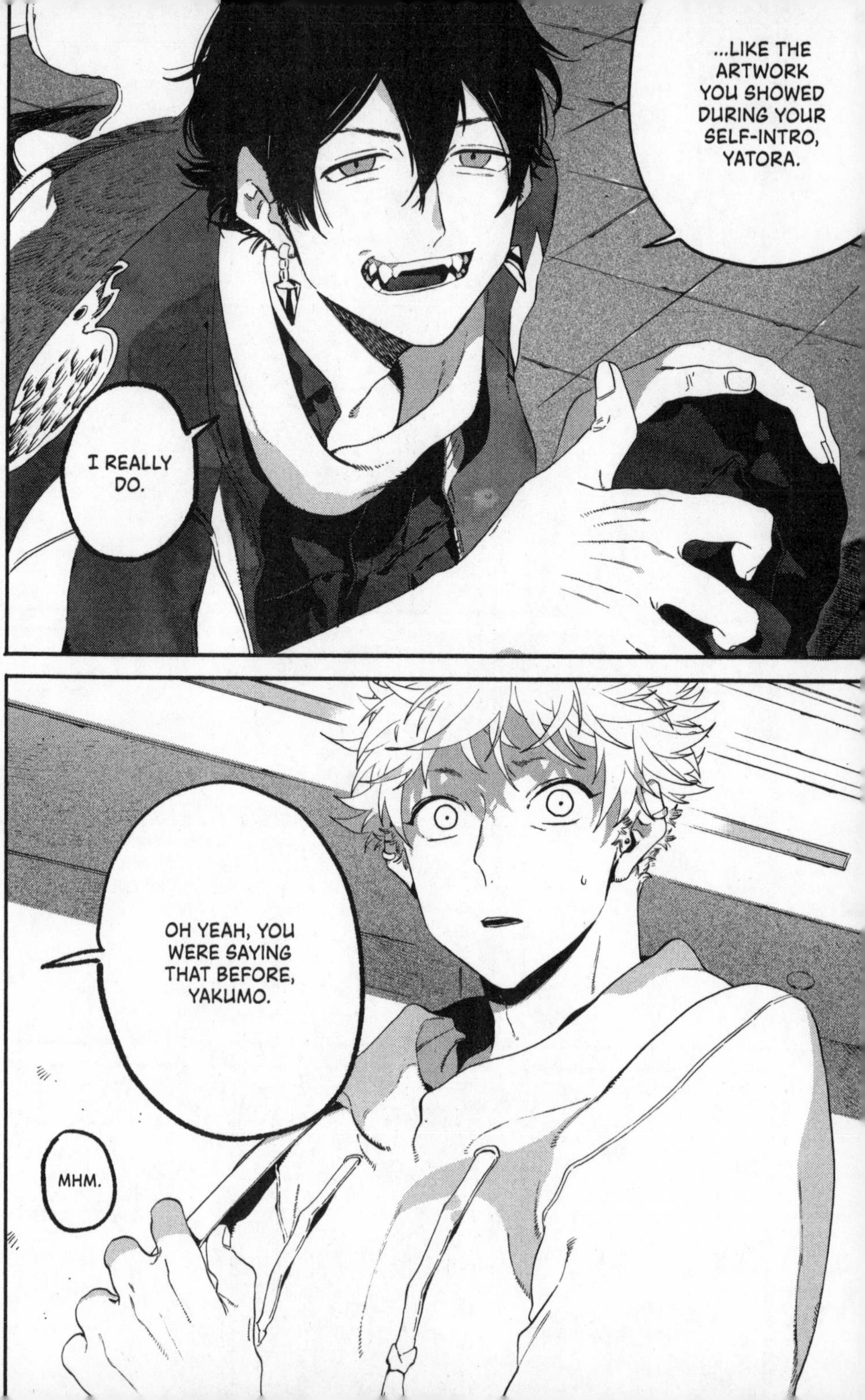
...LIKE THE ARTWORK YOU SHOWED DURING YOUR SELF-INTRO, YATORA.
I REALLY DO.
OH YEAH, YOU WERE SAYING THAT BEFORE, YAKUMO.
MHM.

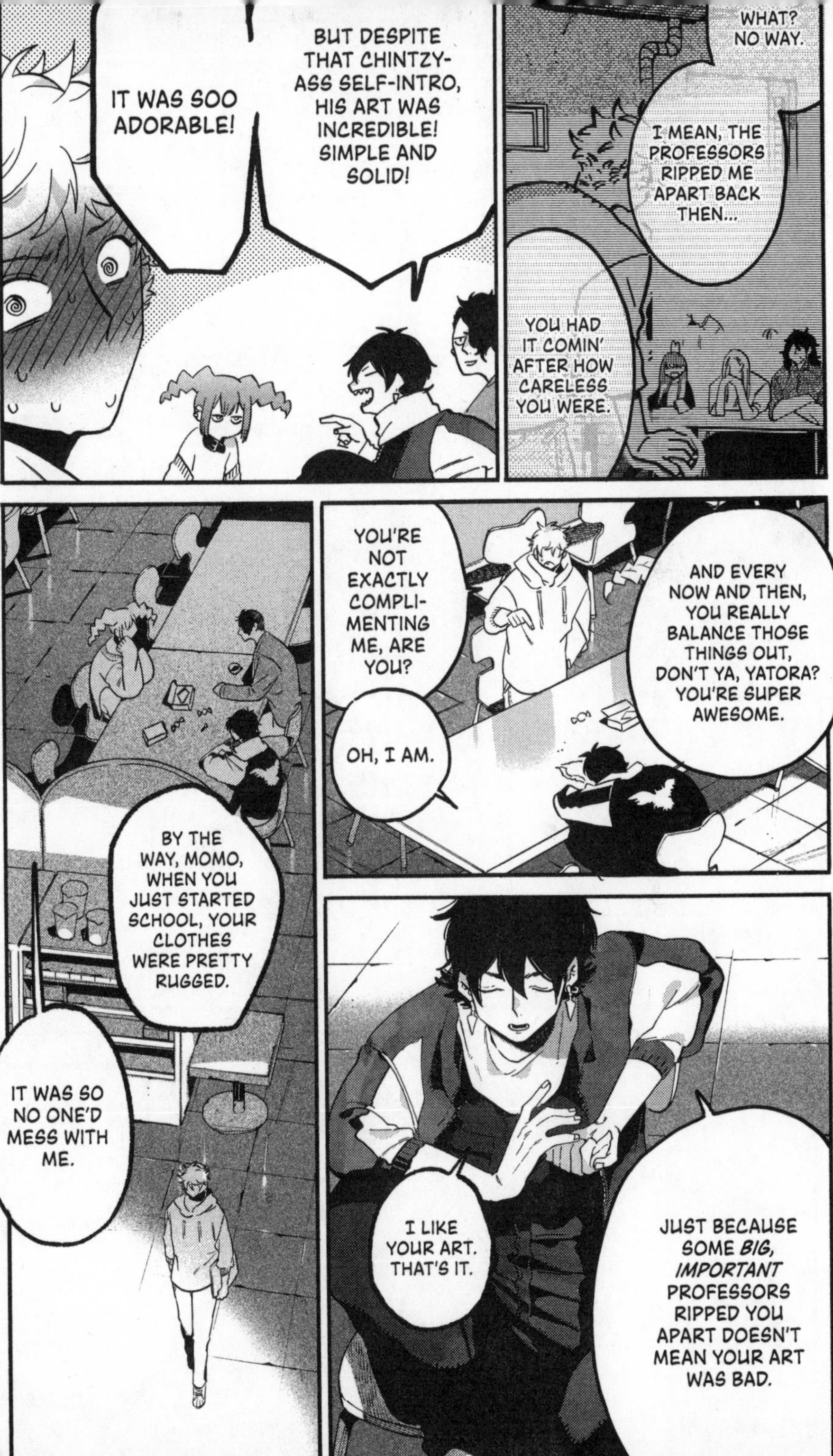
WHAT? NO WAY.
I MEAN, THE PROFESSORS RIPPED ME APART BACK THEN...
YOU HAD IT COMIN' AFTER HOW CARELESS YOU WERE.
BUT DESPITE THAT CHINTZY-ASS SELF-INTRO, HIS ART WAS INCREDIBLE! SIMPLE AND SOLID!
IT WAS SOO ADORABLE!
AND EVERY NOW AND THEN, YOU REALLY BALANCE THOSE THINGS OUT, DON'T YA, YATORA? YOU'RE SUPER AWESOME.
YOU'RE NOT EXACTLY COMPLIMENTING ME, ARE YOU?
OH, I AM.
JUST BECAUSE SOME *BIG, IMPORTANT* PROFESSORS RIPPED YOU APART DOESN'T MEAN YOUR ART WAS BAD.
I LIKE YOUR ART. THAT'S IT.
BY THE WAY, MOMO, WHEN YOU JUST STARTED SCHOOL, YOUR CLOTHES WERE PRETTY RUGGED.
IT WAS SO NO ONE'D MESS WITH ME.

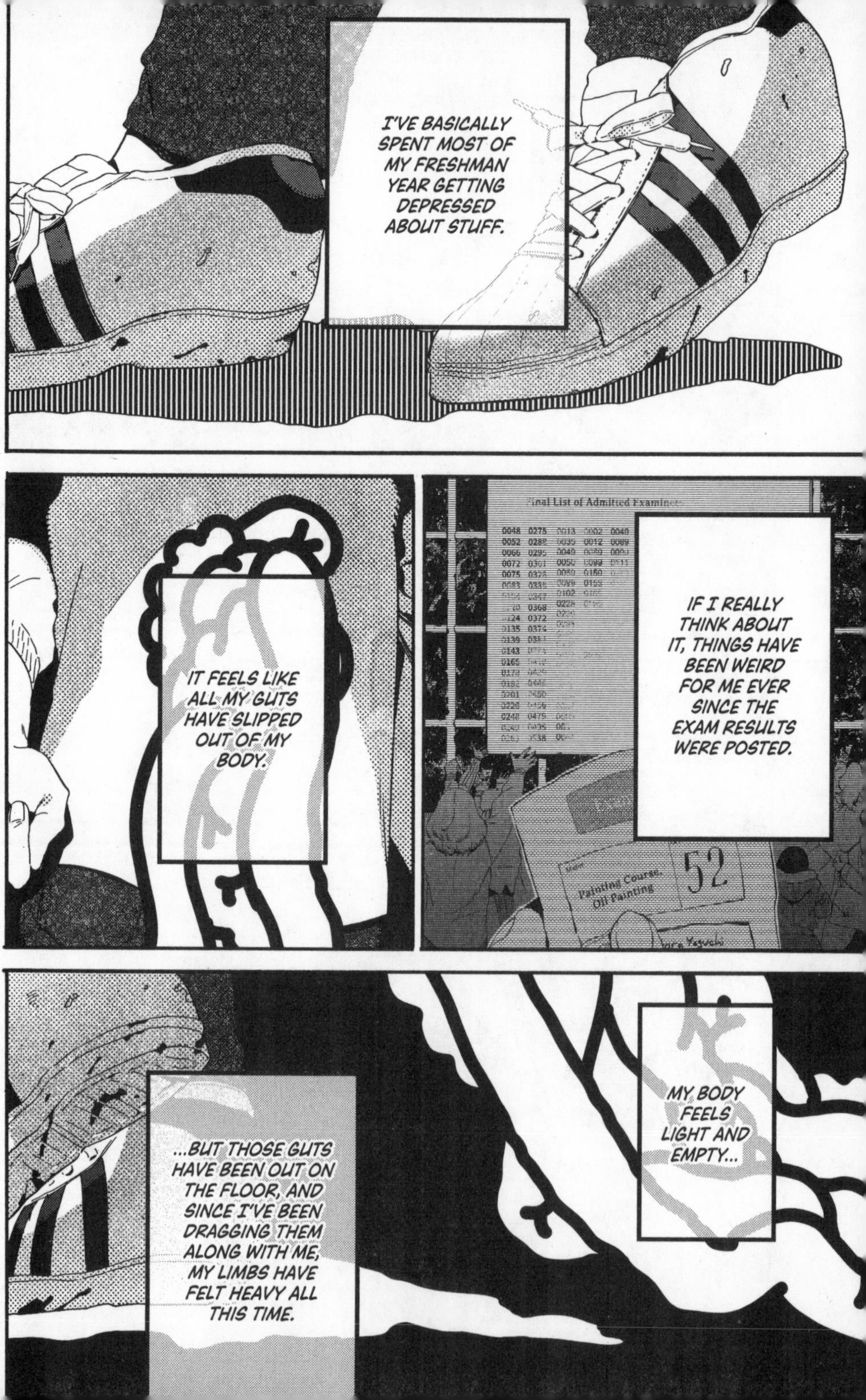
I'VE BASICALLY SPENT MOST OF MY FRESHMAN YEAR GETTING DEPRESSED ABOUT STUFF.
IF I REALLY THINK ABOUT IT, THINGS HAVE BEEN WEIRD FOR ME EVER SINCE THE EXAM RESULTS WERE POSTED.
Painting Course, Oil Painting
52
IT FEELS LIKE ALL MY GUTS HAVE SLIPPED OUT OF MY BODY.
MY BODY FEELS LIGHT AND EMPTY...
...BUT THOSE GUTS HAVE BEEN OUT ON THE FLOOR, AND SINCE I'VE BEEN DRAGGING THEM ALONG WITH ME, MY LIMBS HAVE FELT HEAVY ALL THIS TIME.

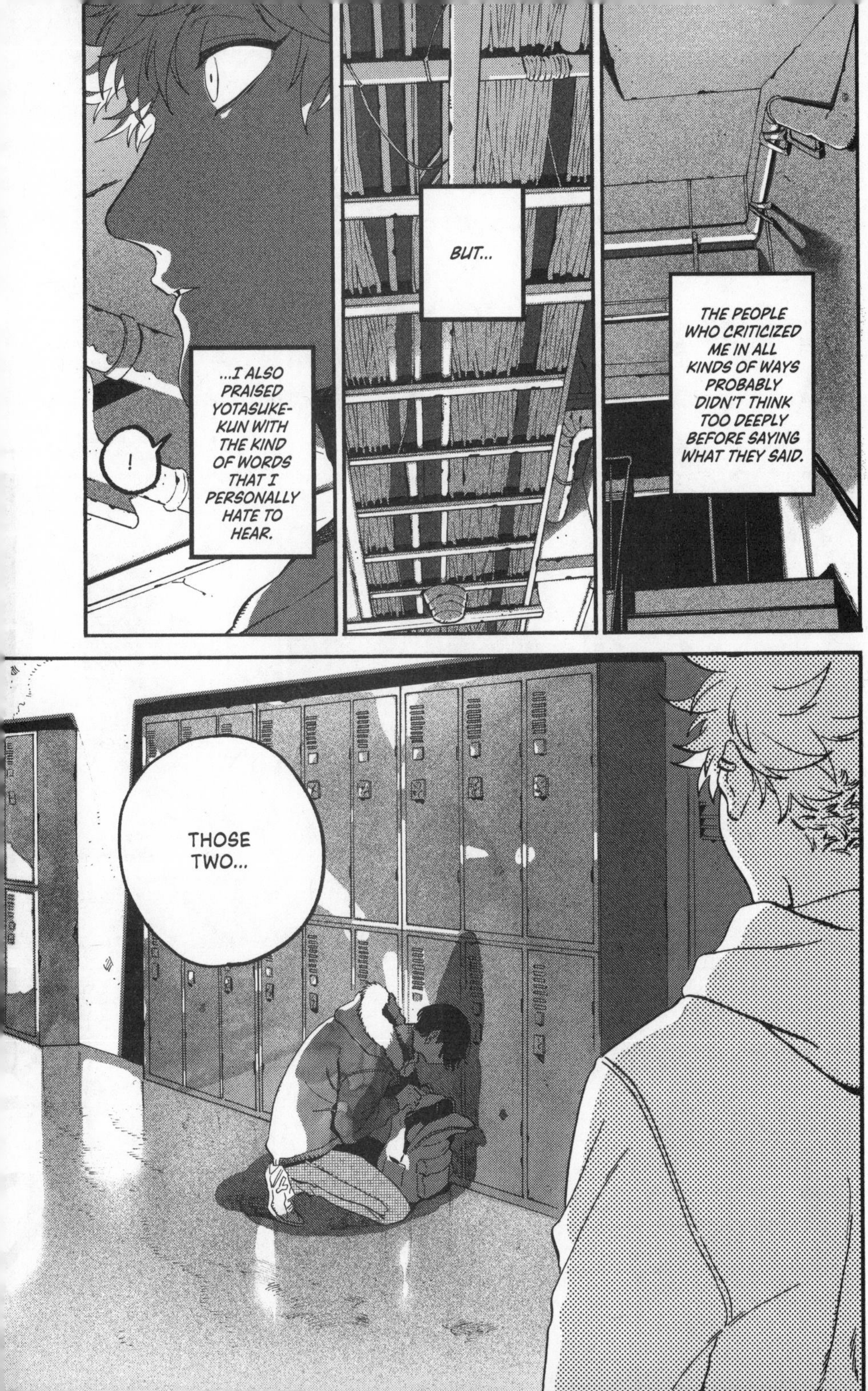
THE PEOPLE WHO CRITICIZED ME IN ALL KINDS OF WAYS PROBABLY DIDN'T THINK TOO DEEPLY BEFORE SAYING WHAT THEY SAID.
BUT...
...I ALSO PRAISED YOTASUKE-KUN WITH THE KIND OF WORDS THAT I PERSONALLY HATE TO HEAR.
!
THOSE TWO...

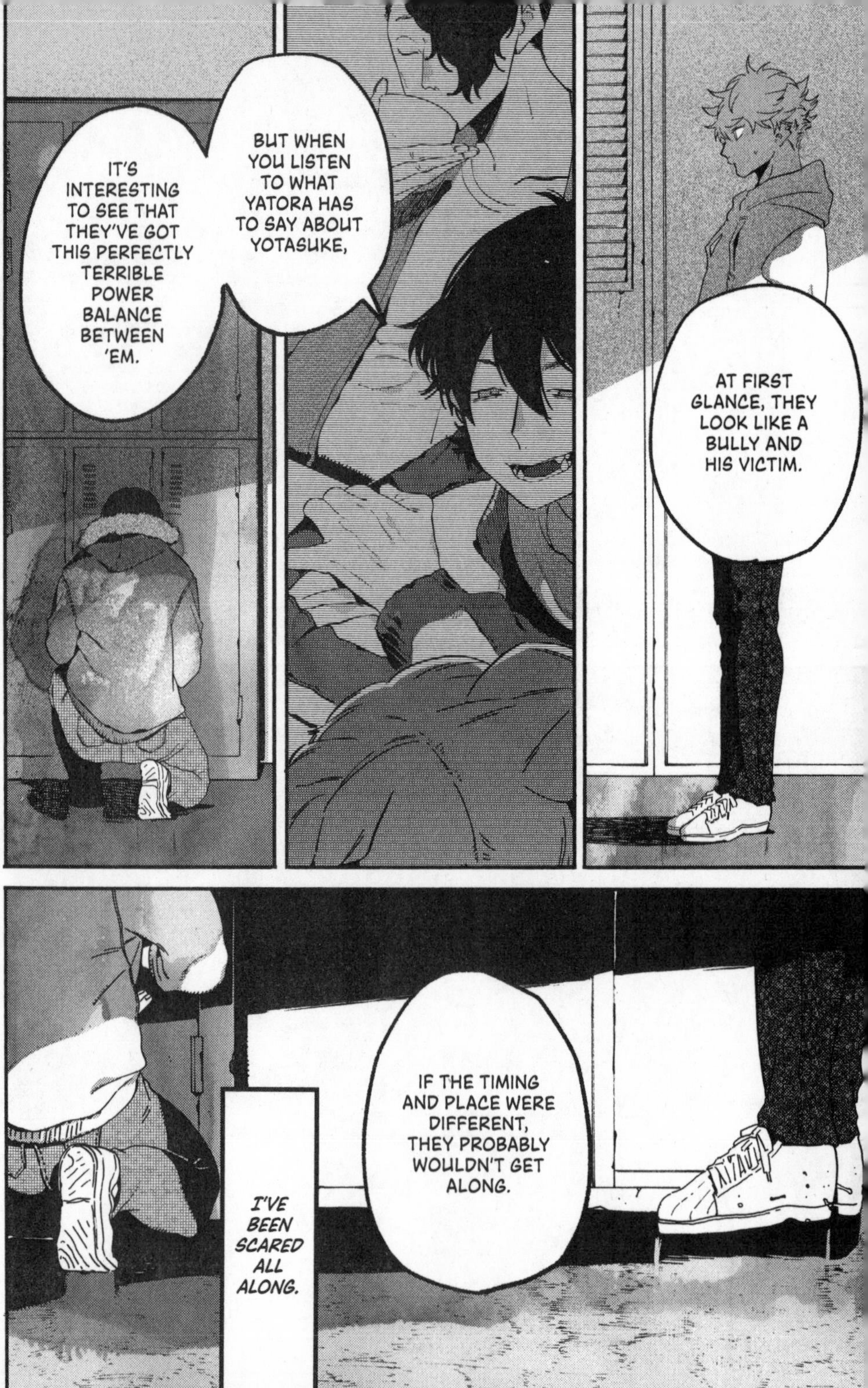
AT FIRST GLANCE, THEY LOOK LIKE A BULLY AND HIS VICTIM.
BUT WHEN YOU LISTEN TO WHAT YATORA HAS TO SAY ABOUT YOTASUKE,
IT'S INTERESTING TO SEE THAT THEY'VE GOT THIS PERFECTLY TERRIBLE POWER BALANCE BETWEEN 'EM.
IF THE TIMING AND PLACE WERE DIFFERENT, THEY PROBABLY WOULDN'T GET ALONG.
I'VE BEEN SCARED ALL ALONG.

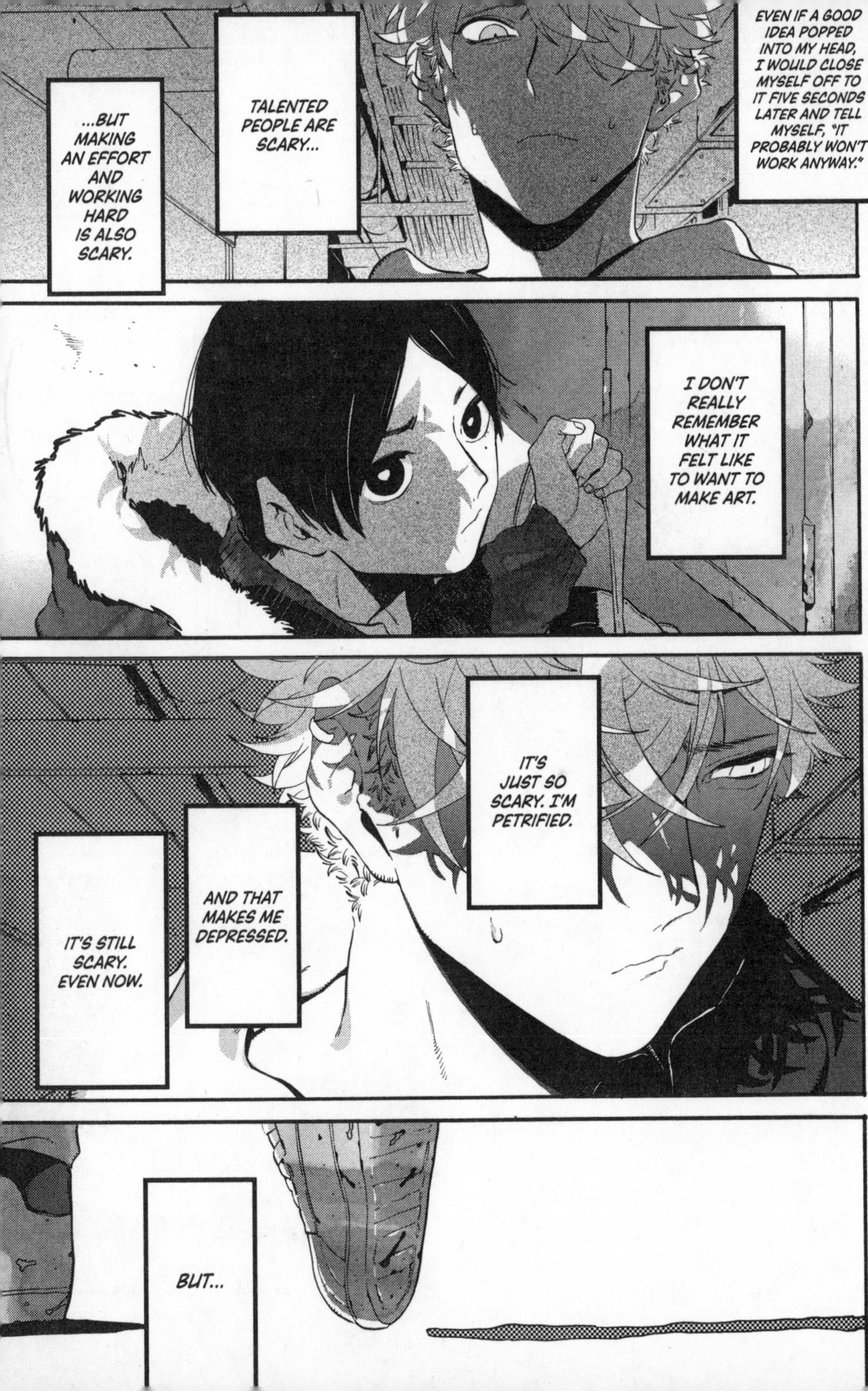
EVEN IF A GOOD IDEA POPPED INTO MY HEAD, I WOULD CLOSE MYSELF OFF TO IT FIVE SECONDS LATER AND TELL MYSELF, "IT PROBABLY WON'T WORK ANYWAY."
TALENTED PEOPLE ARE SCARY...
...BUT MAKING AN EFFORT AND WORKING HARD IS ALSO SCARY.
I DON'T REALLY REMEMBER WHAT IT FELT LIKE TO WANT TO MAKE ART.
IT'S JUST SO SCARY. I'M PETRIFIED.
AND THAT MAKES ME DEPRESSED.
IT'S STILL SCARY. EVEN NOW.
BUT...

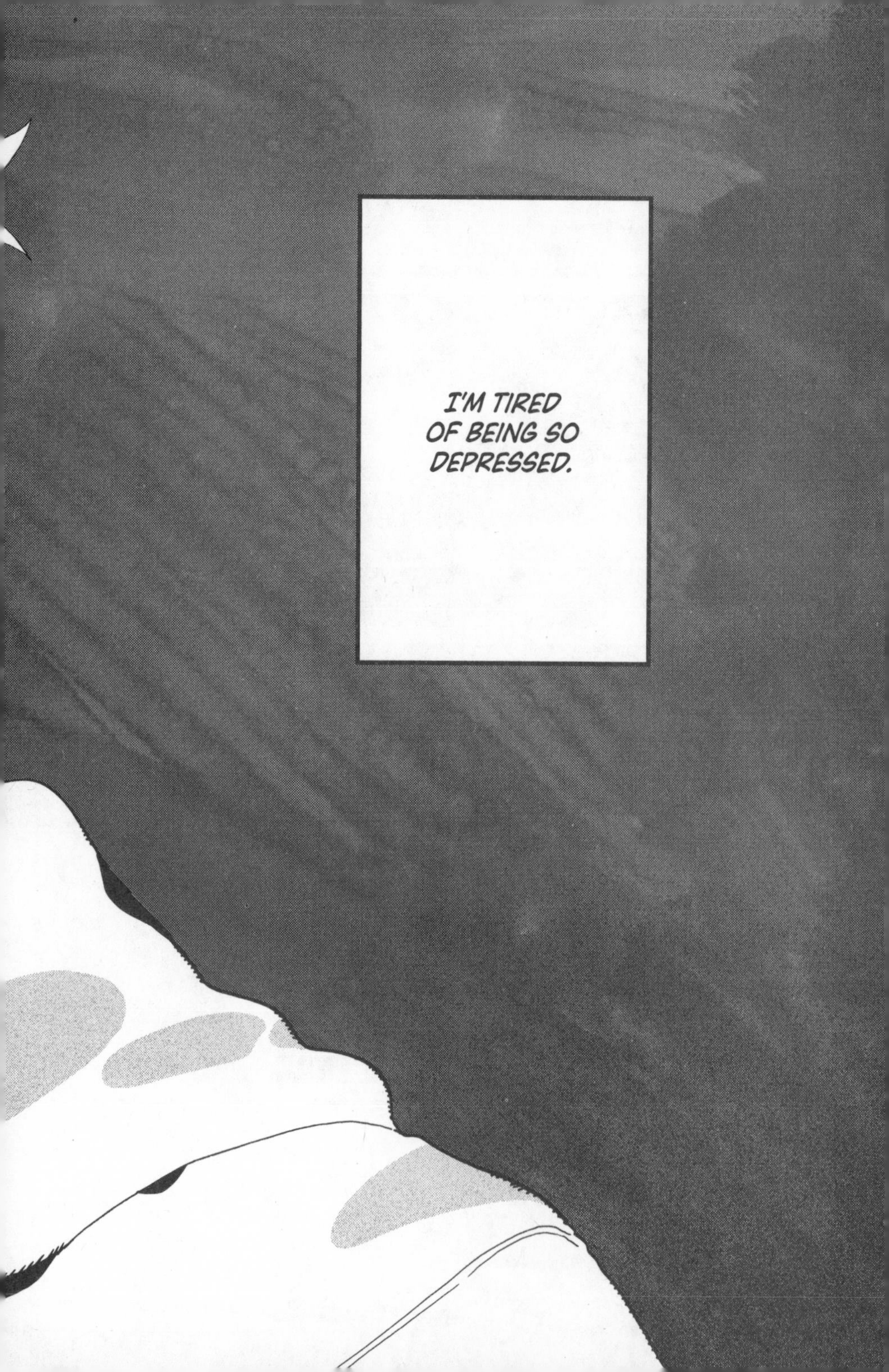
I'M TIRED OF BEING SO DEPRESSED.

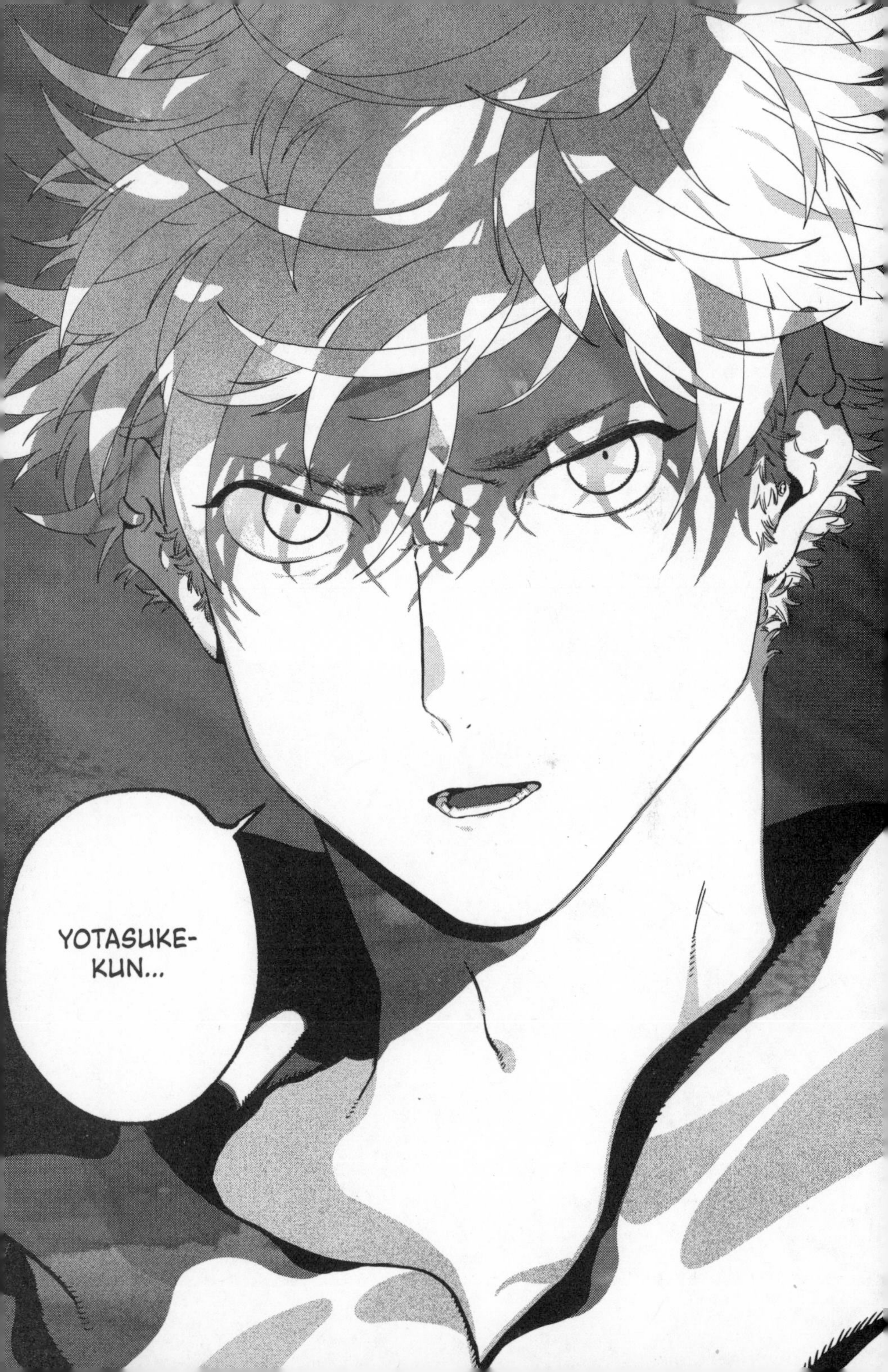
YOTASUKE-KUN...

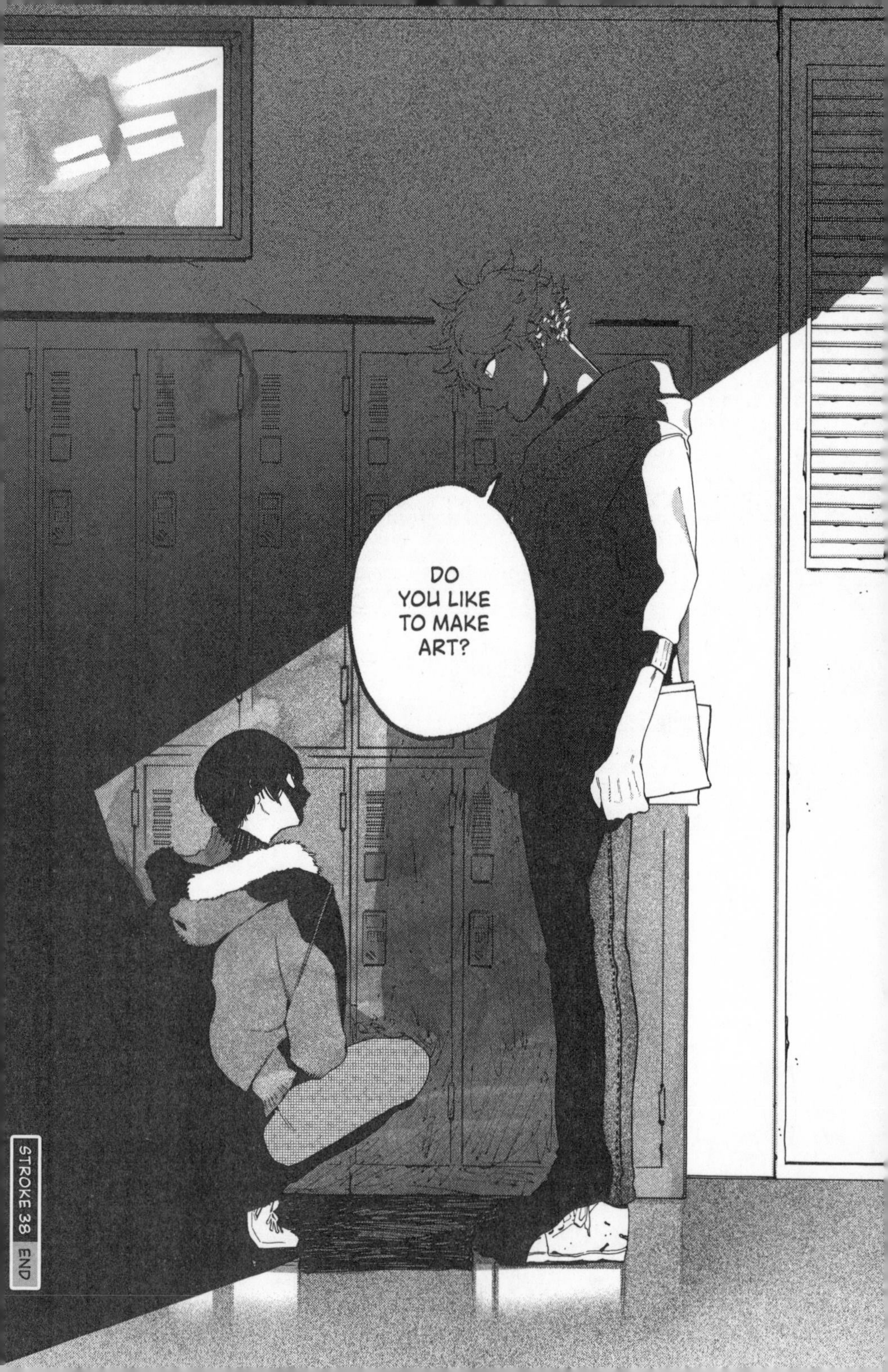
DO YOU LIKE TO MAKE ART?
STROKE 38 END

Blue Period was created with the support of many people!

Special Thanks

Thank you so very much!

Mei Tanimoto-san
Meimeiiii! That you for lending me your art! I love your mosaics, so I would be so happy if you would show me your artwork again. I know that's difficult, given the circumstances, but let's go out to eat again!

Chiharu Otsuka-san
Thank you for lending me your old artwork...! Let's go out and eat a bunch of delicious food while we still live so close to each other!

Yakumo-san
Thank you for coming up with the logos and T-shirts!
It was incredibly cute, so let's print some T-shirts next time!

UNIVERSITY FRIENDS (5)

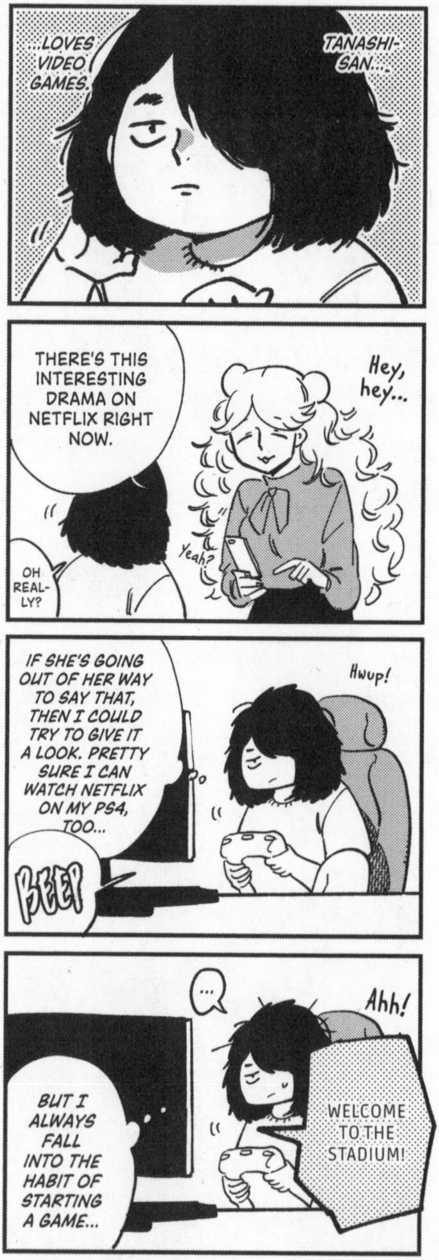
TANASHI-SAN...
...LOVES VIDEO GAMES.
Hey, hey...
THERE'S THIS INTERESTING DRAMA ON NETFLIX RIGHT NOW.
Yeah?
OH REALLY?
Hwup!
IF SHE'S GOING OUT OF HER WAY TO SAY THAT, THEN I COULD TRY TO GIVE IT A LOOK. PRETTY SURE I CAN WATCH NETFLIX ON MY PS4, TOO...
BEEP
Ahh!
...
WELCOME TO THE STADIUM!
BUT I ALWAYS FALL INTO THE HABIT OF STARTING A GAME...

THE FIRST-YEAR PROFESSORS (1)

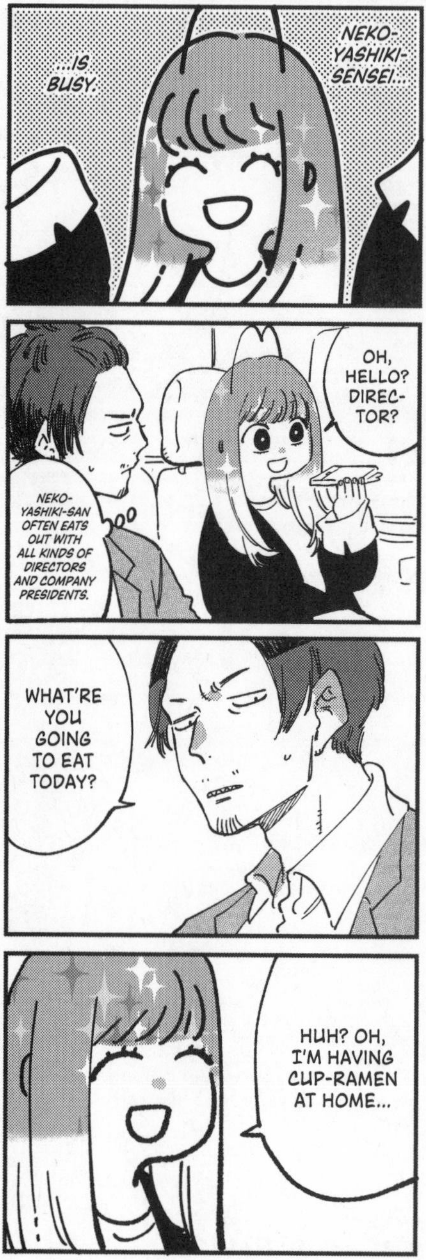
NEKO-YASHIKI-SENSEI...
...IS BUSY.
OH, HELLO? DIRECTOR?
NEKO-YASHIKI-SAN OFTEN EATS OUT WITH ALL KINDS OF DIRECTORS AND COMPANY PRESIDENTS.
WHAT'RE YOU GOING TO EAT TODAY?
HUH? OH, I'M HAVING CUP-RAMEN AT HOME...

THE FIRST-YEAR PROFESSORS (2)

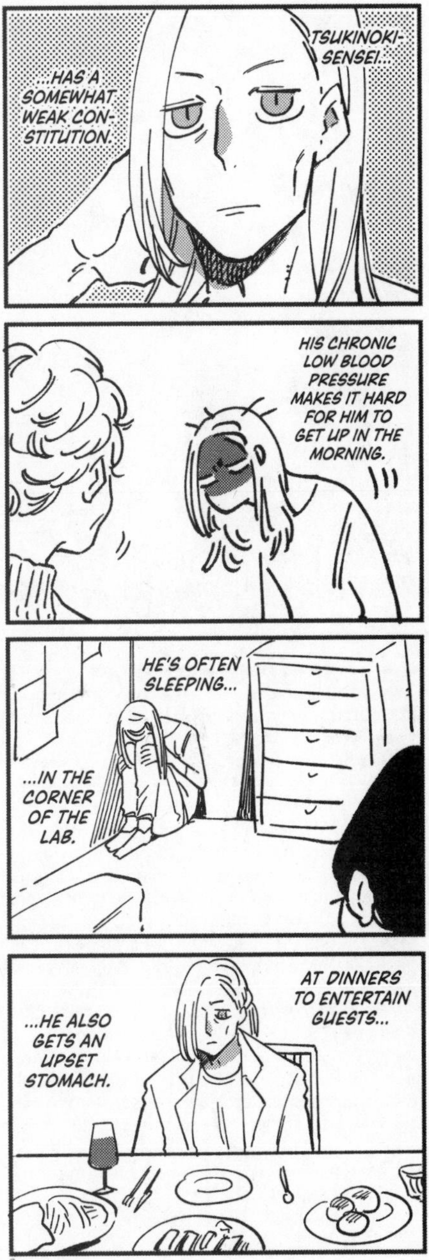
TSUKINOKI-SENSEI...
...HAS A SOMEWHAT WEAK CON-STITUTION.
HIS CHRONIC LOW BLOOD PRESSURE MAKES IT HARD FOR HIM TO GET UP IN THE MORNING.
HE'S OFTEN SLEEPING...
...IN THE CORNER OF THE LAB.
AT DINNERS TO ENTERTAIN GUESTS...
...HE ALSO GETS AN UPSET STOMACH.

THE FIRST-YEAR PROFESSORS (3)

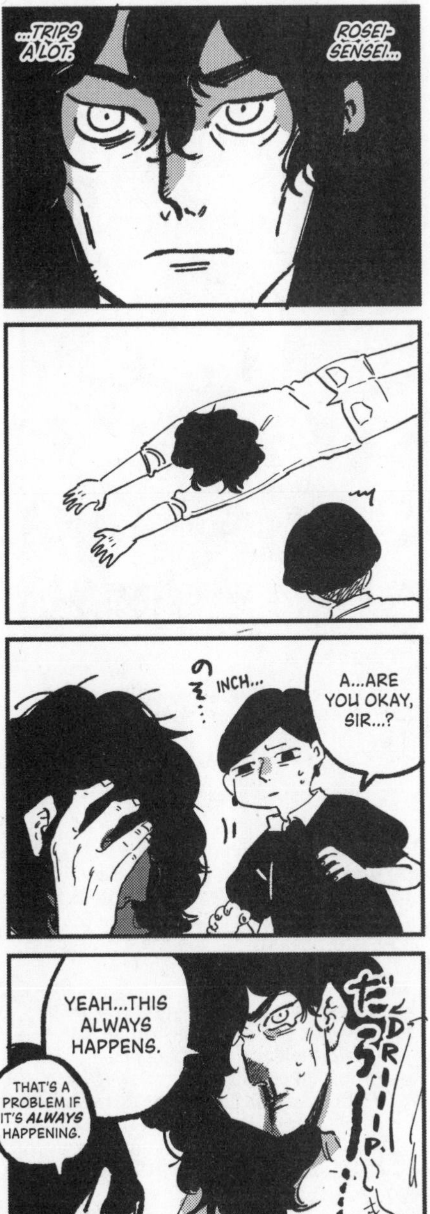
ROSEI-SENSEI...
...TRIPS A LOT.
A...ARE YOU OKAY, SIR...?
INCH...
DRIIIIP...
YEAH...THIS ALWAYS HAPPENS.
THAT'S A PROBLEM IF IT'S *ALWAYS* HAPPENING.

TRANSLATION NOTES

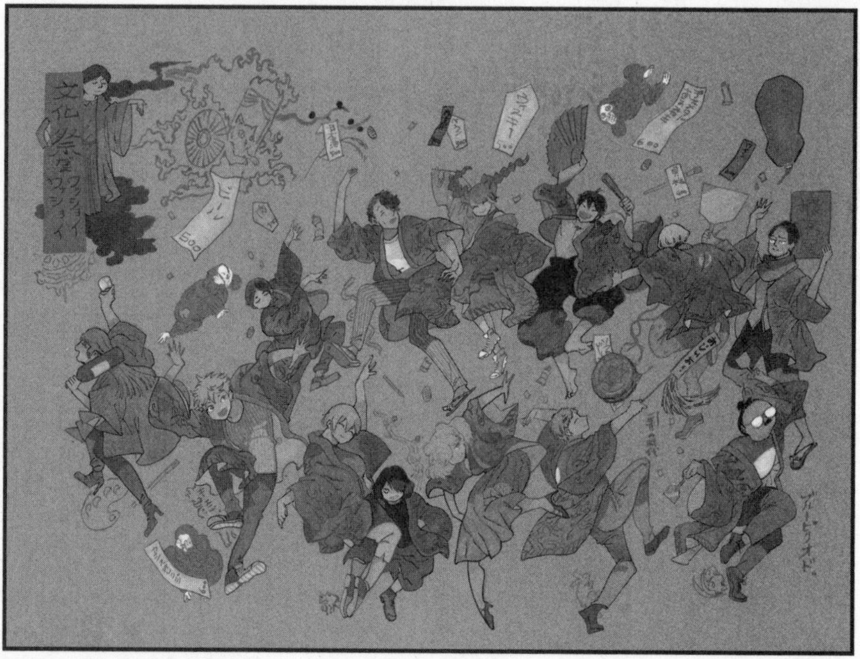
文化祭だワッショイワッショイ

It's a Sign of Happy Events to Come, page 4-5

The various smaller menu banners on the top row read, from right to left: Wine, Scallops, Death Metal Okonomiyaki, Whisky, Bacon, Tea, Sake, Meat, Beer. The menu banners on the bottom row read, from right to left: Tasty! Soft Drinks, Cassis Orange. The large sign on the right reads, "End of line." And the large sign on the left reads, "It's the culture festival! *Wasshoi, wasshoi!*" The two bottom captions read: Blue Period, Blue Age.

Both the opening image and the title of Stroke 34 are related to *Ee ja nai ka*, which could be described as both a dance craze and social protest that spread mostly along the Tokaido highway connecting Kyoto to Edo (modern day Tokyo) for a short time between 1867 and 1868. The opening illustration is an homage to a Kawanabe Kyosai painting that also carries the same title as the movement and depicts an *Ee ja nai ka* party. Though the exact origins are unclear, these celebrations took place during a tense time in the history of Japan between the end of the Edo period and the beginning of the Meiji Restoration. With Japan opening up to foreign trade and a shift in the political atmosphere, there was unrest among many Japanese citizens, so when a flurry of Shinto talismans appeared to rain down from the heavens upon the capital city of Edo, many people saw it a sign of auspicious events to come as well as cause for celebration. This event essentially went viral, and similar happenings occurred in major cities along Japan's main highway at the time. Each *Ee ja nai ka* event started with a shower of talismans followed by dancing, chanting, and a generally festive atmosphere. The phrase *ee ja nai ka* loosely translates to "why not" and relates to the attitude of many people in those turbulent times—a carefree attitude in face of what was seen as negative changes to Japan and the hope that the gods will make things better (including by smiting the foreigners and bringing Japan back to "normal").

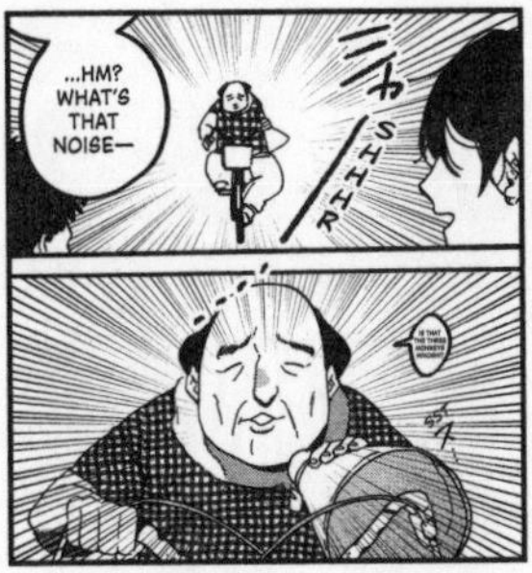
SHHHR
...HM? WHAT'S THAT NOISE—

City bike, page 25

A city bike here refers to what is commonly called a *mama-chari* ("mama chariot") in Japan. It's a relatively cheap and practical bicycle that's built for comfortable rides over short distances. They also tend to come with baskets. For those reasons, city bikes are often associated with housewives who use them to run errands and get around the city during the day, hence the "mama" in "mama chariot."

Donki, page 30

Donki refers to the store Don Quijote, which describes itself as the "biggest discount store in Japan." Don Quijote is not only well known and regarded for its reasonable prices but also for its stores that are jam-packed with a wide variety of products that include everything from food and houseware to costumes and even luxury items like watches.

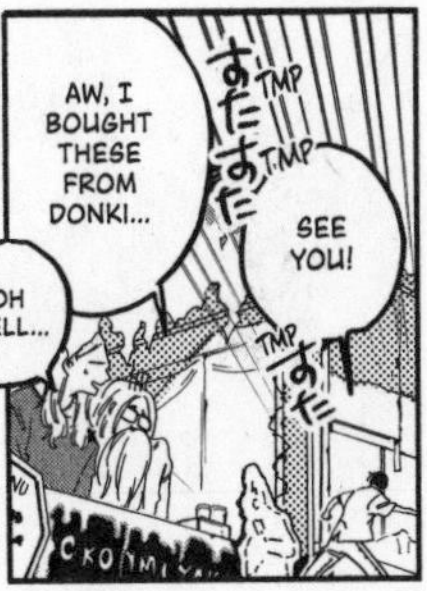
TMP TMP
SEE YOU!
TMP
AW, I BOUGHT THESE FROM DONKI...
OH WELL...

BLUE PERIOD

◄ KAMOME ►
SHIRAHAMA

Witch Hat Atelier

A magical manga
adventure for
fans of Disney
and Studio
Ghibli!

Witch Hat Atelier © Kamome Shirahama/Kodansha Ltd.

The magical adventure that took Japan by storm is finally here, from acclaimed DC and Marvel cover artist Kamome Shirahama!

In a world where everyone takes wonders like magic spells and dragons for granted, Coco is a girl with a simple dream: She wants to be a witch. But everybody knows magicians are born, not made, and Coco was not born with a gift for magic. Resigned to her un-magical life, Coco is about to give up on her dream to become a witch...until the day she meets Qifrey, a mysterious, traveling magician. After secretly seeing Qifrey perform magic in a way she's never seen before, Coco soon learns what everybody "knows" might not be the truth, and discovers that her magical dream may not be as far away as it may seem...

Princess Jellyfish

Akiko Higashimura

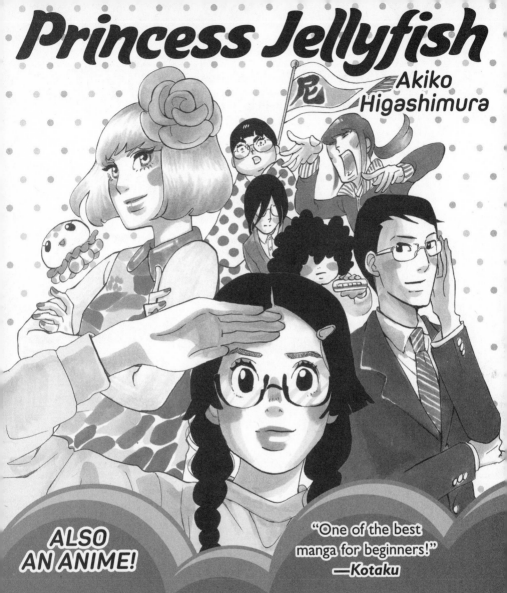

**ALSO
AN ANIME!**

Tsukimi Kurashita is fascinated with jellyfish. She's loved them from a
young age and has carried that love with her to her new life in the
big city of Tokyo. There, she resides in Amamizukan, a safe-haven for
geek girls where no boys are allowed. One day, Tsukimi crosses paths
with a beautiful and fashionable woman, but there's much more to
this woman than her trendy clothes...!

**KC
KODANSHA
COMICS**

A Kodansha Comics Trade Paperback Original
Blue Period 9 copyright © 2021 Tsubasa Yamaguchi
English translation copyright © 2022 Tsubasa Yamaguchi

All rights reserved.

Published in the United States by Kodansha Comics, an imprint of Kodansha USA Publishing, LLC, New York.

Publication rights for this English edition arranged through Kodansha Ltd., Tokyo.

First published in Japan in 2021 by Kodansha Ltd., Tokyo.

ISBN 978-1-64651-395-6

Printed in the United States of America.

www.kodansha.us

1st Printing
Translation: Ajani Oloye
Lettering: Lys Blakeslee
Editing: Haruko Hashimoto
Kodansha Comics edition cover design by Matthew Akuginow

Publisher: Kiichiro Sugawara

Director of publishing services: Ben Applegate
Director of publishing operations: Dave Barrett
Associate director, publishing operations: Stephen Pakula
Publishing services managing editors: Madison Salters, Alanna Ruse
Production managers: Emi Lotto, Angela Zurlo
Logo and character art ©Kodansha USA Publishing, LLC